WORKING MEMORIES

Technological developments during the Second World War led to an approach that linked ideas from computer science to neuroscience, linguistics, philosophy and psychology, known today as the Cognitive Revolution. Leaving behind traditional behaviourist approaches popular at the time, psychology began to utilise artificial intelligence and computer science to develop testable theories and design groundbreaking new experiments. The Cognitive Revolution dramatically changed the way that psychological research and studies were conducted and proposed a new way of thinking about the mind.

In *Working Memories*, Alan Baddeley, one of the world's leading authorities on Human Memory, draws on his own personal experience of this time, recounting the radical development of a pioneering science in parallel with his own transatlantic, vibrant and distinguished career.

Detailing the excitement and sometimes frustration experienced in taking psychology into the world beyond the laboratory, *Working Memories* presents unique insights into the mind and psychological achievements of one of the most influential psychologists of our time.

Alan Baddeley is Professor of Psychology at the University of York and one of the world's leading authorities on Human Memory. He is celebrated for devising the groundbreaking and highly influential working memory model with Graham Hitch in the early 1970s, a model which has been cited over 10,000 times to date. He was awarded a CBE for his contributions to the study of memory and is a Fellow of the Royal Society, of the British Academy, of the Academy of Medical Sciences and of the American Academy of Arts and Sciences. His outstanding record of personal achievements and significant contributions to the advancement of psychological knowledge were recognised in 2001 by the American Psychological Association Distinguished Contribution Award, in 2012 by the Lifetime Achievement Award of the British Psychological Society and in 2016 by the International Union of Psychological Sciences Award for Major Achievement in Psychological Science.

WORKING MEMORIES

Postmen, Divers and the Cognitive Revolution

Alan Baddeley

Routledge
Taylor & Francis Group

LONDON AND NEW YORK

First published 2019
by Routledge
2 Park Square, Milton Park, Abingdon, Oxon OX14 4RN

and by Routledge
711 Third Avenue, New York, NY 10017

Routledge is an imprint of the Taylor & Francis Group, an informa business

British Library Cataloguing-in-Publication Data
A catalogue record for this book is available from the British Library

Library of Congress Cataloging-in-Publication Data
Names: Baddeley, Alan D., 1934- author.
Title: Working memories: postmen, divers and the cognitive revolution / Alan Baddeley.
Description: 1 Edition. | New York: Routledge, 2019. | Includes index.
Identifiers: LCCN 2018014431 | ISBN 9781138646346 (hardback) | ISBN 9781138646353 (pbk.) | ISBN 9781315627601 (ebook) | ISBN 9781317238539 (Web PDF) | ISBN 9781317238522 (ePub) | ISBN 9781317238515 (Mobipocket)
Subjects: LCSH: Cognitive science. | Psychology, Applied. | Neurosciences. | Memory.
Classification: LCC BF311 .B254 2019 | DDC 153—dc23
LC record available at https://lccn.loc.gov/2018014431

ISBN: 978-1-138-64634-6 (hbk)
ISBN: 978-1-138-64635-3 (pbk)
ISBN: 978-1-315-62760-1 (ebk)

Typeset in Bembo
by codeMantra

MIX
Paper from
responsible sources
FSC® C013056
www.fsc.org

Printed and bound in Great Britain by
TJ International Ltd, Padstow, Cornwall

To Hilary, for over 50 years of love and support.

CONTENTS

PREFACE

What follows attempts to do three things. First, to present a personal view of the period of rapid scientific change sometimes termed the cognitive revolution. In doing so I try to give an impression of what it was like to be a scientist during that period, a time when the influence of the digital computer dramatically changed the way in which we think about ourselves. I try to give an account of the experience of scientific research by embedding the account within my own life as a scientist, intent on combining basic and applied questions, having spent much of my career in an environment specifically focussed on bridging the two. My own field, the psychology of human memory, is I believe particularly appropriate for this purpose since the questions it poses, the methods of tackling them and resulting theoretical concepts are close enough to everyday life to be readily understandable, providing an account of the way in which the scientific method can be applied to understanding the human mind. I was inspired in this aim by G H Hardy's *A Mathematician's Apology*, which succeeded in conveying the excitement of his field, even to someone as limited mathematically as myself. Unlike Hardy, however, I enjoy the challenge of taking theoretical ideas and applying them to practical problems, although as will be seen, this often is a far from easy task.

Finally, I have tried to relate the development of the field of cognitive science more generally to its broad historical context. The ever-increasing current pressure to publish and the ever-expanding scientific literature have had the unfortunate tendency to narrow the research scientist's focus of attention to work that is both recent and fashionable. In ignoring the history of our field, however, we are in danger not only of rediscovering what is already known but more importantly of repeating costly mistakes. Topics that seem of crucial importance now represent only a thin slice of what has gone before and as such, potentially provide an unduly limited basis for future progress. If, as Newton proposed, we are pygmies standing on the shoulders of giants, it is as well to understand where we stand.

Attempting to cover the personal, the scientific and the historical, and to combine them into an integrated story has proved a challenge, though an enjoyable one. I hope the reader will find the result both interesting and worthwhile. If, however, you are primarily interested in the scientific rather than the personal or the theoretical rather than the practical, the structure is such that you should be able to focus on your principal interest while skimming the rest. But I hope you won't!

What follows is not a scholarly account of the cognitive revolution, complete with footnotes and references, but rather one person's account of working in one area that was profoundly influenced by it: namely the psychology of human memory. Even within this narrower area, it did not prove feasible to provide the references that would be expected in a scholarly approach from either an historian or indeed a scientific paper. Furthermore, although I am someone who has gained enormously from collaboration over the 60 years of my scientific life, the sheer number of joint publications makes it impossible to acknowledge more than a few of the many people whose work has contributed to my own scientific development. It certainly does not mean that I am not aware of this debt. I have been able to include a limited number of photographs, and here the problem becomes particularly acute. Rather than choosing pictures of eminent figures who have influenced the field, I have opted to select photographs of more personal interest, hence dodging the question of who is eminent enough to be included.

As the title suggests, much of the content of my account is based on memory, which you do not need to be a psychologist to realise is far from infallible. I was, however, fortunate in finding that letters to my mother over two extended visits to the US had been kept and was able to use these extensively in the relevant chapters, noting at the same time that those features that I remembered spontaneously were typically ones that I had described to others at one time or another. My memory seems to comprise a series of relatively well-remembered items, islands of memory in a sea of forgetting, and I take comfort from the fact that the islands of memory do match the accounts in my letters reasonably closely, although they, in turn, will inevitably be biased by my own viewpoint (and by what it is appropriate to tell one's mother!). I try to check the scientific part of the account by looking back at papers, although with around 500 publications I cannot by any means guarantee that everything I report has been carefully checked. I have, however, been fortunate in the colleagues and friends who have agreed to read all or part of the book, in particular noting any errors, which I have then corrected. It is inevitable in a book of this type, however, that much of the content cannot be checked by those who have not experienced it. These are indeed working memories. I am particularly grateful for the help of Graham Hitch and Robert Logie for reading the whole manuscript, while individual sections were read by my brother Keith Baddeley, Philip Barnard, Dorothy Bishop, Douglas Candland, Sergio Della Sala, Michael Posner, Raymond Nickerson and Wolfgang Prinz. They are not of course responsible for any errors or misinterpretations that remain.

I write by dictating and am extremely grateful to Lindsey Bowes, not only for her ability to turn my perambulatory mumblings into relatively readable prose but also for her considerable photographic and IT skills. I have been fortunate in my publisher, and in particular I owe a debt of gratitude to Michael Forster, now retired, whose enthusiasm for the idea behind this book encouraged me to tackle what seemed a rather daunting task. Michael's support has been continued under the enthusiastic and very helpful editorship of Ceri McLardy and Sophie Crowe. Finally and most importantly, I must thank my wife Hilary, without whose love and support neither this account nor many of the events within it would have been possible.

FURTHER READING

Baars, B.J. (1986). *The Cognitive Revolution in Psychology.* New York: Guilford Press.

An account of the influence of the cognitive revolution on psychology, together with a number of interviews with influential North American psychologists.

Gardner, H. (1987). *The Mind's New Science: A History of the Cognitive Revolution.* New York: Basic Books.

A broad overview of the cognitive revolution, providing an account of its impact on philosophy, linguistics, anthropology, artificial intelligence and psychology, together with discussion of future prospects of the field as seen in the mid-1980s.

Mandler, G. (2011). *A History of Modern Experimental Psychology: From James and Wundt to Cognitive Science.* Cambridge, MA: MIT Press.

Places the development of experimental psychology in its broad historical context.

Miller, G.A. (2003). The Cognitive Revolution: A Historical Perspective. *Trends in Cognitive Sciences,* 7 (3), 141–144.

A brief account by George Miller, who played a major role in developing a link between the cognitive revolution and psychology.

Rabbitt, P.M.A. (2009). *Inside Psychology: A Science Over 50 years.* Oxford: Oxford University Press.

A collection of articles by a range of distinguished mainly British cognitive psychologists, describing the development of their particular field over the latter half of the twentieth century.

Much of the detail and references linked to the scientific content of my account are included in one or other of the three memory texts I have produced, with the emphasis of course changing over the years. They are:

Baddeley, A.D. (1986). *The Psychology of Memory.* New York: Basic Books. This covers the early years including the influence of interference theory.

Baddeley, A.D. (1990). *Human Memory Theory and Practice.* Hove: Lawrence Erlbaum Associates. This introduces later developments and stresses the link between psychological theory and its application beyond the laboratory.

Baddeley, A.D., Eysenck, M.W. & Anderson, M.C. Second Edition (2015). Hove: Psychology Press. This reflects the substantial increase in our understanding of Memory and links it to the related neuroscience.

LEEDS 1934–53

1

Growing Up in Yorkshire

I was born on 23rd of March 1934 in Hunslet, an industrial district of the Yorkshire city of Leeds. My mother's side of the family were solidly Yorkshire, her father, Henry Hanson, coming from the adjoining district of Holbeck, from a family that I was told was seen as slightly superior on the grounds that they kept a pig. Her mother's family hailed from Richmond in North Yorkshire, where it was rumoured that some of them had been in service down in London, again a minor source of distinction in mid-19th-century working-class culture. My grandfather had a series of jobs, ranging from steel worker to driving a "steam derrick" engaged in building the high school that I subsequently attended.

My father's origins were somewhat more complex. My grandparents both worked in the theatre in Liverpool, where my grandmother was a dancer in the ballets that were routinely included in operatic performances at the time, and my grandfather was a stagehand, known as Henry Hughes. According to family tradition, it was only when signing the marriage register that he turned into Henry Israel, a name he kept from then onwards. It appears that Hughes was the name of his mother, whose family were apparently originally fisher folk from the Isle of Anglesey, North Wales.

The origin of the Israel part of the family remained a mystery, with family speculations favouring a wealthy Jewish family who had disinherited their son. My father occasionally pointed out facial similarities between various members of his extended family and Benjamin Disraeli, the 19th-century Victorian novelist who became one of Britain's greatest prime ministers. Alas, our family historian, my brother Keith, discovered that the link was not to the distinguished prime minister but to the improbably named Israel Israel, a "general dealer" from the Elephant and Castle, one of the rather seedier districts of London. He seems to have married a gentile back in the 1850s. Since Jewish identity is assumed to pass through the female line, while the name of course passes down the male, the family was left with a 100 years of prejudice, with none of the cultural advantage. My grandfather died at a relatively young age, though not before fathering 18 children, of whom 12 survived. The girls all changed their name automatically on marriage, and the boys did so once they reached the age of 21 and became legally entitled to do so, adopting the name of their mother, Baddeley, whose side of the family seems to have been rather more middle class in origin and even owned land in Devon until the latter half of the 19th century. This belonged originally to John Baddeley, who in 1745 was the rector of the small village of Throwleigh on the edge of Dartmoor in Devon. His son William moved to London, where he is said to have invested unwisely in the theatre; there is a Baddeley Cake that is annually enjoyed by the actors at the Drury Lane Theatre in London on the Twelfth Night after Christmas, though whether this is the result of William's investment is unclear. There certainly have been distinguished actors called Baddeley, though I suspect that the link may be no stronger than our apocryphal association with Victorian prime ministers. The name is not hugely rare, particularly in the area around Stoke on Trent in Staffordshire, where there is a village called Baddeley Green and apparently a local church with a gravestone inscribed "God protect us from the Baddeleys". So, I suspect that we were all run out of town, though just why remains a mystery.

William's son Alfred seems to have had a more practical bent as an inventor, as was Alfred's son, my great-grandfather. He combined inventing with a job as a patent officer, registering many patents himself, but had a particular interest in firefighting. He helped set up the Holborn Fire Brigade in London, which had numerous patents, including one for a fire engine, before in due course moving to Manchester as Deputy Head of their fire service. Unfortunately he had to retire from the post after falling off a roof, moving to Liverpool and taking up a range of clerical jobs. He apparently disapproved of the marriage between my two grandparents but agreed to provide money for them to emigrate to Canada, instead of which they moved to Leeds, where my parents were born. Curiously, both my paternal and my maternal grandfather were said to have subsequently travelled to Canada alone but then returned for reasons that remain obscure. Had they stayed, I suppose I would now be a Canadian.

Instead I grew up in Hunslet, a smoky industrial part of Leeds locally known as "mucky (dirty) 'unslet". The local factories built railway engines, produced ready-made garments and were involved in printing and unfortunately also in manufacturing sulphuric acid, something you could feel on your face when the wind was in the wrong direction. To outsiders it was seen as a prime example of a slum. When, at the age of 13, I was in hospital suffering from scarlet fever in a somewhat rumbustious children's ward, we were rebuked by the fierce Ward Sister who declared, "you are like children from the back streets of Hunslet!" I had the good sense not to make the obvious response; it was best not to get the wrong side of Sister.

Hunslet was one of the largest industrial parishes in the country and tended to attract idealistic and ambitious clergymen. One, commemorated in a book entitled "Turbulent Priest", was a major advocate of better housing, while two who I knew as curates moved on to very different posts, one to a professorship in Theology at Oxford and the other, via a chaplaincy at the University of London, to become the priest in charge of the English Church in Nice, perhaps feeling that he had done his stint of northern missionary work. A move in the other direction was made by the Reverend Vaughan Wilkes, who moved to Hunslet from a position as Headmaster of Radley, a public (i.e. private residential) school in the Thames Valley, causing the local newspaper to compare his move to a descent into hell. This, in turn, led to my first publication: a letter in rather orotund prose, pointing out that we had refrained from eating our last two vicars, signed Satan's Minion.

Despite its reputation, Hunslet was in fact quite a good place to live; as one of the curates said, "When I arrived I was struck by the number of dogs and fat women, but after a while I began to like it because it seemed so friendly and cosy". Housewives, very few women worked after marriage, regarded cleanliness as extremely important, coping with the soot from the factories and domestic coal fires with frequent dusting and by scrubbing floors regularly. This included the front doorstep, which was then typically edged with a "donkey stone", a soft brown sandstone. Our house was a classic northern back-to-back house, a terrace divided down the centre so that we had neighbours to the left, to the right and behind us, with outside toilets shared between pairs of houses; it was rather a chilly arrangement in winter, but in other respects our house was rather like a two-storey apartment.

I remember no crime or violence, with one exception. The elder brother of a boy I knew killed his girlfriend, a Hunslet version of *Carmen* enacted not in the bullring but in a brush factory. Around the middle years of the last century Hunslet also produced a number of good writers: novelists Keith Waterhouse and Willis Hall; the actor Peter O'Toole; and the influential cultural critic and historian Richard Hoggart,[1] whose book "The Uses of Literacy" focussed on Hunslet, offering a study of working-class life. I found it rather like the accounts of African or Melanesian tribes that I encountered in my university social anthropology course. I read Hoggart's book with guilty fascination; it seemed like staring at yourself in the mirror: not the sort of thing a Yorkshireman should do! Hoggart went on to have a distinguished academic career, eventually becoming head of Goldsmiths College, one of the group of universities that make up the University of London. I recently reread the book. It is principally concerned with the impact of literacy on a northern working-class population that still had remote links to earlier agricultural roots, perhaps reflected in my great-grandfather's pig? While I recognise many of his descriptions of the expressions and attitudes, the patterns of holidays and singing in pubs on Friday and Saturday nights, my family belonged to a little-mentioned subgroup he refers to rather dismissively as the "earnest minority".

My father grew up in relative poverty; my grandmother apparently took in other people's washing to help support the 12 children who survived out of a total of 18. He was highly intelligent and had what was probably the most intellectual job that could be found for anyone in his circumstances: namely that of a compositor, the person in the printing trade who used to have the responsibility for designing the page, which included choosing the typeface and layout that then went on to be printed. This was a respected though not particularly well-paid job that has disappeared with the advent of the computer. He was self-educated via the public library and the type of weekly magazine that could be put together eventually to make up a multivolume encyclopaedia, a History of England or of ancient Egypt and the Pharaohs. He read widely and was a trade unionist at a time when being found with a left-wing newspaper could threaten your job. He was determined that my brother and I should have the education and opportunities that he himself had missed.

My father was apparently a very good "comp" and was promoted to foreman, unfortunately at a time when the small family firm for which he worked was taken over by a much larger enterprise with an enthusiasm for American management methods. This all happened during a period when the print unions had become strong and militant. My father was caught between the union he had defended but which he felt now was behaving unreasonably and an equally unreasonable management. He went into a period of deep depression, gradually recovering, helped by the long walks he took, during which I felt I really got to know him properly. He returned to work and was treated well, being allowed to return to his trade as a compositor, which he enjoyed, without a reduction in salary.

By this stage, I was at university, while my brother was working as a power station engineer. My parents finally had a little spare money and began to enjoy country holidays, and my father began to develop his interest in photography, when he suddenly died of a heart attack, aged only 56. My mother then had to find a job, some 30 years after leaving the garment industry to become a full-time housewife. She differed from my father in being intelligent but not intellectual, more interested in people than ideas, observing life with a wry but benevolent humour. It was a very strong marriage, and it must have been very hard to cope with a situation that had quite rapidly changed from having a husband and two sons at home to living alone with the eldest having married and the youngest, myself, about to graduate from university and move to the US, a move my mother later admitted she thought would probably be permanent. Characteristically, she was pleased at my success and made no attempt to dissuade me. She found a job in a well-known cake shop, initially struggling to remember all the prices but soon settling in and enjoying the company of the other "girls". The rented house where I grew up was bulldozed while I was at university to create a new road, and my mother moved to a more modern municipally developed house, which she loved, rapidly making friends. She enjoyed the fact that unlike our first house, it had indoor bathroom facilities and a garden. She lived independently until dying from a stroke at the age of 92, although by that stage she declared herself tired of growing old and ready to be "taken".

I began school in the infants' class at the age of three. I have a very clear memory of lying on the classroom floor, kicking and screaming because my mother had failed to wave when she left, while on another occasion I apparently threatened the teacher, Miss Murray, that my Uncle Jim, a saintly man, would put her on a bonfire. A short break in my schooling occurred at the outbreak of the Second World War, and there was talk of evacuation of children from the city of Leeds, which had important war-related industries. This prospect caused great excitement among us as there was a rumour that you got to leave in a lifeboat from Blackpool, a popular seaside resort. My Uncle Archie in Seattle offered to take my brother and myself, but in fact Leeds proved to be remarkably safe. It lies in a hollow, and the smoke from its many factories apparently made it invisible from the air, so an early visit to the US proved unnecessary.

Moving up to the junior school, I had the advantage of an older brother who could initiate me into its mysteries. One was that the pecking order among boys within a class was determined by fighting, not the sort of knife and gun fighting that appears to occur in some inner cities today but a rather formalised type of wrestling, in which the aim is to pin your opponent to the ground, with rules very much like the college wrestling I discovered when I later went to Princeton. Tutored by my brother, I became quite good at this, eventually leading to a fight-off, surrounded by a shouting crowd of classmates who, when I managed to win, pursued my opponent as he ran home. Not unreasonably, his mother complained, and I was called into the headmaster's study and required to shake hands and make peace. Somewhat remarkably, this worked, and the two of us became best friends. We remained friends for many years, eventually losing contact when he moved away to help his father set up a small plumbing business in a nearby town. This was my last fight; I simply ignored challenges from those anxious to move up the pecking order, and it seemed to work.

I grew up during the Second World War, which had two positive features. The first was food rationing; Britain was and is a net food importer, and when submarine warfare began to take a heavy toll on merchant shipping, the government brought in rationing to ensure that the food was distributed fairly. This meant that meat, eggs and butter were available to everyone equally, though in limited amounts, supplemented by lots of unrationed vegetables from allotments that people were encouraged to develop in land previously used for other purposes, such as public parks. This resulted in a largely centrally planned diet that was healthier than before and probably better than is typical today. This was reflected in child development; I, for example, am about eight inches taller than my father was.

The second source of good fortune was the Education Act passed in 1944 in anticipation of the end of the war. Up to that time, there were three types of schools: Public Schools (which are in fact private and fee-paying) were typically residential and involved expensive fees; Grammar Schools were non-residential and typically charged modest fees, affordable for middle class but not for typical working-class parents. The only free education was provided by State Schools, where pupils were educated up to the age of 14, unlike the Public and Grammar Schools, which provided education up to the age of 16 or 18, hence serving as preparation for the professions and for university. In fact, only about 5 per cent of the population entered university.

The new law left Public Schools untouched, in my view, a mistake that continues to perpetuate the class system by allowing richer people to buy an education that provides better access to universities and professions. The Grammar Schools became state funded in 1945, fees were abolished and admission was based on an examination taken at age 11, which was largely a form of intelligence test. I became 11 in 1945 and was part of the first cohort to take the test, and since it was based on intelligence rather than scholastic achievement, I managed to pass it, despite having spent my final year in Primary School under the care of a pathetically inadequate teacher; I received my first black eye when standing behind him at a point where an object was thrown at him, and he ducked. I think I was one of only two in my class to be selected, the other being a very clever girl whose parents refused to allow her to take up the place. My own parents were delighted. They had managed to find the modest fees for my elder brother and would have done the same for me. Very few of my fellow pupils came from Hunslet; some travelled across the city, but most came from the newer more middle-class areas beyond the school.

I was also fortunate in going to my Grammar School when it was entering a particularly good period. It had been built around 1900, located between Hunslet and a newer and slightly more upmarket part of Leeds. It was initially billed as "the working man's university", specialising in more technical subjects and named "Cockburn High School", presumably after a now-forgotten local figure. By the mid-1940s it had become a general Grammar School, though probably the least prestigious in the city. We were fortunate, however, in having some excellent teachers and at least one outstanding headmaster. The class intake was streamed, based initially on the scores achieved during the entrance exam. I had apparently done well, although I didn't realise it, and was put in the A stream but did not flourish. Homework was an important part of the system and a part that I initially always skimped, with the result that I was usually placed somewhere between the 26th and 32nd of a class of 32. Happily however, as we got towards the first crucial set of exams at age 16, I started to move up the rankings, or as it seemed to me, everybody else was gradually getting worse. By 16 I was enthusiastic and doing well and wanted to go to university.

The subjects I enjoyed most were Geography, English and History. I found Science boring. I can still remember my first physics lesson. It was a co-educational school, unusual at the time, and at the beginning of the second year, we boys were instructed to go to one lecture theatre and the girls to another. The boys were then told that we would study Physics, and the girls would study Biology. One of my friends who wanted to become a pharmacist complained. He was grudgingly told that provided he got a letter from his parents, he could go and study Biology with the girls. The first lesson then began with the demonstration that if you mix hot water and cold water you get lukewarm water, and you can measure this, wow! It did get a little better, unlike Chemistry, which seemed to get steadily worse. Whenever a new substance was presented for which we had to describe the smell, if I was summoned to be the sniffer, I knew it was going to be bad. I gave Chemistry up at the age of 14. Maths was a little better; I quite liked geometry but couldn't see the point of algebra, where I used to turn the equations into their verbal equivalent in order to solve them – not a good long-term strategy! In contrast I liked the fact that Geography, English and History all allowed you to think for yourself in writing essay answers.

I was also intensely curious about the world and how it had got to be the way it is. I regularly read a publication called *The Wide World Magazine* that was full of yarns that purported to come from expatriates living in exotic and challenging parts of the world. I thought I would rather like to be an explorer or failing that a District Commissioner helping run part of the British Empire, which was of course, at the time, being hastily handed back to the locals, given that we could hardly afford to run Britain! I kept all this to myself when careers were discussed, having noted the scorn that greeted a timid and self-effacing lad who declared an interest in becoming a big-game hunter (perhaps he succeeded?). I stuck to the safe answer whenever questioned by saying that I wanted to be a teacher.

I did well enough at 16 to move on to what was known as the Sixth Form, leading to the next academic rung. This involved the Advanced Level Exams, together with a third-rung Scholarship Level, which if negotiated successfully could earn you a grant to go to university, providing enough to live on for three years and likely to guarantee you entrance to all but the top universities. We were a particularly good year, and four of us were awarded State Scholarships and decided to stay on and try for Oxford and Cambridge.

Entrance to Oxbridge, as it is sometimes known, depended on selection by one of a large number of individual colleges, each of which had their own scholarship examinations from which they selected one or two scholars who would receive financial support and a range of other unfunded entrants. Given my State Scholarship, funding was not a problem for me, but what *was* problematic was the fact that admission in the arts subjects typically depended upon focussing on a specific subject: History or English, for example, with only a few colleges offering a general examination analogous to the three-subject package required for a State Scholarship. Public (i.e. private) Schools were largely staffed by Oxbridge graduates who were adept at training their pupils for the more specialised Oxbridge exam system and indeed often had close links with particular colleges. I opted to do the general examination offered by Christ's College Cambridge. One aspect was a general paper, for which our headmaster prepared us well; we spent the three months before the exam doing lots of interesting things, such as attending a series of lectures on modern art at the Leeds Art College, writing essays on issues of current political importance and even spending a day in court, where, by chance, we encountered a trial for homosexual behaviour that in this case occurred between a bus driver and his conductor, and was alleged to have occurred regularly at the bus terminus – not quite what the headmaster had envisaged, I suspect.

I duly went to Cambridge sitting in a large hall full of fellow Grammar School types all doing the general paper and duly appearing for interview. I was wearing a new suit; it was brown with yellow zigzags in a style known at the time as *zoot suit with a drape shape*. I was not offered a place; nor it appears were any of the hall full of general candidates. In the case of Oxford, I never got as far as being called for interview. However, two of my colleagues who opted for science were both accepted at Cambridge.

So, what to do next? I began to wonder about whether I really wanted to spend the rest of my life as a geographer; it did not at the time seem to have a great deal of depth. Furthermore, I had become interested in philosophy, largely as a result of a new course taught in my final years with the rather clunky title of "Greek and Roman literature in translation", taught by the Latin teacher who earlier had tried unsuccessfully to persuade me *not* to take Latin. I found that I really enjoyed reading translations of classics by Aeschylus and Pliny, Virgil and even Caesar's Gallic Wars, but I was particularly intrigued by the philosophy which included Plato's *Republic* and the atomic theory proposed by Lucretius. I also really enjoyed Bertrand Russell's popular philosophy books, written in a clear and lucid style that eventually won him the Nobel Prize for literature. As Russell explained, having established his credentials with the hugely erudite Principia Mathematica, he was able to write clearly and still be taken seriously.

I liked the idea of studying philosophy but thought incorrectly that this would involve reading texts in Latin and Greek. A second factor was the concern that I might find it difficult to earn a living as a philosopher. What about psychology? A chap a couple of years ahead of me at school had gone to do psychology at the London School of Economics; I also heard a talk on amnesic patients on the radio which I found fascinating; finally my hero,

Bertrand Russell, in a radio interview said if he were starting again he would be a psychologist. Well, if it's good enough for Bertrand, why not?

I was again fortunate in that the father of one of my friends had a psychology degree from Edinburgh. He was a local Methodist minister and lent me his psychology books from the 1930s, which I read with considerable interest. This encouraged me to approach the headmaster with the idea of switching subjects, though I did so with some trepidation. To my surprise he was very encouraging, mentioning that his next-door neighbour was a lecturer in psychology at Leeds University and that he would arrange for me to go and talk to him. I can still remember the day; the department was in a large Victorian house, and I timidly knocked on the outer door – no answer. I went inside, and there was another door; as I was deciding whether to knock, the first door flew open, pinning me to the wall. I felt like a character in a Charlie Chaplin film, peeling myself off and going in pursuit of the lecturer, a Mr Joslyn, who proved extremely helpful. I explained that I did not want to go to university in Leeds but wanted to have the experience of living away from home, where would he suggest? He mentioned three places: University College London (UCL), Reading and Manchester. All allowed psychology to be done as an arts or science subject, but Reading required Advanced Level French for some reason. UCL required a slightly higher level of Latin, but it was possible to do that when you got there.

I travelled down to UCL where I was put through a range of selection tests and rather terrifying discussion groups with other candidates. I had not entirely given up the idea of Cambridge; my headmaster had mentioned, to my surprise, that he could probably get me into a less fashionable college than Christ's, so I wrote to the Professor of Psychology, Oliver Zangwill, explaining my situation. He replied, pointing out that psychology only became a substantial part of the Cambridge degree in the third and final year of study, advising that if I wanted to be a professional psychologist he would not recommend Cambridge. I was offered a place at UCL, and I accepted.

On balance, I think I had a good school education, though, given my subsequent career, a rather odd one. I must be one of the few Fellows of the Royal Society, the UK's Academy of Science, with no maths or science qualification beyond the age of 16. Do I regret my educational limitations? I think I would have enjoyed studying Biology at school, and I certainly regret my limited mathematical education, although my lack of maths has been less of a handicap than might have been expected; I am comfortable with the principles underlying statistics, although not with their mathematical derivation.

I have, however, reason to regret my lack of physics. In the early days of computers, programming in Cambridge was taught to any interested researchers from a wide range of departments in a single large lecture theatre. For homework we were required to write programs and hand them in, being told the following week whether they had worked or not. I was spared this daunting activity by the fact that all the examples assumed that everybody had studied Physics at least until the age of 18. I have never really caught up with even elementary programming and am still very dependent on others to cope with any form of information technology. So yes, on balance, my lack of maths and basic science has been a nuisance. It is tempting to blame the quality of teaching that I received. It certainly did not inspire me, but two students of my year gained Oxbridge places in science, so I suspect it may simply reflect the very rocky start I made, coupled with the greater dependence of science on solid foundations created during the early years of schooling.

What did I gain from Geography, English and History? First of all, a freedom to question established opinion, provided that the criticism is backed up by some form of evidence and a coherent argument. This still seems to me much nearer to what I do for a living than the learning about other people's discoveries that seemed to constitute my science courses; I like the process of exploration and discovery perhaps more than the discovery itself. Geography and History appealed to my interest in other countries and the people who lived in them, and how they, and we ourselves, have changed over the years. These topics continue to interest me and give me pleasure from reading and travel. Scientifically, I think of what I do as a form of exploration and of theories as intellectual maps.

My social life was almost entirely separate from school; I was not very good at soccer or cricket, and my one attempt to audition for a major part in the school play failed because I was unable to modulate the thick Yorkshire accent I had at the time. I ended up in a role that involved carrying a corpse on a plank onto the stage and uttering the immortal lines "Are there nails with it?" in an attempted Irish accent. Much more important was my membership in a Scout group attached to the Hunslet parish church. The Boy Scouts seem now often to be regarded as figures of fun, but in my own case they provided an important social focus from childhood until my twenties. It was particularly important to me during my later teenage years, when I progressed to the older scouting group known as *rovers*, an appropriate name since we did rove, not only over the countryside but occasionally to the City Varieties, a surviving remnant of the music hall (British vaudeville). Ages ranged from 18 to late 20s, and activities largely involved hiking in the Yorkshire Dales, usually on Sundays but sometimes including midnight hikes. There were two great advantages to membership: the first was that we had exclusive use of a large loft where we could sit around and talk, and the second was that we had access to communal camping equipment that we would not ourselves have been able to afford. A friend, Brian Scarth, and I were particularly fond of hike camping, where we carried everything in our ex-army rucksacks, often travelling by hitch-hiking.

Looking at the atlas of Europe, it occurred to me that the Island of Majorca seemed potentially interesting and that the tiny republic of Andorra, high up in the Pyrenees, seemed more or less on the way. I proposed that my friend and I would hitch-hike there, and somewhat to my surprise my parents agreed and even allowed me to draw out all my savings, a grand total of £20 ($30). It was clear by mid-France that progress was too slow, and we had to take trains, buses and a ship. I had my first taste of garlic in Andorra – it made me feel sick! I experienced my first stay in a hotel; it had cockroaches, and the proprietors tried to cheat us. Barcelona provided my first experience of a Mediterranean port district where everyone seemed to be living and working on the crowded streets, after which we slept on deck for the overnight passage to Majorca. Tourism in Majorca was in its infancy, and walking in the principal city of Palma, we were handed a card by the police explaining that the shorts we were wearing (standard issue for scouts) were regarded as indecent, and would we please return to our hotel and don long trousers? We didn't have a hotel or long trousers but discovered that outside the main city nobody cared. Money was running low, but having heard that real coffee was very scarce in Europe, we had taken a pound tin of coffee with us, and by visiting one or two hotels and bargaining, we were able to obtain a good enough price to extend our stay by a couple more days before heading back home. It was a great trip!

On subsequent years we went to the Black Forest in Germany, encountering a man with a black cap trudging by with a look of intense concentration. We were told that this was the famous philosopher Heideger and that all he ever said to anyone was "Cnn". "What did that mean?" we asked, "Nobody knows!" The following year we built a folding canoe. I had seen adverts for canoe kits, which turned out simply to involve the plans, but fortunately my friend is considerably more practical than I am. He worked at the technical support section for Leeds Tramways, and with the help of my mother's sewing skills, we ended up with a canoe that could be folded up and placed in an ex-army kitbag, mounted on pram wheels and taken around the country. We had a splendid holiday canoeing down the Moselle from France, via a portage round an unexpected large dam, into Germany, ending at the Rhine, where the sight of an enormous river with huge barges persuaded us to terminate our trip. Finally, we took our home-made canoe to Devon and Cornwall, where we learnt something about sea canoeing and the problem of turning a kayak around in choppy conditions. We also tried spear fishing. My friend had built a spear gun of enormous power that fired a harpoon suitable for whaling. Sadly (or perhaps happily?) our only success was a tiny fish that appeared to have died of fright.

My friend, Brian, and I are different; he is very practical, whereas I had lots of ideas as to things we might do but lacked the skills to do them. However, we shared a sense of adventure and a very similar sense of humour. He went on to an engineering apprenticeship, moving from trams to missiles and remaining in the same company until his retirement. Our only contact for the next 40 years was an annual Christmas card, but on my return to Yorkshire in my late sixties I contacted him. Our annual Christmas card is now supplemented with an annual pub crawl.

Note

1 Hoggart, R. (1957). *The Uses of Literacy: Aspects of Working-class Life.* London: Chatto & Windus.

2

Psychology in the 1950s

Seeds of the Cognitive Revolution

I was fortunate in choosing University College London (UCL), an exciting and rejuvenated department in an exciting rejuvenated city. UCL was founded in the early years of the 19th century by a group of free-thinking intellectuals, notably including the utilitarian philosophers John Stuart Mill and Jeremy Bentham who kindly bequeathed his skeleton to the college. He sits there to this day clad in his best suit, with his gloved hands poised over his walking stick with a high crowned hat above the wax mask of his face. The purpose of UCL's foundation was to break the tight link between the only other English universities, Oxford and Cambridge, and the Church of England. This did not go without opposition; with no chapel and no theology department, it was deemed "the godless house in Gower Street" and led in due course to the creation of a rival institution, Kings College London located in The Strand, with close links to the Anglican Church.

The UC psychology department had a new professor, Roger Russell, an American who had come to work in London during the war and liked it. He was an open-minded man with broad interests and considerable energy who created a department that in retrospect was a microcosm of the varied approaches to psychology at that time. Most of the research and many of our textbooks came from the US following the demise of German psychology under the Nazis and the disruption of psychology in the rest of Europe during the war. The teaching staff came from a wide range of backgrounds, including a number appointed by the previous professor,

Sir Cyril Burt, part of the psychometric tradition in British psychology based on the task of assessing cognitive capacities, and developing tests of intelligence. Earlier figures at UC included Karl Pearson and Charles Spearman, both with major international reputations for their work on psychometrics and the study of intelligence.

The recent department head, Cyril Burt, was originally an educational psychologist who did pioneering work on what was then known as "mental deficiency", setting a London-wide child-guidance system. He carried out an early twin study concluding that intelligence had a strong genetic component. This was questioned after his death with evidence that some of his data might have been invented, provoking a major controversy in the 1990s; although his conclusions have been largely supported by later and more adequate twin studies, Burt's own evidence is still open to question. The psychometric influence within the department continued, largely through lecturers, mainly female, who in my recollection taught the practical aspects of psychological testing, requiring us to familiarise ourselves with various tests by measuring each other's intelligence and personality. Related lectures went under the rubric of "child psychology", which I remember principally as learning, or in my case failing to learn, a series of "milestones" describing what children might be expected to achieve at a given age. Happily, the rest of the departmental syllabus was rather more exciting.

The most influential teachers were two young lecturers, with contrasting personalities. Henry James (we also had a William James, in the department) had been a student of Sir Frederick Bartlett in Cambridge. Henry had a rather reserved self-questioning approach to psychology. His lectures were full of challenges, focussing on things that we didn't yet understand. I really liked this approach; it was based on intriguing puzzles, not just the answers, while some of my fellow students were less enthusiastic. His friend Jonckheere was an extrovert enthusiast who came originally from the Channel Islands, just off the French coast, despite his Dutch-sounding name. He had been appointed by Burt and was an expert psychometrician and an enthusiastic statistics teacher. He had wide-ranging interests which he was very good at communicating. I can still remember his lectures in "animal psychology", which included demonstrations that very simple basic mechanisms, for example the tendency to move consistently up a slope or away from light, could lead to apparently purposive behaviour in snails or maggots, a process often illustrated by vigorous miming.

This was a golden age for ethology, the careful empirical study of animals in their natural habitat, led by Konrad Lorenz in Austria and Niko

Tinbergen who had recently moved from the Netherlands to Oxford. Using an ingenious combination of natural history and experimental manipulations, they were able to tease apart the mechanisms whereby a whole range of instinctive behaviours were controlled. In the case of the herring gull for example, Tinbergen showed that the red spot on the parent's bill was a trigger for a feeding response in the chick; furthermore, the crucial importance of the redness was shown when the chick responded even more vigorously to a red pencil held by the experimenter. Meanwhile, Lorenz demonstrated the dramatic phenomenon of imprinting, showing that geese would become attached to whatever stimulus was presented during the first hours of life, whether this was Lorenz himself or even a towed cardboard box.

Neither James nor Jonckheere would do very well in the current British academic climate, which demands copious publications in "high impact" journals. Henry James complained that his experiments never seemed to work, and shortly afterwards emigrated to Canada, where I understand he proved to be an extremely good head of department. He was subsequently promoted to Dean, a post for which he seems to have proved quite unsuited. He retired from the fray, devoting his time to studying harp seals off the Canadian coast, before eventually becoming a successful psychology department head in a different university. Jonckheere remained at UC, helping many generations of young scientists with his enthusiasm, probing questions and statistical expertise but publishing little himself. When people want to make the obvious point, that departments need good and committed teachers as well as research grant-getters, Jonckheere's name is often the first to be brought up in evidence.

Another influential teacher was Peter Kelvin who came from Oxford where Psychology was then taught as part of a degree known as *Modern Greats*. *Greats* was the term applied to the traditional Oxford education for gentlemen, which involved studying the Greek and Roman classics of philosophy and literature in their original form, and was regarded as providing an ideal general education. By the 1950s, this had changed, allowing the study of Philosophy, Politics and Economics (PPE) or Philosophy, Physiology and Psychology (PPP). In addition to lectures, we were taught in tutorial groups of four or five and required to write an essay every week. Kelvin initially set philosophical topics which he explained would help our essay writing skills. I enjoyed that, although I found myself increasingly drawn to evidence-based psychology. He also taught physiological psychology, presumably reflecting his PPP background. He seemed, however, to be someone who thought largely in words taking a perverse pleasure in rolling off the names of various parts of the brain, as if reciting verse, while, so far as I remember, paying little attention to their spatial arrangement. He subsequently focussed on social psychology to which he was I believe, more attuned.

The reader in the department (a reader is a research-oriented position just below the rank of full professor) was John Whitfield. Mr Whitfield was somewhat older and more experienced than other lecturers and had done research ranging from work on absenteeism in industry to the study of "thinking", a popular topic at the time, to which he applied the newly developed concepts and measures of information theory (of which more later). Unfortunately, by the time I reached UC he seemed rather to have run out of steam. His lectures on statistics were so bad that virtually no one attended, causing him after a few weeks to leave a note saying, "Anyone wishing to discuss nonparametric statistics with Mr Whitfield should come to his room at 11am". Few did. His tutorials were little better. And yet he seemed to be someone of real talent; at my first Experimental Psychology Society meeting in Cambridge, during question time he walked to the front, said a few words and wrote an equation of the blackboard whereupon everyone applauded! I have no idea why. He was, I suspect, a talented man in the wrong job.

The department was growing. New arrivals included Bob Green, from the University of Hull, a tiny department at the time with no full professor but one that produced a number of individuals who later became talented though somewhat maverick professors. Bob had strong anarchist sympathies and joined us in a student protest march, advising on the potential use of ball bearings when confronting police horses. We had, however, neglected to bring ball bearings, and the horses of the mounted police proved very friendly and open to bribery with sweeties. The march was part of a protest against the banning of the annual student "rag" in which students from UC and King's would dress up in carnival mode and collect money for charity, meanwhile throwing flour at each other and attempting to steal the other sides' mascot, a wooden lion named Reggie for Kings and the figure of a highlander named Phineas Mclino for UCL, followed by a bonfire and a party. Affronted by the ban, King's and UC planned joint marches that would converge on Piccadilly Circus at 7 pm, bringing the West End of London to a complete halt around the time that theatregoers were arriving. It was well-organised, good-humoured, apart from the odd cross policeman (and theatregoer no doubt). It worked remarkably well in bringing our protest to the notice of the national press. It had, however, no effect whatsoever on bringing back the rag and was forgotten by the following year.

A few years later, Bob Green became the first professor of psychology at the Open University, newly founded and pioneering a distance learning approach to university education for the many people who had not had the opportunity to attend a traditional university. The appointment did not appear to work well. I suspect that his anarchist views may not have been a good match with the need to organise distance teaching for many thousands of students. Fortunately, other less anarchistically inclined staff were subsequently appointed and psychology at the Open University has been a great success. Another colourful addition to the staff was Norman Dixon who, despite losing an arm in the war, drove fast cars with his remaining arm. He did important early research on subliminal perception, the capacity to make accurate judgements of stimuli that appeared to be beneath the level of awareness. He also published an important book on military blunders, perhaps prompted by his own wartime experiences?

Finally, London proved to be a rich source of supplementary teaching for the department. My favourite lecturer was Professor J C Flügel, an early British psychoanalyst who lectured on the rich heritage of psychology's German roots. Although born in London, he had a German father and had spent some time in Wurzburg, famous for a school of thought that rebelled against earlier introspectionism and introduced the concept of "imageless thought". This rejected earlier ideas that the mind could adequately be understood through introspection. Flügel also wrote a book on the psychology of clothes, suggesting that in the future, people would wear fewer of them. His demise in the mid-1950s was marked by a tabloid headline, "Author of the brave nude world dies".

The Wurzburg school was followed by another more clearly influential movement known as Gestalt psychology. Its roots were in perception and in listing the principles whereby separate features would cohere into a *Gestalt*, an organised structure for which it was claimed that "the whole is greater than the sum of its parts". Such principles included continuity, dots that formed a line were likely to be seen together; proximity, near neighbours are more likely to cohere; similarity, like clusters with like and symmetry, symmetrical patterns are more readily perceived. In visual perception, these principles continue to provide a valid account of the way in which visual features cohere as visual objects. We read influential books by Kurt Koffka on perception and Wolfgang Kohler, who applied broad Gestalt principles to problem-solving in apes. Max Wertheimer generalised the Gestalt approach to thinking in humans, while Kurt Lewin developed a highly original approach to social psychology and motivation within this broad framework. The Gestalt approach was, however, deeply inimical to the Nazi party who saw the job of psychologists as being to demonstrate the superiority of the German master race. These highly influential psychologists left, typically for the US, which welcomed them but not their theoretical views that were quite inimical to the neo-behaviourism that was dominant in the US at that time. However, despite the departure of its leading advocates, the Gestalt approach with its emphasis on organisation rather than simple association lived on and was revitalised as part of the cognitive revolution that in due course swept US psychology during the 1960s.

What about research at UCL? This did not play as big a place in the department as it would today. As was common at the time in the UK, the staff were appointed more or less straight from completion of their undergraduate degree, with some universities favouring their own graduates, leading to a disastrous degree of intellectual narrowing. Fortunately, this was not the case at UC. Several lecturers were concurrently working towards a PhD, a process that accelerated when it became clear that Roger Russell, who supervised most of the staff PhDs, was moving to a senior administrative post, as Secretary of the American Psychological Association. Roger himself was a very active researcher, well ahead of his time in studying the effects of cholinesterase on learning and memory and supervising applied work on the recently discovered insecticide DDT. Its effect on the muscle function of rats was studied by providing a tiny harness and requiring the rats to pull weights of different sizes, showing that performance was clearly impaired by DDT. In due course Roger went on from being Secretary of the APA to serving as Vice Chancellor (chief executive) of a new Australian university before returning to the US for a similar role at the University of California Irvine. When I last met him, he was well into his eighties and still pursuing research in what we then called physiological psychology and is now neuroscience.

What was it like to be a psychology student in 1950s London? Exciting, both intellectually and socially. Intellectually, psychology was at a cross-roads with a whole range of new ideas challenging the neo-behaviourist tradition that had dominated US psychology since the 1930s, of which more later. Although influential, neo-behaviourism was much less dominant in European experimental psychology, where Gestalt psychology remained strong in parts of Europe, while Sir Frederick Bartlett was a major influence in Britain. Bartlett was originally a Cambridge philosopher who turned his interest to experimental and social psychology. His most influential book, *Remembering*, was a reaction against the approach to memory originally proposed by Ebbinghaus in Germany in 1885. Ebbinghaus had made the very important step of refuting the then current idea that it was impossible to carry out experiments on such "higher" cognitive functions as remembering. He did so by developing an extremely simple experimental situation, using himself as an experimental subject and rapidly reading a number of nonsense words that were explicitly designed to be devoid of any meaning. By varying the number of repetitions and then measuring retention after various delays, he was able to show very lawful relations between learning and forgetting, in particular demonstrating his classic forgetting curve. This showed a logarithmic relationship between elapsed time and amount lost from memory; forgetting was rapid initially, then levelling off.

Although Ebbinghaus himself abandoned research on memory after a few years, it was taken up in the US where it went under the rubric of *verbal learning*. This approach was dominated by the attempt to plot lawful functions relating learning and remembering and to interpret them in terms of a very limited set of principles based on the acquisition and loss of associations between specific stimuli and specific responses. Such an approach was particularly dominant in US Midwestern universities and sometimes dismissed as "dust bowl empiricism". Although scarcely exciting, the principles derived, focussing on conditions under which one type of learning would disrupt another, remain important in understanding forgetting. Roger Russell made sure that we knew about them, and that we had a firm grounding in experimental methods.

Bartlett rejected the Ebbinghaus approach, arguing that by avoiding the complexities of meaning, Ebbinghaus had thrown out the baby with the bathwater. His approach was completely different. He would present his student participants with complex material, such as a story from native American folklore and then ask them to recall it after varying periods of time. He was less interested in *amount* recalled than in the nature of what was remembered, what was forgotten and in particular in the nature of erroneous recalls, for example "something black came out of this mouth" became "he frothed at the mouth". He proposed that such errors reflected the underlying act of remembering which he suggested was dominated by an *effort after meaning*. This involved the rememberer attempting to integrate the new material with existing knowledge. The organisation of such knowledge was reflected in his concept of a *schema*, a structured mental representation. His emphasis on the active role of the rememberer in making sense of the situation was timely but his concept of a schema was regarded at the time as too vague to be scientifically useful, although as we shall see, this view was dramatically reversed following the development of computers.

Hence, though treated with great respect, Bartlett's ideas were regarded as old-fashioned and impractical in contrast to some of the exciting new ideas that had developed during and after the Second World War. One of these was *information theory*, developed at Bell Laboratories in the US by Claude Shannon and published in 1948. It proposed a method of measuring the flow of information through a limited-capacity communication-based channel, with the information in a message reflecting its capacity to reduce uncertainty, roughly speaking, its news value. Being told whether a coin had come up heads or tails, for example, would convey less information than knowing the result of the roll of a dice, indicating one of six possibilities. The degree of reduction of uncertainty was measured in terms of binary digits or "bits", which could be represented by an on or off switch. Hence, a choice between two equally likely alternatives could be seen as transmitting one bit of information, one of four alternatives transmitting two bits, one of eight transmitting three bits and so on.

Within psychology, excitement came from the application of this measure to human behaviour. If the individual is regarded as an information processor with limited channel capacity, then it would be predicted that time to process and respond to a signal would increase systematically with the uncertainty or information conveyed by that signal. This was tested experimentally by Edmund Hick, in the Cambridge UK psychology department. He required his subject to respond as rapidly as possible to the onset of a light by pressing a specified key. By varying the number of lights and associated keys, he varied the information transmitted, finding that time to respond increased logarithmically with number of keys suggesting the involvement of a system of precisely limited information processing capacity. Psychology at the time was somewhat preoccupied with its claim to be a "true" science, by which it often meant that it should look like physics, hence the enthusiasm for declaring this to be "Hick's Law". The law was in fact based on only two people: Hick himself a psychiatrist, who subsequently retreated into psychoanalysis and to the best of my knowledge published little else of this nature, and Richard Gregory, who subsequently went on to develop a world reputation as a vision scientist, an inventor and a gifted and energetic populariser of science. Fortunately, despite its limited sample size, the findings proved robust and have been replicated many times.

Participating in reaction time studies is not the most exciting way of passing time, particularly if you are studying the effects of extended practice on performance as did two US investigators Mowbray and Rhoades. They enlisted the help of inmates of the local penitentiary who had a good deal of time on their hands. They showed that although reacting to one of eight lights was substantially slower than responding to two at the beginning of the experiment, as practice continued the difference reduced to a point at which the function was flat; it made no difference whether you were responding to one of eight lights or one of two. Had the human information channel acquired infinite capacity?

In a subsequent study Conrad demonstrated that Hick's Law ceased to apply if the stimuli and their associated responses were very familiar, for example reading well-known words, while somewhat later in a highly influential study, Walter Schneider and Richard Shiffrin made an important distinction between the early stages of learning to link a stimulus with the appropriate response and later stages when the link becomes increasingly automatic. The task of learning to drive is a good example; initially it is a very attention-demanding activity which eventually becomes largely automatic.

An elegant extension of the application of information theory to psychology was developed in the US by Paul Fitts, an inspirational figure who, like Bartlett and Broadbent in the UK, believed in combining basic research in psychology with its practical application. He studied a simple tapping task in which the participant has to move from a start point and tap a target disk as rapidly as possible. He was able to show a very lawful relationship between the size of the target, the distance moved and time to respond, known as Fitts' Law. Sadly Fitts died at a young age, although as we shall see later one of his students, Michael Posner went on to become a central figure in 20th-century psychology and neuroscience.

I suspect that few basic psychology courses teach either Hick's or Fitts' laws, not because they are false but because we have become much more interested in the *mechanisms* whereby such relationships occur. One possible objection might be that one rarely has a simple array of equally probable stimuli, each mapped onto a separate response. This is not a valid criticism however, since another way of varying the information load conveyed by a signal is through its probability of occurrence. If a red light comes on eight times as frequently as a green one, the appearance of a red light will convey less information; it has if you like less news value. Time to react in this situation is also lawfully related to the information transmitted as shown by Ray Hyman, another colourful pioneer in this area. Ray is also an extremely skilled conjurer with a very active interest in investigating claims of "psychic" powers such as spoon bending. The fact that information theory can be applied to events differing in probability makes it eminently relevant to the world outside the laboratory where such biases are universal. They were, however, at the time, largely immeasurable; the world was simply too complex a place to readily apply information theory. With the subsequent development of computers with massive data storage capacity this is no longer a problem and information theory now plays a central role in computational approaches to understanding a wide range of human activity.

Another important theoretical development that flourished in the 1950s and has continued to be influential concerns the area known as *cybernetics* after the Greek word for the helmsman of a ship. The term was invented by Norbert Weiner, a brilliant US mathematician who published a highly influential popular book entitled "The human use of human beings" in which he advocated the development of machines capable of performing activities that currently could only be performed by humans. This field has subsequently developed enormously under the terms *Artificial Intelligence* (AI) and robotics. In the 1950s however, its initial influence was through providing a model or theoretical representation of the way in which humans might perform skilled tasks. Behaviour was assumed to be shaped by "feedback" signals, whereby the effects of an action are registered, fed back to the action control system and used to control future actions. For example if I am reaching for my alarm clock in the dark, the touch of the plastic feeds back the information that I have contacted it and initiates future grasping behaviour.

I myself was much influenced by a book entitled "The Living Brain" by Grey Walter, a remarkably creative neurophysiologist who developed a very simple model of the type of learning known as classical conditioning, demonstrating that his simple assembly of wires and a battery showed similar patterns of "learning" to that of people or animals. He also developed a machine he called his "tortoise", which was capable of "searching" a room in order to locate a point at which its batteries could be recharged, an example of "purposive" behaviour that removed some of the philosophical objections to explanations based on the concept of purpose, explanations previously dismissed as unscientific. If a machine can behave in a purposive way, why can the term not be applied to a person? I have described some of the exciting new developments that were starting up in the 1950s. However as mentioned earlier, the vast bulk of work we covered came from America, where psychology was much more firmly established than it was in the UK at the time. This will be described in the next chapter.

My encounter with psychology went on against the background of student life in London, a big exciting city. In my first year I had "digs", a term for accommodation, as a lodger in a semi-detached house in Balham, a rather featureless lower-middle-class suburb of South London. It had the great advantage of being on an underground or tube line that allowed easy and direct access to UC. Our very maternal landlady looked after three of us: myself; another first-year student who was studying English Literature in preparation to become a Church of England curate; and Algy, a middle-aged businessman who would return to his family at weekends. Over our full English breakfasts, he would regale us with tales of his wartime experience as an air raid warden, whiling away the time between raids and serving as a highly inappropriate agony aunt offering advice to distraught young ladies. His main post-war interest was the cinema where he took a perverse pleasure in detecting errors in continuity and other minor mistakes. We never discovered what he did for a living.

My own week was filled with lectures, seminars and time in the library, while on Saturdays I played rugby and in the evening went to the student "hop" a dance in the student refectory, which provided a way of meeting girls. At the time, UCL had more men than women students, but the balance was maintained by nurses who came over from the several local London teaching hospitals and by girls from Bedford College, a women-only college of the University of London that was located in Regents Park, nearby. If you were lucky, you would get to escort a young lady back to her nurse's residence or college while mutually deciding whether further meetings were a good idea; not exactly speed dating but more effective than most other methods of getting together at the time. Sundays tended to be rather quiet at first, with my fellow student at church all day and Algy home with his family and I began to worry about having a day without friends around. After a while however, I began to realise that after six crowded days, it was quite pleasant to have a day of comparative solitude reading the Sunday papers, listening to the radio and going for walks. This pattern changed with my acquiring a regular girlfriend, where Sundays became a time for visiting the many parks and museums that London provides.

In my second and third years I lived in a student hostel in the heart of Bloomsbury, a wonderful area of London, with the whole of the West End in relatively easy walking distance. The hall functioned very much as an Oxbridge college, providing not only accommodation but also breakfast and dinner. Food was still rationed, and I would hand over my ration book at the beginning of term, retrieving it at the end. I made friends both there and at UC more generally, from many different countries. I was the only psychologist in the hall, and each morning would be presented by my friends with their dreams, which I would then "interpret" in the most lurid way, based loosely on cases described by Freud, where I often felt that the link between the dream and its interpretation was distinctly tenuous. Within psychology, I enjoyed the company of my fellow students, but we did not socialise more generally. A good number were mature students, some of whom had had practical experience within psychology and were seeking a formal qualification, while a number of others came from London and tended to have their main contacts around their home. As a group, I found the Zoology students very congenial and they provide the only currently active link to my friends as a student.

Culturally, London in the mid-1950s was a very exciting city. When I arrived there in 1953, virtually all aspects of culture, poetry, novels, plays, opera and music appeared to be the province of the privately educated middle classes. This was changing. The first play I went to was a rather tedious rehashing of a Greek myth in which the principal source of humour came from the anachronistic combination of Greek gods in their robes exchanging witty banter with each other in sub-Noel Coward dialogue. My next play was very different; it was entitled "The Long, the Short and the Tall" and involved an army patrol fighting terrorists in the Malaysian jungle. They spoke like real people facing important issues with insight and humour. I discovered later that its author, Willis Hall, came from the same working class end of Leeds as myself and had based the play on his own experience as an army conscript serving the two years required for all young men in the immediate post-war years, and which I myself expected to have to serve after graduation. This was just one of a wave of plays and books that reflected the post-war break-up of the traditional domination of the Arts by the English class system, a process that has been described as "the rise of the meritocracy".

At the time we seemed to be developing a society based on equality of opportunity rather than class and tradition. It was driven by the remarkable post-war Labour Government that introduced the National Health Service, still hugely valued across British society, free secondary education with university grants for high flyers, together with the nationalisation of traditional industries such coal, steel and the railways. This was all achieved against a background of considerable national poverty following the debts built up in order to fight the war. The Labour Government had little support or sympathy from a US that seemed shocked that the country had chosen not to elect Churchill who was hugely admired in Britain as a wartime leader but regarded as unwilling to produce the fundamental change to society that people wanted. As he subsequently demonstrated as a later Prime Minister, he was much better at fighting a war than running a peacetime government. Times were hard economically, but there was great hope of a fairer and more just society to come.

I read few novels at the time, a reaction against being made to study Jane Austen at school for exam purposes, preferring to read travel books. I did, however, enjoy American novelists, including Hemingway, Steinbeck and Scott Fitzgerald, and began to be interested in the British novel when it broke away from the earlier upper-middle-class pattern set by writers such as E. M. Forster and Virginia Wolfe, with authors such as Kingsley Amis, John Wain and John Braine seeming to reflect the world I myself knew. I arrived in London with an obvious Yorkshire accent. This was not the handicap it would have been a few years before; Harold Wilson, a future Prime Minister, had a Yorkshire accent, and given the way in which the national culture was developing, it could actually be an advantage. The turning point came in my first year when a posh chap with a double-barrelled name complemented me on it, commented on its "quaintness". I decided at that point that quaint or not, I did not want to be pigeonholed by an accent and decided to let it drift into the relatively standard form, as reflected at the time in a typical BBC radio announcer and as spoken by many people around me. I am someone whose accent drifts accord-ing to the ambient environment, so it was not very difficult, and in fact pleased my parents who had complained as my accent became broader dur-ing my childhood years. I remain somewhat bilingual and since returning to Yorkshire, have, for example, when travelling on the bus, reverted to saying "bus pass" with a long *u* and short *a*, rather than the southern equiv-alent a short *u* and a long *a*.

Shortly before starting my degree I had read and been thrilled by a book entitled "Listening with the third ear: The inner experiences of a psycho-analyst" and imagined my future along similar lines. I had too much low cunning to confess this when interviewed for a place at UC, declaring an enthusiasm for experimental psychology, which though feigned, proved prophetic. On starting the course, I rapidly became fascinated by the pos-sibility of experimentally investigating the way in which the mind works, allowing the evidence to decide whether you were right or not, and if not, then changing your theory. I really enjoyed the course and got high marks throughout my degree for the weekly essays we were expected to write. However, at that time, classification of your degree depended on the final part of the final year when everything was tested using a series of about six three-hour examinations each typically requiring the answering of four essay-based questions, together with a research project carried out across the final year. For my project I had opted to be one of a group of students working under the direction of Hannah Steinberg, a psychopharmacologist, on the effects of nitrous oxide, the so-called "laughing gas" then used as an anaesthetic in dentistry. The thought of gassing my friends was intriguing and proved interesting, though it did not yield anything of great originality.

The last exam involved a three-hour essay on a single topic and inspired a good deal of speculation before the exam. The hot topic in UC was "thinking". We were, however, examined jointly with another college of the University of London, Birkbeck, where the hot topic was "skill". I made a bad guess and in the absence of any questions on thinking, rather foolishly tried to answer a question on skill in terms of thought. For whatever reason, I failed to get the first-class degree I expected on the basis of my coursework and was downcast. Should I become a clinical psychologist, which at the time seemed to be an easy way out. I was discouraged by a friend who already was a clinical psychologist and complained that the profession at the time was dominated by psychiatry, with psychologists in the UK simply being expected to perform mental testing of patients who would then be treated by the medically qualified psychiatrists. That did not sound tempting.

Fortunately at that time, a new door opened. I knew that I wanted to go to North America for at least a year, and wrote to Donald Hebb at McGill University in Canada as the psychologist I most admired and would be most pleased to work with. He replied, saying that he could offer me half a graduate studentship. With no other source of funding I sadly had to turn the offer down. I had better luck, however, in applying for a fellowship funded by the English-Speaking Union, a group of Anglophile US citizens who raised funds that would allow British students to spend a year or more in the US. I received two offers, one from Tulane University in New Orleans and one from Princeton. The idea of a year in New Orleans sounded very tempting, but I was advised that although Princeton at that time was not going through a particularly purple patch, it would be a wiser choice, and I duly became the 1956 Princeton University James Theodore Walker fellow.

My fellowship was due to start in September, which left me with two months free to try to earn a few somewhat devalued pounds before I set off. In the UK at the time, unlike the US, it was rare to have a job during term time but common to have a vacation job. Typically, over Christmas I would work as a postman, helping to deliver the seasonal flurry of Christmas cards. Summer jobs were more varied. The year before, I had worked as beach patrol in Blackpool, a very popular seaside resort somewhat similar to Atlantic City. My job was to walk up and down in a scarlet jacket and blue shorts, looking efficient. In fact, the beach sloped so gradually that by the time anyone was in danger of drowning, they were out of sight. In fact our main job was to warn people that the tide was coming in, which it did, so slowly that reluctant movers could safely be left to wade back to the shore.

My final summer job before leaving for Princeton was in the long run, much more significant than my days as a lifeguard. Rather than Blackpool, it involved a summer in Cambridge at a research centre, the Medical Research Council Applied Psychology Unit. Here, I worked under the supervision of Harold Dale, an ex-UC student, on what effectively turned out to be an extended trial for a future job. Once again Roger Russell played an important role in recommending me to a laboratory that was far more distinguished than I realised at the time, as will become clear later.

3

The Trip of a Lifetime

The two months before I set sail for the US were, in retrospect, perhaps the most important two months of my professional life. They introduced me to the Unit, the Medical Research Council Applied Psychology Unit in Cambridge, where, across three separate visits, I was to spend over 30 years of my research career. I was unaware at the time of how scientifically distinguished it was, simply seeing it as a useful summer job that would allow me to earn a little money to take with me on my travels. It had been founded some 12 years earlier, based on a series of ongoing wartime projects under Bartlett's general direction at the department of psychology in Cambridge, with Kenneth Craik as it first director. Craik was a brilliant and highly creative Scottish scientist who was at the forefront of introducing ideas from control engineering to the study of human behaviour but sadly was killed shortly after becoming director in a cycling accident, leaving Bartlett to take over.

Medical Research Council (MRC) Units were typically set up around the work of single individual and were usually expected to disband on his, or more rarely her retirement. There were exceptions, including a couple of institutes in London, together with units that were seen to be pursuing an area of research that was likely to be of continuing interest to the MRC. Given the tragic death of its first director and the proximity of Bartlett to retirement, the Unit must have been in some danger. Happily it survived and continues to thrive as a vigorous 70-year-old institution, now called the Cognition and Brain Sciences Unit.

Bartlett retired in 1951 and his empire was split in two. The new professor of psychology at Cambridge was Oliver Zangwill, whose interests lay principally in neuropsychology, while direction of the Unit passed to Norman Mackworth, who like a number of members of the Unit had a background in medicine, highly relevant to wartime issues such as fatigue and the influence of climatic factors on military performance. Many years later, as director of the Unit I came across correspondence from this period from which it was clear that Bartlett's two heirs, although expressing cordiality, were somewhat suspicious of each other. The Unit was large relative to the academic department, and Zangwill was also somewhat concerned about the scientific quality of the staff, although he observed that two of them, Donald Broadbent and Richard Gregory, "might have some potential". They did indeed, both having careers of great distinction and in due course becoming Fellows of the Royal Society, the UK's prestigious academy of sciences. Oliver was always a very good judge of people. Mackworth was naturally keen to maintain the independence of the Unit, an independence that continued for some 73 years but has just ended with the recent incorporation of the Unit into the university.

It turned out that my summer job was really a somewhat lengthy job interview, although I don't think I saw it that way at the time. The Unit had previously employed a UC graduate, Harold Dale, initially for his statistical expertise but subsequently principally as a scientist; they were happy with Harold, and thought that they would check out another possible recruit, and I was the one recommended by my professor Roger Russell. I was set to work supervised by Harold on the problem of training military personnel to find faults in electronic equipment. I was assigned a bite-sized project and proceeded to carry it out, subsequently writing it up while in the US. I thoroughly enjoyed my time in Cambridge. The Unit was, and still is housed in a splendid late Edwardian villa on the outskirts of Cambridge, complete with croquet lawn and a small apple orchard. It had recently been purchased by Mackworth, who saw it on the market, decided that it would be an ideal place for the Unit, snapped it up providing a deposit from his own money and only then informed the MRC! This highly irregular procedure was almost certainly the only way he could have bought the house since by the time the relevant bureaucrats and committees had had their say, the house would certainly have been sold. I am happy to say that records show only a mild rebuke from the MRC, urging Mackworth not to do it again. He then furnished the house from Heal's, an upmarket London furnishing store, ensuring that everything, including the pictures, was top quality, a wise choice since they lasted for years without looking shabby.

Mack, as he was known, ran the Unit rather as the benign father of an extended family. At lunchtime we would all sit around a large round table and eat our sandwiches. At weekends, occasionally there would be events such as "treasure hunts" whereby people drove around the countryside in cars following clues. Despite, or perhaps because of, its relaxed atmosphere, the Unit was full of interesting ideas, many of which I suspect stemmed from its Deputy Director Donald Broadbent, who was, however, away in America that summer. Mack himself was relatively atheoretical, focussing on largely empirical studies concerned with attention and control in complex tasks, with most of the testing done by his wife Jane, also a medic who seemed at the time to be happy to serve simply as Mack's research assistant.

Mackworth's pet project was the development of measures of eye movement, with a good deal of the Unit's technical capacity devoted to creating a system whereby a large camera was mounted on the head of the subject. This resulted in the scene being viewed by the experimenter on a screen, together with a light spot indicating the direction of gaze of the subject who might, for example, be driving the Unit's experimental car through heavy traffic. A few years later Mark emigrated to Canada, devoting most of his subsequent career to projects based on his eye-movement system. Meanwhile his wife Jane, who had moved with him to Canada, suddenly began publishing first-rate papers and a book. It appears that the marriage had hit a rocky patch causing Jane to switch from research assistant mode and operate independently. They then got back together again, and the papers stopped. In terms of scientific output, Mack was probably the least distinguished director of the Unit, but, in my view he made two outstanding contributions, first in his amazingly daring purchase of the house and second in the generation of a warm, intellectually lively but friendly atmosphere that continues to this day.

But what of my forthcoming American adventure? The first thing to do was to get a visa, which involved a trip to the US Embassy in London, having my fingerprints taken, promising not to overthrow the US government and being given a chest X-ray, which I seemed to have failed! Visions of a tuberculosis sanatorium instead of Princeton loomed as I went in for a second X-ray. I passed; it seems that I had shivered at the crucial moment inducing a blur.

I sailed from Southampton in the old liner Queen Mary on September 13th, 1956, for a five-day voyage to New York. During the voyage I wrote a letter to my recently widowed mother, adding something every day and posting it in New York. Throughout my whole stay in the US, I continued to write every week describing my life and wonderful experiences. The letters were kept by my mother and passed back to me when she died. I am only now reading them some 58 years after they were sent. They provide an interesting background to what I now remember and what I have forgotten, and as such play an important role in the next section.

My first surprise on rereading my letters concerns the ship, the old Cunard Line Queen Mary. I recently watched a TV programme on ocean liners, marvelling at their size and luxury; those were the days, I thought, remembering the splendid Art Deco first class lounges. But this is what I wrote:

> perhaps the most striking thing with the Queen Mary was that I find it very difficult to regard her as huge. Inside, she is divided into lots of small cabins and lounges. The atmosphere is similar in many ways to that of the cross Channel ferry, softly lit corridors, brown panelling, the enclosed feeling and the motion of the ship all give this effect.

So much for my memory of splendour!

Rereading my letters, two things did not disappoint: the food and the weather. We had a healthy but somewhat predictable wartime diet that did not change dramatically during the austerity years following the war; in fact food rationing had only recently ended. I was amazed by the richness and variety provided on the ship. My letter carefully listed each day's meals, marvelling at the range and quality. I kept the menu card for the final Gala Dinner and note that it lists multiple courses comprising some 32 items, many of which were new to me. Although our wartime and post-war diet was healthy, our height of luxury comprised roast chicken for Christmas dinner, followed at teatime by canned Canadian salmon and perhaps sliced ham or pressed tongue; but to have such an array of delicious food after austerity Britain was an amazing treat, a treat that could have been, but fortunately was not, ruined by the storms we ran into.

The old Queen Mary was built without stabilisers and was somewhat inclined to pitch and roll in heavy weather, which we duly ran into, with a couple of days of pitching following by two more of rolling, confining many of the passengers, but fortunately not myself, to their cabins. The dining room was well equipped to deal with this, since each table was surrounded by ledges that could be clicked into position so that when the plates slid across, they did not end on the floor. The waiters performed balletic miracles in delivering the plates and clearing away without mishap. Sleeping was a problem, particularly when pitching turned to rolling and you were shifted back and forth within the narrow bunk beds like clothes in an automatic washing machine. Happily the storm abated, and people began to emerge, and social life begun. This included films and dancing, which, since the sea had not entirely settled, demanded a rather flexible style where laboriously dancing uphill was likely suddenly to switch to careering downhill as we went over a wave with the need to avoid sliding into the band. During the day, various deck sports were possible, and I even managed to sprain my wrist playing shuffle board, which seemed to be a cross between bowls, hockey and hopscotch. I got to know more of my fellow passengers, many of whom were fellow students often like me, travelling through the generosity of the US Fulbright Scholarship Scheme.

The ship was rigidly separated into first class, cabin class and tourist (us). I felt cross that we had no access to the swimming pool and gym available to the "high-ups". It was, however, always possible to find a door at one deck level or another that would allow us to infiltrate, and see how the other half was living. On the whole they were living rather boringly, and I remember going to the cabin class dance and noting that all the couples but one were interlopers like myself! Relying on my memory, to some extent supplemented by the letters, three images stand out, all of which involved being on deck. The first was sitting on deck in the storm chatting to a merchant seaman who was returning to his ship and his pointing out that when the ship was pitching, the best place to be was in the middle, which seemed sensible, as we looked at the crashing waves. The second was later in the voyage, going on deck in the evening with a steady warm trade wind blowing, and dark clouds on the horizon criss-crossed with flickering blue lightening. The third was the end of the voyage, with the wonderful sight of the Manhattan skyline and Statue of Liberty. Now the adventure could really begin!

I liked New York, where I stayed for a few days as a guest of a very hospitable member of my host organisation, the English-Speaking Union. He was an academic from New York University who had an apartment just outside Greenwich Village, my first experience of the wonderful hospitality I enjoyed throughout the visit. Another example was a trip around some of the main sights of New York provided by the young lady who organised our reception on arrival, after which I had a few days to explore on my own. It was not just the skyscrapers and museums that impressed me but also the bustle in the streets and feeling of sheer energy. People argued and shouted at each other on the street in a way that would never happen in London, something I found exciting but also slightly unsettling. During my sightseeing I thought I would visit Harlem and was surprised to be stopped by a policeman who suggested that it would *not* be a good idea. All in all, however, I had a wonderful and exciting few days before moving on to Princeton where I arrived to great festivities. This was not another example of US hospitality but a celebration of the 200th anniversary of the foundation of Nassau Hall. The oldest building of the university had, for a three-month period shortly after the War of Independence, been the capitol of the US, an event celebrated by the issue of a postage stamp in the Princeton colours of orange and black.

It was a memorable start to a great year. Princeton is a small and attractive town about 40 miles from New York; it seemed to depend for existence entirely on the college, together with a sprinkling of wealthy commuters. It fully lived up to the concept of an Ivy League College with its Victorian gothic buildings. I lived in the graduate college built very much on the model of an Oxford or Cambridge college, complete with dining hall and tower and separated from the main campus by what I remember as an extensive grassed area. The college provided three excellent meals a day and accommodation typically in suites comprising a living room and bedroom shared by two graduate students.

Things did not start too well. I was sharing with a German student of history who was a devout Catholic and extremely hard working, with a sense of humour I described as like "an elephant dancing". I had come with the intention of studying for a year during which I would learn something of the US, do some research and enjoy myself. Peter was very different, and we simply didn't rub along very well. He agreed that it might make sense for me to transfer but insisted that I request this from the Master of the College rather than the bursar, which I did, to the Master's bemusement. I explained that I would gain more from the experience of sharing with an American roommate and was duly transferred to share with Dave Chapelear, a chemical engineer from Yale who had an admirable liking for parties, Old Crow bourbon whiskey and classical music. We got on well!

Reading through my letters home, I am surprised at what a prominent part parties seemed to play in my life at Princeton; I went to far more than in London and had far more friends or at least acquaintances. There was a good reason for this. In London I tended to have a series of girlfriends with whom I would go to the theatre, the cinema or one of the many London attractions such as the Tower or Kew Gardens. Princeton was an all-male college, with few girls and even fewer local attractions to visit, other than the occasional trip to New York. Happily, the undergraduates seemed to have an unwritten rule that they never dated local girls, relying on the "big weekends" when girlfriends would be imported to watch one of the home football games, or to attend a ball. There *were* girls in Princeton, notably quite a number of Swedish au pair girls over to learn English, which meant that there were plenty of parties. An alternative was to go to a dance at one of the local women's colleges, local being anything from 20 to 200 miles away. I didn't drive but could usually get a lift, one weekend getting back from party in Bryn Mawr College at 4am and leaving that day for another party in a women's college over 100 miles to the north, Smith College, or was it Vassar?

What about work amidst all this junketing? The department was somewhat surprised to note that I had only signed up for one year, as they clearly expected me to stay for a PhD. After some discussion, it was eventually decided that I should do a master's degree, which consisted of a "qualifying examination" involving a range of psychological areas and a language test involving two languages, followed by an exam focussed on a chosen area of specialisation. I learned subsequently that I was not expected to be able to complete this in one year, and there was indeed doubt as to whether such a programme was even legitimate. The department was going through a period of rapid change from a broadly clinically orientation to a much more experimental focus, with the appointment of a number of keen young experimentalists.

Graduate school differs substantially between the UK and the US. In Britain at that time, a PhD student would expect to have completed a first degree focussed intensively on psychology, and hence providing a foundation for three years of full-time research. The US tradition allows a much broader undergraduate curriculum, with people moving into graduate school from many areas other than psychology, with the assumption that the necessary psychology would be taught during the first years of a PhD typically extending over four or five years or indeed even longer. I had already covered a three-year syllabus in London devised by a very good American professor and decided that since I did not intend to stay for a PhD, I did not need to pass. I felt free to enjoy myself. And I did.

So what were the dominant themes in North American experimental psychology at the time? They could broadly be divided into two areas: perception and learning; at UCL we were encouraged to focus on one or the other, but happily I liked both and never got around to choosing. Of the dominant themes in North American psychology in the 1950s, perception was the more interesting and varied, with the broad principles of Gestalt psychology accepted at a descriptive level, while theoretical interpretations were widely varied. Psychophysics, the careful mapping of the physical characteristics of the stimulus onto reported sensation, with its foundations in 19th-century German psychology, continued to be influential. I would, however, regard it as a set of gradually evolving methods and techniques, rather than a theoretical enterprise in itself. As such it continues to play a crucial role in any adequately testable theory of perception in both psychology and neuroscience.

Rather more exciting were the attempts to take perception outside the confines of the laboratory and into the natural world. One such attempt was made by the Hungarian psychologist Egon Brunswik who emigrated to California in the late 1930s, and who could be seen as the forerunner of the more recently developed emphasis on the ecological relevance of psychological concepts. He argued that the real world was complex with many perceptual cues, each giving rather uncertain evidence of the physical world, arguing for a position he called "probabilistic functionalism". He created the term *ecological validity* that has subsequently become so widely used to refer to the capacity of research findings to apply to the complex world beyond the laboratory. He argued against laboratory-based attempts to study perception, which depended on carefully controlling the experimental situation and manipulating one variable at a time, advocating instead a system that involved considering and measuring *all* the variables within a natural scene, not an easy task in the world outside the laboratory. Brunswik sadly committed suicide at an early age, and although the spirit of his work continues to be influential, its direct impact on perception at the time was slight. However, his ideas have continued to influence the area of decision-making, where the need to take into account a range of probabilistic factors before reaching a conclusion is more readily demonstrable.

A far more influential figure in visual perception from this period was J. J. Gibson, who again emphasised the importance of carefully studying the perceived environment; although rather than stressing its probabilistic nature, he stressed the richness of available cues, providing a *direct* rather than probabilistic basis for accurate perception of the environment. Gibson's approach to perception was strongly influenced by his wartime experience of working on the cues that enabled pilots to land planes successfully. He pointed out that this was influenced by aspects of the perceptual world of which we may be unaware but nevertheless use effectively. A good example of this is his concept of *optic flow*. A pilot flying a plane on a horizontal path would be likely to have the visual features of the surrounding environment flowing past in a symmetrical way, rather as the scenery flows past a rail passenger. If the plane begins to dive, then the centre point of flow will change, allowing him to use this changing flow pattern to control its heading. Gibson argued against the earlier idea proposed by Helmholtz that perception is essentially a way in which the brain actively solves problems about an uncertain world. He stressed instead the relatively automatic way in which we navigate our environment, often solving complex geometric problems rapidly, successfully and apparently automatically. Consider for example the response of a baseball or cricket batsman responding to an extremely rapidly projected ball which may well be taking a curved path. There are cues present, including the increasing size of the image of the ball on his retina, but such cues have to be picked up and utilised extremely rapidly. Or consider the trigonometric problem that needs to be solved by a fielder running to catch a skyed ball in the outfield, where success will depend on complex calculations based on the rapid online processing of changing visual cues.

Gibson's work continues to be deservedly influential leading to detailed modelling of highly skilled activities such as those described, leading to theoretical developments that were increasingly influenced by engineering and physics-based models. One curious feature of the area, however, has been the messianic zeal with which, otherwise, very amiable and sensible protagonists have pursued their approach, in particular vehemently denying the need for any kind of internal representation to supplement information from the environment.

Gibson's concept of "direct perception", emphasising the elegant mapping of our perceptual systems onto the physics of the visual world, was and is influential but did not replace the previously dominant view, stemming back to Helmholtz, that perception is a problem-solving task in which what we "see" is a construction based on a range of different perceptual cues, each of which gives an informative but not entirely reliable account of the physical world. This emphasis on less than perfect reliability was often demonstrated through visual illusions in which our perceptual system is misled. This view was championed during the 1930s and 1940s by a group known as "transactionalists" led by Adelbert Ames, an ophthalmologist with broad scientific interests. The group developed a series of room-sized demonstrations of the power of a range of selected visual cues, examples of which I discovered had been constructed in Princeton; though by the time I arrived they seemed to have been left to gather dust underneath the football stadium.

The most well-known of these demonstrations is the Ames room, which when viewed through a peephole looks perfectly normal. It is, however, far from normal; it uses the rules of perspective to create what appears to be normal but is in fact grossly distorted, with the result that when a person enters the room they appear to peephole viewer to be enormous. While the transactionalists seem to have faded from the scene, there continues to be considerable interest in visual illusions, partly because they are dramatic and intriguing, and partly because of what they can potentially tell about the mechanisms and processes underlying visual perception. A more recent enthusiastic proponent of this approach was Richard Gregory, a man of many talents who died recently, having lived a life that had much in common with that of a classic 19th-century polymath. In addition to being a keen collector and explainer of visual illusions, Richard was a prolific inventor, a great populariser of science more generally and of psychology in particular, setting up the UK's first Exploratory, a science centre that successfully offered children a way of learning about science in a hands-on way.

However, although the study of perception continued to be important, the dominant area of experimental psychology during the 1940s and early 1950s was the study of learning, which, strongly influenced by Watson's advocacy of behaviourism, tended to study rats rather than people. Watson was a trenchant critic of the introspectionist approach to psychology that was common in the early years of the 20th century, arguing that psychology could only become a genuine science if it limited itself to observable behaviour. He was forced to resign from his academic post following an affair with a student, who he subsequently married, going on to build a successful career in advertising. His views continued to be influential, particularly in the US, developing into a somewhat less extreme position known as "neo-behaviourism".

A range of theories were developed during the 1930s, most seeking to understand the basic "building blocks" of learning, typically assuming that these would comprise "associations" between external *stimuli* and the actions or *responses*. They basically comprised a modern extension of the "associationist" views of the 18th-century British philosophers John Locke and David Hume. The most ambitious of these approaches was that of the Yale psychologist Clarke L. Hull who proposed that when a stimulus was followed by a response which was, in turn, followed by a reinforcement (reward), a stimulus-response association was formed. Such stimulus-response associations were assumed to constitute the fundamental units of all learning in both animals and people. Hull kept detailed laboratory notebooks, which many years later were published. They reveal that his theory became much more influential when he decided to present it in a form based on Isaac Newton's *Principia*, the classic work that laid the foundation of modern physics. Like Newton, his account involved postulates and equations, generating predictions, most of which were then tested using albino rats in mazes of varying complexity.

Could Hull be psychology's Newton? Not according to his principal opponent, Edward C. Tolman in Berkeley California, who took a more "cognitive" approach. Tolman suggested that in learning a maze, rats formed a mental map, which they then used to navigate it. He showed, for example, that rats allowed to wander through the maze but given no reward, subsequently learned it faster once a reward was provided, a phenomenon known as "latent learning"; the rats had accumulated knowledge about the maze during their early wandering, despite lack of reward, revealed only later when a reward became available. He also showed that when a maze allowed more than one route to the goal box, the rat would learn the shortest (also consistent with Hull's theory), but if that was blocked, it would take the next shortest (less easy for Hull to explain). The situation was further complicated by the fact that Hull and his followers used albino rats with pink eyes and poor vision, while Tolmanians opted for hooded rats with good vision and a reputation for being streetwise.

As a student, I found this evermore heated controversy very convenient for exam purposes; Hull's predictions could be derived from a few simple assumptions, and Tolman's objections by imagining that you yourself were the rat. By the time I got to Princeton, the initial protagonists had retired, and the battle was being carried on by Kenneth Spence on the neo-Hullian side, principally opposed by M.E. (Geoff) Bitterman who happened to be visiting Princeton during my year there, as a scholar at the Institute for Advanced Study. Bitterman taught a course I attended, largely focussing on a recently published series of lectures given by Spence, the Sillerman Lectures, which his opponent described as "The Silly Man Lectures", not a wise kind of joke if your name is Bitterman or indeed Baddeley.

I myself was much more sympathetic to Tolman's views than to Hull's, and am grateful to Geoff Bitterman for providing the rats (the smart, hooded variety) on which my first published paper was based. I constructed a ramshackle set-up involving string, rubber bands and wire mesh, and duly demonstrated that my rats were less stupid than Hull's theory would predict. I was warned that it would be savaged by Hullian referees, but by that stage I was sufficiently streetwise to send it to a journal edited by Bitterman. It duly appeared and has been ignored ever since. In the couple of years between its completion and publication, the whole edifice of the Hull-Tolman controversy had collapsed and the underlying theories abandoned.

A basic problem was that in order to account for Tolman's results, Spence had to postulate non-observable *internal* stimuli and *internal* responses. Such an assumption went against the fundamental behaviourist principle of dealing only with overt stimuli and observable responses. A logical next step might have been for the field at large to accept that there was a need for some type of internal representation and to find ways of investigating this, although admittedly it was far from clear at the time just how this could be achieved. Instead, people simply abandoned the field, many switching to research on human learning, moving from the theoretically lively but frustrating area of rat learning to verbal learning, an area that was relatively little changed since the days of Ebbinghaus, focussing on carefully plotting relationships between variables rather than attempting to test ambitious grand theories. The approach remained neo-behaviourist in spirit however, relying theoretically on the assumption that learning involved linking specified stimuli to observable responses and focussing on the way in which new learning could build on, or potentially disrupt what had already been learned.

I had managed to save enough from my summer working at the Applied Psychology Unit before I left and from my generous student grant, to allow me to see a little of America. I decided to go to Los Angeles and try to extend my stay by getting a job there. I responded to an advert from a student who had agreed to drive the owner's car to Los Angeles, the deal being that he had use of the car but paid for the petrol. Divided between the four of us who made the trip, that was a pretty good deal, and for me a marvellous opportunity to see more of America. The car was a virtually new Chevrolet convertible, pale blue and white, with white wall tyres. I apologetically explained I couldn't drive, something my colleagues refused to believe until they witnessed my driving and its effect on the white wall tyres! So, I moved to the back seat, which, with the top down, still provided marvellous views of the country we were passing through, and some 57 years later I still have vivid memories of the trip, some of them revived by reading my letters home.

Not only could I not drive, but only one of my many relatives back home had a car, so rolling across America in a blue and white convertible felt like being in a Hollywood movie. Interestingly, of the wonderful sights we saw I chose to send an oversized picture delivering "Greetings from Kansas Turnpike", boasting two lanes in each direction, occupied by a single car. It was my first sight of a turnpike/freeway/motorway/autobahn/ autostrada. It was sent from Wichita Kansas from a motel where we had been asked "Are you with the rodeo?" This was real America! Our trip included Bryce Canyon Utah with its rock formations in all shades of red and yellow and the bright lights of Las Vegas at which point it was decided to avoid the heat over the next stage, by driving across the desert at night. I settled down in my spot on the back seat and went to sleep only to be woken up by the sound of a police siren and the sight of the driver waking up at the same time. I doubt that I have ever come closer to death since that point! Happily, the drivers all kept awake from there to LA.

I headed for UCLA and managed to find a place in a student cooperative where, for 53 dollars a month, I had bed, breakfast and an evening meal, provided I did my share of chores. I was surrounded by interesting and like-minded students from many different countries; I was the only Brit. I rapidly made lots of friends, a number with cars, very necessary in LA. I began my search for a job by contacting a US Office of Naval Research group working on fault-finding in electronic systems, a problem I had worked on in Cambridge. Unfortunately however, they could not employ me without security clearance. I tried for a factory job assembling equipment but failed the selection test, which involved picking up screws and putting them in holes as rapidly as possible, not one of my strong points. I joined a long line of applicants for ditch digging with the Southern California Gas Corporation. There were lots of applicants as an aircraft company had recently laid off large numbers of people. We eventually had to do a range of psychological tests where, despite aiming to come out as a stable extrovert with average intelligence, I was rejected. I checked out lifeguard jobs on the beach at Santa Monica. There were no vacancies, which was rather fortunate given that my swimming was restricted to a slow breaststroke.

Perhaps the most bizarre experience of a "job interview" was at a hospital where an English physiologist was working on recording activity from the brain of a living but deeply anaesthetised cat. Instead of an interview, where I could have explained my ignorance, I was asked to take a "protocol" and given a clip board and a pen, leaving me to scribble down the names of various brain structures that I had never heard of and which I certainly misspelled. After a few minutes a more competent graduate student took over the surgery from the blundering medic. Unsurprisingly the poor cat died and was then unceremoniously dumped in a waste bin. Out of curiosity, I tentatively asked what was the job? To receive the answer, "what job?" I was pretty glad that that one got away.

At this point the Office of Naval Research team came to the rescue. They could employ me as a technician, assembling multiple copies of a device for training electronic fault-finding skills. I took it; although I was no more qualified to assemble electronic equipment than I was to rescue drowning bathers or dissect the brains of unfortunate cats, it seemed relatively harmless. It proved extremely harmless since there was a problem with the equipment; it had a fault, and no one could find it! So I spent my days reading a book on electronics for halfwits and searching the literature for papers on the psychology of human-computer interaction; there weren't any at the time. The people in the group were extremely pleasant and although it was frustrating not to be able to contribute as a psychologist, I was very glad of a job. It did, however, have one drawback; I lived on the campus of UCLA, and the job was at the University of Southern California, a one and a half-hour bus ride each way, which involved getting up at 6.30 each morning. As I had just acquired a new girlfriend in West Hollywood, one more hour on the bus each way, I was somewhat short of sleep but managed to nod off during my electronics self-education.

I managed to fit in several visits to the Hollywood Bowl and see all the standard Hollywood and LA sights, including Barney's Beanery, a café that was reputedly the haunt of the beatniks who were just beginning to emerge on the US cultural scene. My somewhat bohemian fellow student friend from London, William James, was a graduate student at UCLA. I described him to one of the professors, who responded, "Oh, you mean the guy who looks like a hobo?" I visited Bill in an elegant but ramshackle house up one of canyons. I have two memories of my visit, one that he was smitten with unrequited love for a ballet dancer, perhaps a not sufficiently Bohemian ballet dancer, and the other of the ride home. This involved sitting on the back of his bicycle, whizzing down the canyon and along Sunset Boulevard, in and out of the traffic. I was terrified.

One pleasant feature of being an English-Speaking Union fellow was the hospitality occasionally received from its US members. One example of this was the generous offer of accommodation when I first arrived in New York and another was an invitation to lunch at a Los Angeles beach club. I had never been to a beach club before and was duly impressed by the surroundings and the generosity of my host (I noticed from the menu that the price of pre-lunch cocktails would have fed me for a week), while my host "reassured" me of its exclusiveness: "We don't admit Jews or movie stars".

This was my first encounter with such direct and overt anti-Semitism. There was certainly prejudice in the society I grew up in, largely based on racial stereotypes, as in jokes that began, "there was an Englishman, a Scotsman, an Irishman and a Jew", followed by a series of assumed characteristic ways in which they dealt with some dilemma. While stereotypes can be limiting and harmful, I discovered on reaching the US that they can also be useful, and I was, I confess, not above enjoying the stereotype of an Englishman generated largely by Hollywood: upper class, sophisticated and clever, and at that time, only rarely the villain. It meant that if I made a social faux pas, it tended not to be interpreted as the result of ignorance or stupidity but as a quaint sign of difference between our two cultures. I found that socially very liberating and was not adverse to occasionally exploiting it, as when I turned to an attractive girl sitting next to me in a lecture I was attending at UCLA and asked whether she had a rubber (eraser in England, condom in the US) I could borrow. The initial shock led to a lively discussion and to acquiring a Californian girlfriend, Jan. She was a philosophy student, attractive and clever, and happy to put up with a boyfriend who had no car, very little money and an odd vocabulary.

I was due to sail back to England in early September; when in early August, Jan announced that her long-standing boyfriend Kirk, a junior Olympic skier prone to jealousy, was coming to LA for two weeks. It seemed a good time to take up an invitation from my Uncle Archie to visit him and his family in Seattle. Archie was older than my father and had fought in the First World War, being gassed before emigrating, first to Montreal and then to Seattle. There he became a successful businessman rising to Vice President of his company with a fine house and a boat. He clearly felt close to my father however, and it was he who had offered to take my brother and myself when the prospect of Nazi invasion threatened in 1940. Despite the differences in lifestyle, he was very much like my father, who had died the previous year. He looked like my father, spoke like him and had very similar temperament and attitudes. It was uncannily like meeting my father once again.

The time came to return, and I took the Greyhound bus on the thousand-mile journey south to Los Angeles. In retrospect, a thousand-mile bus trip seems pretty grim, but somewhat surprisingly I rather enjoyed it. I seemed to fall into a mental zone of half-sleeping, half-waking, watching the scenery go by, and when we stopped automatically leaping to my feet, ensuring I did not have to queue too long for coffee and a cheeseburger. By the time I got back to LA I had less than two weeks left before I was due to sail from New York on the Cunard liner Mauretania. I was rather short of cash since my job paid in arrears. I considered hitchhiking, which sounded interesting, but could I guarantee to hitch 3000 miles in the nine days before we sailed? I decided to use the same method as before, agreeing a lift with a young man and his mother who were driving back to New York. It got me there, although it was a rather less pleasant experience than my trip out since my hosts were constantly quarrelling. However, they were happy for me to sleep in the car, which allowed me to save enough money for shopping in New York.

The return voyage was both better and worse than the outward trip on the Queen Mary. After a year in the US, I was less impressed by the food, but the weather was better and surrounded by other returning students, the five-day voyage seemed like one long party.

LEEDS AND BRISTOL 1957–58

4

In Search of a Job

Although it was good to be home and to catch up with family and friends, it was a time of great uncertainty. I knew that I wanted to do a PhD, preferably on a cognitive approach to learning in rats, but I had no idea how I might achieve this or a related goal. The first obstacle was that conscription to the armed forces was still in full operation, meaning that I would probably have to take a two-year break anyhow. I had maintained contact with Mackworth in Cambridge, and he suggested that if I joined the Air Force, he might be able to suggest that I be seconded to the Royal Airforce Institute of Aviation Medicine in Farnborough, which carried out research on human factors, albeit focussed specifically on aviation. That sounded tempting, although I did not see myself as interested in either flying or aeroplanes, so what if I joined the RAF and didn't make Farnborough? I need not have worried; my family doctor asked if I really wanted to be conscripted (no thanks!), then he would give me a letter that would provide an escape. It appears that the conscription programme was running down, and the recruiters were getting rather more selective. I had had a bad attack of asthma aged 13, which was enough to have me graded C and rejected as unfit.

Great news, but then what? Getting a job was far from easy. My mother's hoard of papers still contains a record of my efforts, discovering that I was "over qualified" to work in the personnel section of a local company and that the autumn was not an ideal time for applying for the very limited number of posts in psychology. I did, however, manage to get a job as a porter at St James' Hospital Leeds, a large institution housed in Victorian buildings. The job was not too bad once I got used to rising at dawn and travelling in a fug of cigarette smoke on the top floor of the early bus. Portering could be rather smelly at times and I never got used to the occasional need to transfer bodies to the morgue, but I liked interacting with the patients and got on quite well with my fellow porters. I had been portering for a month or two when a school friend who was now a teacher suggested that I apply to teach at his school. I applied and was duly appointed despite my complete lack of training; I even got a small salary increment for my Princeton MA.

My newly acquired teaching job was in a state Secondary Modern School in a mining village just outside Leeds, where I was assigned a class of about 30 11-year-olds selected as the least able of that year's intake. It was something of a shock after Princeton undergraduates. My classroom comprised half the school dining hall, separated by a moveable partition from the class taught in the other half by an equally inexperienced teacher who had just left Grammar School and was waiting to enter teacher training college. We rapidly discovered that it was very important to maintain discipline, which was not easy with children who saw school largely as a postponement of starting work, typically in coal mining for the boys and in a local shirt factory for the girls. We soon discovered the advantage of leaving the partition open, so that when one of us was writing on the blackboard, the other could keep an eye on both classes.

The headmaster, Jim Waggott, was a large ex-professional rugby player who ruled the school as a relatively benevolent despot, occasionally using the cane but aware that some of the children had far worst beatings at home. He seemed to be liked by both the children and their parents, and did a decent, although educationally rather limited, job. While some subjects were taught by specialist teachers, I was expected to teach mathematics and religion. As an agnostic of limited mathematical ability, this did not seem ideal. Maths largely comprised simple arithmetic. I soon discovered that attempting to teach Pythagoras' theorem was a little too advanced but had slightly more success in teaching the least able lad in my class to count using his fingers. He was a child with real charm and a remarkable capacity for telling stories, so if I ever needed to keep the class quiet for five or ten minutes while I was doing something else, I could always ask Geoffrey to tell us a story to which everyone listened intently.

The school was short of space, and on two mornings a week I would have to take my flock, together with a very experienced older teacher to a room in a nearby Primary School. There, the day would always start with a religious assembly, involving a reading from the Bible, which I could do, and a hymn, with my colleague playing the piano. As a very sceptical agnostic I was not in a great position to offer the type of instruction expected and reverted to simply reading a story from the Bible and then inviting the children to illustrate it using pencil and coloured crayons. They usually enjoyed this, although they did complain at being asked to draw Christ's entry into Jerusalem mounted on an ass through the thronging crowds.

They were on the whole nice children, although one lad did respond to a gentle tap with the claim that the last chap who had done that was stabbed, happily for me, a much less likely occurrence in those days than it is today I suspect. He was always in trouble, and according to Big Jim, the headmaster was regularly beaten by his parents with a frying pan! Another interesting lad had a father who was a known burglar; on one occasion when no one could find the key of a locked room, he was summoned to pick the lock, which he did. I found teaching to be an exhausting job, in part no doubt because I was totally untrained. Furthermore, some of my colleagues who clearly were effective teachers seemed to have transferred their way of dealing with bored and reluctant teenagers to their approach to their way of interacting with people more generally. Would this happen to me if I stayed?

Meanwhile, I was desperately searching for an alternative way ahead. Among the treasure trove of documents kept by my mother, I recently discovered evidence of my search. This included lists of psychology jobs available nationally. Very few seemed tempting: one in military psychology, one in occupational selection and four in the prison service. I also followed up the possibility of doing a master's course at the Tavistock Institute in London, asking if I might then progress to a PhD. The reply was not encouraging, emphasising the psychoanalytic nature of the institute and stressing that this orientation would be expected of any potential subsequent PhD. And then, out of the blue, my friend Harold in Cambridge forwarded an advertisement for a research position at the Burden Neurological Institute in Bristol to which I immediately replied.

I travelled down and was duly interviewed by the Institute's director, Professor F. L. Golla, a distinguished-looking 81-year-old, who explained that they had received a research grant from the Iveagh Bequest (a charitable foundation linked to the Guinness family), to carry out research into the potential *positive* effects of alcohol. Faced with the thought of returning to the arduous task of keeping rebellious D stream kids in order, I hastily searched through what little I knew about psychology and alcohol. I remembered an experiment on rats and booze which claimed that contented rats were teetotal, but when under stress, they opted for water laced with alcohol, presumably to steady their rodent nerves. I would look at the effects of alcohol on relieving stress in rats. "Splendid" responded Golla. "There was nothing like a tot of rum to help the men go over the top in the war", which I took to mean the 1914–18 war. "We can only offer you a thousand pounds a year, but you should be able to scrape through on that". That was twice what I was earning as a teacher and considerably more than twice a porter's pay, so while trying not to seem too eager, I conceded that I probably would be able to survive on a thousand per year and got the job.

The institute comprised a library and conference room, offices and labs, together with a small ward. It specialised in epilepsy and had links to the nearby Frenchay Hospital where any necessary brain surgery was carried out. I found it a very friendly environment with invitations to collaborate on a range of topics, together with the somewhat worrying assumption that I would also serve as a clinical neuropsychologist; this would not be a problem I was assured, since the previous psychologist had left all the necessary tests. Among a total of nine research staff, by far the most distinguished was Dr W Grey Walter, known to everyone as Grey. He was one of the very few people I have met to whom it seems appropriate to apply the term "genius". As mentioned earlier, I knew about him from reading his book *The Living Brain* as an undergraduate, which I found the most readable of a range of books adopting a cybernetic approach to the brain using concepts such as positive and negative feedback from systems control theory to explain how the brain might work. I suggested to him that we might do some experiments on his machines and Grey enthusiastically agreed, although regretting that his tortoise was long gone and when we dug out the conditioning machine, which comprised a bird's nest of wires and batteries, it was sadly in no condition to learn anything.

Grey was also a brilliant neurophysiologist. His work was applied to epilepsy, a area in which he was the first person to use a process of triangulation based on electrodes placed in a series of different points on the scalp in order to identify the location of the epileptic foci underlying seizures. Grey developed Topsy, a system that involved 22 electrodes, each at a different location on the scalp. This allowed electrical activity to be recorded at many different brain locations at the same time, an important forerunner of today's electrophysiological methods. Topsy did, however, depend on the visual assessment of helical patterns at each location generated, which was not an easy task. The use of computers for the analysis of electrophysiological data subsequently provided a more satisfactory method of analysis. However, the computer-based approach was only just being developed at the time in MIT, one of the few centres technically equipped to do so.

Another development at the Burden Institute that was ahead of its time was the use of electrodes implanted in the brain to identify and potentially deal with areas responsible for triggering epileptic seizures. I had the strange experience of watching a brain operation on a young man I had seen around the Institute, subsequently meeting him with wires emerging from a turban-like head covering. The fact that such methods continue but are still regarded as non-routine suggests that progress on this treatment has been rather slow over the subsequent 50 years.

A later contribution to the field by Grey Walter was his discovery of *contingent negative variation* (CNV), sometimes known as a "readiness potential". It comprises a negative spike of electrical activity that occurs about half a second before awareness of a movement a person is about to make. It was one of the first demonstrations that consistent patterns of electrical response to a specific stimulus can be detected within the brain. It requires averaging over many trials to allow the critical feature to be separated from the extensive electrical background noise. This and related *event-related potential* (ERP) measures now play an increasing part in neuroscience, relying on the computer averaging techniques being developed in MIT at the time.

Given his major contributions to neuroscience, it seems surprising that Grey Walter is not better known. As a young man, he worked with the great neurophysiologist Lord Adrian in Cambridge but failed to be awarded a college fellowship, moving first to London and then to the Burden, combining basic and applied research. It is possible that his comparative academic neglect may have stemmed from his emphasis on combining basic and applied research that was productive but was somewhat unfashionable. However, Grey was always a maverick by the standards of medical academia, described by his son as "a communist fellow-traveller before the Second World War and an anarchist sympathiser after it". He was a brilliant populariser. He appeared regularly on a TV programme called "The Brains Trust" in which a panel of tele-intellectuals would discuss questions sent in by the public. Grey was the only panellist to whom the rest of the team would simply listen rather than argue. However, if it was a topic that I myself understood, I realised that Grey was generating an extremely persuasive mixture of solid evidence and very clever speculation, a style that I suspect might not be welcomed by less eloquent/speculative fellow scientists. Sadly his creative career ended in 1970 when his motor-cycle, rounding a corner on a country road, hit a horse. He survived the resulting head injury for a further seven years but unsurprisingly without the old sparkle.

The prospect of working with Grey Walter was very attractive; he gave me lots of papers to read and clearly enjoyed vigorous discussion. However, I was paid (I assumed) to work on alcohol. I managed to borrow a Skinner box, a standard device for training my rats and to acquire a few rats, although unfortunately they did not seem to respond at all favourably to my attempts to train them, but no doubt the rats and myself would work something out in due course.

Meanwhile my social life was rather more lively than it had been in Leeds. I stayed in a boarding house, together with a number of other young bachelors; as was common at the time, our landlady provided breakfast and an evening meal. My fellow lodgers were mainly engineers from the Bristol Aircraft Company with whom I had relatively little in common. I had, however, even less in common with an impoverished Anglo-Irish peer, who seemed like a character from the Drones Club in a P.G. Wodehouse novel. He was an unfortunate-looking chap, with a pudgy face, specta-cles and red hair, and seemed to revel in his total lack of social skills. He was an army officer seconded to the local territorial regiment comprising part-time volunteer soldiers. His attempt at sociability involved addressing everyone, regardless of age or sex as "mate". We English tend to have a problem in replying to "thanks". The American idioms "you're welcome" and "no problem" are both ways of filling this gap. His lordship's solution to this problem of responding to a "thank you" was to reply, "I would do the same thing for a sick cow". He was very keen on greyhound racing and invited me to join him for an evening at the track. I accepted and found him to be better company than I expected, although I didn't take up his offer to combine funds and buy a greyhound.

A rather more exciting aspect of my social life stemmed from the only research student at the Burden, Maya, an extremely attractive Icelandic girl who was full of vitality and of what in those days was known as "sex appeal"; this came as much from her personality as her very attractive ap-pearance, and I became one of her (several) boyfriends. She was doing research for a master's degree, seconded from Leeds University, that was focussed on the effects of lysergic acid diethylamide (LSD). At the time, LSD was entirely legal and was even being promoted in some quarters as a possible treatment for schizophrenia. The whole issue of consciousness-expanding drugs had been popularised by the recent book by the novelist

Aldous Huxley entitled "The Doors of Perception" in which he described his deep thoughts and vivid hallucinations experienced after taking a related substance, mescaline. I readily volunteered to take part, becoming one of a range of young men whose brain waves had been tested before, during and after LSD, several of whom had apparently proposed marriage to Maya during the proceedings.

It proved to be a fascinating experience. I certainly generated colourful images of multicoloured horses rising from the sea, for example, but I knew they were visual images, not hallucinations; I knew they weren't real! What was wrong with me? I then became deeply introspective, first about my failure to hallucinate but then of my relations with Maya, eventually reaching what seemed like a sensible conclusion to both questions. At this point I was asked to take part in an experiment on conditioning carried out by a visiting Belgian scientist. It involved moving a lever in response to a stimulus, with the wrong response being "punished" by a loud blast of noise. I found that I didn't care at all about the noise but was fascinated by the feel of piece of insulation tape wrapped around the lever and incidentally correctly noticed a flaw in the experimental design that I hadn't detected when discussing the study earlier. On emerging from the laboratory I was struck by just how brilliantly coloured everything seemed. Returning to Maya's flat she played me Beethoven's pathetique sonata, and I wept. We went on to the cinema to watch "St Louis Blues", a wonderful experience!

In retrospect, the experience was very close to the Blake quotation used by Huxley "If the doors of perception were cleansed every thing would appear to man as it is, Infinite. For man has closed himself up, till he sees all things thro' narrow chinks of his cavern".[1] It is as if we normally see the world in a manner that is "smeared" by our past knowledge and our future intentions. The LSD seemed to remove these, leading to a sharp and clear focus on the here-and-now. I am told that this effect tends to wear off with repeated doses, and LSD can of course sometimes lead to the very scary experience of a "bad trip". I have never been tempted to find out.

The Burden was a little way out of Bristol, so I decided that the time had come to buy a car. Through the friend of a friend (now ex-friend), I bought a 1936 Morris Tourer, a red open-topped car of great charm and little reliability that I called Jezebel. I had not passed a driving licence test and my friend offered to give me lessons, rather nobly since it involved several pushed starts, then a puncture followed by the discovery that the spare was also flat, and a total brake failure while coming down a busy hill in the centre of Bristol. It seems that the brake cylinder had been "repaired" using totally inappropriate gunge.

Meanwhile things appeared to be progressing pleasantly, if not rapidly at the Burden. Professor Golla was not much in evidence around the research section of the Burden, so when, a few weeks later, I was summoned to his office, I assumed it was to check on my progress. Alas it was not. "Take a seat!" I did. "Bad news; I'm afraid you'll have to go". Pause. "They really can't treat me like this!" said the Prof. "The money is no longer available, so you'll have to leave; and by-the-way, I wouldn't tell anyone about this". Being an innocent soul I did not discuss the matter with my friends and colleagues, until I noticed that they were treating me as if I had a bad smell. I decided to talk to the Deputy Director, who, it transpired, knew that I was leaving but not why. It seems that I had become part of a power struggle between Professor Golla and the Chairman of the Institute governors; Golla had already told the Iveagh Bequest that he was unable to fill the research post when he interviewed me and was forbidden by his enemy, the Chairman, to ask for the money back. I was firmly told by the Deputy Director to explain to everyone what had happened and the atmosphere instantly lightened. Grey Walter said that he felt sure he could find money to support me from a US Air force grant he held but that this would involve some diplomacy and a little time.

Meanwhile I heard from Cambridge that they had a post available and was invited to attend an interview. Suddenly, things were looking up. Grey Walter was keen for me to stay, and attempted to contact the Board Chairman directly. Unfortunately, he was climbing in Scotland but was due back the day of my interview; Grey would speak to him and send me a telegram telling me whether I had the possibility of staying. I duly travelled to the Unit and in the midst of an interview with Donald Broadbent, and Conrad who would be supervising the project, the telephone rang. It was a telegram for me. "Chairman still not back, signed Walter". When offered the job, I had an easy decision.

So it was decided; I was moving to Cambridge, but what about Jezebel? I still had not had many driving lessons, and had not taken my test. I asked around for anyone who might be prepared to drive her from Bristol to Cambridge but without success. What to do? I decided very unwisely that I myself would drive. After about 20 miles I found myself driving in rain for the first time going around a traffic circle, and with tyres that would be illegal these days, ran out of road. We were going slowly, and I was not hurt, but Jezebel was in no condition to continue, so I arranged to have her towed away to the Crypt Garage in Gloucester, while I went ahead by train. I am ashamed to say that to the best of my knowledge, Jezebel is still in the Crypt.

I was sorry to say goodbye to my new friends in the Burden, but in retrospect I am even more sure that it was the right thing to do. Looking back I feel sure that the alcohol project would have been doomed to failure, as would the invitation to provide testing for studies of brain injury or schizophrenia, interesting areas but too difficult to be likely to yield very much given my degree of expertise as the time. I do, however, regret not working with Grey Walter, which I am sure would have been exciting and quite possibly productive, and despite my initial reluctance, I might have become a psychophysiologist. The group was, however, small and isolated, with little contact with other psychologists in clear contrast to the APU in Cambridge that was just embarking on a programme that was about to make it one of the leading groups in the world in the newly developing field of cognitive psychology.

Note

1 Blake, William, *The Marriage of Heaven and Hell* (1906). Boston, J. W. Luce and Company, p. 26

5

From Cognitive Science to Applied Psychology

The cognitive revolution is widely believed to have begun in 1956 and for one of its most eloquent advocates, George Miller, on a precise day: September 11th, which was the second day of a meeting of the "Special Interest Group in Information Theory" at Massachusets Institute of Technology (MIT) It had a truly stellar array of participants who went on to play important roles in the development of cognitive science. They included Allen Newell and Herbert Simon talking about their computer-based logic machine, a group from MIT described their use of the largest computer yet developed to simulate Hebb's concept of neural cell assemblies, John Swets described the transformation of sensory psychophysics resulting from the application of signal detection theory, of which more later, a statistical analysis of syntax was presented by Victor Yngve and finally Noam Chomsky introduced his revolutionary transformational grammar. It convinced Miller that there was a viable interdisciplinary area that could integrate experimental psychology, theoretical linguistics, computer science and social science into a new discipline. The field initially went by a range of different names, Cognitive Studies in Harvard, Information Processing Psychology at Carnegie Mellon and cognitive science at the University of California San Diego. It was the latter name that was subsequently adopted by a major funder, the Sloane Foundation, in initiating an extensive and ambitious research programme, and cognitive science has since become the dominant name for this broad interdisciplinary field.

It is hard to escape the conclusion that 1956 was a seminal year in the development of the field of cognitive science. This was only possible, however, because its several contributory disciplines were coming to broadly compatible conclusions at approximately the same time. In each case there were earlier within-field investigations and discoveries making this possible. In the area of psychology for example, the picture looks very different when viewed from different sides of the Atlantic. The revolutionary aspect is represented most strongly in the US, where behaviourism had dominated psychological theory for the past 40 years, not in all fields but in the study of learning, seen by many as the central issue within psychology. Here, the change was sufficiently radical as to make the term "revolution" plausible, although as Miller suggests, "counter-revolution" might be more accurate. On the other hand, as Miller points out, behaviourism was never fully accepted in Europe, or indeed Canada, as Hebb's more biological approach illustrates.

A better case for a truly revolutionary change can be made for the broader area of cognitive science, which, as Miller pointed out, links a range of previously disparate areas, where it brought together significant progress that each was making at the time. Although my own interest has been principally in cognitive psychology, there is no doubt that psychology has been very substantially and positively influenced by the broader field of cognitive science, as is well illustrated if we simply look at those presenting at the 1956 meeting. Allen Newell and Herbert Simon's "logic machine" was the forerunner of a very extended theory of cognition based initially on a computer-based model entitled the "General Problem Solver". It comprised an aggregate of subcomponents known as "production systems", each based on the if–then principle; if a given state of affairs occurs, then a given response follows. They argued for the importance of grand architectures, rejecting the idea that cognition should first be studied piecemeal. The approach continued to develop at Carnegie Mellon University, where it still forms the base of an ambitious general theory developed by John Anderson. The emphasis on building models resembles the position advocated by Kenneth Craik in 1944, who was, however, limited to using relatively simple analogue computers, since the digital computer was still being invented. There is no doubt that this approach has led to impressive simulations of tasks ranging from motor skills to expert chess performance. One criticism of this approach, however, is that while production systems may provide a good *engineering* solution to a problem, a way of solving it pragmatically, this does not necessarily imply that the brain solves the problem in the same way. While it still has its adherents, the influence on psychology of the production systems approach seems to have waned in recent years.

This is not the case for the second approach mentioned by Miller, namely the attempt to use a large computer to simulate Hebb's concept of cell assemblies, presented as a viable way in which the brain might operate. Hebb's ideas are still influential, and computer simulation continues to play an important role in cognitive neuroscience. This is also true of signal detection theory as presented in the meeting by John Swets on the study of perception. It offered a way of applying the type of decision theory developed during the war to the task of deciding whether a stimulus is present or not. The method has the advantage of allowing the performance of the person attempting to detect a faint signal to be analysed using two separate measures: one based on perceptual sensitivity and the other on the person's bias or accepted level of risk. Decisions under uncertainty all tend to have this characteristic of being influenced by both sensitivity and bias, and the capacity to measure it offered by signal detection theory has influenced psychology widely, not only in perception but also in memory and in social psychology.

An even more important influence from the engineering field had already been provided by the development in 1948 of *information theory* by Claude Shannon at Bell Laboratories in New Jersey. As mentioned earlier, he was concerned with measuring the capacity to transmit information through a link, such as the telephone line and came up with an ingenious solution based on the extent to which any new information reduces existing uncertainty. The information-processing approach to cognition has continued to be influential, although it rapidly became clear that it was far from easy to produce precise information measures in a complex world where probabilities were hard to estimate, and were likely to change over time. In recent years, with the development of massive computer power it is no longer impossible to estimate such probabilities, and information theory is once again proving highly influential.

The final area identified by Miller concerns the study of language, and in particular grammar. Here, the transformational grammar presented by Chomsky subsequently became extremely influential not only in linguistics but also more widely in attempts, for example, to develop a similar approach to perception and action. The central problem tackled by Chomsky was how a rule-based system might generate an apparently infinite number of grammatical utterances, each one potentially different but all syntactically lawful. He developed an elegant answer to this question, taking the subject of linguistics from the byways of academic discourse to what appeared at the time, to be the cutting edge of cognitive science. Within US psychology, the event often identified as the turning point of the cognitive revolution was Chomsky's demolition of Skinner's attempt to explain language in terms of stimulus–response associations. This was partly, I suspect, because both had relatively rigid views of the value and importance of their own system, backed by strongly committed disciples. While these were by no means limited to North America, elsewhere their views were regarded as much less central to the field of psychology. Skinner's views were never widely influential at a theoretical level, and although there was, for a time, considerable enthusiasm for applying Chomsky's transformational grammar to language comprehension and memory, in the area of memory at least, this approach did not prove very productive. Furthermore, while representing an impressive intellectual feat, Chomsky's assumption that the study of grammar could form a basis for understanding the human mind more generally seems rather overambitious. Even in the case of language, the preoccupation with syntax limits its scope. Given the option in a foreign country of understanding the grammar of its language or its vocabulary, I know which I would choose.

The development of the digital computer during and after the Second World War provided a new and exciting way of thinking about the mind. Originating with the British mathematician Alan Turing's proof that a "simple machine" could in principle carry out any possible computation, interest grew in developing programmable machines, leading, in turn, to the development of digital computers in connection with work leading up to the atomic bomb in the US and the cracking of the German Enigma code in the UK. This, in turn, led to discussions of the possible construction of machines that could "think", a question that Turing had anticipated with his proposal of the *Turing test*. Was it possible to program a computer in such a way that it was impossible for an outside observer to tell by asking the computer questions, whether or not a human being was responding? This presented an exciting challenge and particularly in the US led to the development of the discipline of Artificial Intelligence or AI. The Dartmouth conference on AI also in 1956 rivals the MIT meeting as the seminal moment that launched the cognitive revolution, attended by such leading figures as Claude Shannon, Marvin Minsky and John McCarthy, all of whom had a major influence on the subsequent development of AI. Similar developments were taking place in the UK as reflected in an international meeting two years later on the "Mechanization of Thought Processes". However, its development in Britain was considerably slower, partly because of the sheer cost of computers at a time of considerable austerity following the devastation and economic cost of the Second World War.

However, although 1956 was the year that the various constituents of cognitive science came together, information theory, signal detection theory, psycholinguistics and AI all had earlier roots. These were typically relatively recent, often reflecting developments during the Second World War. In the case of psychology however, as pointed out by both Miller and Mandler in their history of the period, the picture differed between the USA and Europe. Whereas behaviourism had dominated US psychology for the past 40 years, its influence abroad was far weaker, with a range of different approaches characterising different regions of Europe, many having a broadly cognitive flavour in the sense of postulating processes and mechanisms that were not directly observable, and hence would be regarded as "unscientific" by the stricter advocates of behaviourism. During the 1930s, European psychology was almost certainly strongest in Germany, where experimental psychology had originated during the previous century. Here it was characterised by Gestalt psychology, as described earlier. Sadly, scientific psychology in Germany was largely destroyed by the Nazis, and although many leading German psychologists were given asylum in the US, their approach did not fit at all comfortably with somewhat rigid behaviourism that was dominant at the time. They tended to find jobs in small colleges rather than large research universities, and had less direct influence at the time than might have been expected. An element of European influence did, however, emerge some years later through post-war European immigrants such as Endel Tulving and George Mandler in the memory field. Furthermore, although Gestalt psychology was greatly disrupted in Germany, traces of Gestalt psychology clearly remained in other European departments and this approach as mentioned earlier,was taught as part of my own course at University College London and I suspect much more widely.

Other influential sources of cognitive psychology notably included Piaget's influential work on child development in Switzerland, while Paul Fraisse in France worked on time perception, while and in Belgium, Albert Michotte studied perceived causality. A cognitive approach to psychology was, however, strongest post-war in England following Bartlett's naturalistic approach to studying human memory and his explanation of it in terms of schemas, internal representations of the world based on earlier experience. Bartlett's influence within Britain grew during the war as a result of his government advisory work and of the research carried out in Cambridge under his direction.

There were strong links between North American and British psychology both during and after the war, with a focus on common war-related questions, such as optimising the usability of equipment and problems of fatigue. Such issues were not readily addressed by strict behaviourist theory, resulting in the development of a more pragmatic approach that was open to influences from information theory and cybernetics, as well as to existing cognitive approaches. Considered from this viewpoint, it is probably more accurate to use the term cognitive *evolution* in Europe as suggested by Mandler and as a *counter-revolution* in the US where behaviourism was gradually superseded by a broader attitude to theory. There have been a number of good accounts of this counter-revolution from a US perspective but little on the European-based evolution (Baars, 1986; Gardner, 1987; Mandler, 2011; Miller, 2003) (see further readings page xiii–xiv).

Many streams flowed into what subsequently became known as cognitive psychology, with contributions from different countries and different disciplines. However, one important contribution came from the establishment of the Medical Research Council Applied Psychology Unit in Cambridge, stimulated by the wartime research carried out under Bartlett's directorship, and having a brilliant young director in Kenneth Craik. Sadly he was killed in a cycling accident within a year of taking up the post, and for the next five years until his retirement, Bartlett became director. Over the years, the Unit has proved unique in its capacity to combine basic theory with practical application. The theory was heavily influenced by two of its directors, both seminal figures in the development of cognitive psychology, namely Kenneth Craik and Donald Broadbent.[1] My own arrival at the Unit coincided with the beginning of Broadbent's directorship and with the publication of one of psychology's classic texts, Broadbent's *Perception and Communication*. This summarised a wide range of recent work on perception, attention, memory and performance under stress, much of it carried out at the Unit, and attempted to explain it using an information-processing model. At the heart of the model was a theory of attention supported by a wide range of ingenious experiments, demonstrating that this was an important and tractable research area, an area that had been ignored by behaviourism.

One important feature of Broadbent's information-processing model was the assumption of a short-term memory system that can temporarily hold limited amounts of information in order to assist in its further processing. Work at the Unit by Conrad had demonstrated that even a brief delay in retaining a long telephone number will lead to errors, while Poulton showed a similar effect when remembering the content of brief statements. Broadbent's tentative speculation proved prophetic in anticipating the subsequent controversy over how many kinds of memory and our own later concept of working memory, and of course in the influence of concepts from computer science on psychology.

Psychology in the UK was at something of a crossroads. Before the war, there were two major influences: namely Bartlett in Cambridge and a series of influential psychometricians mainly concerned with measurement of intelligence. These included Charles Spearman and Cyril Burt in London and Godfrey Thompson in Scotland. By the mid-1950s all had retired. Psychometrics continued to be of considerable practical importance; Burt, for example, was part of the committee that designed the national selection test for grammar schools at age 11, of which I had been one of the first beneficiaries. However, the link with academic psychology was weakening, although Hans Eysenck, a refugee from the Nazis and protégé of Cyril Burt, carried on the tradition, extending it to the study of personality.

Most UK psychology departments were small at that time, with lecturers typically covering a relatively wide area, often leaving little time for research. I can remember speculating with friends during my early years at the Unit about whether it was possible to be research-active in psychology beyond the age of 40! A successful academic would move up the system to become the sole professor in a small department, required not only to run the department but also to help run the university, leaving no time for research. Happily, by the time I myself reached 40, our hypothesis had clearly been disproved, not least by my older colleagues at the Applied Psychology Unit (APU). As mentioned earlier, the Unit occupied a late Victorian house on a quiet street about a mile from the centre of Cambridge. The main room of the house served as a common room, where we had coffee every morning and tea every afternoon. It overlooked the garden with French windows allowing access to the terrace and lawn. Tea and coffee formed an important part of the Unit's routine, and were always well attended. Much of the conversation was not science-related, but it provided a good way of meeting and contacting people, and led to many fruitful discussions and collaborations.

When I arrived at the Unit, Donald Broadbent had just become director and elected to have two deputy directors, Christopher Poulton and Conrad (who like the TV detective Morse, preferred not to use his first name). All three were highly influential in the work of the Unit and contributed substantially to the development of psychology more generally. They were, however, very different, both in personality and in scientific interests, a brief account of each gives a broad flavour of the Unit at the time I joined it.

Without doubt, the most influential figure in the Unit was Donald Broadbent, whose seminal book *Perception and Communication* combined Kenneth Craik's idea of basing a theory on a potentially realisable physical model, with the information-processing approach stemming from Claude Shannon's mathematical theory of information. However, unlike others using this approach at the time, he attempted to apply it to a very wide range of recent research, much of it carried out at the Unit. This source of evidence presented two valuable constraints; first of all it was not limited to a single experimental paradigm, as is all too often the case. Second, it was based on real-world problems of some practical importance, in stark contrast to most of the theoretically oriented research in psychology at the time and indeed since.

The model he proposed was very ambitious in incorporating perception of the world, its control by attention, the manipulation of the information and the resulting action, together with the effect on these of personality differences and a range of environmental stresses, such as noise, heat and sleep deprivation. He used it as a basis for reporting the Unit's work, and its broad outlines provided a valuable theoretical structure allowing a wide range of evidence to be integrated. At a personal level, he was a somewhat complex man. Originally from Wales, from a relatively modest background, he won a scholarship to Winchester, one of the leading public (that is private) schools with a reputation for producing intellectual and perhaps somewhat austere students, known as *Wykehamists*. From school he went into the air force and served as aircrew before entering Cambridge, initially, I believe, to study engineering. He was, however, one of many students who were inspired by Bartlett to enter the field of psychology, and on graduating he joined the APU, becoming director on Mackworth's resignation in 1958.

Donald Broadbent carried out classic work on attention, stimulated initially by the question of how a pilot could follow the relevant spoken air traffic control message while ignoring other spoken messages, a task that in happier times became known as the *cocktail party problem*. Broadbent used this as a way into the broader issue of attentional control; how do we manage to focus on one message and ignore the other? His principal method, known as dichotic listening, involved different messages played into the two ears. He studied the factors that allowed one message to be distinguished from the other, using this to build a simple model that was able to incorporate the existing evidence. He then went on to apply the model more widely, for example focussing on written while ignoring spoken information, which, in turn, generated further testable predictions. This work provided a clear refutation of the belief dominant in behaviourism that attention was far too vague a concept to merit scientific study.

A separate but related interest concerned the effect of noise on performance, where Broadbent was probably the first to demonstrate a clear decrement in cognitive function as a result of loud noise. This subsequently led him to a much broader interest in other stressors, such as heat and sleep deprivation, and to an attempt to incorporate such effects within an extended version of his model. This principally relied on the physiological concept of *arousal*, which could range from very low, as in sleep, to very high, as in panic, with optimal performance occurring at some midpoint; this inverted U-shape was known as the Yerkes-Dodson Law after its initial proposers. Given that different stressors had different impacts on arousal it was possible to explore these and make practical predictions, for example on the negative effects of sleep deprivation (low arousal) on radar watchkeepers, and the possibility of reversing this via other stressors such as noise (high arousal). This led in 1971 to a second book, *Decision and Stress*, that attempted to provide an account of the by-then very substantial literature in this area. It has understandably had less influence than his first book, which played a seminal role in launching the field of information-processing experimental psychology.

Donald was a great synthesiser with very broad interests. He was sympathetic to animal research in the behaviourist tradition and indeed wrote a book entitled *Behaviour*, summarising the field. He was also abreast of developments in other areas such as Chomsky's work in psycholinguistics. As befits a Wykehamist, Donald was a very moral person; he took part in protests against the Suez invasion and in his later years focussed on the study of stress in Oxford car factory workers and how quality of life might be improved. Scientifically, he was an intellectual as well as an experimentalist, a great synthesiser and someone who took seriously the potentially very destructive development of postmodern ideas in the social sciences, writing a piece entitled "In defence of empirical psychology". I myself remained less worried by the threat from the wilder shores of French philosophy, but then I am an optimist and have perhaps lived a rather sheltered intellectual life.

On a personal level Donald often seemed to be an extrovert, choosing, for example, when invited to provide a photograph for the review of his 1958 book, a picture of himself holding his motorbike in front of the Unit's gates. You could always tell when a visitor was being shown round by gales of laughter, but at heart I suspect, he was much more of an introvert, adopting a more outgoing style that he felt best enabled him to do a good job in making an impact in science and running the Unit.

Donald appointed two deputy directors to help run the Unit, Christopher Poulton and Conrad. They were very different from each other and from Donald. Christopher had a medical degree, and was very interested in both stress and motor control. Unlike Donald, who was short and round-faced, Christopher was tall, thin with prematurely silvery hair, a pallid face and in the early days at least he constantly wore woollen gloves with fingers cut out, presumably to cope with some circulatory problem. Christopher was a great methodologist and experimenter but had no time for theory. He would happily review papers for journals, but he told me that he would never recommend acceptance or rejection for what seemed rather obscure moral reasons. At the time of Mackworth's resignation, he was visiting Harvard working with S. S. Stevens on the measurement of sensory magnitudes such as brightness and sound. He applied for the directorship and was clearly resentful that it went to Donald rather than himself, which as we will see later led to complications. Poulton concluded during his stay at Harvard that there were methodological flaws in the methods used by Stevens and many others in the field. In particular, Poulton was highly critical of the fact that many separate judgements of brightness or loudness were taken from each person and then averaged. Christopher argued, with some justification, that this was invalid since each judgement influenced the next in ways that biased the final result. As a purist he believed that only one observation should be taken from each person, an approach that he himself followed by setting up a folding table in the various Cambridge colleges and inviting passing undergraduates to make a single judgement, gradually accumulating enough judgements to draw what he felt were valid conclusions, which typically did differ from those based on repeated judgements.

Christopher was also interested in the effects of stress on performance, carrying out experiments on a wide range of different sources of stress from effects of high pressure on workers tunnelling beneath the Thames, to the influence of altitude on Everest climbers. Although Christopher prided himself on being able to collect data from extremely unpromising situations, he was always a stickler for proper experimental design, in particular warning against the dangers of what he termed "asymmetrical transfer". This occurs when people are tested on two conditions, A and B, with A influencing B, while B does not influence A. An example comes from a study of fatigue in long-distance pilots. Those tested first when rested before flight subsequently deteriorated when retested after a long flight, whereas those first tested when fatigued did no better when tested after resting. They seemed to simply settle for their earlier level of performance. Christopher's advice was to use separate groups, but if this was not feasible because of lack of an adequate number of pilots for example, testing people twice was permissible provided one looked out for these pernicious inter-test effects. If they occurred, then you should rely only on the first test for each group. As mentioned earlier, Christopher was totally uninterested in theory and if he had, as he certainly hoped, been Mackworth's successor as director, the Unit would have been a very different place.

The second deputy director, Conrad, was again very different from both Broadbent and Poulton. In appearance he was relatively short, dark with wavy hair and horn-rimmed spectacles, and was by temperament less outgoing. While Broadbent's principal contribution was theoretical, and Poulton's was methodological; Conrad was outstanding in applying cognitive psychology to real-world problems and ensuring that the results were implemented. His PhD research involved studying the effect of keeping track of multiple tasks, for example, monitoring a range of dials in a control room, with hands moving at different speeds with potentially different levels of importance. He was able to apply his conclusions to the practical job of telephonists in an exchange, resulting in a solution that both saved money for the Post Office and reduced boredom for the telephonists. He was instrumental in alerting the Post Office to the importance of human factors, and sat on the resulting committee for many years. This allowed him to offer ongoing advice based on existing findings at the same time as tackling new problems. The Post Office recognised this service by providing regular funding for a research post. An upcoming issue in the late 1950s was that of automatic letter sorting, and the resulting need for postal codes. It was this project that allowed me to join the Unit.

This general arrangement with the Post Office had a number of advantages. First, it allowed a constant source of expert advice, together with funding for continuing to build up relevant information for later application. Equally important was the issue of continuity; Conrad knew the Post Office organisation well and was trusted by both management and unions. Furthermore because he sat on the committee for many years, he could remember what questions had been raised and answered previously; in short, he provided both expertise and memory. I suspect that a lack of institutional memory is a problem in many organisations where people are expected to move jobs every three or four years. The arrangement with the Post Office was, however, one that involved mutual trust between the advisor and the organisation, far from common in the more cut-throat capitalist world that followed. When the telephony branch of the Post Office was privatised, they changed the system, demanding a tightly specified research programme, with results that the company then wished to refuse publication, a standard requirement of work carried out in the Unit. At this point the research link lapsed. This attempt at secrecy had little effect since the PhD student who carried out the project then accepted a post to work for Bell Telephones in the US.

Unlike Poulton, Conrad also made important contributions to theory. One influential finding came from an applied study of the memorability of telephone and postal codes. He noted that when asked to remember sequences of letters, errors tended to be similar in sound to the correct item, for example *b* remembered as *v*, even when the letters were presented visually. He suggested that this implied reliance on some form of short-term *acoustic* memory trace that faded over time, with the result that when recalled, the decayed memory trace could be confused with that of an acoustically similar letter. He went on to show that those letters that were most likely to be confused when spoken in a noisy background were also those that tended to substitute for each other in memory tests. Furthermore, he showed that sequences of similar letters such as *b t c v g* were harder to recall correctly than a dissimilar sequence such as *k w x l r*.

In due course, this set of findings came to play a very important part in my own scientific life. Conrad later became interested in the possible role of this acoustic memory system in people who had been deaf since birth, demonstrating that deaf people have reduced capacity for remembering and recalling visually presented sequences of numbers or letters. He went on to show a link between this problem and the difficulties deaf people often had in learning to read. The question of the role of short-term verbal memory and reading acquisition has developed hugely since Conrad's initial discovery. He himself later decided to concentrate entirely on work with the deaf, subsequently moving on to Oxford to do so.

Broadbent, Poulton and Conrad were, however, only the most senior of the scientists working at the Unit, which must have constituted one of the largest groups of cognitive psychologists in the world at that time, and almost certainly the most effective in linking theory with its practical application.

Note

1 Broadbent, D. E. (1958). *Perception and Communication*. London: Pergamon Press.

6

Psychology Under Water

I was leading a very comfortable and enjoyable life in Cambridge with the ideal job in an exciting and supportive environment. In some ways, life seemed too comfortable, although weekly games of rugby kept the adrenalin moving in the winter. However, rugby stopped between April and September and it is hard to work up much of a sweat playing tennis if you are constantly hitting the ball into the net or out of the court, so I looked around for an alternative. The university had a wide range of activities, some of which reached their peak in the summer, and I decided to explore these at the next fresher's fair when the various clubs attempt to recruit new members. I was interested in two in particular, mountaineering and diving. I had done a little climbing both in Britain and in New England, and although Cambridge is badly placed for reaching good climbing country, they had a good programme of summer trips and expeditions, largely illustrated by photographs of hairy men in lumberjack shirts. The diving club, with the promising title of the Cambridge University Underwater Exploration Group, made their case through a film about their activities, which incidentally involved shots of girls in bikinis and the blue Mediterranean. I opted to learn to dive! This had the convenient justification that I could run experiments under the water and perhaps encourage the Medical Research Council (MRC) to make a small contribution to my holidays.

The initial stages of learning to dive were far from glamorous. We would turn up each week at a small indoor school swimming pool and gradually acquire the various skills, together with knowledge of the basic physiology and safety precautions. The whole process culminated around Easter in several days of diving centred at Martin's Haven, an attractive cove in South West Wales which was to become one of the UK's first underwater nature sanctuaries. The water was cold, and we newcomers had to wait for our turn at using the club's limited number of drysuits, diving suits that relied for their insulation on the clothes you wore underneath and on their capacity to seal adequately at wrists and ankles. They depend less on an exact fit than the neoprene wet suits that had been bought by the more experienced divers. We dived from inflatables at depths ranging from 10 to around 90 feet with visibility of around 10 feet, good by UK standards, although not of course by the standards of more tropical conditions. It was a wonderful and exciting experience. I particularly remember the hunt for scallops, which when approached would suddenly open and close their shells so as to hop in the air, or rather water, and were delicious when caught.

Each summer the club tried to set up an expedition or project, and the next one scheduled sounded particularly intriguing. It was organised by Nick Flemming, a charismatic figure with wavy blond hair and a moustache to match who learnt to dive in the toughest section of the Royal Marines known as the SBS (Special Boat Service). He was carrying out a PhD on the sea level of the Mediterranean at different points in history. Sea level has risen in recent millennia, and there were two ways of estimating its previous depth: one based on the ruins of sunken cities and the other on underwater sea caves. Such caves apparently develop only close to the turbulence of the surface; hence if they can be dated, they provide a further indication of change in sea level. Nick had persuaded the BBC to fund a television series based on diving around the Mediterranean, beginning in Gibraltar, proceeding along the Spanish coast to the French Riviera and then on to the eastern Mediterranean and back again to the UK. An added bonus was sponsorship from a wetsuit company that would provide each of us with a made-to-measure suit, very expensive at the time. I could hardly expect the MRC to give me the summer off, but I negotiated three weeks, aiming to join the expedition on the Costa Brava in north-western Spain and continue along the French Riviera.

All seemed to be going well; I duly received my wetsuit and waited for news of how the expedition was going. I learnt that it had left Britain on time, crossed the stormy Bay of Biscay and arrived at Gibraltar on the southern tip of Spain where there seemed to be some kind of hold-up. I was concerned and sought further information from the company that owned the boat we had hired, going to London and discovering them in a small rather seedy office in Soho, an area more noted for lurid night life than navigation. They assured me, not very convincingly, that all was well and that the expedition hoped to meet me as arranged, so off I set to the attractive port of Sant Feliu on the Costa Brava and waited. Nothing. There are, however, worse places to wait than the Costa Brava.

At last, after about a week's delay, the expedition limped into harbour aboard a rather pretty pale blue converted steam yacht named Titania (too close to Titanic for comfort). It transpired that Nick's diving expertise didn't extend to assessing the seaworthiness of yachts, and having finally reached Gibraltar, the captain had declared it unseaworthy and refused take it any further. After considerable negotiation, an alternative captain had been found: a Gibraltarian bar owner, a large, piratical-looking man with a black beard, who had a sideline in delivering yachts around the Mediterranean. He had managed to raise a new crew, hippies who had set off from Ibiza to sail across the Atlantic and given up at Gibraltar, and liked the idea of sailing back into the Mediterranean.

By the time they reached San Feliu, they too had become convinced of the lack of seaworthiness of Titania; both captain and crew refused to leave the harbour. There was, however, another problem; the toilet facilities required pumping the waste material into storage tanks, which in due course had to be emptied. The harbour master was naturally unenthusiastic that this should happen in the harbour and the crew resolutely refused to leave port. An explosion seemed imminent. Eventually a compromise was reached and Titania limped out and around the nearest peninsular to discharge her unwanted cargo. It was clear by this point that the chances of the expedition continuing were nil. The cameramen, experienced underwater professionals, said that they could manage one programme using small boats and the rocky coastline. This they did with the grand series eventually appearing as one cleverly concocted programme. The whole episode would probably have made an excellent comedy.

I had planned to do some experiments on underwater vision and collected a little data of no great significance. I did, however, have an idea for a separate study. I discovered that I was the only person to have actually received a complimentary wetsuit, and many of my fellow members were wearing nothing more than T-shirt tops, fine on the surface of the Mediterranean in August but totally inadequate at depths of over a few feet, when one encounters a thermocline, a clear boundary between the warm water that sits on the surface and the cold water that sits beneath, with the result that people who dived to any depth were chilled to the marrow when they emerged. That reminded me of a somewhat curious paper by a US physiologist, Hudson Hoagland, on the role of temperature in time estimation. On one occasion, his wife had the flu and a markedly raised temperature. When Hoagland had been out relatively briefly she complained that he had been gone for a long time. Instead of simply denying this, he asked her to count from 1 to 60 at a one-second rate, noting the time and taking the measure again when her temperature dropped. He found a clear relationship such that the higher the temperature the faster she counted. Based on this and another participant whose body temperature was artificially raised by diathermy, he derived the hypothesis that time estimation was based on an internal clock, a neural oscillator whose function could be related to the standard equation linking the speed of chemical processes with temperature. Would my frozen comrades therefore count more slowly? They did, although the data were not yet sufficient to justify publication.

The following winter was very cold; I did not plan to go on the spring dive until I heard that the sea temperature was abnormally low, and everybody was chilled after diving. At this point I jumped on a train and joined them, and by testing frozen divers, I turned my earlier observations into a more substantial study, finding that Hoagland was right. I was, however, concerned that the effect might be due to anxiety associated with cold water diving, and delayed publication until I had a chance to check this out. An opportunity occurred in the following summer's expedition when the club was working with army divers in Cyprus. The officer in command said that it should be easy to set up a warm, shallow but anxiety-producing dive. This is what he did; he located a wreck in about 10 feet of water and set up a task whereby the diver was given a piece of explosive attached to a lighted fuse, which would continue to burn under water. The task was to swim to the wreck, attach the explosive and swim back again while waiting for the explosion. If there was no explosion, then the diver was to go and retrieve the charge. This was obviously before the days of ethics committees! People were anxious but perhaps surprisingly, no more so than before a deep dive, as I myself can vouch. The anxiety did not influence counting rate, and I was able to publish my first diving paper, not on diving but on the influence of body temperature on time estimation, a result that is still occasionally cited.

Around this time, I came across a paper by two US Navy investigators on the effect of nitrogen narcosis on diver performance. Nitrogen narcosis, described somewhat poetically by the father of scuba diving Jacque Costeau as *the rapture of the deep* is a form of intoxication that results from breathing air at pressure. A range of so-called noble gases that are inert at normal atmospheric pressure become narcotic as pressure is increased. This can present a major problem for the diver since the pressure of air within the lungs must be equal to that in the surrounding ocean. During the Second World War, military divers known as frogmen breathed pure oxygen, which had the advantage that it could be recirculated and rebreathed, and hence generated no bubbles. However, oxygen under pressure is toxic and can cause convulsions and death at depths of 40 or 50 feet. When mixed with nitrogen however, as in normal air, this effect can be avoided, although the nitrogen itself becomes narcotic at depths of 100 feet and beyond leading to a pleasant but of course potentially dangerous experience.

A second threat to the diver is known as *the bends*. When breathed at pressure, nitrogen is absorbed by the body, and when pressure is relieved it bubbles out, in the same way as bubbles appear in champagne when the cork is removed, and the pressure is reduced. This can cause pain in joints known to divers as *the niggles* and potentially serious and fatal damage to the central nervous system. The way to avoid this is to decompress slowly, gradually allowing the gas to clear from the body. Over the years, tables have been devised specifying the rate of safe decompression as a function of diving time and depth.

The Cambridge University diving club had lots of members eager to take part in summer expeditions but needed a project in order to obtain sponsorship. I proposed a study of nitrogen narcosis to be conducted in the open sea, unlike the US study which, like the bulk of existing research, had been conducted in a dry pressure chamber. This suggestion was seized on with enthusiasm by my fellow divers. A number of them were also members of the university's army cadet corps, and through this we were able to set up a link with the British Army with bases in Cyprus, a member of the Commonwealth that was not at that time riven by the strife between Greek and Turkish populations that was to follow. The army had a proud diving tradition, based I think on the need for their engineers to develop and maintain harbours, and did indeed claim that they had taught the navy to dive. We were able to obtain support from army divers to serve with our own expedition members as subjects in our experiment, which aimed to test whether the degree of impairment shown in the US study would be equivalent to that found in an open-sea test.

Today, Cyprus is a popular holiday destination with frequent flights from the UK, but at the time it was necessary to travel overland and then by sea, which was itself an exciting experience. I went via Italy, staying en route with friends and sailing from Venice on through northern Greece via the steep-sided Corinth Canal to Famagusta, the port in the south-east of Cyprus where we were based. Not having worked under water before, I decided to keep things very simple. The US study had found an effect on manual dexterity; their task would be impractical underwater involving bits and pieces that would rapidly be lost. To avoid this I devised a test involving a simple brass plate with two sets of 16 holes, one of which was occupied by 16 nuts and bolts. The task was simply to transfer them to the other 16 holes, thereby setting up the task for the next subject. All divers, including myself, performed this task in both a shallow water location by the shore, and out in Famagusta Bay, diving from an army ship that had a conveniently flat deck and was equipped by an echo sounder, allowing us to anchor at a point where the bottom was just 100 feet below. We planned to measure completion time in two ways, by tugging a rope to a tester on the service when the test trial started and ended, and also by the underwater tester using a stopwatch in a specially built waterproof case. We reckoned that two methods were better than one, since the tester was likely to be as drunk as the subject.

I decided I would go first with a sergeant, the most experienced diver. Army rules required us both to be on the end of 100-foot ropes with a third rope for signalling. We were just about to enter the water for the first time, clutching the screw plate, the stopwatch case and a folding garden chair bought from Woolworths on which the subject was to be seated, when the local general arrived. Over the side we went, undeterred, reaching the bottom and discovering that the signal rope was tangled and did not work. We pressed on, relying on the underwater stopwatch, eventually emerging to a comment from the general that it "looks absolute chaos to me – ha ha". Happily we were allowed to discard our personal "safety" ropes and found that the signal rope worked, if yanked vigorously. We duly completed the study and after a wonderful holiday with splendid diving elsewhere, I returned with some very interesting results.

Performing the screw plate task underwater slowed down performance quite markedly in shallow water but dramatically more at depth. It seemed that the dry pressure chamber results that characterised earlier research might be totally misleading. On the strength of this, the army allowed us to run another study in their dry pressure chamber back in the UK, where we obtained the same results as found in the US study, confirming our initial conclusion that the effect of narcosis was much greater in the open sea. Happily, my request for extended leave had paid off, resulting in a paper in a major applied psychology journal, and MRC permission to later extend our research to deeper depths and other breathing mixtures.

As part of his PhD in physical geography, Nic Flemming needed to make measurements at depths greater than 100 feet and was frustrated by the unreliability of the process. At about the same time, the Royal Navy was developing a deep diving capability based on mixing oxygen with helium, a gas that was known to be substantially less narcotic than nitrogen. Hydrogen, the least narcotic gas, was unfortunately liable to explode when mixed with oxygen in the wrong proportions. The Navy were happy to have the Cambridge group evaluate the system out in Malta, under conditions whereby happily, they rather than Nic chose the boat. I agreed to set up a study in which we compared the performance of divers breathing either air or oxyhelium near the surface, and at a depth of 200 feet, a depth at which one could certainly expect substantial narcosis in an air diver; indeed it was around the limit of safe diving, and well beyond the recommended maximum for sport diving. Decompression tables for helium were still being developed, and since there are individual differences in susceptibility to the bends, we each had to undergo a preliminary "dive" in the Navy's dry pressure chamber. Only Nic himself developed a niggle, but given modification of the tables, he decided to carry on.

We duly flew out to Malta, arriving in a storm to find that a substantial part of the oxyhelium that had been shipped over by sea appeared to have leaked. I can remember sitting down and thinking, "Why I am here when I could be comfortably back in Cambridge?" Once things began, we felt much better; diving was from a naval ship, a small converted trawler, which succeeded in locating an area just outside the Maltese capital, Valletta, with a depth of exactly 200 feet. The new diving equipment consisted of two large tanks filled with the helium–oxygen mixture together with a small separate oxygen cylinder strapped to the chest. Our 200-foot dive would require a relatively lengthy decompression, which could best be done on pure oxygen. This arrangement was not ideal since it involved hanging onto a rope at the specified decompression depth, switching off the heliox and only then switching on the oxygen. Accidentally switching on the oxygen at depth would lead to instant convulsions, while failing to switch it on during decompression would lead to anoxia. I also discovered that diving to 200 feet seems an awfully long way down, losing sight of the surface before eventually landing on soft, easily disturbed mud that we learned later came from the main sewage outlet for Valletta.

Our tests included the screw plate used earlier together with a series of simple arithmetic sums. I wanted something more intellectually taxing but worried that most reasoning tasks are lengthy and in a shortened form would be unreliable. I decided to borrow an idea from psycholinguistics, which, following Chomsky's ideas, had discovered that processing grammatical forms varied in their demand and in how long they took to comprehend, active sentences being quicker and easier than passives and positives more rapid than negatives. On this basis I invented a syntactic reasoning task that involved deciding whether sentences describing the order of two letters were true or false. These ranged from easy, such as *A follows B* – *BA*, which should be ticked as correct, to more complex syntactic structures, such as *B is not preceded by A* – *AB*. I could either measure how long people took to complete 64 such sentences or run it as a group test allowing a specified time to complete as many as possible. I found that three minutes was about right with only a few finishing all in this time. Conveniently, people make very few errors meaning that simple speed measures can be used.

I later found that a three-minute version provided a brief but useful measure of verbal intelligence, based on a rather limited sample of just 21 soldiers for whom I happened to have IQ data. The test also proved useful when presented auditorily in what I suspect may have been the first test of the influence of telephoning on driving, carried out by my colleague Ivan Brown in the 1960s. I published the test in 1968 in a short non-refereed paper advocating the test as a simple rapid test of verbal intelligence. The effects looked strong and I continued to use it occasionally as a stress test but largely forgot it, focussing my test inventing on memory disorders. The A-B reasoning test, although I had cast it off undeveloped, to make its own way in the world has, however, popped up from time to time as a measure of the effects of stress, although not always wisely. I was somewhat surprised a few years ago to be summoned to meet Lord Victor Rothschild, at that time the government advisor on science policy. He had been responsible for a hugely controversial report that persuaded the government of the time to remove substantial amounts for funding from the Research Councils and hand it to government departments who could then specify what research they wished to contract on what was termed the customer-contractor relationship, the assumption being that market forces would lead to greater efficiency. Commissioning was typically devolved to civil servants with little experience of research or its proper management, something that is all too often still the case.

His lordship had summoned me because of his concern that politicians and civil servants might be making important decisions while under the influence of fatigue or other more liquid stressors. He had heard of the A-B reasoning test from a junior member of his family who was a psychology student and had decided that it provided the answer to his concerns.

He would recommend its use by the great and the good with the test to be taken and scored before deciding whether they were competent to make important decisions. I duly arrived at his rather grand house in Cambridge and was told that the test had not been a success. He found that very few people had responded to his request, and that those who had were people who had completed all the items in the time he specified. Could I advise? I offered some reasons for his lack of success, not least of which was to assume that when weary or under the influence, people with difficult decisions to make would chose to do a demanding test and then send him the result. Undaunted, he went on to pass on the test to the Sunday Times newspaper for readers to test themselves after their Christmas festivities. I could have told him that the test does not seem to be very sensitive to alcohol, not to mention that making tests available to the general public is ethically questionable as it is likely to interfere with their subsequent professional use.

In fact the test does seem to have gone on to be used widely often in a slightly modified form to suit different languages, both as a stress test and as a very brief test of verbal intelligence, as recently I discovered from Adrian Furnham who vigorously carries on the classic mental testing tradition first set up by Pearson and Spearman in my old department, University College London. He mentioned that he had used the test over 2000 times and referred me to two papers published in the last few months: one testing a German version based on 478 participants and a second Iranian group validating a Persian-language version based on 196 participants, happily both finding their language-adapted form of the test to be remarkably good as a test of intelligence when properly analysed using the appropriate statistical methods. I was amazed to discover some 50 years after its invention that my simple test was in fact a respectable measure of intelligence.

Paper and pencil tests such as the syntactic reasoning test are in fact very suitable for use underwater since they can be mounted on a Formica board covered in transparent plastic that can be written on with soft pencil and subsequently erased. The tests again proved useful when, despite the loss of much of our helium supply, we managed to complete the study, comparing performance at murky depths with performance at an equally insalubrious harbour location. Performance on the screw plate showed no difference between air and heliox in the shallow condition, together with a clear impairment at depth which was particularly marked on air. Our other tests showed a broadly similar pattern although impairment tended to be reflected in errors rather than speed. It could, however, be argued that errors are the more crucial measure; a diver taking somewhat longer may well be acceptable, but an error could be catastrophic. This was illustrated in one alarming incident. Divers always formed pairs, with one on air and one on heliox, who would presumably be more clear-headed. On one specific dive, the air diver looked at his gauge and decided that there was not enough air to both complete the experimental task and then reach the surface. He decided to complete the task! Fortunately he was a very strong swimmer and emerged from the sea like a Polaris missile, where he was immediately provided with a full tank of air and sent down to decompress, which happily he did without further mishap.

My final Mediterranean diving expedition was rather less hazardous. I had recently married Hilary, a physiotherapist who I met as a result of an over-theatrical gesture from my colleague John Morton, now a distinguished retired psychologist who continues to be enthusiastically theatrical. His gesture broke his little finger, so he took it to the hospital for physiotherapy, in due course charming the physio and being invited along to the house where she lived with several colleagues including Hilary. This led to parties and to my meeting and eventually marrying Hilary in the small but beautiful Little St Mary's Church in Cambridge.

Hilary came along with me on my final Mediterranean expedition, aimed at further investigation of the mysterious effect resulting from combining the effect of narcosis with that of being tested underwater. I was part of a mixed group of research divers, mainly comprising zoologists with an interest in vision. They were concerned with the practical issue of what the best colour was for fishing nets, which were presumably more effective if the fish did not see them. We worked from the quay of a beautiful fishing village where, by entering the water from the quay, we could readily reach 100 feet by simply following the bottom as it shelved through crystal clear water. The subject and the tester would swim gently down and after the test was completed, surface so as to save air and swim back by snorkel. I tested my colleagues together with a group of trainee naval officers, one of whom, on surfacing from the deep test, confessed that he could not swim! Happily, without a weight belt a diver is very buoyant and we were able to discard his belt and tow him back.

In due course we analysed the results which were surprising. We obtained the usual slowing down of performance underwater, together with an effect of narcosis at depth. However the magnitude of the effect was what you would expect from the dry chamber results; we had lost our dramatic interaction between narcosis and depth. Why should that be? My guess was that it resulted from the very relaxed diving conditions, a shallow start, clear water and lots of other divers around doing other studies, in stark contrast to open-sea diving into the blue, something that even the professional army divers had not encountered before and hence found threatening. In the case of our 200-feet dives, a degree of anxiety was certainly justified. However, if our effect was dependent on anxiety, it becomes harder to justify running studies in the clear blue Mediterranean, rather than in the murkier and more threatening depths around Britain. My wife Hilary had enjoyed the trip but objected to the assumption that as the only woman in the group, she should do the cooking, while the fishing net study had simply found out that the optimal net colour was the one that was already being used by the fishermen.

We had one final attempt to test our anxiety hypothesis. By this time some of the medical students who had taken part in the earlier studies had moved to do their clinical training in London and had joined the London medical schools' diving club. They proposed to carry out a study of nitrogen narcosis off the Scottish coast with both physiological and psychological measures of anxiety. The dive site had already been established off a Scottish island where the sea plunged rapidly to 100 feet. I flew up from England, arriving just as a storm was brewing. There seemed to be some concern to raise a sunken buoy from a depth of around 100 feet. Almost all the experienced divers had already tried and would not be able to dive for decompression reasons until the next day, so somewhat reluctantly I agreed to go down with an enthusiastic young chap from a naval family who was widely known as "the Admiral". I was somewhat nervous, not having dived for some time but reluctantly and anxiously, I agreed. On arrival I felt distinctly woozy and made the signal to surface, planning a gentle float upwards. Instead, the Admiral grasped me firmly and went into full rescue mode at great speed. On emerging, I reflected that I was probably getting a little old for this. Both my own experience and when analysed, the results of the experiment confirmed the link between anxiety and narcosis. They also reinforced my conclusion that open-sea research on narcosis might not be an ideal research area for a chap with a wife and by this stage, two sons, Roland and Gavin.

The sequence of experiments just described extended over a period of seven years and were possible only because of the organisational and entrepreneurial talents of amateur student diving clubs. To carry out similar studies with professional divers would have been incredibly expensive and difficult if not impossible to organise. Over this period, my own situation changed from initially regarding the experiments as a convenient appendage to a diving holiday to the situation where my principal aim was scientific, just one of a range of projects, and my own diving simply a useful adjunct.

Although I moved on from open-sea experiments, I continued to be interested in diver performance, one of a small and diverse international group, of which one of the most interesting was John Adolfson, originally an old time hard hat diver who had worked with a massive helmet and lead boots, typically in harbour situations. This included helping to raise the *Vasa*, a magnificent but unseaworthy Swedish warship that sank on her maiden voyage in 1628. He subsequently became interested in diver performance and eventually registered for a PhD at the world-famous Karolinska Institute in Stockholm, studying nitrogen narcosis. His work was principally carried out in a dry pressure chamber but one that had a well into which the diver could be lowered so as to estimate the effects of being underwater at pressure. His results here were very similar to those we obtained on our Mediterranean shore dive, again suggesting that our previous dramatic effects were due to anxiety. By the time I became active in underwater research, John had largely retired, a pity since it would have been very good to work with him. On a visit to Stockholm, he invited me to lunch at the rather grand hotel where Nobel Prize winners are accommodated, a very Scandinavian lunch of multiple courses, each separated by a tot of vodka and a toast. On another occasion, dinner at his home was followed by a traditional sauna where he explained that clothes were unnecessary, somewhat to the surprise of myself and a young visiting American couple.

A rather more staid but very productive link was with the Royal Navy Physiological Laboratory (RNPL) located close to Portsmouth, the British fleet's home port. RNPL had a long and distinguished record on a wide range of problems from the effect of undersea explosions to ways of escaping from sunken submarines. They did extensive work on developing decompression schedules that allow the diver to surface gradually and avoid the bends. It was RNPL that had provided the tables for our oxyhelium dives and checked us out for susceptibility to the bends. Work on nitrogen narcosis was also being carried out by a physiologist, Peter Bennett, with whom I had a slightly guarded friendship; I was not entirely sure he had got his performance measures right and I suspect he regarded us (rightly) as amateurs in a dangerous field.

Peter subsequently moved to a post in hyperbaric medicine in the US, studying the effects of treating certain medical conditions in a high-pressure oxygen environment. He was also able to continue his work on diving, a topic of interest to both oil companies and the US Navy, both of whom were interested in saturation diving as a means of operating for lengthy periods at depth. Saturation diving takes advantage of the fact that there is a limit to the amount of gas that the body can absorb, before reaching saturation point. Once this point is reached, then it does not matter how much longer the diver stays at pressure; the decompression schedule will be the same. Hence, rather than decompressing after each deep dive, a very lengthy process, the diver lives at pressure, only decompressing at the end of perhaps a week.

The US Navy began to explore the problems of living at depth in their Sealab programme. Sealab I took place at a depth of 200 feet off Florida in 1964 but was abandoned early in the face of an imminent storm. Sealab II, also at 200 feet off La Jolla, California, was more successful. Called the Tiltin Hilton because it landed on a slope, several divers stayed underwater for 15 days, and the astronaut Scott Carpenter stayed underwater for 30 days, encouraging the development of Sealab III at a depth of 1000 feet in 1969. It ran into a number of problems including one fatality and the programme was discontinued, with subsequent research focussing on dry pressure chamber studies to determine appropriate gas mixtures and safe rates of compression and decompression.

Deep diving was becoming increasingly important when it became necessary to go deeper in order to access undersea oil reserves, as the operational depth for extracting oil at the time was set by the maximum depth at which a diver could work. As noted earlier, the usual way to avoid narcosis was to replace air with a mixture of helium and oxygen (heliox). This raised the question of whether heliox itself might become narcotic at sufficient depth. A further problem was a condition known as High-Pressure Nervous Syndrome (HPNS), involving nausea and dizziness that could occur during compression. A solution to the HPNS problem was proposed by Bennett, involving adding a small percentage of nitrogen to the standard heliox, with the three-gas medium known as *trimix*. Using trimix, Bennett reported successful chamber dives to depths exceeding 2000 feet.

Bennett's previous lab in the UK, RNPL, was also interested in saturation diving and in his absence, I was invited to provide performance measures for their programme. By this time I had returned to the APU in Cambridge as director. I was pleased to accept the invitation and to design the studies but had to leave the actual testing, which extended over several days for each dive, to colleagues, initially Vivian Lewis and later Robert Logie. We were involved in a total of 11 dives, all in the RNPL dry pressure chamber. Each study involved just two subjects, who would be confined to a metal cylinder of about 6-feet internal diameter, while the pressure was gradually raised, with performance being measured at successive points, then held at the maximum depth for a specified time followed by the lengthy process of decompression. This process was, by the standards of the time, extremely expensive, given the cost of the helium and 24-hour monitoring by staff, together with all further research costs, totalling about £100,000 per dive. The sizes of the chamber meant only that only two subjects could take part in each separate study, a real challenge to a psychologist like myself used to having a couple of dozen or more subjects per experiment. We did our best to tackle this problem by extensive prior practice to establish a firm baseline, accepting that further learning might occur but noting that this would be likely to minimise any performance decrement we might observe, hence making us more confident in interpreting any drop in performance that might appear.

Across the 11 studies we were able to answer a number of questions. First of all, we found that it was possible to detect cognitive impairment breathing heliox, relatively slight decrement at 1000 feet but increasing as we moved to 2000 feet. However, this was not shown by all tasks; for example an arithmetic test based on how many sums could be done in 15 minutes was sensitive, but our three-minute A-B reasoning task was not. Furthermore, substantial differences between individuals were found in their susceptibility to narcosis. We also monitored mood and sleep patterns and were able to rule these out as responsible for changes in performance efficiency. A further study in which divers were confined at relatively shallow depth for a comparable period of time indicated that this "caging effect" could also be ruled out. Finally, our attempt to use trimix to alleviate the problems was unsuccessful and did indeed lead to much greater decrements. It was not clear at the time quite why our results differed from Bennett's, but subsequent research suggests that factors such as the exact proportions of gas at different depths are critical, and trimix is now used routinely, both commercially and on occasion, for sport diving.

Saturation diving has indeed become standard on deep oil rigs, something I learned more about several years later when I received a letter from the wife of a saturation diver. She had observed that her husband had apparently changed personality since taking up saturation diving from a sensible, well-balanced man to someone who got drunk very easily and more generally behaved erratically. She had contacted the wives of other divers with the questionnaire that backed up her concerns. After several years out of the field, I was unexpectedly invited shortly afterwards to a meeting on diving medicine to be held in Norway, where some of the profits accruing to the nation from North Sea oil had been ploughed into diving medicine.

The meeting had a range of participants, some in underwater medicine, a good representation from the oil industry, and some from a major diving contractor, a respected French company. I presented the questionnaire evidence from the diver's wife. It did not go down well with comments like "everyone knows that divers go on a bender when they get back, nothing to worry about".

After the meeting I was taken aside by a sympathetic medic from the French company, saying that it was very difficult to exercise any control of diving on many oil rigs. A doctor pointing out a dangerous schedule may well be told to accept it or get off the rig. Diving is a lucrative profession and particularly attractive to someone on a Third World income, with the result that it may be easier and cheaper to lose a few divers than to stick to the rules. It seems to be the case that the question of long-term effects of saturation remains controversial. The Norwegian government apparently paid out several million dollars compensation in 2000, presumably linked to work in the North Sea, probably the world's best regulated diving region. It is easy to relate any reported effects to the admittedly very stressful life inevitably lived by the saturation diver for which fatalities are high, though no more so than for fishing or logging, while any long-term effects are likely to be difficult to monitor and hard to link to any specific cause.

My final period of diving research and the one for which I am best known involved a project using trainee divers. As will be explained later, I had the chance of year in San Diego and was invited to spend the following summer working with a diving research group at the University of California Los Angeles. They also did underwater testing, although mainly in a tank that had a refrigeration plant attached, allowing them to study cold water diving. They had a contract to study the effect of cold on skills ranging from reasoning and memory to the capacity to build complex underwater structures. I was responsible for the reasoning and memory tests that each diver performed under both warm and cold conditions. I wanted to test retention of information that was rather more complex than the usual list of unrelated words. I could have used the standard clinical prose memory tests, for example describing how a poor old lady in Boston lost her purse, whereupon the friendly police all contributed to replacing the money. However, I thought this might not go down too well with the would-be professional divers, so instead I invented the Wrecks Test whereby they had to remember a whole series of wrecks, their type (e.g. fishing boat), their names (Lucky Lucy), how deep they were (30 feet) and the nature of the bottom (sandy), testing their memory by asking a series of questions such as "What depth was the Lucky Lucy?"

What did we find? The cold *seemed* to have a major effect in that when the divers emerged their behaviour seemed curiously zombie-like. However, their performance was only mildly impaired; this was also the conclusion from a later study of the effect of cold by the Cambridge student group carried out in a quarry back in England that happened to be fed by an ice-cold spring. Furthermore, in the latter study the effects were greatest early in the dive, suggesting that they were probably due to distraction by the shock of entering cold water, rather than from the subsequent reduction in deep body temperature.

The most dramatic finding from the Californian study, however, was that regardless of whether the water was warm or cold, the divers had great difficulty in remembering on the surface what they learned underwater, although the experiment had not been designed in a way that would allow this particular conclusion to be drawn with any great confidence. However, further support for the possible effects of the underwater environment on memory came on returning and meeting an old university diving colleague, now with a fisheries research station. He was conducting a project in which the diver hung onto a trawl net and observed the behaviour of the fish who did or did not go into the net. There seemed to be lots of information underwater, but it seemed to be forgotten on returning to the surface, resulting in the need to develop a recording system for providing an underwater running commentary.

A chance to explore this curious forgetting effect came when Duncan Godden, who had just finished a PhD under Broadbent, contacted me with a view to possible postdoctoral work on diving. We agreed to put in a grant to explore our underwater effect by testing learning and recall, both underwater and on land. By this time I had moved up to the University of Stirling, which happily had an active diving club. Once again, I found myself working in the waters off Oban in western Scotland but at a depth of only 10 feet, just off a very pleasant beach. This time we used more conventional material, testing memory for lists of unrelated words, presented either on the beach or underwater, with recall tested in the same or the opposite environment. Our results were dramatic. While it made little difference whether the words were learnt on land or underwater, learning and recalling them in the *same* environment, whether both on land or both underwater, gave an advantage of almost 40% when compared to recall in the environmental change conditions: learning on the beach and tested underwater or learning underwater and tested on land.

We went on to conduct another study that was broadly equivalent except that memory was tested by recognition rather than recall. Here we completely lost the original effect; performance was equivalent regardless of where learning and testing took place. We went on to try to recapture the dramatic effect on recall of changing the environment in the laboratory. In one study for example, we used contrasting rooms, one quiet, bright and airy, with little furniture other than a desk and chair. The other comprised a dark cramped basement room with a mis-tuned radio and a piece of smelly fish hung behind the radiator. We got our context effect, but the effect was small. This lack of a robust and reliable effect made it difficult to carry out a more detailed theoretical analysis.

The effect we had found was not new, but what *was* new was the magnitude of the effect produced underwater. We attributed this to the dramatic difference between the land and the underwater environment. Because of the magnitude of our effect and I suspect, the novelty of the link to diving, over the years, our study has been cited in many text books, often accompanied by pictures of colourful diving scenes. The effect in general is known as *context-dependent memory*. What you learn in one context is best recalled in that context, a principle that applies not only to environmental contexts but also to physiological state. One study, for example, showed that what you learn drunk you recall best when drunk, consistent with clinical reports of alcoholics who hide drink when drunk and can no longer find it when sober.

But why is the effect not found when memory is tested by recognition? This is because of the different demands placed on retrieving the appropriate memory trace between recognition and recall. In recognition, the words are present, and the task is to judge which ones are more recently familiar. In recall, the words themselves must be retrieved before an assessment of familiarity is made. Reinstating the environment helps this initial retrieval phase rather than the familiarity decision. There are, however, some situations in which reinstating the context can enhance recognition, but these are typically where the context *determines* what you encode. A simple example might be encoding the word *bank* in the context of fishing, leading to difficulty in recognising it when presented in a financial context.

At a broad theoretical level the results fit the stimulus–response approach to memory and forgetting developed within the verbal learning tradition. If you regard the environment as part of the stimulus, then changing the stimulus will make it harder to produce the previously linked response. However, as we shall see in the next chapter, although the stimulus–response approach works reasonably well when applied to learning pairs of words within the laboratory, attempts to apply it more generally have been less successful.

So what are the further implications of context dependent memory? Should students make sure that they revise in the examination hall? Fortunately not; as our own research showed, effects on land of changing context are typically much smaller, presumably because the context during learning is provided by what is going on in your head rather than the surrounding room. There is, however, one important clinical implication which comes from the extension of the context dependency effect to mood and where, as will be discussed later, depressed patients find it much easier to recall negative memories than positive. Attempting to reverse this effect plays an important role in some treatments of depression.

It is now over 30 years since our open-sea narcosis experiments. I have not been involved in the diving field since, and attempted to get a glimpse of how it had changed in the intervening years, principally using information from the web. The first difference is the sheer amount of sport diving; whereas a relatively small number of us underwent a winter of training before our first open-sea dive, these days anyone spending a holiday in a warm water area such as the West Indies, the Great Barrier Reef or the Red Sea appears to be able to have a very brief training session followed by an open-sea dive. Basic equipment does not seem to be hugely different, except for deep diving, where it appears to be the case that the "technical" diver has access to mixed gas diving ranging from different ratios of oxygen to nitrogen in the diving tanks, to complex trimix systems in which computerised schedules will vary the mix of gases dependent upon depth and time.

Given the sheer number of divers, diving medicine has become more important, and I note that Peter Bennett has played a central role in organising medical resources along the eastern seaboard of the US, while Mike Davies, who as a young medical student played an important part in most of our open-sea dives, went on to specialise in anaesthesiology before emigrating to New Zealand, where he has played a leading role in overseeing diving medicine in the West Pacific. In the commercial field, it appears that saturation diving has become relatively routine. For a while, it seemed as though remotely operated undersea vehicles would displace the diver, but apparently there are still enough complex tasks that demand the skill of a human rather than a robot, with the result that there is still a demand for divers. Despite the dangers, given the rich financial rewards, it seems likely that there will be no shortage of deep saturation divers.

7

Practical Applications and Theoretical Implications

Postmen and Watchkeepers

So, after six moves in two years I was back in Cambridge again. I was delighted. The Unit was full of energy and ideas, many captured in Broadbent's seminal new book, which I read avidly. I had been appointed to work on a project concerned with postal codes. Conrad, my supervisor, assured me that he would look after all the applied aspects of the project, and that I should focus on more theoretical issues, leaving it up to me to decide what these should be. Importantly, my post encouraged combining the project with registration for a Cambridge PhD. The APU was not part of the university but was allowed to host PhD students under the nominal supervision of the director, Donald Broadbent, although in my case this was delegated to Conrad. Before being accepted, I had to convince Oliver Zangwill, the professor of psychology, that I was a suitable candidate, and this involved a year's delay followed by an interview. Zangwill was a rather impressive figure with aquiline features, described by my previous Icelandic girlfriend as very "handsome, like an Indian chief". He was, however, a rather shy person, who rarely made lengthy eye contact. He was also the owner of a borzoi, a large and splendid Russian hunting dog who also attended the interview, and while Oliver looked at the ground between us, his dog came over, placed his head on my knees and gazed soulfully up at me throughout. The dog seemed to approve, and I was duly registered as a PhD student.

It was agreed that my thesis title should be "Some psychological aspects of the coding of information", not a very precise topic. It was generally agreed that coding was an important topic, but there was less agreement on exactly why this was the case, or indeed, just what was meant by "coding". My first free association to with the topic was to the use of codes to disguise messages, so I began by reading a book entitled "Secret and Urgent: The Story of Codes and Ciphers", which was a good read but did not provide an obvious link to the Post Office letter-sorting problem. Codes were of course also an extremely important issue during the Second World War, leading to the development of computing by Alan Turing and colleagues who cracked the German Enigma Code, having a major effect on the outcome of the war.

Coding was also central to Shannon's information theory and to computing more generally. Computers were typically fed information at the time, using rolls of paper tape containing lines of punched holes, the presence or absence of a hole conveying one bit of information. Within the area of neurophysiology, there was also great interest in coding seen as basic to the way in which the brain might convert physical stimuli into nerve impulses and ultimately into conscious experience. Unfortunately however, I was not well equipped to pursue either of these avenues, statistical or neurophysiological, nor was it immediately obvious how information theory might be linked to postal codes.

I was puzzling over the problem of coding when, after a few weeks, I was asked how I was getting on. When I explained, I received some very good practical advice, namely "just do something! You will find that once you start the ideas will come". I started, and they did. I began with the idea that a code is a means of transforming information from one form into another, and chose to require people to transfer between a visual and a verbal code in which the digits 1–9 could be mapped onto the nine cells in a 3 × 3 matrix of the kind used for noughts and crosses/tic-tac-toe. The task was to translate digits into spatial locations, locations into digits or simply copy the code, working as rapidly as possible. I tested 12 sailors over five successive days.

It may seem strange to be testing sailors in Cambridge, which is many miles from the sea, but at the time they formed an important component of the Unit's work. This stemmed from the fact that the Unit did a great deal of work for the Armed Forces in general and the Navy in particular; at one point some 50% of the Unit's projects were military. We had a regular supply of 12 sailors, six coming for two weeks and six for six weeks, the longer stay allowing them to take part in extended studies of watch keeping and sleep deprivation. They lived in a Victorian house a little further out of Cambridge, which functioned as a virtual ship, mustering in the morning when the flag was raised, before what they termed "going ashore" to the Unit.

In addition to the sailors, part of our Post Office contract involved examining novel forms of keyboard which might be more efficient for letter sorting; hence the sailors were joined by postmen, who also had time to spare for testing on other projects. Furthermore, through collaboration with my friend and colleague Harold Dale, I had access to a large number of army recruits who could be tested in groups of about 20 by travelling to their training base. A few years later, a regular panel of volunteers was set up. Finding people to test at the Unit was therefore not a problem, and my thesis ended up containing 17 experiments and a number of sub-studies. Some such studies could be run with a group of up to 20 people tested at the same time, allowing experiments to be set up and run very rapidly. In retrospect, I think I was incredibly fortunate in having the chance to run so many studies so easily; if one study failed, it was easy to set up another correcting whatever error had been made. Very different from the typical PhD setup today when many studies involve neuroimaging, experiments may be full of potential pitfalls but are too expensive to repeat and use as a learning device.

So what did my 12 sailors tell me? The clearest feature of the results was that it was slower to learn to transfer information *into* the matrix code than decode from it into digits. However, it was hard to know whether that reflected a general visual-verbal difference or because the matrix code was less familiar than the number code. Ruling out the visual versus verbal explanation would require that the learning task involved input and output codes that were both in the same modality for example, both verbal, in effect, to adopt the classic paired-associate method from verbal learning. An example of mapping a familiar onto an unfamiliar verbal code would be learning the vocabulary of a foreign language, for instance *horse – cheval, translating from* an English to a French code, in contrast to learning to translate *from* the unfamiliar language into English. However, vocabulary learning involves meaning as well as familiarity, so I decided to use non-words, in effect joining the research field of "verbal learning", a field described by Miller (2003) as "perhaps the dreariest area, psychophysics not excluded, of the whole of psychology". Furthermore the obvious material to use was the consonant-vowel-consonant nonsense syllables invented by Ebbinghaus in 1885, the dreariest of the dreary and explicitly rejected by Bartlett who was responsible for founding the Unit, and still occasionally visited. However, it was at least a field with a potential link to remembering postal codes and one that had relevant previous research literature for guidance.

The nonsense syllable, having been invented by Ebbinghaus in 1885, was taken up enthusiastically in the succeeding century in US laboratories. They noted that some syllables were easier to learn than others and attributed this to meaningful associations: for example *kig* could suggest the word *keg*, and *lam* could suggest a baby sheep. In 1928, an experimenter by the name of Glaze had a group of subjects go through every possible consonant-vowel-consonant triplet, reporting in each case if it suggested a real word. The list was then published with an indication of the percentage of participants reporting an association, providing a measure of "meaningfulness" that successfully predicted the overall difficulty of learning such items. This guaranteed Glaze what these days would be called an extremely high citation rate since his measure was used widely. I went ahead with my next experiment, matching my lists using the Glaze table, manipulating familiarity by giving practice on some items and not others. I found that practicing the responses was more effective than practicing the stimuli, the initial items of each pair consistent with the interpretation of my previous study in terms of response familiarity. However, I also noticed something else. Over and above the measure of meaningfulness, and my manipulation of familiarity, there seemed to be another important factor, namely how readily the last letter of the stimulus "flowed into" the first of the response. Furthermore, this seemed to follow the pattern that one would expect from the letter structure of English; for example, *ZIL-TOV* was easier than *TOV-ZIL*, *LT* being a more frequent sequence than *VZ*, allowing the two components to be combined more readily into a single pronounceable pseudo-word, *ziltov*.

How could I check this? Here, the book on secret codes mentioned earlier provided an answer. Breaking codes typically takes advantage of the fact that the letter and word structure of language is far from random, with letters such as *e* and *s* being much more common than *v* and *z*. Furthermore, pairs of letters differ greatly in frequency, with some letters such as *q* being virtually always followed by *u*, while other pairs such as *q a* are rarely found. The codebreaker is able to take advantage of these regularities to help crack the code. In this connection, the author had provided tables of the frequency of individual letters and of pairs of letters in English, and I was able to demonstrate that this offered a good explanation of my experimental findings; pairs linked by probable letter combinations were easier. This led to a further possibility: if a letter structure *between* syllables was an important factor, what about *within* syllable letter structure?

By this stage, the plot had thickened to a point at which I could plausibly link my findings to the question of developing postal codes. The letter frequency tables I had used were of unknown origin and reliability, and

Conrad persuaded the Post Office to generate more adequate data using the large computer at the Post Office Research Centre (such computers were rare at the time). Two samples of material were fed into the computer: one was based on editorials from *The Times* newspaper, written in rather august prose. This was balanced by feeding in the scripts from a popular soap opera entitled "Mrs Dale's Diary". It turned out that both gave the same answers. The tables were published in the journal *Nature*, and we became part of a small group of enthusiasts, most of whom were using letter structure information to decide whether certain alleged plays by Shakespeare were genuine or which books of the Bible came from similar sources. I was able to use the letter pair frequency information to work out a measure of the extent to which any letter sequence approximated to the structure of English. I did this, following Shannon's proposal for measuring information by counting the number of guesses that would be needed to predict the next letter if you were rationally using the statistics of language. Hence, given the letter *q*, telling you that the next letter was *u* would not be very informative, whereas given the letter *t*, you would be likely to guess several letters before *u*: for example *h*, as in *the*. So telling you that the next letter is *u* would in this case convey more information. In information theory terms language involves a *redundant* code, one that involves more letters and more words than are strictly necessary to convey that amount of information. Such redundancy, however, by spreading the information across characters, makes it more resistant to error and hence less liable to be disrupted by overloading a limited capacity system such as the brain, which is subject to possible interference from "noise" from other sources.

In the case of *predictability*, my own guessing-based measure of redundancy, I was able to show that it gave a much better account of learning nonsense syllables than the measure of meaningfulness provided by Glaze. I was keen to publish my results but was discouraged by my supervisors on the grounds that it would interfere with the writing of my PhD thesis, which should take clear precedence. Alas, shortly afterwards two new tables of meaningfulness were published. They differed from the earlier tables, so my carefully matched material was no longer adequately matched. Furthermore, by the time my thesis was completed and examined, a book had emerged by two of the leading lights in verbal learning, Benton Underwood and Rudy Schultz, taking a similar line to my own (though not, I thought, doing it so well!). I was of the mistaken opinion at the time that if someone else had published, then further publication was inappropriate.

I proposed that the advantage gained from predictability would not be limited to memory and learning. The proposed new postal codes would need to be keyed into the letter-sorting machines, and on the strength of this the Post Office allowed us to test teleprinter operators, people whose normal job was to key in letters and numerals. As predicted, their speed and accuracy increased as the letter sequences became closer to the letter structure of English.

I duly created postal codes for every town in the UK, linked to their name and optimal for memorability according to the structure of English. I was thanked but told by the Post Office that they had already decided on a code; it was disappointing but at least they had paid for my PhD. The code they had chosen comprised the first three letters of the town name, followed by a single digit and two random letters; they did, however, want to know where to put their digit. Being an applied issue, this question was duly and thoroughly tackled by Conrad, comparing the various possibilities and making a prediction based on a phenomenon known as the von Restorff effect, after its discoverer. She had found that if you were trying to remember a mixed sequence of items, such as five letters and one number, then the odd one out is likely to be best remembered. Conrad suggested therefore that the digit should go at the point at which errors were most likely: in the middle; for example, a York address could be YOR 6LK. He demonstrated experimentally that this was indeed the case, and British postal codes have followed this format ever since. In retrospect this might seem obvious, but clearly this is not the case since Canadian postcodes involved alternating letters and digits, which Conrad found to be the worst possible solution, while the US postal service opted to use only digits.

Does it matter whether one uses letters or digits? It does; first of all, the capacity of a code, the number of different codes that can be generated, is considerably greater for letters. A single digit will allow 10 different codes to be set up, a double digit 100 and so forth, so a random sequence of five digits allows one to distinguish between 10,000 postcodes. Given that there are 26 letters, a random five-letter code would allow over 11 million separate postcodes. Most would not be very memorable, but given so much spare capacity, memorable codes can be selected, as in the case of my postcodes.

This issue has become important in recent years through the ever-increasing use of passwords. Yesterday I was required to generate a new password to allow me to update my Apple software. Apple insisted that it comprised at least eight items, comprising at least three types, digits, lowercase and uppercase letters. That meant that each of the eight items had a potential capacity of 62, so the necessary password has $62 \times 62 \times 62 \times 62 \times 62 \times 62$ capacity (I'll leave you to work out how large that is). If I choose a password that I have used before, my suggestion is rejected. Given that such passwords are required increasingly frequently, this places a ridiculous load on human memory. Shortly after writing this section, I was contacted by the Royal Mail in connection with a planned press release based on a survey that they had commissioned on code memorability. They found that the postcode resulting from Conrad's advice was rated most memorable of any remembered code including pin numbers, telephone numbers and birthdays by 92% of respondents and that it is now widely used for identification purposes well beyond its initial postal use. The announcement coincided with Conrad's 100th birthday. The gap between research and its final vindication can be rather lengthy. And who knows how memorable the codes I invented in vain might have been?

One major change in Britain between the early 1960s and the present is in the level of keyboard skills throughout the population. Those who have grown up with computers and iPhones appear to be able to transmit text at a remarkable rate, whereas keyboard skills in Britain in the 1960s were limited to pianists and professional typists, unlike the US where I believe typing was typically taught at High School. Consequently, my PhD, my early papers and my first book were all produced in long hand and then passed on to a typist. Organisations would have a "typing pool" comprising young women (always women) who had the job of turning written text or dictation into typed documents.

The lack of keyboard skills in the population presented a problem for the Post Office. It was assumed that the public would learn and use the new postal codes, but it was clear that automatic recognition of handwritten characters was not feasible at the time. The solution was to have a postman (they were all men), type in the postcode, resulting in a machine-readable dot code on the envelope. The letter could then be sorted automatically, a clear advantage as letters typically require sorting several times between the initial posting and final delivery. This initial stage meant either employing large numbers of trained typists at considerable expense, or teaching postmen the relevant keyboard skills. This, in turn, offered two ways ahead, either teach the postmen using the current QWERTY keyboard, so called because of the order of the letters along the top row, or perhaps devising an alternative keyboard that might be easier to learn and ultimately more efficient.

This second approach had certain attractions. The existing keyboard was designed in the 1870s in order to cope with mechanical limitations of early typewriters. These required a direct mechanical link between the key press and the print via a series of striking arms one for each letter, which converged at a point where the letter was to be imprinted. This meant that certain pairs of keys, based on arms that were close together, could become jammed. The keyboard was designed so that common letter pairs did not coincide with potentially jamable arms. Of course, the mechanical justification disappeared long ago, but the original arrangement has remained. It has in fact been challenged on a number of occasions, notably by the Dvorak Keyboard, which attempted to arrange letters so that the most frequent involved the shortest finger movements. The Dvorak keyboard still has its advocates but has never proved popular, probably because most people who needed to type had already learnt the QWERTY keyboard and had no desire to confuse matters by changing.

The Post Office situation was different, as was the case in the UK more generally where relatively few people typed. Conrad took up the challenge of designing a better keyboard, pointing out that it was not necessary to have finger movements at all, if the operator were allowed to press two keys, or indeed more at the same time, effectively like playing a chord on the piano. With 10 keys, one could use 10 single presses for the 10 most frequent letters. The addition of chords involving two fingers, for example key 1 plus key 2, increases the number of different items to over 50. A prototype chord keyboard was duly constructed, with 10 keys, five each in the shape of the two hands on a sloping desk, and groups of postmen duly began to arrive in Cambridge in order to learn to type using either the chord or the standard keyboard. So what happened? Disappointingly the two keyboards gave similar results. Presumably, the advantage of not needing to move the fingers was offset by the complexity of learning and selecting chords, or possibly of making two finger responses at the same time.

The Post Office was therefore left with the job of training their postmen to type. Could we advise? Was it better to try to fit training in with their regular job, one hour of practice a day for example, or at the other extreme, giving everyone much more intensive training, for perhaps four hours a day? I was tasked with finding out. We were given access to the volunteers at the Croydon sorting office in South London, and proceeded to test volunteers, comparing one hour a day of training with one session of two hours or two sessions of one hour per day, and our most extreme regime of four hours per day. We measured three things, how long it took to learn the keyboard by touch, and subsequent speed and accuracy of typing. Our results were very clear, given the same number of hours practice; the one-hour-per-day group outperformed the two-hour groups, which did not differ, while the four-hour-per-day group was worst. When we returned several months later and retested the postmen, who had not needed to use their skills in the interval, we found that the one-hour-per-day group retained the most. Could it be that the four-hour group grew dissatisfied with the heavy work load? We explored this using a questionnaire, and somewhat to our surprise found that the most dissatisfied were the one-hour-per-day group, who felt that they were learning more slowly. They were of course, if measured in number of days it took to acquire the skill. As in many applied questions, the answer is not straightforward but typically depends on a range of practical constraints: in this case, how soon you need a trained group.

About seven years later, I returned to the Unit as director. We were still advising the Post Office who had by then finally sorted out the engineering practicalities, had convinced the trade unions to accept the change and were at last about to introduce sorting at a national level. They asked me what training schedules they should use. Resisting the temptation to charge them for another study, I pointed to a report in their archives. Once Conrad had left their Human Factors Committee, it had lost its "memory", not uncommon in organisations where people change jobs every few years. Institutional memory would, I think, be a very intriguing and a valuable area of future study.

I have always liked to have more than one line of research operating at the same time. It means that if one line is proving frustrating, I can concentrate on the other in the hope that the break will allow new ideas to emerge. I was fortunate that the scientific atmosphere at the Unit was sympathetic to this and that while working on the design of postcodes I was able to pursue collaborative research on vigilance, the capacity to sustain attention over long periods, an issue that became important during the Second World War, with the need to detect potential attack by aircraft or submarines.

Vigilance formed an important component of the early work of the Unit and in 1950, Norman Mackworth, who succeeded Bartlett as its director, published an extensive series of studies, showing that performance on a two-hour watch keeping session declined substantially after the first half hour, a result that he also found with a closer simulation of a standard radar task. He went on to check with the RAF and discovered that they also found a drop in the likelihood of submarine detection after the first half hour on watch. Mackworth tried a number of ways of reducing this decrement, finding that having two men on watch alternating every half hour seemed to be effective, although more demanding of manpower. Providing feedback after each signal was also effective in reducing the decrement but was not of course practicable in the real situation. Simple exhortation to try harder was ineffective, but a Benzedrine capsule at the start of the watch did prove effective, whereas a non-stimulant placebo did not. During the 1950s other laboratories were also investigating vigilance and in particular the vigilance decrement noted by Mackworth. One study found that the decline was faster when the signals were harder to detect, but the effect of difficulty was not found in all studies.

A number of investigators were academics who had temporarily been seconded to do research on military problems, and this led to a lively interest in understanding the mechanisms behind vigilance and its decrement with explanations tending to reflect the theoretical background of the investigator. Hence, one proposed mechanism reflected the Hullian concept of reactive inhibition, a fatigue-like effect that built up from repeated exposure to a given stimulus. A second approach was influenced by B.F. Skinner's research on conditioning in pigeons, suggesting that the watchkeeper made a succession of observing responses, with the occasional signal serving as a reinforcer, a reward for making such responses. It seems unlikely, however, that the rather rare signals would be sufficiently rewarding to maintain such behaviour. I suspect, however, that a Skinnerian approach might be more applicable to the current generation of Facebook users with the temptation always to check if someone or something interesting has cropped up.

A third account was offered by what Broadbent describes as an "activationist" view in which performance efficiency depends on the level of physiological arousal within the brain, a level that is likely to drop steadily if a normal and variable environment is replaced by the monotony of watch keeping. The positive effect of the arousing drug Benzedrine on performance is consistent with this, as is the stimulation likely to be gained from a fellow watchkeeper, or from providing feedback after each response. Broadbent favoured this arousal level approach, coupling it with his filter theory of attention. He suggested that a lower level of arousal may lead to failure to apply and orient the attentional filter that governs the feeding in of information to his proposed cognitive system. This would lead to lapses of attention and failure to detect any signals that occurred during such lapses.

On arriving at the Unit, I became intrigued by the topic of vigilance but felt intuitively more attracted to a fourth hypothesis based the concept of *expectancy* whereby the chance of detecting a signal is dependent on how likely you think it is to occur. This view was favoured by James Deese and James Jenkins who both subsequently became influential in the field of memory. Broadbent was sympathetic to this view but felt that expectancy did not give a good answer to the question that currently dominated the field of vigilance, that of rapid performance decrement during the initial stages of the watch. I myself disagreed, largely on the highly dubious grounds of my own rather limited exposure to a watch keeping activity through my boyhood experiences as a rather unsuccessful fisherman. On each session, I would begin by earnestly watching my float, perhaps remembering previous occasions (sadly rather rare), when it had disappeared, indicating that a fish had taken the bait. As the day went on my optimism declined, and I would spend less and less time looking at the float and more and more time looking elsewhere.

I am embarrassed to remember the extent to which, on arrival at the Unit, I tried to engage Donald on this topic and persuade him to let me work on vigilance rather than postal codes, for which, as he pointed out, I was funded. He suggested instead that I collaborate with a more established colleague, Peter Colquhoun (pronounced Kerhoon) who was working on industrial inspection, a peacetime occupation requiring vigilance. This I duly did. It worked very well, partly because of our contrasting but compatible personalities. I was a naïve enthusiast preoccupied with theory, whereas Peter was a pragmatic pessimist with a dry wit and a rather gloomy sense of humour. His studies were based on "the great wheel", a piece of equipment simulating industrial inspection using a large wheel which clunked around successively presenting rows of six circular blobs through a slit, the task of the inspector being to detect the occasional deviant blob.

We began with a possible expectancy-based explanation for Mackworth's decrement-based expectancy theory. We noted that in Mackworth's and many other studies, the first phase of the experiment was to practice the watchkeeper on the detection task. This typically involved a high frequency of targets to ensure that the detection task had been adequately mastered. This we argued would set up an unduly high expectancy which would in due course be corrected by experience on the task itself. We set out to test this by specifically setting up a high expectancy by initially presenting frequent signals during practice before moving on to the main test at either the same or a lower frequency, comparing this with a training session in which the relevant frequency was established before the start of the test itself. We duly discovered that by varying signal density during training we could influence the watchkeeper's expectation of what was to follow and hence create or remove the decrement, pointing out that many of the studies in the literature suffered from the design fault of high-density training.

Donald did indeed incorporate our results but went one important step further. You may possibly recall from Chapter 5 that one of the important breakthroughs presented at the meeting launching the cognitive revolution in 1956 was signal detection theory. This resulted from an information processing approach to psychoacoustics that assumes that detecting an acoustic stimulus such as a sonar bleep is not a simple all-or-none process. It involves detecting a signal that may fluctuate in its magnitude because of external factors such as distance and hence loudness of the target, against a background of noise that may also fluctuate as a result of other ships or passing shoals of fish. Hence, there may be occasions when the acoustic input from the fluctuating noise is greater than the signal on other occasions when a genuine submarine is present. This means that it is not possible to discriminate perfectly, however good and diligent the operator. If he is to detect all the submarines, he will also have to make false alarms, reporting a submarine when none was present. Similarly, if operators wish to avoid false alarms, then they will have to miss a number of genuine submarines. A tragic example of the wrong vigilance decision occurred when the radar operator at Pearl Harbour discounted the signal from the oncoming swarms of Japanese bombers as sufficiently improbable as to be regarded as "noise", and failed to report it.

Signal detection theory allows two measures. One, a discriminability measure d' (d prime), is based on the difference between the average stimulus level when there is a signal present and the average when it is absent. The other represents the criterion adopted by the decision maker (β), which can range from very cautious, resulting in few false alarms but many missed signals, to extremely liberal in which case few signals will be missed but potentially at the expense of many false alarms. Broadbent pointed out that this approach could be applied to vigilance, with higher levels of expectancy leading to a lower criterion for accepting a signal, a process that could be separated from the watchkeeper's basic capacity to make the discrimination.

Peter Colquhoun and I went on to apply this to our next study in which we varied the relative probability of signals and non-signals. We found that overall detection rate was higher when targets were frequent than when they comprised only a small proportion of stimuli. However, the high probability condition also induced a high false alarm rate. When analysed using signal detection theory we found that d', the capacity to discriminate a signal, was the same across conditions with the difference in performance entirely attributable to the use of a laxer criterion in the high-frequency conditions, a result entirely consistent with the expectancy hypothesis.

However while expectancy provides a good account of both our expectancy training and our signal frequency results, the effects of drugs and sleep deprivation on vigilance suggest that aroused level is also an important factor. Furthermore, while our account of decrement in terms of an inappropriate level of expectancy built up during training could explain much of the existing data, other studies produced decrements that could not be accounted for in this way. Some years later I was asked to examine a brilliant PhD thesis by Raja Parasuraman from Aston University in Birmingham whose analysis of the extensive vigilance literature suggested a crucial variable. Tasks that were purely perceptual in nature, judging each signal against a constant standard, showed little decrement provided expectancy levels were appropriate. Decrements did, however, occur when there was a short-term memory component, requiring participants to hold information about one event until the next one occurred. He went on to successfully test this hypothesis across a series of experiments. Some 20 years later we ourselves were able to use this distinction to demonstrate that patients with Alzheimer's Disease were able, perhaps surprisingly, to sustain *perceptual* attention over time, while showing marked decrement in the capacity to maintain performance when it required comparing stimuli that were separated by a short delay, that is to sustain working memory-based attention.

However, while Broadbent continued to be interested in vigilance and arousal as reflected in his second major theoretical book "Decision and Stress", the topic of vigilance largely disappeared from main stream cognitive psychology, partly no doubt because the military problem of watch keeping seemed less important, while the task of industrial inspection became increasingly automated. There are currently, however, signs that this is beginning to change following the 9/11 terrorist attack on the World Trade Center and the introduction of airport baggage scanning. In this connection, I was intrigued to be contacted a couple of years ago by Jeremy Wolfe, an expert on visual search. He had just published a paper in the journal *Science* on vigilance and airport security with results that were very similar to those on the effects of signal frequency published by Peter Colquhoun and myself some 40 years earlier. Other vigilance-like tasks are becoming prominent again. We were, for example, recently contacted for advice on preventing the smuggling of drugs and mobile phones into high security prisons, while my colleague Karla Evans is working on improving the capacity of radiologists to detect signs of disease when processing very large numbers of X-ray images.

One problem in the application of psychology at least is the considerable gap there may be between research and its eventual application. In the case of developing memorable codes for example, I was recently approached by a small company developed by a computer scientist and entrepreneur who had previously travelled the world as the manager of a rock band. They had identified a major problem in specifying addresses in areas such as refugee camps or indeed in some cities such as Tokyo. They came up with an interesting potential solution, pointing out that, given a capacity of many thousands of words for almost any language, a sequence of three words would provide enough alternative codes to allow them to specify any location on the surface of the earth to within a few metres. They had already developed this and were rolling it out in a number of countries but wished to add a further refinement, namely to ensure that more memorable triads should be available to areas with lots of people, relegating the less memorable to areas such as the centre of the South Atlantic. What would determine memorability? I was able to tell them about word frequency, sequential redundancy and of course phonological similarity, suggesting that it would be a good idea to test out my proposals empirically, which they agreed to consider; although judging by the speed at which the system was being rolled out, time to run new experiments would be far too slow. This is in fact rather characteristic of much applied work, namely that rapid decisions must be made while experimental evidence accrues more slowing. It may often be the case that the evidence is available based on existing research, but as this may have been done long ago, it is not readily accessible.

In all the cases I have outlined, I was contacted because someone remembered that I was interested in vigilance or codes. Unfortunately, this is not a very reliable or efficient way of storing information since it depends on happening to meet the right person at the right time. Surely one might think that Google is the answer. In fact I tried googling vigilance, encountering many references to vigilance in flocks of starlings or herds of zebra, but I found no links to the extensive research done immediately after the war. I was able to eventually find this literature but only because I could remember one or two of the classic papers and pursue them. Whatever the Google algorithm is, it tends to favour the short term and popular over the long term, regardless of potential importance. It thus tends to reinforce the old too common view found in students and postdocs that what is important is what has been done in the last five years, with little need to worry about longer term research apart from a few frequently cited exceptions. In some cases, this results in rediscovering what is already known, reinventing the wheel, which in itself is not bad thing. In others it results in failure to consider potentially important issues and repeating old mistakes.

8

Acoustic and Semantic Codes

Evidence for Separate Memory Systems?

I had been in Cambridge for four years, the postcode project had finished and my PhD was completed. So what next? At that time, the same government department was responsible for both postal and telephone services and had a very active technical development programme. They were keen on improving the quality of telephone lines and for that purpose needed to measure their efficiency. This was, and I suspect still is, typically done through listening tests whereby potentially confusable items and phrases are spoken, and the quality of the line is measured in terms of the listener's error rate. Might it be possible to obtain an even more sensitive measure, if, in addition to hearing the material, people had to use it? One can think of two possible reasons why this might be the case. It is possible that the effort of decoding a noisy signal might take attention away from other types of processing such as understanding the message. Another possibility is that decoding a noisy auditory signal itself might lead to a noisy memory representation, potentially leading to further error when retrieved.

It was suggested that I should tackle this problem, using a specially designed piece of equipment that exactly simulated the way in which the transmission of the voice became "noisy" over a telephone line. However, the equipment took some time to develop, and meanwhile I felt free to play around, exploring possible methods, using a simple noise source, producing something like a waterfall sound, as a noisy background against which normal speech had to be perceived and processed.

I began, rather ambitiously, with a situation in which people were trying to communicate either in quiet or in noise. I used sailors separated by a screen and gave them a task that I thought they might enjoy. Both had the same array of pictures of girls, and one was supposed to communicate to the other the girl he would most like to date. The idea was that I could then tape the conversation and in some unspecified way analyse it for efficiency. The sailors seemed to enjoy the task but were not particularly communicative, so I switched to our panel of volunteers, having pairs of ladies tell each other about their holidays. This, they really enjoyed but alas there was even less communication. They talked enthusiastically about their holidays but seemed more concerned to relive them, rather than to communicate information; indeed it was not unusual for both to talk at the same time, leaving me with huge amounts of verbiage and no idea how to analyse it. It was time to rethink. I simplified the question and started again, resulting in a series of experiments that subsequently formed the nucleus that grew into my lifelong interest in working memory, the system for temporarily holding and manipulating information that provides the basis for complex thought processes.

Stripping the problem down to its essentials, I argued that what was needed was a task that would combine correctly hearing verbal material under different listening conditions with storing it in memory. The question of the influence of noise on more complex tasks, I left for later investigation. I was of course familiar with Conrad's work on acoustic similarity whereby immediate recall in the correct order of sequences of letters that were similar in sound such as *b g d v t* was less accurate than recall of dissimilar letters such as *k w x r y*. Perhaps combining the need to *hear* the material accurately with the need to *remember*, it would be particularly sensitive to the quality of the acoustic signal?

At the same time, I decided to tackle another question. Conrad interpreted his results as evidence for a specific temporary memory store that was based on sound, and that ran into difficulties when it had to handle items that were acoustically similar; remembering the letters in the right *order* was particularly difficult for the similar letters. Conrad had, however, not looked at other types of similarity. Perhaps *any* kind of similarity would have the same effect? If so, the evidence for a specifically acoustic store would be seriously weakened. Such a position would be much closer to that taken by the dominant approach within verbal learning at the time, which did not differentiate between different types of similarity. I decided to use words and look at similarity of meaning as well as sound.

The resulting experiment was a very simple one. It involved hearing sequences of five words and then writing them down in the same order immediately afterwards. The sequences were all drawn from one of four pools of eight words, with each five-word sequence selected at random. People quickly became familiar with the words, but as in remembering a telephone number, the crucial problem is remembering the *order*. One set used words that were similar in sound, so a typical sequence might be *mat man cat map can*. A second set comprised dissimilar words (*pit day top hen rug*). A third set were similar in meaning but not sound (*huge big large wide tall*), and a fourth involved words that were dissimilar in both meaning and sound, for example (*old wet late thin hot*). In line with Conrad's work with letters, I expected the acoustically similar set to be harder to recall in the correct order than the dissimilar list. The crucial question, however, was whether I would find an effect of similarity of meaning, indicating a more general short-term memory system than the phonological store that Conrad proposed.

It was of course important first of all to test whether participants were actually able to *hear* the various words, so the whole session began with a listening test. The experimental situation would probably horrify anyone working on the psychology of hearing, which typically involves testing a single listener in a small soundproof room isolated from any potential outside noise. I simply recorded the lists of words, and then played them to a room full of about 20 people. They were tested either in quiet, although the room was in the middle of the building and not soundproof, or while accompanied by a noise like a waterfall played from a speaker at the same time as the spoken words that had to be heard and remembered. I reassured myself with the thought that if anything promising emerged, I could do a more carefully controlled study using a soundproof room and the fancy equipment that was still being built.

You may recall I had two questions. The first was practical; could I offer a better way of testing the quality of telephone lines? The second was theoretical; is Conrad's temporary memory system purely acoustic or is it also sensitive to similarity of meaning? The answer to the first question was disappointing; my simple listening test detected a few errors when noise was added, and unsurprisingly these all occurred in the acoustically similar *can man cat* set, but I found no evidence that these led to further problems when the words had to be remembered, so no brilliant new method for the Post Office. In contrast, I got a resoundingly clear answer to my theoretical question. As expected, the acoustically similar items were harder to recall than the dissimilar, but what I had not expected was the sheer magnitude of the effect, with around 80% of the five dissimilar *pit, day,* word sequences remembered correctly, and only about 10% of the similar *man, cat* set. The contrast with the effect of similarity of meaning was dramatic, with the similar *big, large* sequences remembered about 67% of the time, and the dissimilar *old, wet* 73%, a dramatically smaller, though still statistically reliable difference. Conrad was right. I still had some tidying up to do, carrying out further experiments repeating my results and showing that they also occurred when the words were presented visually, to fully rule out any interpretation in terms of mishearing.

Conrad was away on sabbatical in the US during this period, and in borrowing his acoustic similarity effect, I felt a little like the magician's apprentice (played in Disney's Fantasia by Mickey Mouse), who borrowed his master's magic wand to help with his daily chores of carrying water, though happily I had avoided generating the disastrous flood that followed Mickey's efforts. It now occurs to me that things might have been rather more complicated if my results had been totally inconsistent with Conrad's position! In supporting Conrad's model by providing further evidence of the specificity of acoustic coding, I found myself part of a very hot controversy, that of whether to assume a separate short-term storage system as proposed by Conrad, Broadbent and others in both the UK and the US, or to hold on to the traditional verbal learning position that the existing evidence could all be explained within a single memory system. This question led to an obvious next experiment; if Conrad's short-term system favours the importance of sound over meaning, will the long-term memory system give the opposite answer, with long-term memory using a code based on meaning rather than sound?

I tackled this question using a modification of the original experiment. This time, people had to learn lists of 10 words, well beyond their memory span, and hence requiring several learning trials. I found that sequences of words that were similar in meaning (*huge, large,* etc.) were learned consistently more slowly than semantically dissimilar lists (*old, wet,* etc.), whereas similarity of sound made little difference. Exactly the opposite to our short-term results. We were able to repeat this finding using more standard verbal learning interference methods based on paired-associate learning, where people learn to link a list of stimulus words with a specified response as in learning foreign vocabulary. Again, we found that people relied on an acoustic code for remembering small amounts of information over the short term, switching to a dependence on meaning for long-term learning. This all seemed to add up to a simple conclusion, two separate memory systems, one temporary and relying on sound and another more durable system based on meaning. We had our entry ticket for the controversy over how many kinds of memory there are, a question that dominated much of the research on human memory during the 1960s.

Some encouraging results from other groups were beginning to appear that seemed to support the proposal of separate short-term acoustically based and long-term semantically based memory systems. One study was concerned with memory for prose passages, probing for both semantic and syntactic information and testing either the most recent or earlier sentences. Results suggested that syntactic information conveyed by exact word order was well retained across the final sentence, suggesting that it was held, at least temporarily, in a literal form. For all but the last sentence however, only the semantic gist appeared to be retained. Hence a sentence such as "*The boy was chased by the dog*", followed by the test probe "*The dog chased the boy*" was correctly rejected as non-identical when tested immediately but not after intervening sentences, whereas the meaning of the phrase was retained for much longer. A similar distinction was apparent in free recall, where acoustic errors came principally from the short-term recency component. Semantic coding however, reflected in the tendency for items from the same semantic category to be recalled together, was present in the early part of the list but not within recency. So far so good; the data could be readily explained by assuming two separate memory stores, a temporary system based on acoustic coding and a semantically based long-term store.

However, problems had begun to arise with this simple two-store view of memory. One of our studies used a recently developed technique, known as minimal paired-associate learning, in which a small number of pairs of items are presented and tested only once, for example presenting just three pairs probed in turn by giving the first word of each (e.g. Present *dog – hat*; *rose – tin*; *hill – book*: Test; *rose?*). We varied the number of pairs from three to six, expecting the shorter lists to show an acoustic similarity effect and the longer lists to show semantic coding. Instead, we found a consistent effect of acoustic similarity regardless of number of pairs, and no effect of semantic coding. Six pairs of words were well beyond short-term memory capacity, so why were they not encoded semantically?

The next step involved my first postdoctoral visitor, Betty Ann Levy, who joined me from the University of Toronto, probably the most active and successful memory lab in the world at that time. She had been warned by colleagues of my enthusiasm for primitive technology and that if she were not careful she could end up running memory experiments by holding up cards with words written on them. I agreed not to humiliate her in this way. In due course I gave her the choice of a range of methods, which included testing large groups of subjects simultaneously by holding up cards, or individually in a technically more sophisticated way; she opted for testing groups using cards.

We decided to test the hypothesis that the reason why semantic coding was not used in our minimal paired- associate situation because of the difficulty in finding a meaningful link between the words, given a single brief presentation, whereas the standard long-term procedure involving re-peated presentation allowed semantic coding to build up gradually. If this were the case, then choosing material that was easy to link semantically should change the pattern of results. As in our earlier short-term paired-associate experiments, we varied similarity within lists, constructing lists in which all the items were similar in meaning but this time including a condition in which the pairs were easily combined in a meaningful way: for example *priest-pious, vicar-holy*, or *apple-delicious, pear-tasty*, contrasting this with mismatched pairs, such as *priest-delicious, vicar-tasty*. If we were correct, meaning would only influence performance when the words read-ily created a meaningful pair. Hence, holy vicars should become confused with pious priests to produce pious vicars while juicy vicars and tasty priest were just treated as sequences of unrelated words. This is just what we found. People use meaning to help remember even over brief intervals but only when the words can easily be semantically linked. Our original idea of two separate stores each with its own code was clearly too simple, as indeed it had to be, on reflection. If we had no acoustic long-term memory, we would not be able to learn people's names or new words in our native language, while second language learning would be impossible. The fact that immediate memory for *sentences* is substantially greater than for unrelated words, around 15 words versus five, indicates that mean-ing *can* be used over the short intervals required in classic memory span studies. This suggests that the acoustic and semantic memory systems can operate simultaneously and in parallel rather than passing information sequentially from a short-term acoustic to a long-term semantic store as was commonly assumed at the time.

We went on to investigate this by creating three-word mini-sentences that could be either acoustically similar or dissimilar, for example *I might fly* versus *he may jump*. We compared memory for these with word triplets that were matched for frequency but did not make sense: for example *eye fight dry* versus *king wake slip*. We put pairs of these word triplets together to make six-word lists and had our subjects recall them after either a 2- or 20-second delay, filled by a distractor task to prevent subvocal rehearsal.

Our results were clear in showing overall effects of both meaningfulness and acoustic similarity. However, the acoustic similarity effect was only apparent after the *short* delay and had vanished after 20 seconds, whereas the semantic advantage was present after two seconds but then remained strong. Particularly striking was the fact that the "I might fly" condition actually *improved* over the delay. It seems that people initially stored and potentially had access to both sound and meaning but *chose* to rely on the brief though less effective acoustic code after the short delay.

It is not uncommon for people to place too much reliance on verbal rote recall in a long-term learning situation. Verbal rote memory has the advantage that it is simple, rapid and good for storing serial order but is limited in both its capacity and its durability. Semantic coding is more durable but depends on the nature of the material; if items can readily be combined into a meaningful unit, then semantic coding may be rapid, but with arbitrary material, either longer encoding time or repeated presentation is necessary. Finally, our results suggest that acoustic and semantic processes run simultaneously and can be combined when appropriate, as in recalling sentences.

By the early 1970s, people were becoming disenchanted with the field of short-term memory. It seemed to be resulting in many different methods, often accompanied by a separate micro-theory and interest was beginning to switch elsewhere. At this point the field was dramatically changed by what proved to be a hugely influential paper on a topic related to the acoustic-semantic distinction, with the publication by Fergus Craik and Robert Lockhart of a new theoretical framework for memory research based on the concept of Levels of Processing. Fergus (Gus) Craik graduated from Edinburgh and then moved to a post at a Medical Research Council Unit in Liverpool that focussed on ageing. He would visit Cambridge occasionally and, being at similar stages in our careers, he and I would enjoy sorting out psychology, preferably over a pint of beer. At that time Gus worked mainly on short-term memory, whereas I working on long-term memory. He later moved to Birkbeck College London, which had a very active group of young long-term memory researchers. In due course he accepted a one-year fellowship from the University of Toronto, at that time the strongest memory research department in the world. He decided to stay, as have a number of recipients of this generous fellowship, and in collaboration with Bob Lockhart, who himself originated in Australia, produced the paper that changed the way in which many people thought about memory. The Levels of Processing framework moved away from the idea of a succession of memory stores, focussing instead on memory as a by-product of cognitive processing, with memory durability depending on the manner in which material had been processed.

Probably the best way of explaining the concept of levels is through a typical experiment. This would involve visually presenting a series of words, each of which had to be processed in a particular way. One instruction would involve purely visual processing, deciding, for example, whether the word was printed in upper-case or lower-case letters. A second instruction might require a phonological judgement: for example *does the word rhyme with dog?*, while a third would involve "deeper" probably semantic processing. *Would the word fit the sentence "the man stroked the"*? Whether tested by recognition or recall, the most superficial visual judgement led to poor retention, the acoustic judgement led to better performance but not nearly as effective as a judgement based on meaning.

This result proved easily replicable across "deep" processing tasks ranging from semantic category judgement to the assessment of pleasantness. Furthermore, it made little difference whether or not people were warned before making the judgements that memory for the words would be tested later. Although Craik and Lockhart rejected the existing concept of separate long- and short-term memory stores, their interpretation was very much in the information-processing tradition. It continued to assume a short-term *primary memory* system of limited capacity but emphasised its attentional nature rather than its storage capacity, stressing its role, not only in encoding but also in rehearsal and retrieval.

Rehearsal was assumed to take two forms, *maintenance rehearsal* and *elaboration*. Maintenance rehearsal involved simply recycling the stimulus at the same level of processing. Verbally repeating a word sequence to prevent forgetting would be an example of this. Maintenance rehearsal was assumed to reduce forgetting in the short term but not to increase the probability of long-term retention. This requires elaborative rehearsal, actively processing the incoming material and transforming it into some deeper code, for example linking the word dog to its meaning, and perhaps then linking it semantically to the next word in the sequence. Note that this is very different from the role of rehearsal in the models of short-term memory at the time such as that proposed by Atkinson and Shiffrin where simple maintenance by repetition was assumed to lead directly to enhanced learning. This was tested in a series of studies by Craik and others, which in general supported the levels of hypothesis, typically suggesting very little long-term benefit from mere rote repetition.

The Levels paper caused great interest, leading to a wide range of replications, typically using concrete words and showing dramatic effects. At a theoretical level, its underlying assumptions fitted neatly into theories, popular at the time, that assumed a sequence of ever deeper stages from peripheral sensory processing to perception and then to meaning and broader semantic interpretation. It was also welcomed by the traditional verbal learning community who suggested that it removed the need to assume separate long- and short-term memory systems, although this was not a position Craik and Lockhart themselves held, emphasising the importance of a short-term primary memory system for the initial stage of learning.

The Levels approach was not, however, without its critics, of which I was one. Secretly I felt that it was simply a way of rephrasing the acoustic-semantic distinction and linking it to an unproven set of assumptions about the processes occurring between perception and memory. Furthermore, I argued that it would prove impossible to provide an independent measure of processing depth, and that it was therefore liable to lead to a circular argument by assuming that if something led to better learning, it *must* have involved deeper processing. It did prove difficult to develop an independent measure of depth, and an attempt by Craik and Tulving to use processing *time* as a measure of depth proved unsuccessful, but this did not however lead to the circularity I predicted but rather to the abandonment of the assumption of a fixed sequence of ever deeper separable stages. Indeed, evidence from elsewhere seemed increasingly to point to parallel perceptual and semantic processes operating at the same time, with information flowing in both directions from semantic to perceptual as well as the reverse. Craik himself has backed off from the concept of successive levels, stressing rather the importance of elaboration, providing an increase in associative links, hence adding redundancy and robustness to the encoded memory, which, in turn, facilitates retrieval. This view has much in common with the views of William James from the 1890s, who thought of such links as resembling hooks that enabled more richly encoded memories to be retrieved more readily and reliably.

Despite my initial criticisms, I find that whenever I have to give a talk to a general audience about memory, Craik and Lockhart's work always features prominently. It demonstrates very robustly that what you remember depends on how you process the material, not on how determined you are to retain it. Indeed such determination often encourages an attempt at rote learning which gives the illusion of good retention after a short delay but little durability. At a more theoretical level, I think the emphasis on *processes* rather than memory *stores* was a timely one. The term "store" tends to suggest a location into which memories are placed and kept, passively until required. It has been known however, at least since Bartlett's research, that remembering involves highly active processing, not only during encoding but also at retrieval, with both involving a search for meaning that will link new learning with old. The term "store" does, however, capture the fact the *something* must persist. This is true both logically and physiologically, where consolidation involves both a consolidation process and something that is consolidated for which the rather abstract term "memory trace" seems appropriate.

Hence, the assumption that explanations should rely on *either* processes *or* stores seems simplistic. Memory is not an abstraction but depends on the human brain. which involves both anatomical structures and neurophysiological processes, both of which must feature in an adequate theory of memory. It is interesting to note in this respect that theorists influenced by neuropsychology, with its necessary link to the brain, rarely seem to reject the need for the concepts of memory storage, while proceduralist approaches rejecting the concept of storage appear to be more common among more behaviourally oriented experimental psychologists.

So what about my original task of measuring acoustic quality of telephone lines? Given the theoretical promise of my demonstration of a link between coding and memory, I was encouraged to continue to pursue this line of research. The telephony project was transferred to Patrick Rabbitt, who had just joined the Unit; using the newly built noise-creating equipment he was able to show a clear though small effect of noise on immediate memory, attributable to the demands placed on memory by the need to discriminate the noisy items; Pat has gone on to develop a distinguished career in the field of ageing, and went on to show that this noise effect becomes increasingly important with age. Recent research shows that simple tests of hearing are not good predictors of the capacity of older people to follow a conversation in a noisy environment such as a party or a supermarket. What determines this capacity is a joint effect of hearing loss and the listeners' short-term working memory, which is needed to make sense of the stream of poorly heard speech. Importantly however, it has recently been shown that working memory capacity only has a substantial effect on comprehension as we age. If only I had tested older people 40 years ago, I would have shown a clear effect! But then, I would probably have missed joining the long-term/short-term controversy, and all that has followed.

9

From Full-Time Research to a New University

I had been at the Applied Psychology Unit for around seven years. I was enjoying life at the Unit, but I had always assumed that at some point I would move over to a university post and if so, given my lack of teaching experience, it might be sensible to move sooner rather than later. The mid-sixties was a good time to move as the university system had greatly expanded following the foundation of six or seven new universities, almost all of which had psychology departments. Furthermore, departments were getting larger with more emphasis on research, breaking away from the old system of one professor per department who was then doomed to spend the rest of his or her career in administration.

I began to look around for posts in good departments in pleasant locations and in due course was shortlisted for two lectureships, a lecturer being the first of three rungs on the academic ladder. One post was at Oxford and the other at Sussex. I was interviewed at Oxford and it did not go well; I managed to get lost trying to find the interview room and having found my way, responded to a question about amnesia by confessing my total ignorance, not a good move in Oxford! Things went rather better at Sussex where teaching was more specialised and where the head of department was familiar with my memory research as a result of recent talks I had given. I was offered a job and duly accepted, with the agreement that I could take early sabbatical leave in response to an invitation I had received to spend a year in California.

By this stage I had spent nine years in Cambridge and looked on the prospect of a move with enthusiasm. Hilary and I had two sons, Roland

and Gavin, with Bart, a third son arriving a year or two later. Our first job was to find a house, not an easy task since the housing market was going through a period of stasis; we could not find a single appropriate house in Brighton and ended up living in Hassocks, a commuter village a few miles north, which involved a very pleasant drive across the South Downs to the university. Hassocks was a little dull, basically a dormitory village with many of its inhabitants commuting to London, but our house was pleasant, and the schools were good. Brighton itself is a very interesting city, initially a small fishing village that developed during the eighteenth century, first through claims of the health-giving effects of sea bathing and later when the rakish Prince Regent chose it as a place to bring his numerous lady friends, in due course building the Brighton Pavilion, an exotic palace built in a dramatically oriental style. As Brighton developed, it continued to blend the grand and the rakish, a classic place for an illicit weekend, and with the development of the railways, providing a lively day at the seaside for Londoners, complete with a racecourse for those keen on a flutter at a time when off-course betting was illegal.

The university was founded in 1961, the trendiest (good 1960s word!) of the new universities with a campus designed by a famous architect in a fold in the downs just outside the city. Unlike most universities, which had individual departments organised within loosely organised faculties, such as science, arts and medicine, Sussex had a number of interdisciplinary Schools, each of which was supposed to share first-year teaching across subjects within the School. This meant that there were three psychology departments, one in the School of Education, one in Social Sciences and my own department of experimental psychology located within the School of Biology. This model did not in the long-term prove to be a great success. In the case of biology, it involved a common first-year course in biochemistry attended both by students who intended to become biochemists and psychology students who might have neither biology nor chemistry in their background. Furthermore, it meant that within the psychology curriculum the same topic, for example memory, had to be taught separately in education, social science and experimental psychology, not all of which could afford to have anyone with expertise in the area. The system gradually changed, resulting after many years in a single psychology department, a cautionary tale perhaps for the grand bureaucratic schemes that are inflicted on universities from time to time.

The experimental psychology department (although we were not supposed to call it a department) did have the advantage in my case of allowing a focus on a relatively limited range of psychological issues, with a strong emphasis on research. The department was founded and developed by Stuart Sutherland, a charismatic figure from Oxford who was intent on making it the best in the country. He recruited well, if not with great breadth; when I arrived I was actually the only person who was not working principally with animals. However, everyone took very seriously the task of covering the range of experimental psychology, except myself where somewhat remarkably, I was able to claim ignorance and avoid teaching anything other than memory. This involved a grand total of eight lectures per year linked with a second series of eight lectures on psycholinguistics. These were taught by Bob Boakes whose research was principally on pigeons but who had been bitten by the Chomsky bug while doing a PhD at Harvard and was happy to teach psycholinguistics.

I made up for lack of lectures by teaching the second-year practical course. Students were trained in standard experimental procedures in the first year and were expected to develop this in the second, going on to carry out individual supervised projects in the third. The second-year course traditionally involved performing a series of standard "classic" experiments, which people found rather boring. Instead I decided to use it as a communal research activity, typically choosing a series of topics, each typically based on a well-understood component that *ought* to work combined with the addition of a new question that would add to current knowledge. I typically used paper and pencil methods, explaining the design one week and instructing everyone to test two subjects. The following week we would analyse the data, typically using very simple robust statistics. On a couple of occasions, the results looked solid enough and interesting enough to justify a modest paper, which raised the question of who should be the authors. I solved the problem by putting all the students' names in a hat and drawing out about four as co-authors, a procedure that I am sure would be regarded with horror these days on many different grounds, but it was fun and engaged the students far more than the traditional approach of simply replicating standard studies.

The department was very interactive, with everyone interested in each other's research. This, together with the need to teach and explain things to students, had a very positive effect on my thinking about the field. Much of the zest in the department came from Stuart Sutherland's leadership. On first encounter he seemed a somewhat unlikely figure, burly and balding, often clad in an ancient gabardine raincoat with a moth-eaten fur collar. He was a heavy smoker, and would attempt to give up from time to time; this meant giving up *buying* cigarettes, but he was not above going into the departmental library and "borrowing" a cigarette from an undergraduate.

His office contained a bed and a half-full gin bottle (in fact half-full of water), and he had a growl that could reduce students to tears. In fact he was very caring, and when some miscreant was about to be kicked out, it was usually Stuart who said, "well we did let them in, so it is our job to sort them out".

We had many distinguished visitors to the department, particularly from North America, and it was Stuart's custom to offer them a job, which they always rejected with thanks. This could, however, occasionally lead to problems, compounded by Stuart's inability to remember names and faces. On one occasion he offered a job to a postdoc in the department by the name of Angus Craig, mistaking him for Fergus Craik who was at the time doing classic memory research in Toronto. Angus, on discovering the mistake, sensibly declined the offer. It was, however, a happy department since we knew that Stuart would always support his staff and stand up for the department in the university more generally. It was also a very sociable department and staff meetings, which can potentially be interminable, were always started one hour before the pub opened, providing a very strong motivation to keep things brief.

Stuart kept well abreast of developments in cognitive psychology and artificial intelligence (AI). His own prime interest was in a cognitive approach to animal learning, where he published an influential book with Nick Macintosh who later joined the department. He also had an interest in, and lectured on, vision, and was very supportive of research on AI and on attempts to develop computer-based models of both language and vision. He appointed Max Clowes who developed a model of visual processing that involved combining lower level visual features into shapes and then "parsing" the shapes into objects within a scene, all based on a logical structure resembling that developed by Chomsky for language. He persuaded the university to create a department of cognitive science focussing on AI, initially assuming that it would form part of the School of biology. Unfortunately, at the time the government somewhat surprisingly did not want to create more science departments, and when a "department" of Cognitive Science was founded, it was within the School of Arts, with the excuse that it would help make arts students more computer literate. It subsequently evolved into a separate School of Cognitive Science, where two of my sons eventually took degrees in AI.

Meanwhile, with a light teaching load and plenty of student volunteers to test, my research continued apace. A good deal of the research on acoustic and semantic coding in short-term and long-term memory described earlier was carried out during my early years at Sussex. It seemed to fit neatly into the case for separate memory systems, in what was, and some claim remains a very controversial issue, that of how many different kinds of memory we should assume. As mentioned earlier, by the late 1950s, attempts to develop a grand theory of learning based on rats running mazes were beginning to falter, with investigators increasingly looking elsewhere for more tractable problems. This led to more and more people switching their interest to human learning in general, and in particular to the dominant approach at the time in the US, the verbal learning tradition. This assumed that all learning was based on the association of stimuli with responses, not only in the case of language where one might learn that the French word *lait* is equivalent to the English word *milk* but also in the world more generally, where we learn the association between fire and heat, for example, and between clouds and rain. *Associationism*, the view that all knowledge is based on such links, had its roots in the work of the eighteenth-century British philosophers John Locke and David Hume. It was reflected in the mid-twentieth century by an approach that saw the role of psychology as attempting to work out in detail the principles whereby new associations were formed, and old associations forgotten. It relied largely on studies requiring the learning and retention of lists of either meaningless syllables or words and was hence commonly referred to as the verbal learning approach.

Forgetting was assumed to occur through a process of interference, whereby old stimuli became attached to new responses, with the result that the old association was disrupted. The degree of interference was assumed to depend on the similarity between what has already been learned and the new learning, with similar interference being more disruptive than dissimilar. In one study for example, people learned lists of words for later recall; one group then went on to learn lists of numbers, while a second group learned a new list of words. When later asked to recall the first list, the number learners recalled more of the initial words. The intervening numbers were less similar to the first word list and hence caused less interference.

There is no doubt that interference effects occur. In my own case for example, as a result of travel, I have acquired a smattering of Italian, French and German. Italian and Spanish are much the more similar languages, and when I try to speak one, I find it hard to keep out intrusions from the other, whereas this is not a problem for Italian and German. Such an interaction between different tasks goes under the name of *transfer of training*, and the language interference between Italian and Spanish would be a case of *negative transfer*. There are of course positive effects; having learned Latin at school, I find that it helps with both Spanish and Italian vocabularies, while

English vocabulary helps with both German, for example *hund-hound*, and French, as in *mouton-mutton*. So, there is no doubt that such effects do occur and influence both learning and forgetting, but are they the whole story?

By the early 1960s, the verbal learning approach had developed a well-established series of principles, which were assumed to apply to all learning and memory. Consequently, when people lost faith in the grand theories of learning based on maze learning in rats, verbal learning seemed to offer a more solid alternative. However, at the same time, the psychology of memory was beginning to be influenced by the cognitive revolution, which had an impact on two fronts. One concerned the influence of linguistics, which will be discussed later, while the other reflected the information processing tradition as typified by Donald Broadbent in the UK and Paul Fitts, Michael Posner and Ulrich Neisser in the US. The case for a separate short-term memory system relied on several lines of evidence of which three seemed initially particularly compelling: namely (1) some tasks appear to have two separate components, one durable and the other more fragile; (2) evidence from brain-damaged patients that showed that gross impairment of one of these systems could occur, while the other remained unaffected; and (3) differential coding, with the short-term system apparently depending on acoustic and the long-term system depending on semantic processing. As we saw in the last chapter this proposed coding distinction proved more complex than at first seemed likely. As we shall see this also proved to be the case for the other two lines of evidence.

During the 1950s, the generally accepted view of memory in the US at least was that it involved a single system based on the formation of associations with forgetting resulting from the capacity of associations to interfere with each other. However, in the late 1950s, the standard view of a single unitary memory system was challenged by experimental evidence from both sides of the Atlantic that seemed to suggest a separate short-term memory system based on a memory trace that faded spontaneously over time, rather than being disrupted by interference from other similar material. John Brown in Cambridge, England, presented evidence for the forgetting of verbal material over an interval of a few seconds filled with a purely visual task. At around the same time, Lloyd and Jean Peterson in Indiana developed a new experimental paradigm that proved to be extremely influential over the next few years. This involved presenting a consonant triplet such as *B Q J*, which then had to be recalled after delays ranging from 2 to 18 seconds, filled by backward counting in threes, to prevent people from rehearsing the items during the delay. Since the intervening task involved digits that were quite dissimilar to letters, an interpretation in terms of interference was regarded as implausible. Both Brown and the Petersons interpreted their results in terms of a spontaneously decaying memory trace. This seemed to fit neatly into the previously described information processing model developed by Broadbent in his studies of selective attention. The Peterson task became very popular as an apparently elegant demonstration of the fading over delay of a short-term memory trace. The method was used across a range of materials and modalities with broadly similar results. However, as in the case of the evidence for a separate short-term system based on acoustic versus semantic coding, the situation proved more complex on closer investigation.

As early as 1962, Arthur Melton, a leading figure in the verbal learning tradition, launched a counter-attack on the need for separate memory systems. One of his most powerful arguments came from an ingenious demonstration by himself and Geoffrey Keppel that the rapid forgetting of consonant triplets shown by the Petersons did not apply to the very first triplet presented, which appeared to show no forgetting. Forgetting did, however, build up over the first four or five test items, after which it remained stable. They suggested that forgetting was due to interference from *earlier* items, an established effect in long-term memory known as *proactive interference*.

Further evidence for this view came from studies in which triplets of *words* from specific semantic categories were used, beginning, for example, with animals and then after five trials switching to vegetables, then to birds. Under these conditions, the very first item of each new category showed very little forgetting, with amount of forgetting gradually building up, only to be reversed when the next category was presented. Such a result was entirely consistent with the assumption that interference between successive items comes from the greater *similarity* between items within the same category. This explains why the very first item shows no forgetting over the 18-second delay. However, the fact that longer delays result in more forgetting requires the further assumption that proactive interference *increases* over elapsed time, an existing assumption within interference theory but not one that is particularly well theoretically justified. Interference theory, however, had a further problem. Simply leaving a few seconds between the testing of one item and the presentation of the next memory item greatly reduced forgetting. If, as suggested, proactive interference increases over time, such pauses should impair performance and not improve it. Time to think again.

The Peterson task basically requires the rememberer to recall the *last* item presented from among many other earlier items. But how does he or she decide which was the last? When there are no earlier items, the task is easy. When all the other items are from a different semantic category it also seems easy, suggesting the importance of *discrimination* among potential items at retrieval. The capacity to pick out the wanted item seems likely to depend on three factors: Is it distinctive? How long ago did it happen? How long ago were the nearest competing items? I and others showed that this could be calculated by the ratio between the time of occurrence of the wanted last item and that of the next most recent prior item.

A neat demonstration of this comes from a study in which each of several groups of people was tested repeatedly after the *same* delay, some having repeated delays of two seconds, while others had a repeated five-second delay, while a further group was always tested after 20 seconds. Because the delay was always the same over successive trials, the ratio of delays between the correct item and the item immediately before remained the same. As predicted by the ratio hypothesis, amount of forgetting was the same for all of them. So, was there any evidence of trace decay? With only three-item sequences, performance on the first item tested was around 100%, resulting in what is known as *ceiling effect*. Suppose one item was much easier than another, *abc* versus *zxq*; on Trial 1, this could not be detected because both would be correctly recalled. We decided to use longer sequences for which performance would be less than perfect to see if any forgetting of a single item occurred over time. As each subject could be tested on only one item, we needed lots of volunteers. This we achieved by towing the departments' mobile test caravan into the centre of campus and offering a very small sum to a popular charity for each person tested. We succeeded in meeting our target of several hundred before officialdom demanded that we withdraw from our unauthorised location. After all our efforts we did find forgetting of the first item but very little and only over the first five seconds.

So where does this leave us? Clearly the idea of a memory trace simply fading continuously over 18 seconds will not account for the range of results now available. We need to assume that the rememberer is trying to pick out the most recent item from prior items and that these may well reside in long-term memory. In teaching this material I would usually do a demonstration of the effect of switching semantic categories, and then a week later ask my students if they could recall any of the material used. They usually could, indicating that much of it was indeed in long-term memory. By this point, it was clear that the Peterson task that formed one of the principle challenges to a unitary view of memory could be seen as largely if not entirely based on long-term memory.

The evidence for tasks having both a long- and short-term component was not, however, limited to the Peterson effect. Further evidence for more than one kind of memory came from an experiment using the method known as free recall. This involves presenting a list of items, usually words, then requesting that the participants recall them in any order they wish. In an influential early study, different lengths of list were tested, and all showed the same pattern, with somewhat better recall of the first few words, poorer recall of the intermediate words followed by excellent recall of the last few, the so-called *recency effect*. When recall was delayed by a brief activity such as recalling a telephone number, the recency effect disappeared, while the delay had no effect on earlier words. This pattern of results was consistent with the assumption of two kinds of memory, a short-term recency effect that fades rapidly over a brief delay, coupled with a much more robust long-term component.

I myself set out to collect further evidence for this, but my efforts were overtaken by an influential paper by Murray Glanzer from New York University which made a strong case for the two-component view. I settled for a less ambitious paper emphasising the importance of order of recall suggesting that the act of recalling one item might disrupt the short-term storage of earlier items, stressing the importance of recall strategy in making the most of such brief and fragile memory representations. Studies of recency became very popular, with Glanzer and his group being particularly active. They showed, for example, that any of a wide range of factors known to influence long-term learning would influence the earlier part of the serial position curve but leave recency unaffected. Such factors included length of list, with items in long lists being less likely to be recalled, rate of presentation, with more time leading to better recall, age, with older children performing better than young, and elderly people showing poorer performance, while none of those influenced the most recent items. Drugs such as alcohol and marihuana would typically affect the earlier part of the curve as would a concurrent task, with the heavier load leading to greater impairment while leaving the recency component intact. The recency component was, however, very sensitive to a brief delay, provided it was filled by other activities to prevent rehearsal.

Once again however, the picture became more complex under further investigation. For example, Glanzer's group showed a standard recency effect when people were remembering a list of proverbs such as "Too many cooks spoil the broth", with the last few proverbs being well recalled. How could the many words contained in several proverbs be fitted into a limited capacity short-term system? Michael Watkins and Zehra Peynircioglu showed that people could show up to three simultaneous recency effects across different tasks, provided the three were sufficiently distinctive. For example people could be given three successive lists to remember, one of favourite foods, one of riddles and a third of simple actions to be performed and then required to recall all three. All showed a recency effect. In each of these cases, presenting further examples from within that category whether foods, riddles or actions would disrupt recency. Again, an apparently clear demonstration of separate long- and short-term systems became much less clear on further investigation.

The occurrence of interference effects might at first sight appear to support the classic associationist approach. However, a more plausible alternative was proposed by Nancy Waugh and Donald Norman who developed a new task which involved presenting people with digit sequences of unknown length. The sequence would occasionally stop and a "probe" digit specified. The task was to recall which digit had followed the probe within the sequence. Hence given the sequence 7 9 6 1 8 3 5 and the probe 8, the answer should be 3. By varying the number of items that had followed the memory probe, they showed marked recency. They explained this in terms of a limited capacity memory store that was constantly being fed with new items which then pushed out the old. They presented the digits at two rates, suggesting that if forgetting reflected decay of the memory trace over time, then faster presentation should allow less time for decay leading to better performance. This was not the case, leading them to favour an interpretation of short-term forgetting based on displacement of items from a limited capacity system; once the store was at capacity, each new item would push out the older item. The effect of presentation rate was rather small, with both rates showing marked recency, together with a much lower flat level of performance on earlier items, which they attributed to a long-term component, concluding that both types of memory could occur at the same time.

By this point, it was becoming clear that neither the Peterson task nor the recency effect presented clear evidence for the two-component view of memory, and while interference effects are easily demonstrable, they do not fit readily into a simple associationist theory. However, the strongest evidence for separating long- and short-term memory did not come from the experimental psychology laboratory but from the study of amnesic patients who appeared to have preserved short-term memory together with a grossly impaired capacity to create new long-term memories. The possibility to study such patients arose shortly after I moved to Sussex and is described in the next chapter.

10
Amnesia

There is a long history of attempts to throw light on the mechanisms of normal cognition based on its breakdown in brain-damaged patients. In the 19th century, a number of German neurologists attempted to create models that would explain the deficits shown by their patients, linking behaviour to the neuroanatomy of the brain. This approach had much in common with the information-processing "box and arrow" models that were beginning to influence cognitive psychology in the 1960s, particularly in the UK, where patient-based data relevant to cognitive models were increasingly presented at experimental psychology meetings. Such individual cases can be highly intriguing, as subsequently demonstrated by Oliver Sacks in the various books describing his patients. My own initial view, however, was that they were likely to be too complex to provide useful theoretical guidance. Hence, when asked by Elizabeth Warrington, who I knew from student days at University College, if I would like to work with amnesic patients I replied that it seemed unlikely that they would be obliging enough to have their lesions in theoretically interesting locations and declined. I did, however, agree to go along and demonstrate a technique I had developed that Elizabeth thought might prove theoretically interesting when applied to patients.

I duly travelled up from Brighton to the main UK centre for neurology, the National Hospital in London, and duly tested an elderly lady who was densely amnesic. It was very rapidly clear that she could do my task perfectly well, thus rejecting Elizabeth's tentative hypothesis. So, what should we do next? I asked Elizabeth to tell me about the amnesic syndrome, and she explained that amnesic patients have normal digit spans, indicating preserved short-term memory (STM), but then forget immediately that they are distracted. I suggested that forgetting should not be so immediate, according to current theories, so we decided to test this. We sent our patient to have a cup of tea and proceeded to devise an experiment, cutting up cards to make material for the Peterson task which at this point was regarded as a classic measure of STM. She was briefly shown a hastily prepared card with a consonant triplet such as BZH. She then had to process digits, presented on a succession of further cards, to prevent rehearsal. She did this for varying periods of time before being asked to recall the consonants. Far from forgetting immediately, she showed the normal pattern of gradual forgetting over a 60-second delay, despite being densely amnesic on standard tests of long-term memory. I was impressed and intrigued, and we decided to go ahead and test a group of amnesic patients, not only on this task but also on a range of tasks that had recently been developed as measures of STM.

The National Hospital as its name suggests is the principal centre for neurology in the country, receiving patients whose patterns of symptoms seem puzzling and require further investigation. It was a rather starchy institution, relying on past glories to keep its status high while training rather few young neurologists. The psychology department was under the wing of the consultant in psychiatry and housed in a prefabricated building situated on the roof of an earlier building. I was told that any publications that might result from our joint work should be published solely as coming from the National Hospital, although I was kindly allowed a footnote to explain that I came from the University of Sussex. Elizabeth has spent her whole career there during which her clinical sensitivity coupled with her astuteness in linking theories of cognitive psychology with patient deficits has been enormously productive in discovering new and theoretically revealing groups of patients. I was very fortunate to have the opportunity to work with her and to develop a lifelong involvement with neuropsychology.

Elizabeth had identified a group of six patients who were densely amnesic while being otherwise intellectually unimpaired, a rare group, and ideal for exploring the possible link between amnesia and the theories of memory that were developing in cognitive psychology. At about this time, the dramatic relevance of amnesia to the proposed distinction between long- and short-term memory was becoming apparent. Some years earlier, Oliver Zangwill in England had shown that densely amnesic patients suffering from alcoholic Korsakoff's syndrome had an intact capacity to hear and immediately repeat sentences, suggesting preserved STM. A similar case was made by David Drachman, a US neurologist using a simple technique whereby patients and healthy controls were required to repeat back digit sequences, being given repeated trials on the same sequence until it was correctly recalled. He found that amnesic patients performed normally on short sequences within memory span that could be repeated straight back but became more and more impaired as sequence length increased indicating preserved immediate memory together with greatly impaired learning of longer sequences.

By far the most influential evidence, however, came from a single case, Henry Molaison known by his initials HM. He was studied extensively by Brenda Milner, who, after receiving an undergraduate degree in Cambridge, England, had emigrated to Montreal, where she worked at the world-famous Montreal Neurological Institute. The institute was particularly renowned for the neurosurgical treatment of epilepsy, a highly disabling disease involving seizures that can make normal life intolerable. In some cases seizures can be triggered by scar tissue within the brain, which can be removed surgically, leading to considerable improvement. HM had undergone a somewhat drastic operation by William Beecher Scoville at Hartford Hospital, Connecticut, which involved removal of tissue from both sides of his brain, including much of the hippocampus, a structure forming part of the medial temporal lobe. This reduced HM's seizures but left him desperately amnesic. He lost his capacity to retain ongoing events and rapidly forgot any experiences that occurred after his operation in 1953. He could not tell you what day of the week it was or who the current US President was and would fail to recognise in the afternoon the psychologist who had tested him all morning. He showed normal immediate memory on tasks such as digit span but performed extremely badly on standard tests of long-term memory such as remembering a brief story or recalling a list of words.

On moving into a new house, he could never remember where anything was kept. He could read the same magazine repeatedly without noticing. This lack of memory made it difficult for him to follow plays or sports on television, and he did not retain even dramatic current news items such as the Watergate scandal. However, he remembered much of what he had learned before his operation. He knew his parents and relatives; retained historical facts learned at school; and preserved language and daily habits, such as brushing his teeth. HM was also able to acquire new skills, for example learning to trace a star shape that he could only see via a mirror or learning to keep a stylus in contact with a moving target. His case generated enormous interest internationally and continued to do so until his recent death, recorded in obituaries worldwide as possibly the scientifically most influential patient ever.

HM's misfortune led to two very important conclusions, one anatomical and the other psychological. The first concerns the longstanding question of how memory is registered in the brain. Earlier research by Karl Lashley on rats had consistently failed to find "the engram", the physical structure within the brain where memories were stored. This he interpreted in terms of two "principles": one was entitled *mass action*, the proposal that the brain operated as a whole rather than as a cluster of separate modules. The second principle was that of *equipotentiality*, which proposed that all parts of the brain had a similar function, with the result that performance impairment was a simple result of the amount of brain tissue removed. This clearly did not apply to HM since many patients had lost more brain tissue as a result of accidents or surgery without being nearly as amnesic. Furthermore, HM's case demonstrated very clearly that the hippocampus plays a crucial role in memory, a finding of importance both scientifically and practically to neurosurgeons. At a psychological level, HM's preserved STM, as reflected in his normal digit span, provided very clear evidence for the separation of STM from his dramatically impaired long-term memory.

While Brenda Milner's work was strongly linked to neurosurgery and to identifying the function of specific anatomical areas, Elizabeth's was more closely linked to the developing field of cognitive neuropsychology and at an applied level to the diagnosis of the wide range of cases that were referred to the National Hospital. One of the cases of "pure" amnesia within Elizabeth's group had, like HM, undergone surgery to relieve intractable epilepsy, leading to a dense amnesia, while four of the other cases suffered from alcoholic Korsakoff syndrome, a disease that can result from drinking too much and eating too little. This, in turn, leads to a deficit in vitamin A (thiamine) and to the destruction of brain tissue. Damage is particularly likely to occur in the hippocampus and the related mammillary bodies, both of which play an important role in long-term memory. It is typically the case, however, that other areas of the brain will also be affected by this syndrome, leading to much more general cognitive problems. Very occasionally however, patients have problems that are entirely limited to memory as in the cases that Elizabeth had identified.

We chose to investigate the performance of our patients on a range of tasks that had recently become relevant to the proposed distinction between long- and short-term memory systems. One was the Peterson task; a second was the minimal paired-associate learning task mentioned earlier, in which three pairs of words are presented, and one pair is then tested before moving to another set of pairs. We also looked at free recall for 10 unrelated words with recall tested immediately or after a brief filled delay to eliminate the recency effect. We went on to study the Hebb effect. This is a variant on digit span discovered by Hebb which involves presenting sequences of digits slightly beyond span. Most sequences are random, but unbeknown to the rememberer, the same sequence crops up repeatedly but always after new interpolated random sequences. This typically leads to gradual improvement on the repeated sequence, regardless of whether or not the rememberer notices the repetition. It therefore demonstrates that even digit span, the classic STM task, has a long-term component that builds up over trials. We were interested in whether amnesic patients would show this classic long-term learning effect and used sequences of eight digits with the sequence presented second always repeated on alternative trials up to Trial 24. Finally, all patients were extensively tested on standardised tests of long-term memory and on digit span. We compared the performance of our patients on these tasks with that of a group suffering from peripheral nerve injuries but with normal memory.

Most of our results were in line with our predictions based on the assumption of separate systems. All patients showed good digit span, and Peterson performance, even at the longest 60-second delay. They also showed normal performance on minimal paired-associate learning. As expected, the patients were substantially poorer overall than a group of control patients with peripheral lesions on overall free recall performance but had intact recency, as predicted by the two-component theory. We were surprised, however, to find that our patients showed a normal Hebb effect, indicating gradual build-up of long-term memory over trials. Hence, although our results were broadly in line with the assumption of separate long- and short-term memory systems, some puzzles remained. Why was the Hebb effect preserved, and why was Peterson performance normal even after a filled delay that was clearly sufficient to remove the recency effect in free recall?

I was by this time convinced of the theoretical value of studying neuropsychological patients, and intrigued by the consistency of our results across patients but felt challenged, by the points at which our results did *not* fit expectations. I also found patients themselves fascinating; some were all too aware of their problems, while one lady, whenever she failed to remember something, exclaimed, "How strange, I pride myself on my memory!" forgetting that she had already said this several times in the last few minutes. For the most part our patients were very willing to be tested although it was explained that our study was part of the process of trying to understand their problem, and was not a form of treatment.

We published our results in a mainstream experimental journal, where it had reasonable impact, given its topicality, although the more traditional verbal learning community tended to argue that brain-damaged patients were atypical and hence irrelevant to the development of theory. Meanwhile, a similar line of research was being pursued by colleagues in Boston focussing on veterans with Korsakoff syndrome, and producing rather different results. Our counterparts were Nelson Butters, a neuropsychologist at the Boston Vetarans Hospital, and Laird Cermak, who, like me, was a cognitive psychologist. Their patients performed rather badly on the Peterson task and failed to show release from PI, even with a semantic category switch, from animals to flowers, for example; based on this, they interpreted the amnesic deficit in terms of a failure to encode semantically.

While such a result would fit my own theoretical position at the time very neatly, it was not characteristic of our own patients who seemed to have no difficulty in encoding semantically. This was brought out very clearly in a further series of experiments in which we showed that our patients were able to take advantage of semantic coding when recalling lists comprising sets of four words selected from each of several semantic categories such as four animals, four flowers and four colours. They showed the standard enhancement from semantic categorisation when compared to recall of uncategorised lists. Unlike the control group however, they were unable to take advantage of a third condition that used an imagery mnemonic whereby patients and controls were asked to visualise a series of simple scenes. Each scene involved a cluster of four critical words, for example "The *Irishman* gave a *penny* to the *monkey* playing a *violin*", where the underlined words were to be recalled. Our patients were thus clearly able to take advantage of semantic categorisation but gained nothing from the visual imagery condition, despite reporting that they were quite able to form the image and having demonstrated normal short-term visuospatial memory in another study. We concluded that they were able to encode semantically and take advantage of pre-existing associations but could not store newly formed links between words.

In attempting to explain our Peterson results, our Boston colleagues published a sequence of papers raising a series of methodological objections to the way in which we had carried out our Peterson task. None of the objections seemed plausible to me at least, and by that time I had in any case abandoned the idea that the Peterson task offered a simple measure of STM, while Elizabeth suggested that the Boston patients had other more subtle deficits that were responsible for their poor performance. Eventually, she was proved correct when Laird Cermak published a paper showing preserved Peterson performance in a patient suffering from encephalitis, a brain infection that left him with a dense amnesia but otherwise intellectually unimpaired. It proved to be the case that the Boston Korsakoff patients were in fact suffering from additional frontal lobe damage that impaired their performance on the Peterson task and reduced their capacity to use semantic cues to enhance memory performance. The silver lining for the Boston group was that they could then use the Peterson task as a sensitive measure of the subtle associated deficits when assessing patients.

So it appeared to be the case that our demonstration of good Peterson performance in our amnesic patients was not due to poor experimental design, nor was amnesia generally explicable in terms of failure to encode semantically, but we were still left with the problem of why Peterson test performance at our longest delay, 60 seconds, was preserved and well above chance, and what could explain the clear evidence of long-term learning on the Hebb repeated digit sequence task. These were, however, not the only evidence that amnesic patients were capable of some types of long-term learning. HM had been shown by Susan Corkin at MIT to demonstrate normal learning of a motor skill, while Elizabeth and Lawrence Weiskrantz had carried out a number of studies demonstrating that her patient group had preserved long-term memory for both verbal and visual learning under certain critical conditions.

A typical such study might involve presenting the patients and matched controls with a sequence of words: for example *STAMP* and *GREEN*. As expected, when later asked to recognise the words they had just seen amongst a mix of old and new items, the patients did very badly. However, when given a word fragment such as *ST_ _ _* or *GR_ _ _* and invited to guess, they responded with the words that had been presented, while having no memory of having recently seen them. Similarly, if shown a series of line drawings of objects followed by an incomplete drawing and asked to guess the item on the basis of the fragments, they again performed as well as controls in "guessing" the previously seen objects. So, despite extremely dense amnesia, patients showed preserved Hebb learning, normal Peterson performance, together with preserved visual and verbal fragment completion on material that they could not recognise and, in HM's case, preserved skill acquisition.

How could all this evidence of preserved learning be tied together? Once again the initial distinction between preserved short-term and impaired long-term memory was proving more complex than it first seemed, although in this case, the complexity came from the long-term component, not from the short-term. Even this, however, was open to a possible objection. Could it be that the short-term tasks were simply easier and hence more resistant to brain damage? Fortunately a response to this objection was at hand through a study carried out by Elizabeth and Tim Shallice on another patient KF.

KF was a young man who had suffered damage to an area around the junction between the temporal and parietal lobes of his left hemisphere. His general intellect and long-term memory were well preserved, but his digit span was reduced from the normal six or seven digits to one or two. On free recall, his performance on early items was normal but he showed little evidence of recency. KF therefore shows exactly the opposite pattern to our amnesic patients, a distinction that is readily explained by the assumption of separate long- and short-term memory systems but not by the suggestion that short-term tasks are easier.

By this time the study of STM had become extremely popular with many new methods developed, often linked to attempts to present theoretical accounts in terms of mathematical models. The most influential of these was developed by Richard Atkinson and Richard Shiffrin and is shown in Figure 10.1. The model assumes that information comes in from the environment through the first of three separate stages, each involving memory storage. The first of these comprises a range of

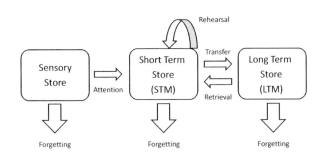

The multi-store model of memory
(Atkinson & Shiffrin, 1968)

FIGURE 10.1 The multi-store model of memory (Atkinson & Shiffrin, 1968).

temporary sensory storage systems that could best be regarded as part of the process of perception rather than memory. The most extensively investigated of these were the temporary visual system sometimes known as *iconic memory* and its auditory equivalent, *echoic memory*. These operate in parallel, passing information on to the second system, the *short-term store*. This is assumed to hold information and to process it, selecting and using strategies to optimise later recall, a role that had been described by Miller, Galanter and Pribram in 1960 as *working memory*. Information can be actively maintained in the short-term store but may be displaced by later information. While it is being maintained, the information is assumed to be gradually transferred to the more permanent long-term store.

A mathematical model of this process was proposed and illustrated using standard verbal learning material. As Atkinson and Shiffrin acknowledged, the model has much in common with Broadbent's original but was much further developed in the light of extensive subsequent research, and was accompanied by a more detailed mathematical specification. It captured the essence of a range of models created at the time and was hence dubbed the "modal model" and was to dominate the field for several years to come. Its authors did not, however, develop it further; Richard Atkinson moved into academic administration and Richard Shiffrin to the mathematical modelling of long-term memory.

Meanwhile, as already noted, the apparently simple question of how many kinds of memory to assume was proving to be rather more complicated. Although the modal model was widely accepted and featured prominently in text books for a number of years, it was encountering problems of which two were acute. The assumption that simply holding information in the short-term store would guarantee long-term learning proved mistaken as simple time held in the short-term store was a poor predictor of later long-term recall. A second problem came from patients such as KF. Despite their grossly impaired STM capacity, their long-term memory was good, quite inconsistent with the assumption that long-term learning depended on short-term storage. Furthermore, the assumption that the short-term store acted as a working memory, essential for many cognitive functions, would predict major cognitive problems for such patients. They were, however, typically remarkably unaffected in their everyday life; one such patient worked as a secretary, another worked as a taxi driver, while a third ran a shop and looked after her family.

At this point, a number of years had passed and my collaboration with Elizabeth had ended with my appointment to a professorship at the new University of Stirling in Scotland. I was anxious to continue working with patients and Elizabeth suggested that I contact Neil Brooks who ran a neuropsychology course at the Southern General Hospital in Glasgow a few miles from Stirling. I knew that it was unlikely that we would have access to a group of pure amnesic patients who combined a dense amnesia with otherwise preserved intellectual capacity as such patients are rare. Bearing in mind the lesson of the Boston Korsakoffs, this created problems for any attempt to identify any specific deficits that might explain the source of their amnesia, as any deficit we found could potentially be the result of their additional cognitive impairments. This is a common problem in drawing theoretical conclusions from patients with more than one deficit. I argued, however, that if we were to study what was *preserved* in amnesia, then the impact of any further deficits could be discounted, given that the preserved learning capacity existed *despite* other potential problems. And so, Neil Brooks and I asked what *can* amnesia patients learn?

Glasgow is not renowned for its sobriety, and I assumed that there would be plenty of Korsakoff cases. I was wrong, possibly because of the tendency to drink beer, which, I was told by a nutritionist colleague, could be "hopping with vitamins", although this is not always the case (a prominent US brand springs to mind). In line with this hypothesis was the fact that most of our London Korsakoff patients were spirit drinkers somewhat atypical given the greater expense of spirits; the nearest we came to a classic Korsakoff was a charming shepherd from the Highlands who used whisky to while away the cold winter evenings. With some support from colleagues in Edinburgh, we managed to assemble a group of five amnesic patients, all of whom had a degree of more general cognitive impairment, three with alcoholic Korsakoff syndrome and two teenage boys, both of whom had suffered from encephalitis resulting in both amnesia and more extensive executive problems reflecting frontal lobe damage. We chose to study the acquisition of a motor skill, keeping a stylus in contact with a moving spot of light which on the basis of earlier work with HM we expected might be preserved, together with two further tasks. One of these, the Porteus maze task was originally devised as a measure of nonverbal intelligence, in which the maze was always visible, and the same maze was presented repeatedly, with learning shown by an increase in speed over successive trials. A third task involved assembling a child's jigsaw puzzle, which again gets faster with practice. We also included two standard verbal learning tasks, free recall and paired-associate learning. As expected both of these showed a clear deficit though with preserved recency in free recall as found in our earlier study.

Our main focus, however, was on the three tasks involving long-term learning. Here, we replicated the preserved learning of a motor skill, shown by HM with good acquisition of the pursuit tracking task. Speed of performing the visual maze also increased as did performance on the jigsaw puzzle test. Our results were shortly followed by a growing number of reports from different groups reporting an increasing range of tasks for which performance improved at a normal rate in densely amnesic patients. Putting together these results with our earlier findings from the Peterson task, the Hebb repeated digits procedure and the evidence of preserved verbal and visual learning demonstrated by Warrington and Weizcrantz indicated that the amnesic syndrome left a wide range of types of learning unimpaired.

The Warrington and Weiskrantz priming effects, where prior experience of the stimulus enhanced subsequent "guessing" responses, were widely replicated. Normal learning rates were also found in more complex skills such as reading mirror-reversed script. Serial reaction time studies in which subjects responded as rapidly as possible to lights by pressing associated keys showed that amnesic patients were able to take advantage of bias, responding increasingly quickly to lights that occurred more frequently, even though, unlike most people, they were not consciously aware of the bias. Classical eye blink conditioning also proved to be preserved when a tone is followed by a puff of air to the eye, people rapidly learn to blink in anticipation following the tone. This also occurs in densely amnesic patients who are nevertheless unable to recall the event or explain the repeatedly experienced function of the air nozzle. Patients also showed a normal capacity to modify their aesthetic judgements as a result of experience. Patients and controls were required to judge the pleasantness of unfamiliar Korean melodies. With repeated hearing of the melodies, both groups showed a similar gradual increase in reported pleasantness, although amnesic patients denied having ever encountered such melodies before.

This range of evidence was subsequently followed by extensive further support from studies on normal participants, leading to a distinction being made between *explicit memory*, in which the rememberer can consciously retrieve the information, and *implicit memory*, where learning is demonstrated by a change in performance rather than the ability to consciously remember the prior experience. Meanwhile, as will be discussed later, the distinction between implicit and explicit memory was becoming a major topic beyond the neuropsychology community. However, much of this development was still to come. Furthermore, while some theorists regarded the neuropsychological studies as providing convincing evidence for separate long- and short-term memory stores, others remained un-convinced even of the relevance of data based on individual patients for theories of normal memory. Such patients are rare, and few investigators have access to them; consequently most of the research in the area used data from healthy young subjects as will be described in the next chapter.

SAN DIEGO 1970–71

11

California and New Directions in Memory Research

The work on code design stemming from my PhD project led to an increasing involvement with the largely US-based verbal learning community. It was traditionally rather conservative, focussing on the detailed analysis of a limited number of experimental paradigms and their interpretation in strict stimulus-response terms. By the 1960s however, it began to attract a growing number of investigators who were influenced both by earlier ideas from Gestalt psychology and by later developments from an information-processing viewpoint. Although I could not afford the considerable expense at the time of travelling to North America, I was part of the extended group who exchanged publications and ideas and who eventually decided to set up a journal entitled *The Journal of Verbal Learning and Verbal Behavior*, which I found a more congenial outlet for publishing than the rather more staid *Journal of Experimental Psychology*. The Unit had a stream of visitors from North America, many of them with interests in memory, so I felt very much a part of an international group in an exciting area.

I was therefore delighted to be invited to spend a year in the US by George Mandler, who was playing an important part in moving the field forward from its conservative roots. George had recently become the first head of the department of psychology in the recently founded University of California San Diego (UCSD). The University of California had a range of nine campuses of excellent quality, with the most established being Berkeley just outside San Francisco and UCSD being among the most recent. George was able to attract a stellar group of founding professors and to set up within the department the Center for Human Information Processing (CHIP). On accepting my new post in Sussex, it was agreed that I should take up this sabbatical offer in due course, and I chose to do so for the 1970–71 academic year. We were helped to arrange housing near the UCSD campus, an arrangement involving one house before and one after Christmas, only then to discover that the appointment in fact started in the summer, not in September as I had assumed. This involved more house hunting, greatly helped by my hosts. As was the case from my Princeton year, I wrote regular letters back to my widowed mother during our year in California and my memories of this important time in my life have been refreshed by rereading them.

By this time my wife Hilary and I had three sons, Roland the eldest was aged 5, Gavin 3 and Bart almost 2. I still have vivid memories of our flight out, which for all of us was a novel experience. We obtained a very inexpensive flight with Caledonian Airways, a Scottish company whose air hostesses wore natty tartan uniforms. It was pouring with rain when we left home (according to our neighbours leaving the front door of our house wide open!). The plane seemed rather ancient and I noticed before take-off that water was dripping onto my head, apparently from the downpour. Was a leaky plane safe to fly across the Atlantic I wondered, but one of the stewardesses assured me that it would stop once we were pressurised, which made sense but was still not very reassuring. I now realise that it was simply condensation, not a leaky plane!

Hilary had prepared for the long journey by making a series of packages that each child should open, one every hour, and this worked remarkably well in keeping the kids happy. We duly arrived in New York and had time for a brief sightseeing walk, marvelling at the skyscrapers before starting the next leg to Los Angeles. George Mandler kindly met us on arrival and took us to our house in a very modern development north of the campus in Del Mar, at that time a relaxed horse racing and beach town, though now I believe a suburb of San Diego.

Our house felt really luxurious, and our next-door neighbour proved very hospitable, welcoming us with tumblers full of bourbon whisky; Hilary later confessed that feeling it might be uncivil to refuse, she coped by pouring most of hers into a convenient plant pot when no one was looking. Despite his amiability, meeting our neighbour was something of a culture shock. He had recently retired from the US Air Force, where his job had been to root out homosexuals, presumably as potential blackmail risks, given that homosexuality at the time was illegal in the US, as it was in Britain. He also expressed extreme disgust and contempt for "draft dodgers", young men who refused to lay down their life in Vietnam on Uncle Sam's behalf! I had many American friends, but this was a new type of American; no doubt his equivalent existed in Britain, but I had just not had them as neighbours. He also explained the mysterious instruction in our new home that was to "remember to water the ice plants". Were "ice plants" gadgets for turning water into ice cubes? No. The houses were built on a slope and as he explained, the ice plants were indeed plants; they provided ground cover on the steep parts of the garden, and their roots bound the soil and prevented us from slipping down onto the house below but only if they were regularly watered. This we did, and happily our house did not slide away.

My very generous invitation came jointly from George Mandler and Donald Norman whose research on short-term memory I knew very well. Don invited the family to a departmental beach party on our first weekend, telling us not to worry about bringing food and drink. We duly turned up, very pallid among the sun tanned throng and in due course watched people unloading food and drinking wine. We explained to the children that it was rude to go and take someone else's food. Happily someone noticed and pointed out the Californian custom of everyone helping themselves. At the time in Britain wine was expensive and it would be seen as very impolite to simply help yourself uninvited to someone else's wine. With increasing prosperity we have now all become more Californian!

We settled in, with Roland going to a primary school, Gavin to a Montessori preschool and Bart staying home with Hilary. At that time it was normal for wives to give up work when children arrived, sometimes permanently, as in the case of both Hilary's mother and my own. By this time however, it was increasingly common in the UK for married women to return to work, though typically only when the children were all of school age, a convenient arrangement for husbands, though creating major career development problems for wives. Meanwhile I had an office in the new building that housed CHIP and began work. I had set myself three targets. The first was to write up the substantial backlog of papers that had accumulated, the second was to take the opportunity of meeting as many of my North American colleagues as possible and the third was to write a book. A couple of years before I had signed a contract with Oxford University Press for a book on short-term memory. Unfortunately however, they refused to provide an advance. Consequently when approached by Sam Glucksberg, one of the APU sabbatical visitors, in a pub appropriately called *The Friend at Hand* to ask if I was interested in writing a memory text, I readily agreed, provided the advance was sufficient to buy a second hand car in California. It was, and I duly accepted, expecting that turning my memory lecture notes into a book would be quick and easy. Little did I know…

Around September, we moved to the house in La Jolla that we were due to occupy until Christmas. La Jolla, as its Spanish name "The Jewel" suggests, is a beautiful coastal town built around an idyllic cove. It had expanded considerably from its original Spanish-style centre, and we had a comfortable ranch-style house in the suburbs. It was about 20 years old and some of the domestic appliances were becoming a little unreliable, hence the instruction from our landlord, a theoretical physicist away on sabbatical, that should any of it break down, we were to ring the professor of Experimental Physics, who would come and fix it. He did a very good job on the cooker, and if you ever have problems with your kitchen appliances, I can recommend contracting your local physics department. His remit did not, however, extend to drains, where we discovered another quirk of the Southern California climate. Because of lack of rain, tree roots seek out any sort of moisture eagerly seizing on any leaks from drains, then following the leak to its source and eventually causing a blockage. We were advised to call up a firm called Speedy Rooter. Hilary mentioned this to her French friend Monique who exclaimed in horror "Non; not Speedy Rooter, every metre a dollar!" They did the trick and we had no further drainage problems, but we did have one more Californian incident. While I was at the university, one of children playing on the patio came in and told my wife that "there's a snake out there!" Hilary looked out, and there on the patio was a rattlesnake; shutting the children in, she went next door to seek help. They sent a 10-year-old child around with a big stick. He nonchalantly dealt with the unfortunate beast, and by the time I returned home, all that was left was a snake-shaped stain on the patio.

It is of course almost impossible to live in Southern California without a car. I myself am not an enthusiastic driver, and regard cars as simply a relatively convenient way of getting around provided there is not too much traffic. So whenever I need to buy a car I talk to friendly enthusiasts who I find are usually happy to help with suggestions. I was told that I should aim to get a Dodge Dart, a car that we were assured was small (by Californian standards), economical and reliable. I also took advice on car dealers, then explaining to the dealer my source of advice, hoping he would feel some interest in maintaining this good reputation. He did indeed have a Dodge Dart in a vivid turquoise colour that at least had the advantage of making it easy to locate it in a crowded supermarket car park. It had, he claimed, been owned by a little old lady; if so, she seemed to have been a very heavy smoker from the smell, and also a member of the armed forces if the documents left inside had anything to go by. But it served us extremely well, and remarkably, at the end of the year we sold it for virtually the price for which we bought it. I can certainly recommend Dodge Darts from the 1960s.

And so, we settled in with the children at school and endless sunny days to spend on the beach or making the most of our chance to see as much as possible of Southern California with its wonderfully varied landscape of beaches, forests, mountains and deserts. Meanwhile I took full advantage of the year free of any duties other than the enjoyable ones of writing and sitting in on George and Don's lab discussion groups.

My year at UCSD came at a crucial juncture in the development of the field of memory, a time when the old associationist approach to verbal learning was apparently on its last legs, while at the same time a new form of associationism was being created under the influence of artificial intelligence, with George Mandler and Don Norman both playing importance roles, and UCSD providing ideal place to observe the change.

Throughout my career I have watched the demise of two major theoretical traditions. To the outsider at least, one of these was rather sudden in the disappearance of Clark Hull's attempt to create a grand overarching theory of learning based on his studies of maze learning in the white rat. The other was the verbal learning tradition, where the decline was a much more gradual process. Indeed, judging by some of the comments on my papers from journal referees over the years, I would suggest that the parsimonious spirit of traditional verbal learning lives on. George Mandler played an active part in the evolution of the verbal learning field and summarises it in his recent *History of Experimental Psychology*. Here, he traces the transformation of the study of memory from the traditional stimulus–response Ebbinghaus tradition through to the broad cognitive approach that characterises the field today. He describes a series of meetings, all in the US with most resulting in published proceedings that reflect this transformation. I myself read the various proceedings with great interest, although coming from a blend of the Bartlett and the information-processing traditions, and not being a participant, was unaware of the intensity of the theoretical battles within the US group.

Much of the early discussion focussed on the question of serial order; how can we maintain, reproduce and control sequential behaviour, with the most obvious and dramatic example of this capacity presented by the use of language. The classic stimulus–response associationist view envisages sequential behaviour as based on a chain of stimuli, each one followed by a response, which, in turn, serves as the stimulus for the next item in the chain. This view was strongly rejected in a now much-quoted paper by Carl Lashley at the Hixon Symposium, a meeting involving major figures in psychology, neurophysiology and computer science that was held in Pasadena, California, in 1948. There were no traditional associationists present, and the issue of the contrast between the conclusions drawn and the standard verbal learning approach went largely unremarked until the 1960s, when Lashley's paper finally began to be quoted; it has since that time become highly influential.

Verbal learning had long continued to be a very constrained and inward-looking field, making it difficult to publish results that were at all controversial. A good example is the case of the observation made by Weston Bousfield in 1953 that when a scrambled list of words drawn from different semantic categories was recalled, the words emerged in semantically related clusters, even though the categories were separated at presentation, suggesting the possibility of some form of active organisation by the rememberer. Such active organisation was seen as inconsistent with associationist theory and although regarded later as an important paper, it was at that time, only publishable in a low status journal.

Under the influence of the growing cognitive revolution described earlier, things began to change. In the area of memory, this was reflected in a symposium in Minnesota held in 1955 that mixed people interested in memory with others concerned with language. It generated enough lively discussion to persuade the US Office of Naval Research (ONR) to fund what proved to be a series of further symposia. The ONR has a remit that extends well beyond naval matters, and over the years has funded a great deal of innovative basic research. In 1959, they funded an important meeting in upper New York State involving 19 presenters who were a mix of those favouring the traditional associationist verbal learning approach including Arthur Melton described by Mandler as the "eminence grise" of the field and other hard line verbal learners, together with what Mandler describes as "the young Turks", James Deese, James Jenkins who you may recall had previously proposed an expectancy theory of vigilance and Mandler himself, all of whom were intent on opening up the field to outside influences. Finally, there was also a sprinkling of people principally interested in language at both syntactic and semantic levels. Among the topics discussed in the memory field was free recall where a list of items is read and must be recalled in any order, a method that did not fit neatly into stimulus–response theorising since it appeared to involve responses without stimuli, and which, as Weston Bousfield had shown, leads to semantic clustering at recall. This and other data pointed to the *active* role of the learner in *constructing* memory representations based on *meaning*, concepts that were much closer to Bartlett and to Gestalt theory than to orthodox stimulus–response psychology.

Enough heat and light was generated to justify a further meeting in 1961 with a wider range of participants and topics, often accompanied by theorisation that paid no attention to the classic associationist views. Topics included an analysis of recognition, a discussion of the acquisition of syntax and a paper by Peterson on immediate memory, which you may recall was seminal in stimulating further controversy on the need to separate long- and short-term memory. A particularly striking departure was the presentation by George Miller of what was perhaps the first computational model of learning, *EPAM* (Elementary Perceiver and Memorizer), a model that had been built and applied to data by Edward Feigenbaum and Herbert Simon in 1959. The editors of the resulting proceedings summarised the meeting as a conflict between the traditional stimulus–response associationist presenters who were looking for problems that their theory could address versus a range of other approaches choosing to approach a range of new problems, regardless of their relevance for current associationist theory.

One final symposium attempted to put the Humpty Dumpty of associationist theory together again by attempting to integrate a range of work within a broad stimulus–response framework. It was too late, with the editors concluding with the question "Is anybody really willing to assume that the general laws of habits, as developed in simple behavior in lower animals apply to verbal behavior in man?" (Dixon & Horton, 1968, p. 110).[1] The answer is that some participants still were stubbornly objecting to the new ideas, which they claimed were based on "improper methods", interpreted with "mentalist overtones" (Staats, 1968). However by this time, the concept of language as a simple chain of verbal associations had been abandoned by most theorists following Chomsky's publication of his classical book *Syntactic Structures* in 1957 and his devastating 1959 review of Skinner's attempt to explain language in his book *Verbal Behavior.*

However, the traditional verbal learners could reasonably argue that their aim was not to generate a theory of language but rather to explain the basic laws of association that underpin human *learning* rather than language. Given that Chomsky claimed that the capacity for syntax is genetically based, it could be argued that it was unrelated to the issues addressed within the verbal learning tradition, and although the controversies surrounding language had some influence, the meetings just described were mainly concerned with explaining human learning and memory. The conflict here was less confrontational than in linguistics, with Mandler's young Turks coming from within the verbal learning community but arguing for the acceptance of new ideas rather than proposing the overthrow of the traditional approach.

Mandler himself, for example, was clearly influenced by Gestalt psychology and stressed the active role of the rememberer in organising the material to be subsequently recalled. This position had been strongly argued in a book published in 1940 by George Katona, a refugee from Nazi persecution, whose work was largely ignored in the neo-behaviourist climate, leading him to quit the memory field. Like Katona, Mandler stressed the importance of active organisation in memory. In one experiment he presented subjects with a pile of cards with each card containing a different word. One group was told to look through the cards and to memorise the words; a second group was told to sort the cards into semantically based categories, with no instruction to remember. A third group sorted and was also told to remember, while a fourth group simply sorted words into neat columns, regardless of meaning. Although they had no expectation of subsequent test, the semantic sorting group remembered just as much as those given memory instructions and did considerably better than the group who simply sorted the words into neat piles. This and other studies demonstrated that active organisation leads to good memory regardless of intention to learn.

The role of organisation in memory was a major research theme over the 1960s and 1970s. Gordon Bower at Stanford University, for example, demonstrated the powerful effect on subsequent recall of organising words such as the names of metals into a hierarchical structure, and went on to show that many of the traditional memory improvement techniques, long ignored by the verbal learning tradition, could be explained in terms of organisation. A good example is provided by the use of visual imagery by Roman orators to remember their speeches. This would involve memorising a complex building and identifying a fixed sequence of locations in the building. A visual image would then be created for each point to be made and then linked to the appropriate location, for example a sword representing a military campaign in the first location, a sheaf of corn representing the need for a food supply for the campaign in the second and so forth tying the succession of themes within the speech to the pre-learned sequence of features within the building. In medieval times churches often acted as structures for mnemonics, while modern improve-your-memory courses tend to be more prosaic, suggesting using locations in your own home, for example, to remember a shopping list. As the last example suggests, what was once known as the art of memory lost its importance with the development of widespread literacy.

The question of why basing the method on visual imagery was so effective, however, remained an intriguing question that was explored by Alan Paivio, a Canadian of Finnish extraction whose muscular physique as a bodybuilder had earlier earned him a Mr Canada title. He apparently was, however, advised by his PhD supervisor, Donald Hebb, that it might prove difficult to sustain a joint career in bodybuilding and verbal learning. Paivio chose verbal learning! He demonstrated very clearly that the ease of learning words could be predicted by asking people how readily each word could lead to a visual image; words like *rabbit* and *table* can easily be visualised in contrast to abstract words such as hope and *justice,* and are much easier to remember when presented in word lists. Despite a strong hint of the "mentalist overtones" denounced by traditionalists, Paivio managed to publish extensively in journals that were wedded to the neo-behaviourist verbal learning approach. He avoided the stigma of "mentalism" by pointing out that he was simply predicting one kind of observable behaviour, that of remembering from another, making verbal judgement responses, and that he made no claims about the nature of the processes underlying such verbal judgements. In order to explain his results he developed a dual coding hypothesis, arguing that imageable words had both verbal and visual associations, whereas abstract words were limited to the verbal, an interpretation that was sufficiently close to a traditional approach to allow him to escape censure.

Mandler, Bower and Paivio all demonstrated ways in which organisation was crucial for learning, but why should that be? An answer was provided by Endel Tulving, like Mandler, a post-war immigrant, in Tulving's case from Estonia. Like Mandler, he was at the time part of the very powerful and innovative group of memory researchers at the University of Toronto. Tulving also advocated the importance of organisation in learning, showing that if people are given a list of perhaps 24 randomly selected words to remember in any order, with the same words being presented over several successive trials, then the words recalled will gradually form clusters or chunks, with the same words recalled together even though presentation order was changed each time the list was presented. Furthermore, as learning proceeded, such clusters became gradually larger, supporting the view that active organisation plays a crucial role in learning. This emphasis on organisation based on meaning was broadly consistent with my own stress on the role of semantic coding in long-term memory.

By this point, the importance of organisation in memory had been firmly established. But why is organisation so helpful? The answer came through the concept of *retrieval*, the process whereby the information in memory is accessed and reproduced. While the importance of retrieval may now seem obvious, this was not the case at that time; I was part of a PhD thesis committee while at UCSD, that of Karalyn Patterson who was supervised by George Mandler. The concept of retrieval was central to her dissertation, but we had some difficulty convincing an eminent neurobiologist on the committee that consolidating a memory trace was not the end of the story and that forgetting may reflect the failure to *access* a memory that has been encoded and consolidated, not necessarily the loss of the memory trace. A simple illustration of this point comes from the observation that recognition typically leads to higher scores than recall. In one study, Mandler presented a list of list of 100 words five times finding an average successful recall score of 38 words. A second group was tested by recognition of the 100 old words mixed with a 100 new words. They recognised 96 of the 100 words, with just seven new words falsely recognised. This means that many of the words that had failed to be recalled were in fact *known* as indicated by recognition; they were potentially *available* but could not be *accessed* at the appropriate time.

Further evidence for the importance of retrieval was provided by a number of elegant experiments carried out by Tulving during the 1960s. One source of evidence came from simply observing *which* words were recalled on successive trials in a multi-trial free recall learning study such as that used to demonstrate clustering. Tulving noted that although the overall number of words recalled gradually increased, some words recalled on Trial 1 would not be recalled on Trial 2 but might reappear on Trial 3 or 4, suggesting that they had been learnt but were not consistently accessible. In another free recall learning study, Tulving repeatedly presented a list of words in one condition, while in a second condition he followed the initial learning trial with three successive retrieval trials. Performance from the two groups was equivalent, suggesting that the act of retrieval was just as effective as an additional learning trial, a result that emphasises the importance of practicing retrieval.

In recent years, the importance of testing knowledge has become a major issue in education, with demonstrations across a range of educational topics, that the act of retrieving material by testing students may often be a better way of learning than repeating learning trials. Further evidence for the importance of retrieval comes from the tip-of-the-tongue effect whereby you are sure you know a word, often a name, but cannot produce it although quite often you have some idea how many syllables it contains and perhaps of the initial letter. Given a range of possible answers you are immediately sure which is the correct one; it had been stored, and you knew that you knew it, but you could not retrieve it at the time.

Tulving went on to develop a theory of retrieval which he termed the *encoding specificity hypothesis*. He suggests that when we learn something we encode a range of cues comprising features of the item and its context, and that retrieval occurs when one or more of these contextual cues is presented and evokes the original memory. The more retrieval cues present, the higher the probability of recall. Tulving carried out a range of experiments to explore this hypothesis. In one study, people were presented with lists of words coming from a number of different semantic categories, for example animals, birds, furniture, flowers, metals and clothing. At recall, half the people were cued by being given the category names, and half were not. Providing the category names greatly enhanced recall. When in due course, the uncued group was provided with the category names, they then recalled substantially more words. The category names acted as retrieval cues, providing the semantic context that allowed retrieval of learned but previously inaccessible words. Tulving's emphasis on the importance of context in memory retrieval is of course directly applicable to the previously described experiment on divers where recall was better when it occurred in the same context, what was learnt underwater was best recalled underwater.

By this stage, the defenders of the old verbal learning faith were faced with the problem of whether to adapt or retire from the field. The two most influential figures in the field of verbal learning, Benton J. Underwood and Leo Postman, came up with a dramatic proposal by attempting to demonstrate that the principles of stimulus-response associationism could be linked to the field of language through what they termed the *extra experimental interference hypothesis*. This proposed that most forgetting shown in studies of verbal learning was the result of interference from existing language habits. They generated a range of very clear and strong hypotheses on this basis and proceeded to test them, resulting in a very clear answer. Their results completely failed to match their predictions, and to their credit, they published these very negative results in one of the major journals.

At this point the traditional verbal learning approach retreated from the field, although not from the field of reviewing. Both of these consequences were unfortunate since there is no doubt that the phenomenon of interference is of great importance, far too important to neglect. However, as I discovered to my cost, attempting to address the issue along any but the narrowest traditional lines was likely to lead to stiff opposition from referees of the old school. In my own case for example, our demonstration that remembering where you parked your car on successive occasions fitted into the traditional interference paradigm rather well was met with enthusiasm by Ulric Neisser reviewing the paper from a cognitive viewpoint but was rejected in the face of objections from other referees claiming that the design did not strictly adhere to what was a classically acceptable verbal learning paradigm. At this point the field known as verbal *learning*, which was principally concerned with *forgetting* was increasingly referred to by cognitive psychologists as the study of *memory*. Paradoxically, the new lines of research were in fact largely concerned with *learning*. After many years of comparative neglect, I am happy to say that the study of forgetting is once more becoming acceptable, and may indeed be in danger of becoming fashionable.

We have talked about "learning" lists of words, but the learners did, of course, already know the words. Had the experiment involved Finnish or Hungarian words, the results from the English-speaking rememberers would have been very different. What they were learning was not the words themselves but that they had just been presented in the list that they were asked to recall. This point was stressed in a very influential paper in which Tulving distinguished these two kinds of memory, and which he termed *semantic memory* and *episodic memory*. Semantic memory refers to stored knowledge of the world. This includes not only the meaning of the words but also non-linguistic knowledge such as the colour of a banana or knowing the appropriate way to behave in a restaurant. Episodic memory refers to the capacity to recollect a *specific* incident or episode, for example what you had for breakfast *today*, as distinct from what you usually have for breakfast. In a standard verbal memory experiment you would try to recall the words that occurred in that *specific* list, hence involving episodic memory. This would almost certainly, however, also depend on knowing the meaning of the words, illustrating the fact that semantic and episodic memory work together. Knowing the meaning of the words allows you to create new clusters that allow that specific list to be distinguished from other occasions when those words have been used. We move on to semantic memory in the next chapter.

Note

1 Dixon, T. R., & Horton, D. L. (Eds.). (1968). *Verbal Behavior and General Behavior Theory.* Englewood Cliffs, NJ: Prentice-Hall.

12
The Emergence of Semantic Memory

Tulving's classic paper reflected a major change in the memory field, the acceptance that the standard approaches to memory depended critically on an underlying knowledge base, and that this in itself was an important area to study. Investigating semantic memory benefitted from the development of measures of memory based on speed of access rather than errors, an approach initiated by Saul Sternberg's influential work in short-term memory where he varied the number of items being held in short-term memory, finding that the time to recognise a test item increased regularly with the number of items being held. Tom Landauer and Jonathan Freedman attempted to show a broadly similar effect in semantic memory. While it is difficult to know exactly how large set sizes are, they argued that a category such as *animal* had to be substantially larger than one such as *dog*, since dogs and many other categories were part of the animal kingdom. Their task involved deciding whether a particular example such as *Labrador* was a member of the specified category, *DOG* in one case or *ANIMAL* in another. They duly found that it was quicker to decide that a Labrador was a dog than that it was an animal, concluding that this reflected a search through either the limited *DOG* or the much larger *ANIMAL* category within semantic long-term memory.

Their simple search hypothesis was, however, attacked on two grounds. Their theory involved simply searching a category, such as *DOG* or *ANIMAL* for the presence of the target word Labrador and detecting if a "hit" occurred. The specific nature of the negative items should not matter as they would simply not be encountered as they do not form part of the category set. In fact, the nature of the negative items *was* important. It takes much longer to decide that an *oak* is not a *FLOWER* than to decide that a *chair* does not belong to that category. Furthermore, the precise nature of the *positive* items also had a powerful effect. Hence it takes longer to decide that a *penguin* is a *BIRD* than to make a similar decision about a *robin*. Instances that are typical of the category are processed more rapidly. It became increasingly clear that such category judgement tasks were in fact quite complex, more analogous to a simple reasoning task than to a direct lookup in a passive database.

The experimental psychology department at Sussex has a master's programme that enables people with good degrees in other subjects to undergo an intense training in experimental psychology. It resembles the initial part of a standard US PhD programme and is necessary in the UK since a typical psychology PhD assumes that the candidate will already have extensive undergraduate training in psychology. The master's course attracted strong and interesting candidates, and has over the years had a major input into British psychology. One such student came from a very active AI group, keen to add some psychology to his computer science skills. He turned up one day with a PhD thesis dissertation from MIT entitled *The Teachable Language Comprehender* by Ross Quillian. It had the remarkably ambitious aim of teaching a computer to understand prose. In order to do so it had to handle the question of how to incorporate meaning, in short, to develop and operate some form of semantic memory.

In an attempt to economise storage capacity, the computer-based model used a hierarchical system in which the relevant features that comprise each level are stored at that point, with more detailed features being stored lower in the hierarchy. For example an item such as *shark* would have features such as *living, moves*, etc., at the general level of *ANIMAL* since initially all animals have these characteristics leading down to the next level of *FISH*, which would have *swims, has fins*, etc., down to *shark*, the specific instance, which would have features such as *dangerous, has teeth*, etc. When asked to verify information about a shark, excitation within the model would move from the presented instance word *shark* up to a level at which the statement could be verified. Hence *has teeth* would take fewer steps and be more rapid than verifying that the shark *swims* or that it is an *ANIMAL*. In collaboration with psychologist Alan Collins, Quillian published experimental data that seemed to provide elegant support for the hierarchical hypothesis. Alas, other investigators, including ourselves, failed to find such a clear relationship and it eventually turned out to be the case that the sentences they had selected were not typical of language more generally.

Despite the failure of Quillian's cognitive economy hypothesis, his work was important for two reasons. First, because of the openness of this computer model to empirical test, which encouraged the growing interest by experimental psychologists in the problems of semantic memory. Second, despite its ultimate failure it was a programming tour de force that encouraged others in AI to tackle the challenging question of simulating the comprehension of language. An influential later attempt to tackle the problem, again based on a PhD dissertation from MIT came from Terry Winograd who simplified the question of semantic memory by limiting his system to "block world", requiring it to move around and manipulate a series of blocks of different sizes. Even so, the model required three components: one concerned with syntax, one with the semantics of the block world and a third responsible for reasoning. The model was impressive in that it linked language to action, albeit in a very constrained toy world.

Meanwhile, within psychology, a number of groups were creating models of the human semantic system, typically using computer simulation and assuming various types of inter-item association. These models began to appear in the early 1970s. John Anderson and Gordon Bower's model HAM (Human Associative Memory) from Stanford appeared in 1973, Walter Kintsch from Colorado published his model in 1974 and on the east coast of the US, Alan Collins and Elizabeth Loftus modified Quillian's model replacing the previous assumption of hierarchical storage with one of "spreading activation" whereby activation of one node within the network would begin to influence surrounding nodes. The first of this sequence of models, however, came from UCSD, published shortly after I left by David Rumelhart, Peter Lindsay and Donald Norman in 1972. I had the good fortune to sit in on their group seminars, although as an observer rather than an active participant. This was a seminal period for the group who went on to play a central role in the development of a new approach to modelling learning, based on the assumption of *parallel distributed processing*.

Like most of the models, their model was complex and involved a range of different types of association, all reflecting different semantic properties. Examples include "ISA" links as in *John is a man* and "HAS links" as in *John has a dog*. These link two types of units represented as nodes in a semantic network, each of which can convey three types of information. A distinctive feature of the model was its assumption that information is processed in *parallel*, with a range of different activities proceeding at the same time, in contrast to the methods that were standard at the time which assumed a *sequence* of processing stages. This approach to modelling was, for a time, extremely influential, in part because it is clear that the brain is a parallel processing system and hence it is tempting to assume that parallel models are inherently more biologically plausible than sequential models. In fact, there is no reason to assume a simple one-to-one mapping of nodes within such networks with neurons in the brain, which probably uses a mix of parallel and sequential processing.

Parallel distributed processing systems did in fact originate considerably earlier than the 1970s with Oliver Selfridge's concept of *pandemonium* as a model of perception. Applied to an activity such as reading, it would assume layers of "demons", detectors that were each assigned a job. The lower layer of demons would, for example, detect either the horizontal, vertical or oblique marks within each letter, shouting out when they detect such a mark. A layer above comprised demons who would each be listening for a given letter, and once the appropriate combination of strokes had been shouted to them would themselves shout out the letter to the layer above. These higher level demons would be listening for clusters of letters and would, in turn, shout up to the word detecting demons.

The question then arises as to how to model this system. A basic unit for this was proposed by Frank Rosenblatt in 1958 and named a *perceptron*. Each perceptron had two inputs and was hence able to detect the presence of one of two stimulus features, passing this information on and responding to feedback in order to allow learning to occur. However, in a highly influential paper from MIT, Marvin Minsky and Seymour Papert declared the perceptron unworkable on the grounds that it could not handle the situation in which both features occurred at the same time. This seemed to convince the field and for many years parallel processing was regarded as unworkable until a simple solution was provided. This assumed a third level of "hidden units" capable of responding to such conjunctions, allowing the development of a range of computational models of learning. These assumed an artificial neural network comprising a web of interconnected nodes, connections through which activation could flow, hence its popular title of *connectionism*. Learning occurs through the modification of such connections as a result of feedback. Geoffrey Hinton and John A. Anderson advocated this approach in an influential book in 1981, showing that it allowed the development of very powerful ways in which a computer could be made to learn.

Connectionism represented a radically different way of thinking about both the brain and the mind, allowing, for example, much more plausible ways of thinking about retrieval than the existing sequential processing AI models. These typically saw retrieval as a systematic serial search through an array of storage locations, plausible perhaps for limited sets but less so for the massive amounts of information stored in long-term memory. For a while, it was hugely fashionable, and it seemed that connectionism might take over the whole field of cognition. As an approach to psychological theory however, it has a number of limitations, in particular that the original learning procedure that was proposed, known as *back propagation*, appeared to be far too slow to be a candidate for human learning. More importantly, models that are developed on the basis of connectionism are often very difficult to interpret in psychological terms since the same problem can often be solved by the computer in a range of very different ways, any one of which might or might not be equivalent to the way in which the brain tackles the specified task, which can of course also be a problem for the earlier serial processing AI models. Hence, a good engineering solution that might solve a specific practical problem is not necessarily a good scientific solution to the question of how the brain tackles that problem. Consequently, while computer-based learning has now become extremely successful at an applied level, its contribution to understanding the brain is better seen as providing a potentially valuable *tool* for developing theories rather than itself providing a model.

To return to the psychological question of semantic memory, some of the most compelling evidence was beginning to come from neuropsychology in the 1970s where patients suffering from what later became known as semantic dementia appeared to lose access to the meaning of words and objects in a systematic way. Elizabeth Warrington and Tim Shallice at the National Hospital in London noted that their patients would lose information progressively, initially, for example, being able to recognise a dog picture as that of a Labrador; as time went on they would still know it was a dog but not which type. Yet later they knew that it was a living thing but not what kind of living thing. Such a decline was not limited to words or pictures, reflecting a general loss of meaning. An even more interesting group of patients seemed to show differential loss depending on the type of item. One patient might, for instance, have difficulty with abstract words such as *love* or *justice*, while another might have problems with concrete words such as *house* and *crocodile*, and patients were later discovered with even more constrained deficits, for example, for fruit or household objects.

These neuropsychological clues as to the nature of semantic memory have been gradually extended over the years, more recently using neuro-imaging and leading to a broad model of semantic memory known as the hub and spokes model. This assumes that individual sensory features are stored across the brain in regions responsible for perceiving and processing that dimension but are linked to a common hub in the frontal region of the left temporal lobe, which brings together the features into a coherent conceptual representation. The general loss of semantic detail is assumed to come from overall deterioration, while more specific deficits involving brain regions, reflecting, for example, visual features or those features responsible for manually manipulating objects. This broad theory has more recently been combined with the previously described parallel processing simulation techniques to provide more detailed models of semantic memory.

But such developments were all for the future; suffice it to say that UCSD was a very stimulating environment, not only because of my interactions with the Mandler and semantic memory groups but also because of the chance to learn about neurobiological approaches to learning from Tony Deutsch and about psychology and music from Diana, his wife, together with the opportunity to interact with Ursula Bellugi at the Salk Institute along the road and learn about her work on sign language and deafness. UCSD was an exciting place to be in 1970.

Meanwhile we continued to enjoy the apparently endless sunny days and even began to make the subtle distinction between an ordinary sunny day and a "nice day", although I did begin to miss the contrast between seasons. Furthermore, despite the sunshine, we were rather less healthy than usual. In particular my middle son Gavin and I both suffered from asthma, in Gavin's case sufficiently seriously that he had to be hospitalised on a number of occasions. In this respect we were very grateful to be members of the University of California's health insurance programme, covering what otherwise would probably been a ruinously expensive year. It appears to be the case that, because of the "benevolent" climate, many plants flower at different times of year. As a result it is a very poor climate for allergies in general and asthma in particular. It was, however, a wonderful climate for sightseeing, and we took full advantage, amazed that we could travel from hot desert to mountain snows in little over an hour.

CHIP offered an ideal working environment, with plenty of intellectual stimulation, no demands from teaching or administration, and I see from one of my letters that I apparently finished writing nine papers before Christmas. This allowed me to get on with the proposed book based on my lectures. Rather overambitiously, I planned to finish it by Easter and then move on to writing the short-term memory book that I had offered to Oxford University Press. It did not quite work out that way. As I began to write, I kept coming up against the need to reread papers, which then sparked off ideas that led to further reading until the whole enterprise became more ambitious but also much more interesting.

By Christmas, we needed to move again, with a gap to fill before taking up our second main let, a one-year-old house in Del Mar owned by David Rumelhart, a prominent member of the semantic memory group at UCSD who was due to spend the next semester at Princeton. Meanwhile, our theoretical physicist landlord returned for Christmas and we prepared to move into a motel. Happily, two graduate students in the department offered us use of their house while they returned to Boston for Christmas, provided we looked after their pets. These proved to be two ducks and two monkeys, one of whom had already escaped and disappeared before we moved in. We were advised not to let the remaining monkey, Amos, out of his cage, a situation that understandably made him rather cross. His cage faced the television, and he was particularly enraged when a certain used-car salesman appeared, for reasons that we could never fathom. The two older children really enjoyed what they describe as "Christmas in the monkey house" but Bart seemed to have monkey nightmares waking up calling out "Amy Amy!"

We had a very good Christmas, which included an unexpected visit from departmental carol singers, invitations to drinks and overall, a memorably happy time. It was, however, good to move after Christmas from the colourful but rather ramshackle monkey house to a large modern house back in Del Mar and close to the university. It had the added bonus of lots of toys left behind by the Rumelhart children, and as a toy for me, Dave's red Austin Healey 3000 sports car. This proved to be a slightly mixed blessing. The problem was partly that I was far from sure that my driving merited a sports car, together with the fact that it was rather ancient and had a problem with its cooling system. Consequently, in hot weather it was necessary to put the heater on full blast to prevent the radiator boiling over, making driving a somewhat torrid experience. However it did allow me to leave the Dodge Dart for Hilary while I drove sweatily into the university.

By this time, although the writing was going reasonably well, and I was enjoying interacting with people in the department, I had not done much towards my aim of taking full advantage of the fact that I was in the US to meet as many people in other departments as possible. The problem was one of distance, the east coast of the US being no closer to San Diego than it is to Sussex. The best way to cope with this problem seemed to plan a small number of long trips that combined visits to as many good departments as possible. As I wanted to minimise the time that I was away from my family, this resulted in rather hectic schedules.

My first trip was to Canada, based on Toronto, an outstanding department for memory research where I had a number of friends and that was surrounded by several relatively close universities with good cognitive psychologists. Here I note from my letter home that over a 10-day trip, I averaged one talk per day, returning hoarse and unsurprisingly exhausted. Talks on the west coast and the Rockies proved less demanding and I had a very enjoyable visit to Berkeley where Leo Postman, a major figure in the verbal learning tradition, introduced my talk with the words "we have had our differences in the past but nonetheless we are very pleased to welcome…", which left me wondering what differences he had in mind and whether they would feature in my talk. Leo was, however, extremely friendly and a very good host.

My talk led to an invitation to Stanford by Gordon Bower, a leading memory theorist in what was at that time, probably the outstanding cognitive department in the world. I accepted and in due course flew North again to the Bay Area and gave my talk. As I was leaving, a friend I had known in England gave me a package that I opened on the plane. It contained an envelope full of what seemed like dried grass and a paperback which turned out to be a manual on preparing and consuming marijuana. Since this was definitely illegal, I hurriedly hid the package, first in my luggage and later among Dave Rumelhart's books, making sure to place it out of reach of the children, while I decided what to do with it. Next came a trip to Colorado, complete with a blizzard. I was then due to fly on to Albuquerque to visit the University of New Mexico. However, I received a phone call from Hilary telling me that Gavin had had to go in to hospital with pneumonia and that the two other boys were also ill. I immediately flew back, by which time Hilary was also ill. All in all we had a very unhealthy February, with a succession of bugs.

My final marathon trip was to the east coast, organised with the help of Dick Neisser who I knew from the time he had spent in Sussex. It was a splendid trip, with memories recently refreshed by rereading the letters I sent home to England. I began in Washington DC, staying with a friend from Cambridge days and giving a talk at the University of Maryland before spending time sightseeing over the weekend. My visit coincided with a Peace March, with a quarter of a million people protesting about the Vietnam War. Should I join in I wondered, or was it inappropriate as a visitor and guest of the country? However, I remembered the old slogan from the American Revolution/War of Independence that claimed,

"No taxation without representation". I was indeed being taxed by the US government and so joined the throng of Vietnam vets, grannies holding placards, dancing Hari Krishna devotees, men with swastika armbands and jack boots, together with lots of very ordinary people. The march just happened to go by the National Gallery and since it seemed as though it would go on for a long time, I dropped in seeing some great paintings and buying some very good reproductions that I still have. I then resumed the march. And in due course, the war ended!

From Washington I flew to Princeton in a 15-seater plane, a new experience and an enjoyable one since it flew so close to the ground that you could see far more than you can from a jumbo jet. From Princeton, which had changed quite a lot in the 14 years since my time as a graduate student, I hired a car and drove to Bell Laboratories, which at the time had outstanding cognitive psychologists doing basic research, notably including Saul Sternberg, whose model I disagreed with, having collected evidence that was inconsistent with its predictions. I was finding difficulty in persuading the more staid US journals to accept the resulting paper, eventually publishing it in a British journal of rather more liberal views. Saul was a wonderful person to discuss this and much else, very open-minded and very clever. I really regret the fact that he appears to have done little further work in cognitive psychology. I then drove a large hire car to Newark airport in the rush hour realising how much easier it was to drive our modest Dodge Dart through the comparatively empty roads of Southern California.

From Newark I flew on to Hartford, Connecticut, to be met by Michael Turvey, an old friend who had originally moved from Britain to the US on an athletic scholarship from Ohio State. He then became intrigued by psychology and went on to carry out some elegant and theoretically important memory experiments within a cognitive psychology framework, before rejecting the cognitive approach in favour of a particularly fundamentalist Gibsonian approach to perception and action. He remained excellent company, despite his eccentric views, about which we would regularly happily disagree, preferably over one or two beers. We went back to the colonial mansion he was renting, complete with Doric columns 200 acres of land and a pond full of peepers, amorous frogs who spend the whole night serenading their loved ones. I envied them their voices as by this time my voice, which had started somewhat croakily, was beginning to give out. I croaked my way through a talk at the University of Connecticut and went on to Yale where I had dinner with Endel Tulving, someone with whom I love to dispute, although our arguments usually end up as a tie, on the basis that we tend to have similar ideas but express them in very different terms. Alas by this time I had lost my voice and had to sit passively, while Endel (wrongly) put the world of psychology to rights.

From Yale I went to the nearby Haskins Laboratories, which specialises in speech and hearing. Among other things, I was shown a device that it was claimed could tell whether you had throat cancer. Its inventor was away; otherwise, it was explained I could have tried it out. As I later realised it would probably have detected a polyp that had developed on my vocal chords that might or might not have been cancerous. Happily, when my polyp was later diagnosed and subsequently removed, it proved not to be malignant.

My final stop was at Cornell University in Upper State New York, where my host was Dick Neisser who had been largely responsible for arranging the trip. My voice had almost vanished by then but using what seemed to be left of my vocal chords I grunted another talk. I enjoyed the usual splendid hospitality and particularly an invitation from James Gibson and his wife, Jackie, to visit their lab and try out various devices such as spectacles that invert the visual world. I was particularly pleased, partly because he was known not to be enthusiastic about cognitive approaches to memory, or indeed verbal learning. When he had visited Sussex a couple of years earlier, Stuart Sutherland had introduced me as "This is Alan Baddeley, our verbal learner". To which Gibson replied glumly, "I suppose everyone has have one". Gibson proved to be both friendly and seemed much more open-minded than his more radical disciples such as my friend Mike Turvey.

That was the end of my east coast tour, but I had included one more stop, to give the talk in New Mexico that had been postponed on my previous trip. I duly arrived and was struck at the difference between Cornell and Albuquerque. I remember visiting a psychophysiology lab in an adobe house that looked more like the film set of a Mexican village from a cowboy film than the Gothic Ivy League buildings I had recently visited. After my talk I returned to the motel, so exhausted that when I flung myself down on the bed, I missed. I arrived back in San Diego at 9.15 the next evening, and the following morning I went into the university to find 20 letters waiting to be answered, in longhand as I did not type. Looking back, although it was a wonderful experience, I was amazed at the energy I must have had and at Hilary's patience in coping with the children while I was away.

By this time we were coming to the end of our stay in San Diego, continuing with family outings to Disneyland, where our two-year-old showed an alarming enthusiasm for the more terrifying rides, and a visit to a cousin in Orange County who I remembered as a rather dashing Canadian soldier in the kilt of the Black Watch, who used to spend his leave with my aunt in Leeds, eventually returning to Canada with a Yorkshire bride. He was now a milk delivery man in Orange County.

I was due to spend the summer in Los Angeles, working on a diving project at UCLA at the invitation of one of the very few groups carrying out research on diver performance at that time. However, Gavin was still having asthma attacks and Hilary decided to take the children home rather than to set up house again in Los Angeles. She had a somewhat damp return since Bart, our youngest, managed to pour a can of 7-Up all over her, stickily arriving home with Gavin still wheezing. She took him to the Brighton Hospital, where the staff took a somewhat laissez-faire approach reducing his drug dose, and within a day or so he was fine. Whether this was a result of removing the drugs or escaping the pollen-filled atmosphere of Southern California, we shall never know.

Meanwhile, back in California, I had an appointment to have the polyp removed from my vocal chords under a general anaesthetic. This involved arriving at a hospital in the desert outside San Diego early in the morning. I still have a clear memory of sitting in the car worrying, both about the general anaesthetic and also as to whether the polyp would prove to be cancerous or not. Rather dramatically, I remember writing a "last letter", which happily proved unnecessary since the polyp was benign. However the operation required a week of vocal rest, in a state of Trappist silence. Happily I was taken in by Roy and Karalyn Patterson, two graduate students with whom we had become very friendly. They looked after me until I had recovered sufficiently to head up the coast to Los Angeles.

I moved to Los Angeles for the summer, finding an apartment near the UCLA campus, to work with the diving research group, which was headed by Gershon Weltman and Glen Egstrom. Gershon was a psychologist who ran a small research and consulting group and Glen held an academic position in sports science and was trained as a physiologist. He was a large and imposing figure who was said to be the second most influential diver in California. The number one, who was located in San Diego, had the added distinction of having had his arm bitten off by a shark.

I missed my family, but there were advantages to living a bachelor life, which included going back to diving. Glen, who was I believe the diving safety officer for California, reckoned that since I had done open-sea experiments down to 200 feet, I was probably reasonably safe without re-training, a view that differed from that of the shark-bitten head of diving at

UCSD, who had insisted that I would have to be retrained. I had some very enjoyable dives both from the coast and from the offshore islands, which had wonderful kelp forests. On the boat over to the islands I was surprised to see the skipper pick up a rifle and start shooting. "Oh, he is just shooting at sharks" I was told. Happily, the only shark I saw when diving was rather small and at some distance.

In moving to Los Angeles, I had taken my stash of marijuana, complete with instruction book, and one evening decided to read the book and find out what to do. I discovered that "weed" had to be heated to work. I therefore decided to heat it in a frying pan and ate it on toast with marmalade. I then set out on a walk to see what would happen; sadly, nothing happened. I eventually put the remaining weed and the book in an envelope, which I deposited in a box in Westwood Village that requested books and related contributions to Brandeis University, where I was sure there would be people who could make better use of it. In due course we finished the diving study and I returned to my family and Sussex.

RETURNING TO SUSSEX
1971–72

13

Working Memory and the Phonological Loop

Up to this point, my account has attempted to use a structure that links the events of my own scientific career with the developments within cognitive psychology that were happening at the time, mapping both onto my geographical location at that time. From this point, it becomes more difficult to sustain such a framework. Within a period of about four years I moved from Sussex to San Diego to Los Angeles back to Sussex to Stirling and then to Cambridge where I stayed for the next 20 years. Spread across the last three of these locations was the development of the concept of working memory, a theme that has continued to evolve over the last 40 years. However, I continue to find the geographical structure a useful way of linking my research to my life more generally since both develop in parallel. In the case of working memory I have chosen to link the three initial components with the place most closely associated with its early development, respectively, Sussex for the phonological loop, Stirling for the sketchpad and Cambridge for later developments including the central executive. There were of course many other issues that cropped up during my 20 years in Cambridge. These will be described using a topic-based approach, while my later chapters revert to a more chronological structure.

I returned to Sussex where I had agreed while in California to be the temporary Head of Department while Stuart Sutherland was on sabbatical leave at MIT. I was somewhat surprised to be asked, but the proposal probably reflected the fact that no one else wanted the job, and since I had just had a sabbatical myself, it would seem churlish not to help Stuart do the same. In fact the department was very well organised, and I just needed to keep things ticking over. The only problem I can remember is when Stuart wanted us to employ a well-known US developmental psycholinguist for six months on a salary that would soak up all our spare teaching money. The department was firmly against the idea, doubting whether the distinguished visitor would in fact do the substantial amount of teaching that was promised. So I was deputed to deliver a firm "no" to our famously irascible leader. We waited in some trepidation for Stuart's response, which we expected to be somewhat explosive. To his credit he responded that we were totally stupid, but since he had put me in charge, he would respect my decision.

One reason why chairing the department did not prove too onerous was that we were not strictly speaking a department but rather one component of the School of Biology. This was led by a Dean, in this case, the distinguished evolutionary theorist John Maynard Smith, an amiable and fair-minded man who ran the school well. It was an interesting and challenging time for universities worldwide. In 1968 the students of Paris had come out on the streets in traditional French revolutionary mode, resulting in a substantial impact on French politics. Student protests against Vietnam were also prominent in the US, including the tragic events on the Kent State campus in Ohio. In tune with the spirit of the times, the Sussex students felt that they too should protest, but about what? They decided that the university Vice Chancellor (Chief Executive) should formally declare that the University of Sussex was against the war in Vietnam. They staged an occupation of the administration building to drive home their daring revolutionary point. The Vice Chancellor, a wily old social historian, who I am pretty sure was against the war in Vietnam anyhow, declined to be pushed into making empty gestures about this or anything else. He realised that most students were relatively moderate, and rather than heavy-handedly removing the sitters-in, simply waited for them to get bored. We had a similar "event" in the School of Biology, where the students convened a meeting of the whole school, declaring that the School of Biology should function as a commune with all decisions made by vote and all members from the cleaning staff to the Dean having an equal say. This was passed "by acclaim", followed by a question from one of the students. "May I propose a motion?" "Of course" responded the self-appointed chairman. "The proposal is that this commune hereby disbands itself". This was passed by a substantial majority and everyone except the disgruntled organisers then went happily home.

Meanwhile, in addition to my rather light administrative and teaching loads, I was quite busy with three new PhD students, with a continuation of my work on amnesia in London and with the start of two new research grants. One was on context-dependent memory in divers as described in Chapter 6 and the other on short-term memory. This stemmed from an earlier hint from my boss that it was about time I applied for a research grant. By this time I was in my late thirties having spent most of my research career at the APU where the rule was that as we were already funded by the Medical Research Council, applying for additional funding from the research councils who support basic research in the UK was forbidden. Stuart suggested I apply for a research assistant and a postdoctoral fellow, which I did, nominating Graham Hitch, a physicist who, following the MSc in Experimental Psychology at Sussex, had become interested in memory and completed a PhD under Broadbent at the APU. The grants committee was broadly favourable but thought found my proposal too expensive and cut one of the posts, happily the assistant. Had it been the postdoc, my future research career might have been very different.

Graham returned to Sussex and we began to think about just what we should do. We had claimed that we would look at the link between short-term and long-term memory, a topic that had become increasingly complex with a growing number of experimental methods linked to an ever-increasing range of different models. As mentioned earlier, the most influential of these was Atkinson and Shiffrin's modal model, but this was facing criticism for its assumption regarding the transfer of information from short-term to long-term storage. The assumption that simply maintaining information guaranteed learning was inconsistent with Craik and Lockhart's demonstration of the importance of deep elaborate processing. Furthermore the discovery of patients with normal long-term memory despite having grossly impaired short-term by Shallice and Warrington was also inconsistent with the model. At this point, people began to abandon the study of short-term memory, attracted by the new concept of semantic memory and subsequently by a rapidly increasing interest in levels of processing.

In the light of growing confusion in the field we decided to focus on a single question. What useful *function* might short-term memory serve, if any? We did not have access to the rare but highly informative patients with impaired short-term and normal long-term memory (LTM) but came up with the idea of simulating such patients using our students. Rather than removing chunks of their left hemisphere, we would keep the part of the brain responsible for STM busy, by giving them sequences of digits to remember. One thing that all the modellers and theorists agreed on was that memory span for digits depended on a limited-capacity STM. We argued that as we increased the number of digits to be remembered, we should gradually reduce the capacity left for other tasks. This would then gradually impair performance on any tasks that were assumed to depend on STM such as reasoning, comprehension and learning.

We began by presenting the digit sequence first, then giving a brief test of reasoning, after which the digits had to be recalled. This produced messy results as some people would do a couple of quick rehearsals and then switch to the reasoning task, going back later to recall any of the digits remaining, while other people continued to keep the digits in mind throughout the reasoning task as we had intended. We therefore adopted a method that we have used ever since, which is to require the subject to continuously repeat the sequence aloud, while performing the reasoning or learning task. By increasing the number of digits to be maintained, we could reduce systematically the short-term memory capacity available for reasoning. Once we adopted this overt rehearsal approach, we began to get clear results.

We were interested in the role of STM as a general processing resource, used across a wide range of cognitive activities and chose to study three, namely reasoning, learning and comprehension. By using a range of different experimental tasks we ensured that we were not simply learning about performance on a single laboratory paradigm, an all-too common occurrence in the field. For purposes of explanation however, I will focus on a single task based on a simple test of verbal reasoning. We chose to use a task that I had originally developed to study the influence of nitrogen narcosis on divers. It was borrowed from psycholinguistic studies of grammar and involved deciding whether a sentence does or does not correctly describe the order of a pair of letters; for example *A follows B – BA*, for which the answer is "true", or using more complex syntax, *B is not preceded by A – AB*, which is false. A good number of sentences can be presented in a short time, error rates tend to be low and speed of reasoning offers a sensitive measure of performance. As you may recall, we found that processing speed correlated quite highly with verbal intelligence scores, rather surprising for a test that only takes three minutes. Unlike most intelligence tests, the syntactic reasoning test comprises a series of very brief subtests, one for each sentence, thus providing many separate measures of performance. This allows a more reliable estimate than might have been obtained by more complex reasoning tasks of the type often used in standard intelligence batteries, where the individual component tests take longer and are more variable in nature.

We began by showing each sentence visually and measuring the speed and accuracy with which people responded while holding and repeating zero, three or six digits. We found little effect of three concurrent digits but a clear effect of six. In a later study we systematically varied the sequence length from zero to eight digits, finding a very nice linear increase in reasoning time as the length increased, suggesting that the system required for holding and repeating back digit sequences was indeed involved in our reasoning task. However, the effect was far from catastrophic, with response time increasing by about 50% from the zero to the longest eight-digit sequence. Even more remarkably, error rates remained low at 5%, regardless of number of concurrent digits.

We obtained broadly similar results with a comprehension task that involved understanding a passage of prose while reciting sequences of zero, three or six digits. Another series of studies combined concurrent digit load with the learning and immediate free recall of lists of unrelated words. An interesting feature of this latter condition was that, although the concurrent digit load reduced overall recall, it did not influence the recency effect. This was a particularly striking result, given that, as previously described in Chapter 10, the predominant view at the time, including that of the modal model, was that both digit span and recency reflected the same short-term memory system.

We decided to develop an alternative model, which we termed *working memory*, a name that highlights its function, to serve as a cognitive workspace, holding and manipulating information as required to perform a wide range of complex activities. We did not invent the term but acquired it from Atkinson and Shiffrin who, in turn, seem to have borrowed it from a very influential book entitled "Plans and the structure of behaviour" by George Miller, Eugene Galanter and Karl Pribram, which briefly outlines the need for a working memory system but does not take the concept further. Although their book was very influential, I myself must confess that I briefly dipped into it but did not read it, preferring a less speculative and more closely evidence-based approach to theorising such as that typified by Broadbent's work.

We decided that our model needed at least three components, resolving to keep it as simple as possible, adding new components only if the evidence was clearly beyond the explanatory scope of our original set of three. We proposed an attentional control system which we called the *central executive*. This was assumed to be limited in capacity and to be aided by two subsidiary short-term memory systems for which we initially used the engineering term *slave systems*. We have now abandoned the term, partly under pressure from advocates of political correctness but also because, under certain circumstances, these subsystems can be used to control the executive, a helpful alliance rather than a slave's revolt. We assumed that one of the subsystems was verbally based and closely allied to the earlier concept of verbal STM. We proposed that it was this system that had principally featured in our concurrent digit span experiments. We assumed in addition, however, that the need to run the reasoning and memory tasks simultaneously would also place demands on the central executive. We then broke the verbal system down into two probable components, a temporary store and a rehearsal system based on subvocal articulation. Indeed we began by calling this system the *articulatory loop*, later changing this to the *phonological loop* to emphasise the mode of storage rather than rehearsal.

In postulating a temporary verbal or acoustic storage system we were confronted with a number of questions. First of all, what was the precise nature of the information being stored? Conrad had used the term "acoustic", but since "acoustic" similarity effects also occurred when letters or words were presented visually, in the absence of any acoustic input, this seemed inappropriate. We suspected that determining the nature of the underlying code would require a knowledge of speech perception and production that went considerably beyond our own expertise and looked for what we hoped was a more neutral term. We tried "phonemic", but this proved not to be at all theoretically neutral subsequently switching to "phonological", which I am told is not neutral either. At this point rather than change again we gave up the search and settled for the term *phonological loop*.

A second question concerned the nature of forgetting in the phonological store. This took us back to the old controversy of whether forgetting is due to the gradual decay of a memory trace over time, or to interference from later items that might overshadow or possibly actively suppress memory of the earlier items. We opted for trace decay on the grounds that an interference interpretation would require us to come up with a more detailed specification, which we did not feel able to do. Some 40 years later, the question of trace decay versus interference in verbal STM continues to be controversial, with a range of competing views. Fortunately, it is not one that is crucial to the overall viability of our working memory model.

This was broadly the state of play when I received an invitation from Gordon Bower in Stanford to contribute a chapter to an influential annual series entitled *Recent Advances in Learning and Motivation*. Should we accept the invitation, given that our working memory model was far from complete? It seemed too good an opportunity to miss. This indeed proved to be the case since our paper which appeared in 1974 has apparently now been cited over 10,000 times.

We have of course continued to develop the concept of a phonological loop, and for reasons of coherence I will mention here two later developments, one of which occurred in Stirling and the other in Cambridge. I was interested in how I might investigate the rehearsal component of the loop and hit on the idea of testing whether memory span for words might depend on how long the words were. Longer words should take longer to articulate, hence allowing more time for the trace to decay during rehearsal. It is clear, however, that long and short words can differ in many ways, and for that reason, I was almost tempted not to carry out the experiment but decided that such complexities could be sorted out later. In collaboration with a colleague, Neil Thomson and a student Mary Buchanan, we ran a series of studies in Stirling, finding that there was indeed a marked effect of word length on short-term recall. In one study for example, we chose words of one, two, three or five syllables, controlling for semantic factors by having words of each length from a series of different categories, for example diseases and US states, ranging in length from *mumps* to *tuberculosis* and from *Maine* to *Louisiana*. We also checked pronunciation time by requiring our subjects to read out sequences of such items as rapidly as possible. Our results were very clear. Immediate memory for five-word sequences declined systematically from 90% of sequences correctly recalled for single-syllable words to around 50% for five-syllable words from the same semantic categories. We found a similar relationship between the speed at which the words could be read and per cent recall. We also found that faster talkers remembered more than slower speakers, in line with our hypothesis that slower rehearsal allows more decay of the memory trace. Our results could be summarised as showing that across the range of lengths, people can remember about many words as they can say in two seconds.

An interesting practical consequence of the word length effect comes from the fact that the names of numerals differ in length from one language to another. In Hebrew and Arabic for example digits average more than two syllables; in English they average one syllable, while in Chinese it appears to be possible to pack more than one digit into a single syllable. A recent study of our own, for example, found an average digit span of 6.7 for English students compared with 8.3 for Chinese, with articulation rates of 1.4 versus 1.9 digits per second. It is clear that digit span varies quite substantially from one language to another, an important factor when comparing the span measure of patients speaking different languages.

Our own interpretation of the word length effect was in terms of a fading trace. All the time that rehearsal is proceeding, the memory trace is fading. However, if articulation is sufficiently rapid it will still be possible to pick up and refresh the memory trace before it is degraded beyond retrieval. We attempted to test this hypothesis by comparing memory for sequences of two-syllable words that had a long pronunciation such as *Friday* and *harpoon* with shorter words such as *bishop* and *wicket*. We duly found that memory for short word sequences was better, concluding that trace decay was supported. Unfortunately, others using different words failed to replicate our results. It is in fact difficult to find words that provide a clear test, particularly since it is necessary to balance other factors such as acoustic similarity and frequency in the language. Consequently, after 40 years this still remains a controversial issue with some investigators supporting our result and others rejecting it. My own view is that the difficulty of finding samples of suitable words and of balancing factors other than spoken duration means that this method is simply not sensitive enough to answer the question reliably. So on the question of decay or some form of interference in the phonological store, I remain open-minded but currently opt for decay as the simplest assumption.

It is possible to stop people rehearsing subvocally by requiring them to continue to utter some irrelevant sound such as the word "the". This removes the effect of word length, as indeed it should according to our theory. Such articulatory suppression also disrupts the phonological similarity effect when material is presented visually, presumably because it interferes with the process of turning a visual stimulus such as a letter into a phonological code, its spoken name. Interestingly, a similar disruptive effect can be induced by requiring the subject to tap out a syncopated rhythm, although there is no such effect for regular tapping, a phenomenon first noted by my friend Satoru Saito when attempting to sing at the same time as providing a somewhat overambitious syncopated accompaniment on the guitar. He later demonstrated this effect in the more controlled environment of the psychological laboratory. It seems likely that the control of rhythmic phrases overlaps at some point with the timing mechanism for controlling speech production, which then interferes with the process of turning a visually presented letter or word into its vocal equivalent.

At this point it might be appropriate to mention another aspect of the phonological loop that impinges on music and speech: namely the irrelevant sound effect. Some years later, during my time at the Applied Psychology Unit, I received a request from a French psychologist, Pierre Salame, who wanted to spend a year at the Unit. Pierre duly arrived with the remit to work with me on the effects of noise on memory, as part of a more extended PhD program. This created a problem since my earlier work attempting to use STM as a measure of telephone line quality had shown no clear noise effects, even with auditory presentation. We eventually agreed that speech could, for present purposes, be regarded as noise, potentially allowing a rather wider, and I hoped more promising range of questions to be asked. We went ahead and designed an experiment in which people tried to remember sequences of digits while avoiding distraction from either meaningful words or nonsense words. Pierre predicted that only meaning would disrupt STM, while I predicted that neither would impair performance. We were both wrong. Nonsense syllables and words both impaired performance to an equivalent extent. We discovered later that this had already been discovered a few years earlier by Herbert Colle but not widely taken up, and so we continued to explore our effect.

We carried out a series of experiments which seemed to tell a coherent story that fitted neatly into our concept of a phonological loop, with irrelevant sound disrupting the storage component. We found no difference between the disruptive effects of concurrent long or short words, suggesting that the articulatory rehearsal component was not important. Further evidence of the unimportance of either semantic or lexical effects came from an experiment in which we compared the effect on recall of sequences of visually presented digits of other auditorily presented digits, or of words made up by the recombining phonemes that occur in digits, namely *tun* (one), *gnu* (two), *tea* (three), *saw* (four), *thrive* (five), *fix* (six), *heaven* (seven), *fate* (eight) and *sign* (nine). If disruption occurs at a lexical or semantic level, then these should interfere less with digit recall than irrelevant concurrent digits. If however, interference operated at the level of the sounds that make up the words, then they should be just as disruptive as concurrent spoken digits. Words and digits proved to have the same effects. Like Herbert Colle we interpreted our results as reflecting some kind of interference operating at a phonological rather than semantic level. We went on to explore this interpretation further, finding that the memory disruption effect was not limited to interference from speech since memory for digit sequences could be disrupted by concurrent music, with a stronger effect for vocal music than instrumental, while unpatterned noise had no effect, consistent with our explanation in terms of interference with *phonological* storage.

Meanwhile, over in Cardiff, Dylan Jones who had worked on the effects of noise on behaviour with Donald Broadbent became interested in the irrelevant sound effect. He and Bill Macken tested our phonological masking hypothesis directly by varying the phonological similarity between the irrelevant auditory items and the visual items that had to be recalled. Similar auditory items should interfere more: they did not, a result later replicated by several others including ourselves. Dylan and his group took over the exploration of the irrelevant sound effect, devoting considerable attention to mapping out the characteristics of irrelevant sounds that can disrupt performance, producing their *changing state hypothesis* whereby *fluctuations* in the irrelevant sound were responsible for its capacity to disrupt memory for serial order. Consistent with this view, they found that even fluctuating sequences of pure tones would impair serial digit recall.

Dylan proposed an explanation of his results based on auditory perception, suggesting that sequences of sound formed paths through a system involving what he describes as an *Object-Oriented Episodic Record*. The irrelevant sounds formed competing paths, which then disrupted the path left by the remembered sequence, and hence recall of the order in which they had been presented. He proposed that this was a multi-modal system recording visual as well as auditory sequences. The Cardiff group reported evidence for cross-modal interference, but this has not been easy to replicate, with evidence for separate visual and verbal systems being much more typical. Neuropsychological data also suggest very clear evidence for a visual-verbal separation, with some patients showing grossly impaired verbal but normal visual STM, as in the classic cases reported by Shallice and Warrington, while others showed the opposite pattern. Interestingly, Jones and Macken now appear to have abandoned their original position in favour of an approach that emphasises what they term "perception" and "action", a view that in my own opinion (although not theirs) maps readily onto the phonological storage and articulatory rehearsal components of the phonological loop.

So where did this leave our own explanation of the irrelevant speech effect? A major problem for us was the fact that the effect operated by disrupting memory for the *order* in which items were presented, and our model had no explanation of how order was retained. One possibility was in terms of stimulus-response chaining. The first item serves as a stimulus which is associated with the second, which, in turn, links to the third and so forth. Both phonological similarity and irrelevant sound could be assumed to interfere with this, causing the chain to break and forgetting to occur.

The problem of maintaining serial order is a classic problem, not only in memory but also in generating language and in fluent complex motor skills such as playing the piano for which an explanation in terms of a simple chain of stimulus–response–stimulus associations seems inadequate. In this context digit span has proved to be a convenient test for a range of theories, since it involves two very basic questions, the first of which concerns how serial order is stored and retrieved. The second involves the phenomenon of "chunking", whereby a number of items can be combined and then appear to act as a single item in terms of their representation within the limited-capacity short-term storage system, an important idea first proposed by George Miller in his classic 1956 paper entitled *The magic number seven*. In the case of language for example, immediate memory span for a random letter string is around five. If the letters comprise five three-letter words however, span increased to around 15 letters (five words). If the words form a typical meaningful sentence, then span can increase to around 50 letters. Both serial order and chunking have led to extensive theorising, much, though by no means all within a broad phonological loop framework, with the irrelevant sound effect now attributed to a separate serial order component rather than to phonological storage.

It seems likely that a full explanation of the operation of the phonological loop will depend on and integrate with a more detailed understanding of the speech perception and production systems from which it presumably evolved. However, the concept has continued to be a very fruitful one, providing a simple account of a limited but extremely useful memory subsystem, as will become clear from the chapters that follow.

Our only picture of Grandma Israel (nee Baddeley) with friend. It would have been good to have a picture of her in her days as a dancer some 18 children earlier.

My parents at the seaside. Note the cane and cigarette: very 1920s!

My parent's wedding including my maternal grandfather, the best man, Uncle Clarence, previously the 84lb boxing champion of Yorkshire, together with the bridesmaid, my Aunt Daisy, known as big Daisy to distinguish her from her daughter who rapidly outgrew her.

A wartime picture with my father a member of the Home Guard behind my brother and next to my grandfather. I am between my mother and the jar of caterpillars on the window ledge.

Our extended family, minus the five uncles who emigrated, at my parent's Silver Wedding. My brother Keith is far left, and I am fourth from the left, lurking behind my uncles John and Jim.

The MRC Applied Psychology Unit.

My PhD involved studying codes that could be used on this Post Office letter sorting machine.

Peter Colquhoun and the wheel which simulated a very boring inspection task.

A study of the effects of telephoning on driving conducted by Ivan Brown in the 1960s. Drivers followed a route on an airfield, which involved driving through narrow gaps or avoiding them if they were too narrow while performing a simple reasoning task that I originally invented for testing divers, their steering was unaffected, but their judgement was impaired.

Hilary in her physiotherapist uniform around the time that we met.

Discussion between Donald Broadbent (R), myself and Fergus Craik (L) at the Nato meeting on short-term memory in Cambridge 1967.

The Mediterranean is not always blue. My attempts to perform the screw plate test at 200 feet are hampered by our choosing a site too close to the main sewage output from Valletta.

Delmar California 1971: I demonstrate my lack of success in either carving a joint or growing a decent beard.

Our three sons Gavin (L), Bart and Roland around the time of our year in San Diego.

All change at the Unit: Donald Broadbent leaves for Oxford and I lurk in the bushes. Cartoon by Clive Frankish.

Hilary and I at the Unit Christmas party in 1975.

Developing tests for the parasite study in Kingston Jamaica.

One of the classrooms in Tanzania where we ran the parasitic infection study.

Hilary outside our hotel room in Bagamoyo Tanzania.

The "Gang of Five" founders of the European Society for Cognitive Psychology at the first meeting in Nijmegen 1985. From the left: Wolfgang Prinz, Janet Jackson, John Michon, myself and Paul Bertelson.

Annual working memory discussion meeting at Satterthwaite in the Lake District, mid 1980s. Back row Graham Hitch and myself. Front right seated Dorothy Bishop and Susan Gathercole, standing with arms folded, Robert Logie.

The 2016 annual working memory meeting at Parcevall Hall in the Yorkshire Dales. Myself, Bob Logie and Graham Hitch are front left.

Feeling cheerful 2008, having finally published "Working Memory, Thought and Action".

Richard Allen, myself, Faraneh Vargha-Khadem and Jon whose memory capacity challenged several theories including my own (London 2017).

14

Working Memory and Visual Imagery

Shortly after our return from California, I was invited to give a talk at the University of Stirling in Scotland, a university founded a few years earlier on an idyllic campus with the university buildings scattered around a loch with a hill behind that formed the southern edge of the Highlands. I was invited by Bill Phillips an old friend from Sussex who explained that the department had now sorted out its teaching and wanted to build up its research, planning to appoint six new professors. At a time when most departments had one or at most two professorships, this was indeed ambitious. Was I interested in running the research side of the department? Hilary and I travelled up and liked both the university and the neighbouring town of Bridge of Allan, a Victorian resort town just outside Stirling, and despite Stuart's offer to attempt to get me a professorship back in Sussex, it seemed too exciting a development to miss.

We duly moved up and were delighted to discover that house prices were substantially less than those around Brighton, deciding on a rather grand Victorian house up-the-hill in the posher part of Bridge of Allan. The Scottish system of house buying is rather different from that in England where the seller's price is advertised and is typically broadly achieved. In Scotland, potential buyers make a sealed bid to a solicitor who on the appointed day opens all of the bids and awards the property to the highest bidder. We were instructed by the University's senior administrator, a retired general to offer exactly £11,000, which to us, used to Brighton prices, seemed very low. We did as we were told, adding a few hundred for luck, and as instructed appeared at the solicitors at the appointed time. After a brief delay, the solicitor appeared looking flustered and declaring that the general would be very upset about this but that someone had bid more than us! It seemed that there had been some sort of pact between the retired general and the solicitor that had come unstuck – good luck to whoever had beaten the system I thought. We eventually bought a house at the bottom of the hill that was less grand but extremely pleasant with friendly neighbours and a magnificent garden maintained by the efforts of a blind Canadian gardener. We never did work out how he came to be gardening in Scotland, or how, being blind, he did such a splendid job.

We only spent two years in Stirling, but they were very happy years which began with a big house-warming party for the friendly and enthusiastic young department. My research was going well, and Hilary rapidly made friends with congenial neighbours. The children also settled in at school, once the tricky question of which of the two Glasgow soccer teams they supported was settled, was it Rangers (Protestant) or Celtic (Catholic)? They diplomatically settled for Leeds United, at that time, a very successful team from my home town which just happened to have a charismatic captain who came from Stirling.

Scotland was different; initially the houses and countryside seemed to be all greys and greens, but after a few days, the eye seemed to adapt and on returning to England, the red brick houses at first seemed very garish. There were unexpected cultural differences; instead of the traditional English pub, there tended to be bars where serious drinking was expected. Fish and chip shops were more frequent and had a more varied menu in-cluding fried black pudding, white pudding and haggis. Politically things seemed to be run at that time by a moderately left-wing but very compla-cent Labour Party, with the result that I voted Scottish Nationalist as a mild contribution towards gingering things up, not a problem today with the resurgent Scot Nats having replaced Labour throughout Scotland.

The educational system was also different. Instead of the A level exams taken in England at age 18, Scottish students took Highers, a broader range of subjects taken at 17. They could then start a four-year university degree in which the first year involved a range of different subjects, in my view an advantage compared to the early specialisation that happens in the three-year English system. The students were also somewhat different from those in Sussex, needing more encouragement before they would speak in tutorials. Student politics was even more lively than at Sussex with elec-tions typically resulting in student union officers who seemed to reflect a toxic mixture of Trotskyists and Maoists, with the odd anarchist thrown in for good measure. The university had been founded in 1968, the year of student protests in Paris, and the students saw themselves as "Red Stirling".

This was not a recipe for good student government. The annual pattern seemed to involve staging an obligatory protest demonstration at the beginning of the first semester, typically followed by doctrinal disagreements resulting in multiple resignations by students who would then spend the rest of their sabbatical year travelling the world. However, 1972 was a rather special year, when the Queen was due to visit and officially open the university. It was to be a high point in the career of the Principal who had moved from a post in industry to run the university. He was a friendly man who had thoroughly enjoyed the early years when there were few students; he knew them all and could teach them sailing on the university loch. He was, however, rather less comfortable with the stroppier students that followed. As a professor, I was on the university council and the question was raised as to what we would do about the inevitable early-year protest. The ex-military university secretary declared that there would be no problem and if there was, then the police would deal with it, a response greeted with worried scepticism.

When the day dawned, a large number of students gathered on the central square of the campus hours before the Queen was due to arrive. They persuaded the campus supermarket to sell them bottles of wine, and to open them (not strictly legal), and by the arrival of her majesty, many of them were drunk. The Queen happily sailed through them with great aplomb, while the police did nothing other than prevent the builders working on the site from attacking the students. Next day it was all over the national newspapers, including the picture of a "mature" psychology student who appeared to be threatening the Queen but was actually, he insisted, toasting her in Gaelic.

It was a huge embarrassment, greatly resented by the local community, and of course by the Principal. He felt that he had to act and did so, not wisely but too well. He first of all closed down all bars on the campus, which, as none had been responsible, was not particularly helpful. Much more problematic was his use of the university's new disciplinary procedures, which involved carrying out the whole disciplinary process in secret, presumably intended to keep the innocent from a public accusation that might prove to be untrue. In this case however, it meant that initially, hardly anyone at the university knew what was happening. It then became clear that the Principal was using a new and untried piece of anti-union legislation recently introduced by the Conservative government. This held that actions by individual members of an organisation were the legal responsibility of that organisation even though the organisation had not approved the action and was not directly involved. Given that the legislation was highly controversial and had not been tried in court before, this seemed to promise an extremely prominent lengthy and acrimonious legal case between the university and the student union.

What had started as a rather naïve mistake by both administration and students was in danger of becoming a legal disaster. Fortunately at this point, the University Court, its overall supervisory body, proved its worth by intervening. Its chairman, an experienced Scottish law lord, stepped in and promptly sorted things out. The Principal took a year's sabbatical, during which he tragically died of a heart attack. The following year, instead of the usual Maoists or Trotskyists, the students elected a mature student, a tough trade unionist from the Glasgow shipyards who would stand no nonsense from naïve student revolutionaries, and everything calmed down.

By this time also, the political climate across universities had changed with the arrival of Margaret Thatcher as Minister of Education. It rapidly became clear that the good years were over and the chances of Stirling appointing six professors in the foreseeable future were vanishingly small. At about this time, Donald Broadbent retired from the Directorship of the MRC Applied Psychology Unit in Cambridge and the advertisement went out for a new director. Should I apply? We really liked Stirling, but it was clearly not going to be a leading research university at least within the next few years. Furthermore, the combination of theoretical and applied research at the Unit suited me perfectly, as did the prospect of directing a world-leading institution at the cutting edge of cognitive psychology. I would feel guilty at abandoning Stirling but was advised to take the opportunity and not to feel guilty about it by Peter McEwen, our kindly head of department (no, I really don't think he wanted to get rid of me!).

I applied, together with Derek Corcoran, a friend who had started his PhD at the Unit the same year as I did and who was currently Professor at Glasgow, together with several more experienced candidates. After the interviews Derek and I went on a London pub crawl that also involved dropping in at the Scientology Centre on Charing Cross Road. They thought that they could help Derek but seemed to regard me as a hopeless case. Happily the Medical Research Council had a higher opinion and I was offered the Directorship but would first have to have a security vetting since the Unit did military work. I was duly visited by a man in a raincoat of the type commonly assumed to be worn by spies, after which … nothing! As the weeks rolled by I began to search my conscience for anything that might make me a suspicious character in the eyes of the military, without success. Eventually the MRC said they would appoint me anyhow and Christopher Poulton, the deputy director, could look after military matters if necessary. It subsequently emerged that the spooks had been investigating a complex case involving Russians, politicians, aristocracy and sex, much more interesting than checking out a simple psychologist like myself.

On the research front, it had been an extremely productive two years. We had carried out the previously described study on the influence of the underwater context on memory in divers, we continued our work on recency and it was in Stirling that we discovered the powerful effect of word length on verbal STM. However, the principal focus of research was concerned with the visuospatial sketch pad. During the 1960s, inspired by the Peterson and Peterson demonstration that verbal material would be forgotten over a matter of seconds when rehearsal was prevented, a number of studies had been carried out extending this to other modalities. My friend Harold Dale in Cambridge showed that a similar pattern of rapid forgetting applied to remembering the location of a dot in an otherwise empty field and Elizabeth Warrington and I had noted that this capacity was preserved in densely amnesic patients, who were nevertheless clearly impaired in a more long-term task that involved learning the location of a more complex dot pattern. Michael Posner showed a similar forgetting function for memory of the location of a dot on an extended line, and with the help of a Sussex student, Elizabeth Gilson, I extended this to the tactile domain.

Perhaps the most interesting of our visual memory studies while still at Sussex, however, stemmed from an influential paper by Michael Posner and Stephen Keele published in the journal *Science*. They chose to use reaction time as a measure of the strength of the underlying memory trace, devising a task that exploited the fact that some letters are visually similar in upper-case and lower-case forms (e.g. *Cc* and *Xx*), whereas others differ (e.g. *Aa* and *Gg*). Subjects were presented with pairs of letters and required to decide as rapidly as possible whether the two had the same *name*, ignoring whether they were printed in upper-case or lower-case; hence, *AA*, *Aa* and *aa* should be judged the "same", while *AB Ab*, *aB* or *ab* should not. This was then converted into a memory test by separating the first and second letters by a delay. Posner and Keele found reliably faster responses when the two were visually identical, even though case was not directly relevant, but only for delays up to 1.5 seconds, after which the case effect vanished. They interpreted this as reflecting judgement based on a visual trace that is readily accessed but fades rapidly, leaving a more durable verbal trace as the basis for later judgements.

At about this time I began to work with Bill Phillips who had joined Sussex having completed a PhD on visual memory in Australia. We were concerned that such a rapidly fading visual trace did not seem consistent with other work on visual memory, and suggested another possibility, namely that the verbal memory trace dominated but took longer to develop, with the result that brief delays favoured visual and longer delays verbal. We decided to avoid letter material and look again at visual short-term memory, employing complex material that could not be verbalised. We chose to use 5×5 chequer board patterns in which each of the 25 cells had a 0.5 probability of being filled. A pattern mask followed to rule out iconic visual sensory memory. This, in turn, was followed by a delay ranging from 0.5 to 9.0 seconds. A second chequer board was then presented that was either identical, or had one cell changed. The subject had to decide whether it was the same or different. We found gradual forgetting over the whole 9-second period, suggesting a much more durable visual code than the 1.5 seconds proposed by Posner and Keele. We published our results in *Psychonomic Science*, a journal that did not require referees to decide whether it was a good paper or not. It was published and has since been ignored. Fortunately however, Bill, who had by this time moved on to Stirling, went on to do a much more systematic study published in a more influential journal. He studied matrices ranging from 16 to 64 cells, over delays up to 9 seconds, finding that amount of forgetting increased systematically with the size of the matrix, which he duly reported in a paper that became deservedly influential.

The method used by Posner and ourselves, known as change detection, had been around at least since the early years of the 20th century, when it was used by psychophysicists to study perception. After a number of years of neglect, the change detection task has become extremely common in the study of visual working memory, principally following the seminal work of Stephen Luck and Edward Vogel that prompted a major surge of papers on visual working memory, of which more later.

Bill continued this line of research after he had moved to Stirling, while Graham Hitch and I, still in Sussex, focussed mainly on exploring the phonological loop. At about this time, people began to investigate the phenomenon of visual imagery, "seeing things in the mind's eye", a topic that would not have been regarded as respectable by traditional neo-behaviourist verbal learners. A step in the direction of respectability came with an elegant demonstration by Roger Shepard, a very creative psychophysicist with immaculate mathematical credentials, who devised a task that became known as mental rotation. The subject was shown a figure representing a complex object followed after varying delays by a second object in a different orientation. The task was to decide whether the represented object was the same or different. The stimuli were chosen so that the negative items were similar to the target except for a leftward or rightward rotation of one of the object's features. Time to make this decision increased linearly with the difference in orientation between the target and the test item, just as if the objects were being mentally rotated at a constant rate before being lined up and then compared with the target. Other paradigms were more complex: for example imagining the folding of a flat piece of paper so as to form a three-dimensional object and then judging the object, a task sometimes used to measure the visuospatial component of intelligence. Here again time and accuracy scores were consistent with the idea of a mental equivalent of manual folding.

A somewhat more surprising claim came from a paper published in 1971 by George Atwood whose study involved memory for a series of brief sentences that were either abstract (e.g. *The intellect of Einstein was a miracle*) or concrete (e.g. *Nudist devours bird*). Each sentence was followed either by a very brief and simple auditory judgement or a simple visual judgement. He found that memory for the abstract sentences was impaired more by the verbal and the concrete sentences by the visual judgement. He interpreted his results in terms of a model that had separate visual and verbal processing and memory components, somewhat similar to our own working memory model. The work generated considerable interest, but we and others were unable to replicate the findings and Atwood himself left the field.

I myself continued to be interested in the area partly as a result of a personal experience. While I was in California, I developed an interest in American football and was listening to the big game between UCLA and Stanford on the radio while driving along the freeway. Spatial location is of course of great importance in the game and I had a very clear visual image of the proceedings when I noticed that the car was weaving from one lane to another. I rapidly switched to music and survived. In Stirling, I decided to try to investigate further this apparent interference between imaging and steering. We did not have a driving simulator but did possess an ancient piece of equipment known as a pursuit rotor. This involved a spot of light following a circular track, with the subject required to keep a stylus in contact with the moving spot. Level of difficulty could be varied by adjusting the speed of rotation with performance measured by time in contact with the light spot.

For my equivalent of the American football game, I capitalised on some ingenious work by the Canadian psychologist Lee Brooks. He studied verbal short-term memory for a series of short phrases, some of which could be assisted by the use of visual imagery while others could not. In one study for example a 4 × 4 matrix is presented with one of the cells deemed the starting square. Subjects must then hear and repeat back a series of sentences such as the following *In the starting square put a one. In the next square to the right put a two. In the next square down put a three. In the next square to the right put a four*, where it is possible to supplement verbal memory by imagining a path traced through the matrix. This strategy can be prevented by substituting non-spatial adjectives for *right, left, up* and *down*, hence *In the starting square put a one. In the next square to the good put a two. In the next square to the weak put a three. In the next square to the bad put a four etc*. Under these latter conditions using the matrix to imagine a path is hopeless and people simple rely on rote verbal memory. This results in a span of about six sentences compared to eight sentences in the spatially encoded condition. We then combined this spatial memory task with performance on the pursuit rotor. We found that tracking and visual imaging interfered with each other, just as I experienced when driving on the freeway.

We concluded that the memory system underpinning the visuospatial sketch pad was *spatial* in nature, a proposal that was later challenged when I gave a talk describing our work at an Attention and Performance meeting. Daniel Kahneman, a highly creative cognitive psychologist who later moved over to decision-making and won a Nobel Prize for Economics, pointed out that our results were consistent with either a visual or a spatial system. There was of course good evidence from perception for separate visual and spatial processing systems involving different anatomical pathways. I agreed, and returned to Stirling to devise an experiment that might separate these two.

The experiment, which became known locally as the pit and the pendulum study, worked as follows: subjects were led into a dimly lit room and shown a pendulum suspended from the roof at the end of which were a beeper and a light cell. They were then given a flashlight and shown that when the light was on the pendulum bob, the tone changed. They were then given practice at keeping the flashlight in contact with the swinging pendulum, initially while watching it, and after practice, while blindfolded, basing their tracking on the location of the sound. This thus became a tracking task that was spatial but not visual. Would it still interfere with visuospatial imagery? Again, using the Brooks task we showed that it did. Our next problem was to devise a condition in which the judgements were visual but not spatial. For this we again placed our subject in a semi-darkened room, this time containing a screen on which a slide projector was focussed and delivered a sequence of slides yielding either bright or less bright overall illumination. The task was to press a button whenever a bright stimulus appeared. Unlike the pit and the pendulum task, brightness judgement had, if anything, more impact on verbal than visual STM.

Our evidence therefore appeared to point clearly in the direction of a spatial rather than a visual system, at least for the visual imagery tasks that we ourselves had studied. This, in turn, led to the question of whether there was some form of rehearsal mechanism, equivalent to that of subvocal speech in the phonological loop. One possibility, suggested a number of years before by the Canadian psychologist Donald Hebb, was that eye movements might serve this purpose. I began to explore this possibility some years later, with the help of Chris Idzhikowski, a physiological psychologist who was working with me principally on the effects of anxiety on parachutists but who was capable of setting up a basic eye movement recording system. We again used the matrix task in which people had to remember spoken sentences describing a path through the matrix, requiring our subjects at the same time to monitor a computer display on which a spot of light jumped from one location to another. People were required to move their eyes to each new location and report an occasional change in the colour of the spot. We duly found an interference effect that was not present when the eye movements were not required, while eye movements did not affect the non-spatial version of the task.

We went on to ask the question of whether it was eye movements themselves, or the need to control them intentionally that was the problem. We did this by borrowing a rotating seat from the Cambridge physiology department and twirling the subjects around, before then requiring them to perform the matrix task. Such rotation induces nystagmus, a tendency for the eyes to move automatically in order to counter the movement of the visual scene, a tendency that continues when the rotation stops. Would this type of automatic eye movement also disrupt visual imagery? Somewhat to our surprise, although we were successful in generating such eye movements, they did not influence performance. Having replicated and extended our initial result, we submitted a paper to a leading journal, only to have it turned down; the two memory referees were very positive, but the eye movement experts were not sufficiently impressed by our somewhat basic measures of eye movement.

By this time I had become intrigued by a further question, namely whether the important aspect of our disruptive effect was the movements of the *eyes* per se, or moving the focus of *attention*, a distinction that had been made very neatly by Michael Posner who demonstrated convincingly that it was possible to look at one point but attend to another. Again we were somewhat surprised to find that switching attention repeatedly from one location to another did not disrupt our spatial memory task, whereas maintaining stable attention but switching the eyes did, implicating eye movements rather than attentional distraction as the source of the memory interference. This was a very interesting result but one where the task of convincing the eye movement enthusiasts seemed even more daunting.

At this point, the situation was further complicated when we replaced the task of switching the eyes from one spot of light to another, using instead a task that involved following a continuous visual path, a procedure known as optical pursuit. We lost our effect! We later discovered that this type of eye movement is quite separate from the so-called saccadic jumps of the eyes from one target to another and does indeed depend on a different part of the brain. Given that this was very much a research sideline rather than my main concern at the time, I decided that it was all too complicated and put the results in a drawer, leaving it there despite the occasional reminders from the several postdoctoral colleagues who had worked on the project over the years. I did, however, mention the results when I came to report our research in a book published some years later that summarised a decade of working memory research.

Many years later I was asked why the work was never published since it had apparently been replicated several times. I and my long-suffering co-authors agreed that if the enquirer, Brad Postle, was able to do a replication using up-to-date eye movement technology, then we would be very happy to have it resubmitted. This duly happened, and we sent it back to the original journal, which, perhaps unsurprisingly given the 20-year delay, declined the resubmission. Happily another journal was more sympathetic.

All the evidence so far pointed to a purely spatial system, but Bob Logie, one of the several postdocs who had worked on the topic with me, was not convinced and was determined to demonstrate otherwise. This required selecting a task that was visual rather than spatial. He chose a paired-associate task that involved learning to link pairs of concrete words such as *octopus* and *telephone* by forming an interactive image: for example of an octopus making a telephone call. During the learning phase, people attempted to ignore concurrent irrelevant stimuli that comprised either spoken words, expected to interfere with phonological coding or a visual equivalent, line drawings of objects. As he predicted the visual imagery condition was disrupted by the irrelevant drawings but not by irrelevant speech. The case for separate visual and spatial components of working memory is now widely accepted. Gerry Quinn, a PhD student who joined me from Stirling University at Sussex, choosing to remain in Sussex rather than switch back to Stirling, has done extensive work in this area, showing that even a simple flickering visual noise pattern can disrupt visual imagery under appropriate conditions. It seems that the claims of Atwood whose original experiments we failed to replicate might be closer to the mark than we originally thought.

Bob has gone on to elaborate his work over the years, producing a model of the sketch pad that assumes two components, a *visual cache* that holds the memory trace and a *spatial rehearsal* system that performs a similar function to subvocal rehearsal in the phonological loop, and that is disrupted by eye movement tasks. Later work has shown that patients occur in which one component is impaired, while the other is intact. For example we studied a very talented sculptor who, as a result of an autoimmune disease, had lost her capacity for short-term visual memory and visual imagination; her original very realistic approach to sculpture was then abandoned in favour of sculpting much more abstract shapes. This was not simply a stylistic change as it was accompanied by an inability to produce even broadly realistic drawings of well-known objects, together with impaired performance on experimental tasks involving the visual component of the sketch pad. In contrast, her spatial abilities were intact, and she had no difficulty in finding the way and driving herself from her home many miles away to the Applied Psychology Unit in Cambridge where we tested her. Other patients showed exactly the opposite pattern of preserved visual but impaired spatial working memory.

The two years spent at Stirling were happy and fruitful ones. The department was rather different from Sussex with a more strongly developmental and applied orientation. It ran, for example, the only master's degree course in childhood psychological disorders, an important but neglected topic at the time that fell between standard courses in clinical and educational psychology. Stirling also had strength in ethology and a primate laboratory interested in behaviour rather than neuroscience together with strength in main stream experimental psychology including attention, visual memory and psycholinguistics. I am happy to say that the department has continued to produce good research even though the planned six professorships never materialised. We were sad to leave but excited to be returning to Cambridge and to the Unit.

15

Returning to the Unit

And so in 1974, I returned to the Applied Psychology Unit in Cambridge, this time as Director. Was I not daunted, asked one friend, to be succeeding such eminent figures as Bartlett and Broadbent? Perhaps I should have been, but I was not, although I was naturally excited at the prospect of directing a research centre that was at the leading edge of both cognitive psychology and its practical applications. Unlike Broadbent, I had not written one of the classic books that launched the cognitive revolution in psychology, but my research was going really well, with the 1974 paper with Graham Hitch about to appear. I knew a large proportion of the scientific and support staff from the nine happy years I had spent there. Finally, if things did not work out, I was confident that I could move back into the university sector.

My first task was to make a series of scientific appointments. Donald had announced his imminent retirement from the Directorship some two years in advance, which meant that no fewer than seven scientific posts were to be filled, together with a research assistantship to work with myself. Happily, the position for tenured posts had recently changed. The previous system involved a series of non-tenured appointments, each initially lasting for three years, then potentially moving onto five-year posts until possibly achieving tenure around age 40. This contrasted with the system in most universities where tenure was typically achieved within your first couple of years. The problem with the Medical Research Council (MRC) system was the uncertainty, made worse by a lack of clarity as to exactly what factors determined your next contract. Was theoretical work more important or application, and who made the decision? The MRC system was very hierarchical, so everything came through the Director who was clearly under constraints from "Head Office" in London, but what these pressures were and how free the Director was to withstand them remained somewhat mysterious.

Such a system was hardly consistent with the rebellious spirit of the 1960s, a situation that seemed to have led to increasing discontent within the Unit. Caught between an apparently rigid MRC system and increasingly rebellious staff, Donald had decided to move on, suggesting that the staff create their own system of governance and giving them two years to do so. This had led to a proliferation of committees and subcommittees, and happily by the time I arrived, most people had discovered that they would much rather be doing science than attempting to set up and run the Unit as a commune. I was effectively left with a blank slate on the question of running the Unit, provided of course I kept the people in Head Office happy. Most people in the Unit already had their ongoing programmes, but with seven unfilled posts, I had plenty of scope for devising an overall plan for the future development of the Unit, a plan that would have to be approved by the MRC Neurosciences Board, a committee mainly comprising senior academics in the broad field of neuroscience.

It might at this point be useful to briefly sketch the way in which the MRC operated at that time and I assume the way it still does. It was one of several research councils funded by the government but not directly government-controlled; others included a rather smaller Social Sciences Research Council and the very much larger Science Research Council, which at the time encompassed all the non-medical or environmental sciences. It has since been split into a number of smaller research councils, such as physical, biological and environmental sciences, probably wisely since it was excessively large and bureaucratic. Happily, although quite a large organisation, I found the MRC to be caring and flexible; with one exception, decisions that directly impinged on the Treasury, the government's financial arms were always imposed with great rigidity; the Treasury has never been renowned for its sensitivity or flexibility, or to my mind, good sense.

The employment rules for recruiting new scientific staff had fortunately changed. It was still possible to employ people for three years or indeed shorter periods on specific projects, particularly if dependent on outside funding. Potential career posts on the other hand were closer to the US version of a tenure-track position, involving a five-year appointment, after which an application for tenure could be made and would be judged by an academic panel set up by the MRC in London. This made recruiting and directing staff a much easier and more congenial enterprise, since both you and they were motivated to build a strong case for a continued career in research, judged in due course by academics who themselves were familiar with hiring scientific staff. I can vouch for the fact that over my 20 years as Director, it was never difficult to attract good people, although it could be hard to fill posts in specific areas where there was currently little research activity. Indeed, if you are keen on research, what could be better than a life in a pleasant and stimulating academic environment with few demands from teaching or administration?

So how had the Unit changed in the seven years since I left? In some ways it felt just the same, the same lovely house, the same general atmosphere, even the smell was the same, helped perhaps by the fact that the same floor polish was used throughout? The garden was just the same with its mulberry tree and orchard, and many of the staff were the same. But something of course was very different; my previous arrivals had been as a student working on a summer job and then as a prospective PhD student. This time I was expected to run the place.

Two of the three most influential people during my time there, Donald Broadbent and Conrad had both moved to Oxford with Christopher Poulton remaining as an Assistant Director. This concerned me initially since I knew that he had been very disappointed when Donald rather than he became the previous Director. Happily, he seemed to have abandoned the idea of directing the Unit himself and was always friendly and supportive, taking responsibility for a range of administrative jobs including our links with the navy and oversight of the sailors who continued to visit Cambridge as participants in experiments. He also ensured that the house remained in good condition, where he was happy to teeter up ladders to examine the guttering or descend into the depths of the drainage system.

The Unit's remit was to provide a bridge between the theoretical development of psychology and its practical applications, while given considerable freedom as to how this was achieved. As you may recall, it had originally developed from a series of projects carried out for the military during the Second World War and for many years, links with the armed forces and in particular the navy, formed a substantial part of the Unit's work. In peacetime, we could clearly no longer rely solely on military projects and other important links were forged by Conrad with the Post Office, hence my own earlier appointment, and by Ivan Brown with the Transport and Road Research Laboratory, a national organisation staffed largely by engineers but with a keen interest in driver behaviour, a focus of Ivan's work throughout his career. His continued involvement over the years, together with his membership of the committee that advised parliament on matters of road transport, meant that Ivan had a genuine and sustained influence on this important applied field. While the Unit as a whole was assumed to link basic and applied research, individuals varied in the balance of their theoretical and practical contributions. Ivan, for example, was an extremely good applied psychologist and agreed to take on links with the Post Office when Conrad left, while others such as John Morton who had joined the Unit since I left would see himself principally as a theorist. He created a highly influential model of language processing and ran weekly theoretical seminars where ideas were the principal currency of discussion, although empirical evidence was tolerated in moderation.

However, although these sustained applied links were important, they did not dominate. Scientists tended to function as individual researchers, who, as they grew in seniority, might acquire a long-term research assistant. People were encouraged to develop their specific theoretical lines of research at the same time as looking for potential practical applications. These could lead to further funding but need not, provided a case could be made for the promise of the work within a broad Unit framework. The possibility of free advice and potentially of direct help meant that the Unit got a wide range of enquiries, often accompanied by a willingness to facilitate further research. This resulted in a flexible organisation and to the recruitment of people who had a clear personal research agenda, coupled with a willingness to investigate its practical applications and to collaborate as and when appropriate.

This was a very different structure from our German equivalent, the Max Planck Institutes, which typically have two or three tenured directors, each directly responsible for a programme involving a team of non-tenured postdoctoral fellows and PhD students. It also differs from the situation that is most common across science generally, and increasingly within psychology, where the pattern seems increasingly to favour an ever smaller number of larger and larger teams typically led by a single individual whose job it is to justify the continuation of his team over the next three to five years by obtaining a continuous stream of grant funding. This typically seems to involve specifying in detail what the team will do and its expected outcome. Such a model has clear advantages in terms of top–down control. Sadly however, this can come at the expense of turning the team leader into an administrator and severely restricting the horizons of the more junior staff. I resolved to maintain a flat management structure, encouraging collaboration both within the Unit and beyond, a structure that allowed more ambitious and varied programmes to develop without overstretching the Unit's limited space. This could, however, be problematic as the top-down political pressure grew, and on one of the five yearly inspections of the Unit's work, I was warned by a committee member that they were instructed to assume a hierarchical model in their report. That evening I went home and invented a structure, asking the Unit secretary to go around the Unit telling people which group they were in but not to worry as things would then proceed as usual. It seemed to work, and we got a good report.

In my next 20 years as Director I was quite frequently asked by visitors, often from North America, how they could set up a similar unit that combined basic and applied research. My answer was that you first need an equivalent of the MRC who are prepared to run a system flexible enough to allow such interaction. By the time I left in the mid-1990s, the system had already begun to change with increasing pressure towards top-down control with more and more scrutiny of each individual and his or her individual contribution. Since the scrutiny came from a panel of academics they tended to value theoretical rather than practical contributions, and after I left, many of the more applied people were encouraged to "move on". It is interesting to note that applied research in the UK is now greatly in favour with considerable top-down pressure for people to apply their results. The pressure appears to come from politicians and to operate through committees who often appear to have very little understanding of just how complex and lengthy the process of turning theoretical work into its practical implementation is. Happily I did not have these constraints and could place our theoretical achievements in the "shop window" during our five yearly academic assessments while keeping the MRC happy in the interim by being able to respond to a wide range of enquiries and at the same time to entertain visiting dignitaries sent up from London by telling them about the practical problems that we were tackling.

Given this rather broad remit, it was the Director's job to develop a coherent and presentable overall Unit research programme. This was both a challenge and an opportunity, provided you could persuade your colleagues that the direction was a sensible one. But what direction? My own interests focussed principally on the area of learning and memory. This, it could be argued, lies at the centre of education that in Western countries, at least, could go on until the early twenties and have a major influence on a country's prosperity. And yet there were very few links between the rapidly developing field of cognitive psychology and the practical issues of education. I made a number of visits to education departments and found a depressing lack of contact with research on learning. Typically, such departments were staffed by ex-schoolteachers who had very little research experience, working in a field that was complex, methodologically difficult and often driven by fashion rather than evidence.

I decided that at least some of my seven appointments should be educationally oriented, not by appointing people from education, a rather barren field at the time, but by appointing good young cognitive psychologists and encouraging them to apply their theories and techniques to areas of potential educational relevance. I suggested that we start with the basic skills of learning and memory, such as reading, writing and arithmetic. From today's viewpoint, I had a remarkably free hand in filling the seven posts. I chose to use a group of the most senior members of the Unit as an appointment committee, but there were no outside members. They agreed to my overall plan and we chose accordingly. To look at learning and memory I appointed Karolyn Patterson, who I knew from my year at UCSD, and who was then at the University of Toronto, together with her husband Roy, a psychoacoustician who would fit very well into the Unit's traditional concern with the practical application of acoustic theory. To look at writing I appointed Alan Wing, an Edinburgh graduate who had completed a PhD at McMaster University in Canada on the timing and control of fine motor movement. I also appointed my ex-postdoc Graham Hitch and encouraged him to study working memory and arithmetic. Arnold Wilkins who had conducted a PhD on semantic memory at Sussex before moving to the Montreal Neurological Institute to work with Brenda Milner was encouraged to apply developments in the study of semantic memory to the topic of knowledge acquisition. To look at reading, we chose Tony Marcel who had been appointed at Sussex while I was there, largely on the strength of some very clever work on reaction time theory. He had then switched to the highly controversial area of unconscious priming in reading, showing that a word flashed so rapidly that it could not be consciously detected was nonetheless able to influence the interpretation of a later word. This proved to be a highly controversial area partly because of its apparent link to the Freudian concept of *the unconscious*, in fact a very different concept. The non-conscious processing of information is now widely accepted.

Our seventh and most unlikely appointment was Tay Wilson, a Canadian social psychologist who I met when he gave a talk at an international conference held in London. Tay worked at a traffic research centre in Ontario where his task was to evaluate the effects on specific communities of local transport changes: for example the closing of a rail commuter line in Canada or the impact of introducing local air connections in Norway. His method was to use what have subsequently become known as focus groups. He would generate discussion within a group of local residents, allowing it to develop and subsequently boiling down the content into a series of salient points illustrated by concrete examples, a method that did appear to have a direct and positive influence on policy. While hardly central to the Unit's focus, I thought that Tay might add another dimension that could make a valuable contribution to our applied research.

Looking back, it seems remarkable that it was possible to make seven such diverse appointments within what seems like a matter of weeks. It was a time of considerable political unrest, with a major miner's strike leading the Conservative Prime Minister Edward Heath, somewhat remarkably, to institute a three-day working week so as to conserve electricity. I am not sure whether this coincided with recruitment, but I have a clear memory of a power cut and the need to interview candidates by the light of a Tilley lamp. I was reminded of the Greek philosopher Diogenes who took to wandering the streets of Athens holding a lamp in the daytime and claiming to search in vain for an honest man. He subsequently developed a philosophy known as Cynicism. As far as I can remember, the selection committee completed our task amicably and without lapsing into cynicism.

This relaxed mode of making five-year appointments provides a huge contrast to the situation today when even minor posts in most universities are likely to involve members of the administrative staff together with major representation from other departments, all required to have taken courses on how to interview, typically run by outside companies with little knowledge of academia. What was also atypical was that I already knew many of the successful applicants. This was partly because when on sabbatical from Sussex, I had been instructed by Stuart to keep an eye open for potential recruits to lectureships while I was in California, a search that I had continued in connection with developing the Stirling Department. Furthermore, the pool of potential candidates was much smaller than today when, for example, our recent advertisement for a lectureship drew 130 applications.

Appointing people you know can, however, be a dangerous business; I can think of at least two British psychology departments with Heads of Department who were themselves talented researchers but who had filled their department with their own students leading to many years of steady decline. An important factor of course was that the appointments were not tenured posts but rather tenure-track research posts with the need at the end of five years to convince an external committee that tenure was justified. With the exception of Tay, our social psychologist who moved on, all achieved tenure and have had or are having distinguished careers. Five of them remained at the Unit for the next 20 years, with three then choosing to take up Chairs and form MRC-funded research groups within a university context, while Graham Hitch left after two or three years to apply our concept of working memory to the study of children.

However, I think I learned most from my wild card Tay the social psychologist, both positive, about how best to organise the Unit's committee structure, and negative, about the perils of being too relaxed about research management. Tay was a very interesting character, tall, bespectacled with long slightly crinkly auburn hair. He was not exactly a dedicated follower of fashion, and on one occasion I complimented him on his bright kingfisher blue sweater. This, he explained, had been sent by his father, a mortician back in Canada. Apparently corpses often come in wearing clothes that the relatives no longer wanted, and any particularly fine ones that looked as though they might fit Tay were posted over to Cambridge, an entirely rational though somewhat odd approach to developing a wardrobe.

I was not entirely sure what to encourage Tay to do but suggested that he look around for potential projects, and in the meantime that he should talk to people at the Unit about their views and come up with suggestions for an organisational structure to replace the proliferation of committees that had grown up during the two years following Donald's announcement of imminent departure. Tay did the rounds and spoke to people, eventually proposing a very simple solution. The scientific staff were very keen to have representation on a committee that determined the scientific broad direction of the Unit and that could also discuss ongoing issues such as appointments. They had little interest in discussing more domestic issues involving the day-to-day running of the Unit, while the technical and administrative staff had an exactly opposite view. The answer seemed to be to keep and reorganise one of the existing committees known as the Research Coordination Group or RCG, and to create a separate more domestically orientated House Committee. In both cases there would be some ex-officio members, but a majority would be elected with a system that ensured that both junior and senior staff would be represented.

I myself chaired the RCG, and over the years, most research staff served at one time or another as elected members. The rules were that I would make the proceedings of the RCG open for general discussion within the Unit wherever possible, except for those involving the discussion of individuals where confidentiality was essential. This worked surprisingly well with remarkably little evidence of "leaking". I found the system very helpful in discussion of matters as they arose. The openness given that anyone was eligible to be elected seemed to lead to a level of trust that made it much easier to deal with potentially disruptive issues than would have been possible in an atmosphere of secrecy.

Meanwhile I asked Tay how he was progressing in developing his own principal project. He seemed rather pleased with it but delayed telling me about it until it was further developed. After a month or two I suggested that it was really time to discuss things in more detail at which point he revealed that he was working on a value-free way of assessing proposals for social change. "That sounds very tricky, how do you manage it?" To which he announced that the first stage was to read the great books of the world and abstract their wisdom. We agreed that the MRC tenure panel might take issue with his plan, and that we should find something a little less ambitious. I did in fact identify a problem from the MRC's Hearing Research Institute in Nottingham, namely to find out why people with age-related hearing loss rapidly abandoned use of the hearing aids provided for them, and Tay agreed that this was a good project. Before it had come to fruition however, he moved to direct a master's degree course in Transport Psychology at neighbouring university. I later learned from someone on his course that he ran a very tight ship, insisting on strong mathematical and statistical skills. I realised that his previous environment, surrounded by engineers, had provided very concrete practical questions within a structured framework that was missing from the Unit. Had I realised this earlier we would have made better use of Tay's talents. I heard from him a few years ago that he was back in Canada and running an institute concerned with social policy and wondered if he had yet finished reading the great books of the world.

Having made my appointments, the next task was to put together a framework for the future direction of the Unit. This I did, emphasising the importance of education and the opportunities offered by the newly developing field of cognitive psychology. The Board made its decision, and I was summoned to London, where I met Bronwen Loader, one of a range of senior administrators who dealt directly with units. Bronwen was a relatively direct Australian who after a research career in biochemistry had moved into administration. She announced that my programme had been rejected by the Board, advising me to go home, have a few drinks and then start again next day. I explained indignantly that I had presented my programme to the Chief Executive of the MRC who had apparently approved it! "Oh, she explained, he likes to be nice to people, do you have anything in writing?" Making a note on the writing part for future use, I returned home surprised but not too dejected. I had appointed people because they were good scientists, not because they worked on education. They and everyone else at the Unit had good ongoing projects, so it was up to me to find a framework that could provide a plausible way ahead.

I decided on neuropsychology, impressed by the way in which the study of single cases had informed and challenged theory in understanding both memory and language and was excited by its future potential. There was one major problem however. There was a complete absence of any strength in neuropsychology at the Cambridge hospital Addenbrooke's, which had only just started the process of moving from a somewhat limited regional hospital to the clinical research arm of a great university, a process that was to take a number of years. I suspect that if I had started with this proposal, it would have been rejected as impractical on that basis. However, since I had been appointed, as had my seven staff, the Neurosciences Board settled for the way ahead that I proposed.

My new proposal had involved a degree of rebranding. In my own case, I had published both theoretical and potentially applied work on amnesia. Arnold Wilkins had just come back from the Montreal Neurological Institute where he had found photosensitive epilepsy to be a more fruitful area than the semantic memory studies from his PhD. He has continued the fruitful study of the effects of visual stress on reading, epilepsy and migraine for his whole career. Karolyn Patterson later became interested in disorders of reading and has had a distinguished career, much of it using single case studies to understand semantic memory, recently acknowledged by her election to the Royal Society. Alan Wing continued to study handwriting as proposed but extended his remit to include a wider range of movement and its disorders, building strong links to physiotherapy.

We aimed to solve the patient access problem through collaboration, providing an input from cognitive psychology to the study of a range of clinical cognitive deficits, and as time went on Addenbrooke's Hospital did indeed develop into a world-class centre for clinical research, allowing a steadily increasing degree of fruitful collaboration. Meanwhile, our need to develop links outside the Unit had two advantages: it allowed expansion of our research programme without needing to increase the limited space available within the Unit, and second it allowed us to export our developing concepts of cognitive psychology into an ever-widening clinical field. In retrospect, I am sure the Board made the right decision in rejecting my first proposals. Financially tough times were ahead, and we would have found it increasingly difficult to justify the spending of funds allocated to neuroscience on educational research, an area that was supposed to be covered by a totally different research council.

So what should my own role be within Tay's suggested restructuring? The MRC saw the Director as solely responsible for the Unit, allowing him or her to choose the way in which their unit was run. In my case, I saw myself as a research scientist with managerial responsibilities rather than an administrator with scientific interests, deciding that it was essential that I continued to function as a very active research scientist. In that connection, I tried to ensure that I published at least as much as my leading colleagues. This raised the question of how best to balance the potentially competing demands of research and management. I remembered that Donald had tackled the problem by discouraging people from approaching him over administrative matters during the daily tea and coffee sessions, instead putting a notice on his door which had a series of specified 10-minute slots for you to sign if you wished to talk to him on administrative matters. I remember feeling uncomfortable about this; sometimes it could just take a minute and sometimes longer than 10 minutes and signing seemed to be making a statement of some sort. I decided that I would let people approach me at anytime, and see how it worked out.

For the most part it worked well. Most of my research involved collaboration and people did not interrupt research-related discussions. The main potential problem was, however, with writing, and I suspect this is what Donald found difficult if people were constantly interrupting. Fortunately, I had discovered a way around this problem. While in Stirling, I was invited to give a talk on theories of amnesia at a conference. This was a very active area and needed a good deal of preparation and thought, which left virtually no time to write the chapter that was invited for the proceedings of the conference. This seemed a pity, given that I had finally gained what seemed like a clear understanding of the field but knew that I would have no time afterwards to write the chapter. As a desperate gamble, I decided that I would try to dictate the chapter, shutting myself in a testing cubicle and as I thought, giving the lecture. To my surprise and relief, the result required little further elaboration and I delivered my chapter on time.

I now know that it was very unlikely that what I produced was equivalent to the lecture that I gave; good writing and speaking styles are very different and my occasional attempts to use a recorded lecture as a basis for a chapter have proved very unsatisfactory. What I had discovered was that I appear to be able to write reasonable prose by dictation, and from that point on, this has been my preferred method of "writing". Furthermore I found that rather than shutting myself in testing cubicle, things worked better if I walked in the open air, preferably through pleasant countryside, perhaps with a pint at a pub at the end of the day. However, if the weather is bad as it is right now, I can pace up and down inside and still produce prose that does not need too much subsequent editing, although the less formal resulting style has occasionally been deemed "unsuitable" by some of the more austere journals.

The fact that I could write in this way meant that I could easily escape potential interruptions by taking one of the very pleasant walks that I found around Cambridge. My writing life became even better a few years later when we bought a cottage about half an hour's drive away. Cambridge is a very attractive city but one that is surrounded by very flat country, fens that were once marshland and have now been drained resulting in very fertile soil but limited in scenic beauty. As a result of our boys going on a summer camp, we discovered that beyond the fens was the county of Norfolk with rolling countryside and a very attractive coast. We had recently tried to buy a larger Cambridge house having discovered that our mortgage could be increased. We were outbid, but assuming we could get a mortgage, we decided to look for a cottage in Norfolk.

We eventually found one on the edge of the royal estate of Sandringham. It was a semi-detached (duplex) brick house that had previously provided accommodation for agricultural workers on the royal estate, becoming redundant when the number of workers was drastically reduced by mech- anisation. It had running water but no bathroom and a toilet that formed part of a jumble of sheds in the back garden. We really liked the house, but it did have a crack in the wall, which was slightly worrying. Reassured by the opinion of a builder who thought it could probably be readily cor- rected, we took a chance on this and put in a bid to the Queen's solicitor, offering a little less than the asking price £2950 (about 4500 $ US). Her Majesty's solicitor replied that the Queen did not haggle, and we agreed to the full price, only to encounter another snag when her solicitor rejected our purchase contract on the grounds that it did not leave sufficient space for Her Majesty's signature! The document was duly amended and went ahead. We were unable to increase our mortgage but obtained a loan from the bank, who were distinctly impressed by our royal document.

The cottage proved to be a wonderful bolt hole with lots of pleasant walks around. It was easy to travel there for the weekend or in the summer, to spend longer periods and it proved ideal for writing. The builder was correct about the crack and because the cottage was in rather a rundown condition, I convinced myself that even someone with my limited skills could improve it. I even discovered a limited talent for tiling, setting up a primitive shower that was fine except that when in use, the showeree kept being attacked by the clammy surrounding plastic curtain. We furnished the place largely from the sales of furniture, often by departing young academics who were leaving the country and were pleased to get rid of their limited possessions, while beds came from a nurses' hostel that was being refurbished. Our children loved the idea that they could bounce up and down on the furniture and I relished the fact that we had no telephone. While staying there I would walk to the public call box in the village and ring my secretary to check if anything urgent had cropped up. If it had, she would ring back when my coins ran out and we could discuss it or if necessary I could drive back in half an hour, although this rarely, if ever, arose. We continued to use the cottage until, after 20 years at the Unit, I resigned the Directorship and moved on, opting for a similar arrangement between our next home in Bristol where we lived midweek and a cottage in a small Devonshire village that offered equally pleasant walks and a rather better pub.

I did of course have administrative responsibilities in running the Unit, which eventually grew in size to almost a 100 people, although my load was lighter than that of the head of a university department, with no teaching to organise and no university committees to attend. The MRC at the time had a policy of appointing directors and then letting them get on with research, provided that the five-yearly assessments indicated that they were doing a good job. This meant that the Director had considerable power, not only to decide how funds and space were allocated, and to recommend promotions but also in determining the scientific course of the Unit. I remembered a conversation with George Mandler and his wife Jean over lunch shortly after I had arrived in California for my stay at UCSD. George asked whether we would prefer to have power or influence; both Jean and I opted for influence and George for power. I think he was feeling withdrawal symptoms after retiring as a period as first head of the new department when he had done a really terrific job in attracting outstanding staff. The cost of power over influence lies in the potential lack of trust. Even if the Director is correct in his decisions, taken on a totally altruistic basis, conspiracy theories will arise. As I believed that the Unit's aims and my own were in line, I resolved to be as open as possible about issues, realising that trust is an extremely powerful facilitator, slow to accumulate and potentially rapidly lost, but which once earned, allows administration to go rapidly and smoothly.

Over time, trust became increasingly important as constant political pressure from a Thatcherite government led the MRC to become more bureaucratic and less trusting. A good example was the government's simplistic attempt to motivate staff by introducing "performance-related pay" whereby each year, everyone was evaluated and, provided their evaluation indicated improvement, given a very modest increase in salary from a very limited pot of money. The system simply led to grade inflation and dissatisfaction; people who had been doing a good, worthwhile job for many years, and hence were highly valuable to the Unit, could not be constantly promoted and tended to feel that they were failing. Indeed one important role as Director was to try to insulate the Unit as far as possible from the effects of such ill-judged attempts at top-down control. Over the years however, I became increasingly involved in various national committees both within and beyond the MRC. Once I understood how things worked both within the Unit and within the council, it proved possible to delegate more and more to senior staff, many of whom proved excellent managers who were happy to take some of the load alongside their scientific programmes.

However, this account is principally about my life as a scientist, and that will provide the focus for most of the remaining chapters. I have always liked to have more than one research theme running at any given time so that a lull or setback in one meant that progress was perhaps being made in others. This approach was well-suited to the Unit with its broad range of applied queries and opportunities running alongside my continuing theoretical focus on memory. Because of this parallel and ever-changing pattern, the next few chapters will switch from a chronologically based structure to one based on a number of broadly based themes that may well have earlier roots, and that often continued after my period at the Unit. This is certainly the case for my continuing theoretical interests in working memory and in amnesia. Other topics were more constrained in time, one example being psychology and the law, where my period of active research has been limited, but where my interest has continued. It provides a good example of the challenges, complexities and often frustrations of attempting to carry out research in areas that might have influence on the world beyond the laboratory and will be described next.

16

Encounters with the Law

Psychologists have been interested in the implications of their work for the legal system since the early years of the last century when in 1908, Hugo Munsterberg published a book entitled "On the Witness Stand". Munsterberg was a German psychologist who became one of the first appointments to the newly developed department in Harvard. He was an enthusiastic experimentalist who favoured taking psychology out of the laboratory and applying it to practical problems, unlike his professor William James, who was more attracted to the philosophical implications of the subject, and who seems to have regarded experiments as rather boring. Happily James also liked to have around him talented people with different views. Many of the points made in Munsterberg's book are sadly all too familiar today, as when he warned against "the blind confidence in the observations of the average normal man" and argued strongly against the current ways of interrogating suspects, commenting that "brutality is still the favoured method of undermining the mental resistance of the accused". He went on to argue that "the method is ineffective in bringing out the real truth", with the result that "crimes that were never committed have been confessed, infamous lies have been invented, to satisfy the demands of the torturers", alas, a claim that could still be made today, all too frequently.

So how much progress has been made in the last 100 years? Far less than Munsterberg might have hoped, partly at least for reasons that are reflected in my own sporadic encounters with the law. Happily genuine progress has been made, largely due to investigators such as Elizabeth Loftus, who has devoted her whole career to attempting to improve the judicial system and who has certainly made a genuine impact. We will return to this issue at the end of this chapter. However, the main purpose of this chapter is to use my own sporadic involvement with the law to illustrate one aspect of the work of the Unit, namely to respond to requests for help and advice, often from government sources. These may involve difficult questions that do not necessarily have clear answers but which challenge existing knowledge and theories in interesting and sometimes productive ways.

The first of my occasional encounters with the legal system occurred shortly after I arrived back at the Unit when I received a call from a solicitor representing his client, a professional criminal from the East End of London called George Davis. He was being tried for a violent robbery of which he claimed complete innocence, with the evidence apparently relying heavily on the testimony of a policeman who claimed to recognise the accused as someone he had seen at the scene of the crime some 11 months before. The solicitor wanted me to testify that this would have been impossible because of the delay. I explained that I knew of no evidence on the issue and could not produce the statement he wanted. I asked him a little more about the case and discovered that shortly before picking out George Davis from a police line-up, the witness had been shown a photograph of the accused. I suggested that this was much less defensible, but the solicitor was unconvinced and rung off. Davis was duly tried and found guilty and sentenced to many years in prison.

At this point his friends and family began to organise a massive protest, with marchers carrying placards protesting outside parliament, something unheard of in the London criminal community from which he came, where "spells inside" were regarded as the acceptable cost of their profession. The most dramatic form of protest came during a five-day cricket match between England and Australia, one of the sporting highlights of the English summer, when protesters climbed over the wall of the ground one night and dug up the cricket pitch. This caused the whole match to be abandoned since it is crucial that the same strip of turf be used throughout the game since its gradual deterioration throughout the match plays an important role in the outcome. The Appeals Court refused a retrial, but very exceptionally, this was overturned by the Home Secretary, the senior relevant government minister, on the grounds that it was an "unsafe committal", although he did not rule that Davis was innocent. He was duly released, only to be rearrested some two years later when caught driving the getaway car from a raid on the Bank of Cyprus, with firearms on the seat next to him. He pleaded guilty and in due course served his time, subsequently returning to prison again after pleading guilty to yet another robbery. It was not prison his family had protested about, but being "fitted up" by the Metropolitan Police. The unreliability of the eyewitness evidence that falsely convicted Davis was increasingly recognised at around this time. It led to the setting up of a Royal Commission, an official investigation into the issue, that questioned the soundness of much eyewitness testimony, noting the powerful influence based on claims of person recognition on the outcome of trials, recommending that no one should be found guilty on eyewitness testimony alone.

My own involvement with the related issue of face recognition came shortly afterwards with a request to advise on the possibility of developing a means of improving face recognition performance. This certainly seemed an interesting project but one that raised an unexpected moral dilemma since the request came from the British Army, who were interested in identifying at passport and checkpoints known members of the Irish Republican Army (IRA) who were heavily involved in a bombing campaign both in Northern Ireland and in England. It raised two dilemmas: should I work for the army? And should I work on this particular project? The first was relatively easy to solve. I am not a pacifist. I appreciate that passive resistance can be an effective tool, as in latter days of the British presence in India. However, it is only likely to work with a government that is capable of being shamed and hence would be unlikely to have had much influence on more ruthless regimes such as those imposed by Stalin or Hitler. Therefore I feel that I should support our armed forces if asked, in connection with projects that themselves seem ethically justifiable. I had, for example, served briefly as a consultant on the control of antitank missiles, on grounds that anyone approaching us in tanks is unlikely to be an innocent victim.

Improving face recognition, however, might potentially develop skills that could be employed by a dictatorship against the innocent, as indeed could any of many scientific developments. So what about the IRA? As a high school student of 19th-century British history, the "Irish Question" had loomed large with the repeated attempts by successive governments to provide home rule, being frustrated by the problem of the northern six counties, where a majority of the population were Protestants who were just as unenthusiastic about joining an Ireland that was heavily influenced by a very conservative branch of the Roman Catholic Church as the Ulster Catholics were to remain part of Great Britain rather than Ireland. Both sides were committing atrocities, which in the case of the IRA involved blowing up a shopping centre in Manchester and a pub in Birmingham, and attempting an assassination of Prime Minister Margaret Thatcher by placing a bomb beneath the room she was occupying at a party conference in Brighton. If better face recognition could do anything to make such atrocities less likely to happen, then I reckoned the project was justified but preferably kept rather quiet since we would have been the softest of soft potential targets.

The army already had their own course aimed at training people to recognise faces using a system developed by Jacques Penry, an entrepreneur who had developed a system called photofit that claimed to enable witnesses to communicate faces they had seen to an investigative team. It was based on the assumption that any face can be broken down into a number of different features, such as overall shape, eyes, nose, chin, etc. Multiple photographic representations of each were provided which could then be individually selected and fitted together by an eyewitness to represent the remembered face. A group of psychologists at Aberdeen University were investigating this system on behalf of the Home Office, the department of government concerned with policing crime.

The basis of the Army course was to teach participants how to "read" a face, that it is to break it down into its constituent features, in each case noting the relevant characteristics and any peculiarities, the assumption being that this analysis would enhance later memory of the face. It was a thorough course lasting three days, and we were allowed to test participants both before and after so as to measure its effectiveness. We conducted three studies, each using a slightly different method of assessment, and each comparing trainees with a similar group who had not undergone training. Only our third study produced any difference, and that was in the wrong direction, the course made people very slightly worse at remembering faces.

So could we do any better? We decided to apply the concept of Levels of Processing to face recognition; you may recall that memory for words is substantially better if the word is processed in terms of its meaning rather than its appearance or sound. There was already a little evidence that something similar might work for face memory. In one study, judging the personality of the person pictured led to better subsequent recognition than a more superficial judgement of their sex, while another study found pleasantness judgements to be somewhat better than estimating the person's probable height, although neither of these results was particularly strong and both were open to possible objections.

I set up a series of experiments in collaboration with Karalyn Patterson who came with a background in long-term memory although principally using verbal materials. We compared two conditions. In one, people had to judge the physical characteristics of each face, whether the lips were thin or full, the nose small or large, eyes close together or far apart and whether the face shape was long or round. The second group made "deeper" judgements as to whether the person depicted was nice or nasty, reliable or unreliable, intelligent or not and lively or dull. The "deeper" processing helped later recognition, but the size of the effect was tiny. We next tried to enhance the depth of processing by providing relatively rich information about the character portrayed, his background, habits, strengths and weaknesses: for example a *sailor from Portsmouth, a keen fisherman but with a quick temper.* All to no avail, we did get a higher detection rate when the person's picture was presented alongside such a description, but unfortunately this went along with a higher false positive rate since people were also liable to judge *new* faces as familiar when presented alongside an old character description.

We carried out a range of other experiments on the effects of disguise, changing aspects such as hairstyle and the presence or absence of a beard, a moustache or spectacles. We found that each changed feature lowered the probability of later recognition, something more useful to the IRA than the army. As part of this study we also manipulated the pose adopted in the original target picture, either frontal, three-quarter or profile. We found a clear three-quarter view advantage. I became quite excited by this finding; should passport photos all be three-quarter rather than full face? I was even more intrigued on visiting the National Portrait Gallery in London to discover that traditional painters strongly favoured a three-quarter view, although somewhat mysteriously this effect disappeared in modern portraits. I contacted a Professor at the Slade School of Fine Art in London who was himself a renowned portrait painter and he kindly invited me along to lunch to discuss the matter. Far from supporting my hypothesis regarding the wisdom of the historic portrait painters in selecting a three-quarter view, he attributed the change to the increasing use of photographs by modern portraitists, suggesting that frontal views are hard to do well but are greatly helped by an appropriate photograph.

Somewhat disappointed at the rather prosaic end to my foray into the art world, I reminded myself that the three-quarter view was still better, even with photographs, and set out to demonstrate that this was an effect of sufficient size to be taken seriously in the world outside, perhaps even changing the nature of passport photographs. Bob Logie and I decided to take advantage of a contact I had with the local newspaper, the Cambridge News to set up a field study in which the newspaper would publish pictures of "targets", people who would be in their local area at a specific time, who they were encouraged to look out for, detect and report. The Cambridge News assured me that they always had lots of responses to any such competition. Furthermore, they offered to print different pictures for each of three editions of the paper, one for each of three surrounding towns so that if person A was frontal in one town, he would be profile in the second and three-quarter in the third. The experiment was put out on the Friday evening edition for the following day and I sat at the telephone all Saturday awaiting the promised large number of responses.

After many hours I had amassed one single response, which in fact came from a profile view. Perhaps we should not have been so surprised. I then remembered that a somewhat similar situation had been used in the 1920s and 1930s initially by the Westminster Gazette, which was concerned by falling sales, particularly during holiday weeks when people would cancel their normal weekly subscription. Their scheme involved showing a picture of a reporter, "Lobby Lud" who would then wander around a seaside town. Readers were encouraged to look for him while carrying a copy of the Westminster Gazette and on detecting him to tap him with the newspaper, declaring, "you are Lobby Lud and I claim my five pounds". Not many prizes were claimed.

Undeterred, we decided to try again, this time in Cambridge, relying on our panel of volunteer participants who we knew we could trust to do their best to help. We confined the targets to a central region of the city and asked our volunteers to spend at least 15 minutes in that area, paying them the usual subject participation fee. A total of 43 people took part, of whom 34 detected no one; there were two correct detections, one frontal and one three-quarter, and 28 false alarms. We had taken the precaution of asking two of our colleagues to join the search; they would have the advantage of knowing the targets, but even their detection rate was very low, one target each. They did, however, make the useful comment that people simply don't look at faces when shopping. We had one final experiment in which 145 volunteers were looking for a single target, a third were given a frontal, a third profile and a third three-quarter photograph. They were instructed to follow a circular route and were told that the target would be circulating in the opposite direction. We finally got a reasonable detection rate with 70% identifying and reporting the target correctly. There was, however, no pose effect. So, were we wrong about the three-quarter view?

We went back to the laboratory using a live target with participants being introduced to the individual and then later required to select that person from a large set of photographs with a third of people tested encountering the target in each pose. Our three-quarter advantage returned. So what had we learnt from our foray into the real world? We had learnt that effects consistently detected in the laboratory do not necessarily survive outside, a valuable lesion for any would-be applied psychologist. We had learnt that the army course was unsuccessful but had failed to find a good replacement. The training problem has not gone away, and extensive courses still exist, together with a detailed syllabus of what they should contain, as formulated by an international organisation involving law enforcement agencies from around the world. There appears, however, to be no adequate validation of its effectiveness, and attempts to validate the component parts appear to have been unsuccessful. Furthermore, I suspect that disguise is still highly effective, should it be needed. There has, however, been some progress in training people to detect individual target faces from photographs, where presenting multiple views of the same face does increase the chance of subsequent detection.

By the end of our programme we had tested 400 different people and noticed substantial differences in how well they performed. We decided to call back 19 of the best detectors and 19 of the worst and retest them seeing how well they could remember and recognise 50 pictures of unfamiliar faces, 50 paintings of objects and scenes and 50 concrete words. We then tested each of these sets of 50 items, pairing each old item with a new item from the same category and asking people to detect which they had seen before. As expected, the good face recognisers were still good and were also better at recognising pictures, whereas no difference occurred in word recognition. Interestingly, when we asked people whether they were better at visual or verbal memory, both good and poor face recognisers reported that their visual memory was better. Although we did not realise it at the time, our detection of large differences in how good people are at recognising faces offers a hint as to one of the very few effective ways of improving face recognition performance, namely by testing applicants for the job and excluding those with poor face memory, a strategy currently employed in London by the Metropolitan Police who have a very effective team of carefully selected "super-recognisers".

However, by far the most important outcome from work associated with the project came not from me but from my PhD student Vicky Bruce, who was studying visual long-term memory. She began by looking at memory for simple scenes and comparing retention of different aspects such as colour, object shape and location. Not finding anything exciting she decided that she would also look at faces and after one or two experiments came up with the question of how we recognise *familiar* faces. She developed a method she called the "face in the crowd" technique in which the task is to look for one or more people amongst an array of pictured individuals using the nature of the non-targets to understand what sorts of factors were important. In one study, the task was to look for the last four British Prime Ministers amidst an array of either other politicians or equally familiar TV actors and personalities. She found that the presence of other politicians rather than actors or TV personalities of a similar age slowed down performance. Although this might appear to be a purely visual task, the semantic feature of occupation seemed to enter the judgement.

Another method resembled that of waiting at the gate of a train station and looking for a friend passing through. She again found that looking for a recent Prime Minister, Harold Wilson, led to slower responses when he was mixed in with other politicians but only when the distractors were visually similar to the target. In a further study she replicated our previously observed three-quarter view advantage but only for unfamiliar faces; familiar people were equally well recognised regardless of viewpoint. This pattern of results suggests a crucial distinction between the way in which we remember and recognise unfamiliar people, and our recognition of those people who are known to us. Furthermore, it indicated that semantic factors such as profession influence the apparently purely visual decision of whether this photograph fits the target or not. This distinction is somewhat similar to that between an unfamiliar nonsense syllable such as *nog* and a meaningful word such as *dog*, both conveying a similar amount of visual and phonological information, but one taps into a rich array of associated knowledge.

Following this line of argument, she and Andrew Young subsequently developed an information-processing model similar to that proposed for word recognition. Their model assumes a first stage of encoding the visual structure of the face, followed by extraction of information on expression, age, gender and speech. In the case of a familiar face, they assume that stored representations of that face already exist in long-term memory, which contain semantic information about the person, potentially also linking the face to a body of knowledge about that person, often including a name. The model has proved extremely fruitful and influential in investigating a wide range of aspects of face recognition from the encoding of emotion through to neuropsychological disorders of face recognition.

Although exciting, the model was necessarily quite complex, not likely to lead to an area of research that should be undertaken lightly. In view of my other commitments I myself decided to drop out of the field of face recognition. It has since, expanded hugely. Much of the research continues to be focussed on photographs of unfamiliar faces, which seem to be processed by the brain as a particular kind of complex visual pattern in contrast to the rich and meaningful three-dimensional representation of familiar faces. As my colleague Rob Jenkins has recently shown, people are extremely bad at deciding from an array of photographs of unfamiliar people, which ones represent the same person, even having difficulty in deciding whether a simultaneously presented array of faces comprises one, two or many people. This has serious implications for law enforcement, since the capacity to decide whether an individual is the same as that shown on their passport is distinctly limited, as is the ability to identify someone from a video clip. However, if you know the person, then performance in such situations can be very high.

So, although our search for a way of training people to recognise faces was ultimately fruitless, it did indirectly lead to a theoretical breakthrough. Unfortunately, no such claim can be made to our response to the next request for research on matters concerning the law. The Medical Research Council was asked by the judiciary to advise on the question of whether the jury in complex financial fraud trials could reasonably be assumed to understand the issues on which their final judgement was made. As such trials could go on for several weeks and concerned arcane points of law and accountancy, the answer would seem to be clear, but we said that we would do our best. The obvious starting point seemed to be to question jurors who had taken part in such trials. This we were told would be totally illegal. I can understand why talking to jurors before the trial should be banned, but why not talk to them afterwards? I suspect that it is because the jury's deliberations need to be kept private for fear of reprisals from convicted criminals or indeed potential embarrassment to the judiciary.

We would clearly need some kind of simulation but could not, within the limited budget, expect a sufficiently large number of people to sit through a trial potentially of many weeks, so eventually we settled for listening to a judge's summing up, a mere hour and a half in length, combining it with the relatively innocuous question of whether rest breaks every 20 minutes might help. They didn't. We tested over 50 people, some carefully selected to match a typical jury and some simply using our regular volunteers. The two groups gave the same results, with only four of the 50 claiming that they understood the proceedings and a further three reporting "some general understanding", whereas the remainder reported little or no comprehension. These self-ratings were closely linked to the individual's performance on a multiple choice questionnaire on features on the trial. Under 50% of answers were correct, which, given that a score of 25% would be obtained purely by guessing, is not impressive. It is of course entirely possible that if our volunteers had spent the previous several weeks listening to the case they may have understood and possibly also remembered sufficient to make an informed judgement, but I doubt it.

Many weeks after the submission of our report, the judiciary decided that denying those accused of financial chicanery the privilege of a jury trial, in favour of judgement by informed experts, would be too big a step to take and that the situation should remain the same. The conviction rate following fraud trials in the UK is extremely low, they are very expensive, and it is very hard to prove guilt, given a sufficiently clever and well-remunerated defence counsel. At present, we seem to rely on the fraud having implications for the US, where conviction rates are much higher. Interestingly, the issue of jurors and fraud trials cropped up again recently, around 25 years after our study. The law moves very slowly, and I expect a similar conclusion.

Another request for advice that arrived via MRC Head Office came directly from Prime Minister Margaret Thatcher. It was a period when she and Ronald Reagan appeared to be on particularly good terms. There had been one of the spy scandals that crop up from time to time, and Reagan apparently advocated that our government should employ lie detector tests in order to avoid such embarrassments. I was summoned to the Cabinet Office in Whitehall and briefed by one of her civil servants, requesting that we provide a reasoned and balanced assessment of the strengths and weaknesses of lie detectors. I was a little concerned that our advice might be ignored, and the decision nonetheless attributed to the Medical Research Council. I explained my concern, referring to the incident when Tony Benn, as Minister in charge of Telecommunications, had asked the Unit whether London telephone numbers should be changed from geographically based names such as WHI (for Whitehall) 1212 to an all-digit system. My boss Conrad had investigated and found that this would make them *harder* to remember and use. Benn went ahead regardless with the change, reporting it as "following the recommendation of the Medical Research Council". When Conrad complained, Benn justified this on the grounds that the change did come *after* our recommendation. Benn had, by the time of the lie detector enquiry, become a holier-than-thou left-wing figure, certainly not someone that Thatcher would want to emulate. I explained that if the government did a "Tony Benn", then I would feel obliged to make it clear what had happened and was reassured it would not.

The Unit was fortunate at the time to have an amiable Canadian psychophysiologist, Archie Levey, who had joined us when his old Unit closed due to the retirement of its director. He undertook the task and did a brilliant job scientifically in producing a balanced account of the evidence. Lie detectors pick up the emotional responses of the person being questioned, and much of the time this can detect someone who is deliberately trying to lie. He pointed out, however, that some people show an emotional response when not lying and that this constitutes a sufficiently large proportion of the population as to be distinctly worrying. How many loyal civil servants would the PM be prepared to lose because they were unduly nervous at the wrong time and what would be the impact on their colleagues? Furthermore, it is possible to fool the lie detector test by inducing an emotional response at the wrong moment. Finally, certain individuals do not show such a response, either through careful training or because of their personality, the charming psychopath who might incidentally make an excellent spy. Archie did mention a couple of further points that he suspected might be of background interest, namely that the origin of the lie detector test came from collaboration between a Police Chief and a Harvard academic who subsequently left academia becoming the inventor of the comic book character Wonder Woman. The report was duly submitted, and Margaret Thatcher decided against adopting the lie detector, crediting advice from the Medical Research Council. There were in fact other reports coming to similar conclusions, but I suspect having the right person produce the right report at the right time helped the UK to avoid a major policy change.

My final encounter with the legal system came many years later when I was contacted by a solicitor who was appealing against a judgement of infanticide by a young mother, Sally Clark, who had lost two children as a result of what is known in Britain as *cot death* and in the US as *Sudden Infant Death Syndrome* (SIDS). She had been tried and found guilty, it was claimed, largely on the strength of the testimony of a paediatrician, Professor Roy Meadow, who was regularly called in such cases. He had proposed what became known as *Meadow's Law*, which asserted that one such infant death is a tragedy, two highly suspicious and three is murder unless proved otherwise. He based this conclusion on the totally unfounded assumption that such happily rare events were entirely due to chance, and hence that it was vanishingly unlikely that the same person would be unlucky more than once. The possibility, indeed probability, that there might be an underlying genetic or environmental basis to such events was completely ignored.

I was consulted because Meadow had another less well-known law, namely that if the mother did not have a clear memory of the situation, then this was also a sign of guilt. This conclusion was based on his own observations of cases that had been found guilty, typically following Meadow's Law. There was no comparison group of innocent people with clear memories, nor was there any sensible measure of precision of memory.

I was asked if I was prepared to comment on this and agreed. The case came to appeal, and the previous judgement was happily thrown out, together with extensive criticism of Meadow and his reasoning. Meadow's earlier cases were reopened and the whole situation re-evaluated. I did not need to testify and to the best of my knowledge, Meadow's eccentric views on memory have now been forgotten.

I was, however, horrified at the quality of "expert" evidence that could sway such a case. I was told that judges had been known to chastise defence counsels for their impunity in challenging the "distinguished" Professor Meadow. I myself had consistently over the years refused to testify in court on the grounds that my evidence would be neither black nor white, and hence unlikely to help either the prosecution or the defence. This case seemed to reinforce my position. I decided to try to question the position of the expert witness in the British system, a grossly overambitious aim but one that seemed more realistic when I happened to be sitting next to the President of the Royal Society, the principal scientific establishment in Britain. I mentioned my concern and it turned out that he had recently met up with an old friend from Australia who had come over to investigate just how expert witnesses were handled in the UK. His friend had concluded that the situation was even worse in the Britain than in Australia. I received a sympathetic hearing and it was agreed that he would set up a meeting between the Royal Society and a senior law lord.

He succeeded, and we duly turned up at the Old Bailey, the centre of the British legal establishment, going through shadowy corridors to a meeting room where not one but several law lords appeared. They too were concerned about the quality of expert witnesses, and had a plan. They wanted the Royal Society to set up and run a system for vetting expert witnesses. Alas, this was not the sort of thing the RS felt it could or should do. The meeting concluded with an agreement that further meetings should be arranged. I am still waiting.

The British legal system does not seem to emerge from this account with any great credit. This reflects my own opinion, that it is extremely conservative. The judiciary is certainly drawn principally from a narrow and privileged stratum of society, and takes an inordinate amount of time and money, to reach what are not necessarily particularly safe conclusions. It is however, probably the case that you would be very unwise to try to bribe a British judge, and through a number of observations on committees over the years, I have been impressed by the astuteness and fair-mindedness of those who reach the highest range within the judicial system. But the system does need to change.

So, throughout a lifetime in research, my contact with the law has been at best sporadic, and any influence minimal. Why then should I write about it? I think it reflects some of the problems of attempting to interact with and influence long-standing systems in the world outside the laboratory. It is significant that the one point of genuine impact, advice on lie detection reflected work done by many people in different countries over many years rather than the outcome of a specific research project. Individual projects can be useful as providing the accumulation of evidence that eventually may justify a change to the system. This has occurred in the case of eyewitness testimony where Elizabeth Loftus's career has been devoted to informing the judiciary about the fallibility and the potential suggestibility of witnesses of dramatic events. A striking example in the problem arose from the widespread but poorly justified assumption that adult mental illness often results from repressed experiences of childhood abuse. This can lead to the conclusion that such illness implies abuse and that uncovering it will be therapeutic. Loftus has shown that such a situation can readily give rise to the creation of false memories that can have devastating effects on both patients and their families. This is a complex and highly emotive area demanding both courage and persistence over many years but one in which Loftus has had a genuine influence on the US legal system.

Other psychologists have also made a genuine impact on the legal process, as in the case of Gisli Gudjonson a London-based Icelander, who has devoted much of his career to the issue of false confession, how it can be avoided and if not avoided, then detected against a natural tendency for law enforcement agencies to look for a clear and simple way of "solving" a crime. The forensic application of cognitive psychology is likely to continue to be important, with substantial contributions made from those who devote their career to it, and a lesser but still one hopes useful contribution being made by more sporadic and less sustained attempts to apply the developing field of cognitive psychology to legal problems.

17

Stress

From Sky Diving to Anaesthetics

The Applied Psychology Unit was founded during the Second World War, based on a range of projects concerned with issues of military importance. Many of these were stress-related ranging from the impact of repeated combat missions on air crew to the effects of heat and acclimatisation on infantry and from the problems of maintaining alertness in radar operatives to coping with an overload of information in control rooms. Several of these problems continued to occupy the Unit after the war, with extensive research on watch keeping, sleep deprivation and shift work forming a sustained part of the Unit's programme. One of the achievements of Donald Broadbent's classic book *Perception and Communication* was his proposal of an overarching theoretical framework that would encompass the classic issues of attention perception and memory, together with their potential changes under stress. An important part of Broadbent's approach concerned the differences between individuals in the way in which they respond, linking this to differences in personality. This remained a focal interest of Donald's after he left the Unit, as reflected in his substantial later work *Decision and Stress* and his subsequent work in Oxford, relating stress to the quality of life of production line workers in the car industry.

Central to Donald's thesis was the concept of *arousal*, which, in turn, depended on the level of activation of the reticular formation deep within the brain, with level of arousal potentially varying from somnolence to panic. The influence of arousal on performance was assumed by Donald to follow the Yerkes-Dodson Law. This proposed that performance would show an inverted U function, being poor at low levels of arousal, improving as arousal increased to a maximum, after which performance begins to deteriorate. An example might be the attempt of an experienced golfer to make a simple putt, likely to be unreliable if he were too relaxed, to improve with concentration but deteriorating as the stress level passes a certain point, the effect known as "choking", with the golfer missing a putt on the last hole when the championship is at stake. Different tasks were assumed to peak at different points; hence a level of arousal that is optimal for running fast might not be the best level for solving a puzzle. Furthermore, evidence seemed to suggest that people differ in their resting arousal level, with extroverts, the life and soul of the party, having a lower basal arousal level than introverts who would rather curl up in a corner with a book. The situation is further complicated when people are exposed to more than one stressor; hence both sleep deprivation and noise can impair performance but, when combined, may lead to a reduced level of disruption, presumably because sleep deprivation lowers arousal level, and noise has the opposite effect, hence cancelling each other out.

This framework proved useful, though difficult to test since an increase in arousal may result in either improved or impaired performance, depending on the point on the inverted U at which arousal is increased. In principle of course, it is possible to plot out a whole range of different points across the inverted U, but in practice this is hard to do, particularly given that different individuals may peak at different points on different tasks. Finally, although the concept of arousal is part of the answer, it lacks motivational directionality; you can be aroused by excitement because you are successfully performing an activity that you enjoy and do well or aroused and full of dread because you are failing to cope. Both will increase level of arousal but are unlikely to lead to the same behaviour. We clearly need a more adequate way of thinking about and measuring not only arousal but also its valence, positive or negative and how it is controlled. We need a better understanding of both mental energy and motivation. It is important to note, however, that much of the Unit's work was not specifically targeted at answering theoretical questions but rather at providing information that might be useful in attempting to understand and alleviate the effects of stress on performance. Donald Broadbent's attempt to base a coherent framework on the work of the Unit was a major achievement, but theoretical development was not an aim that characterised most people working in the area at that time.

At the other extreme stood Christopher Poulton, one of the two deputy directors whose approach to science was much more atheoretical.

Christopher was a very good experimenter and an outstanding methodologist. He also produced a number of very thorough and focussed reviews on specific topics, commenting on the quality of the evidence, not always entirely judiciously where personal grudges were concerned. Several years after my arrival as director, Christopher decided to review research on the question of whether performance was impaired by loud noise. Here he convinced himself that a study carried out by Donald Broadbent was flawed and had played a crucial part in Donald's rather than his becoming Director of the APU. I am sure he was wrong on both counts, but it led to what was probably the most difficult situation of my 20 years as director, before it eventually died down. I wondered if he would feel similar resentment against my becoming Director but happily that appeared not to be the case; it helped, I suspect, that we shared an enthusiasm for devising ways of carrying out practical studies in unusual environments.

My own interest in performance under stress, resulting initially from my open-sea diving research, was rekindled after my return to the Unit by an application from a Scottish student to carry out a PhD at the Unit on stress in parachuting. This seemed a promising research area where people voluntarily place themselves in an obviously anxiety-generating situation and one in which they are likely to have the time and motivation to take part in brief relevant experiments. Our new PhD student Arthur Grierson came with a first-class degree and a stunning recommendation from Edinburgh. This stated that he had completed his degree the year before but had not applied to do research since he was predicted not to get a good degree as he appeared to spend so much time skydiving. He then confounded expectations by achieving a First Class degree. His undergraduate project involved recording heart rate during a skydive, using a heart rate monitor that could be remotely detected but unfortunately only over relatively short distances. This meant that Arthur would jump alongside the participant, maintaining a suitable distance while falling, so as to ensure good data. This was obviously before the days of ethics committees.

On arrival he discovered that Cambridge did not have a free fall parachuting club, whereupon he set about to create one, meanwhile doing research on the rather less-exciting topic of noise. Within a year he had created a club that had a professional full-time instructor and was jumping competitively at a national level. The instructor was about to be married, with Arthur as his best man. They planned to arrive at the wedding by skydiving onto Midsummer Common, a park in the centre of Cambridge. Tragically, Arthur was killed in a rehearsal jump. He had been given a new parachute by a well-wisher. He and the bridegroom became entangled just after leaving the plane, a standard emergency that he was well trained to handle, having made literally hundreds of successful jumps. According to standard protocol he cut away his existing parachute and attempted to open the reserve. It was, however, a new model and had an unfamiliar release mechanism. By the time he had worked this out it was too late. I can remember no sadder event than attending his funeral in South West Scotland, where his family was joined by large numbers of skydivers who knew and greatly respected him.

By this point, I had persuaded the army to fund a postdoctoral fellow to look at stress using parachutists as the relevant participants. Part of Arthur's contribution to the Cambridge club was to set up a training scheme whereby people could come for the weekend and jump, allowing them to decide whether they would like to take up the sport. The postdoc appointed was Chris Idzikowski, also from Edinburgh but with a background in physiological measures of performance acquired through research on sleep. What should we do following the tragic event? Should we abandon the project leaving Chris without a job? We felt sure that Arthur would want us to go on, potential skydivers would be coming anyhow and testing them on the ground before and after would in no way increase the risk. We decided to press on as before, except that Chris wisely decided that he himself would not be jumping. So what did we find?

We found first of all just how difficult it is to design and carry out an experiment under the constraints imposed by the training programme. It involved people arriving on a Saturday, undergoing instruction during the rest of the day and the following morning, and finally jumping on the Sunday afternoon. A good experimental design would have half of the jumpers tested first in the low-anxiety condition followed by the pre-jump test and half tested in the opposite order on a second weekend. However data from the US suggested that 85% of trainees do not return, and this proved to be the case in Cambridge; for most people who jumped, once was enough! We had to modify the design accordingly. A final very important factor was the weather since bad weather and in particular high winds would make the jump impossible, which it did on all too many weekends.

Altogether, it took Chris two years to test a total of 114 jumpers of whom 90 were men. The crucial test for half was on the relatively unstressed Saturday and half immediately before the Sunday jump, all of whom were tested on the ground. Testing on the plane just before jumping would be likely to involve higher anxiety levels but was likely to prove unacceptability distracting. We measured anxiety in terms of both heart rate and self-ratings, with both measures being maximum in the period leading up to the jump. This was linked to cognitive deficits, but these effects were not large, with a reduction in memory span of 0.8 of a digit; a simple reasoning task was performed at the same rate but with significantly more errors, while a visuospatial task showed a small speed deficit as did a search task involving scanning an array of numbers and crossing out those designated as targets.

Frustrated at the slowness with which we were accumulating data, we decided to run a second study alongside our parachuting project based on anxiety associated with presenting a talk at the Unit, before a keen and well-informed audience. This had the expected effect of producing a level of pre-talk anxiety that was high, though not quite as high as that faced by jumping out of a plane for the first time! The results were broadly similar with digit span reduced and reasoning errors but not speed impaired.

All in all, these were not particularly rich pickings from a demanding two-year project; dangerous environments are inherently difficult to control in an ethically acceptable way, and almost certainly do not attract a random sample of the population. Danger does seem to impair performance though not nearly as much as I would have expected, just as with heat, cold, nitrogen narcosis and fatigue. Furthermore the pattern of results was unexpected. The concept of arousal and the inverted U relationship led me to expect that complex tasks would be the most vulnerable. This was not the case for either the diving studies, where reasoning was less affected by stress than the simple screw plate test, or in parachuting, where the task of simply remembering a digit sequence was most clearly impaired. I remained interested in the way in which cognition is influenced by emotion but resolved to pursue the question, should the possibility arise, by working with clinical psychologists on patients with emotional problems, potentially offering a more productive way ahead from both a practical and theoretical viewpoint. It was through a much later attempt to explain the effects of anxiety and depression on working memory that a possible explanation of these earlier results finally emerged, as will be discussed in Chapter 24.

The possibility of studying a very different source of stress occurred some years later and concerned the possible effects of road traffic fumes on health and performance, presenting an important but difficult research challenge that I attempted to tackle on two occasions, both more notable for the lessons to be learned than from the information gained. The first of these occurred when I was at Sussex and was approached by an engineer from what is now the University of Brighton asking for help. He was concerned that the measures of traffic fumes on which the government based its decisions were inappropriate due to the location of the sensors, which he suggested was determined by convenience rather than validity; some-times, for example, they collected fumes high on a lamp post in a situation where the fumes were probably substantially greater nearer the ground. He had obtained a small grant from *Which*, a consumer magazine that also concerns itself with environmental affairs. He wanted to combine his study with an estimate of the effect of traffic fumes on cognitive performance and I agreed to help. We set up an experiment in which people sat in a van near the centre of Brighton performing a range of tests while breathing either bottled pure "medical" air, or air from the road outside. It came at a diffi-cult time for me with the end of term exams and other commitments, but I managed to fit it in and to find a graduate student to run it. I explained to my colleague that it was very unlikely that we would obtain positive results and that we should be prepared to publish regardless. He agreed.

Somewhat to my astonishment however, we found substantial effects across a number of measures and duly published our results in the prestig-ious scientific journal *Nature*. This caused something of a stir and a meet-ing was organised in London to which I was invited to defend our paper against a range of sceptics, including representation from the Medical Re-search Council Air Pollution Unit in London. Fortunately I had chosen a very good experimental design and was able to respond to all the criti-cisms, but such a large effect *did* seem surprising. I decided that it clearly needed replication and set about trying to find funds, without success until eventually *Which* agreed to fund a follow-up.

I decided this time to collaborate with the MRC Air Pollution Unit who had a test station, located in the men's lavatory beneath Fleet Street in the centre of London, with fumes fed down from above. This time I made sure that I had an experienced research assistant rather than someone who just happened to be available and set about designing a study. Alas, just as we were about to begin the experiment, resurfacing of the road above began with copious tar fumes and no traffic. While they were mending the road, we decided that we would try to do a very simple experiment using bottled roadside air; we accepted that this was far from ideal, but it seemed worth a try. We tested two groups, both of which had a practice run on pure medical air, with one going on to more medical air and the other to the bottled stuff. We found significantly poorer performance in the bottled group. We were delighted, until we looked at the pretest performance. During this pretest practice period when both were breathing pure air, the group that had been assigned to the roadside mixture was already worse! Our apparent effect was simply due to the chance assignment of better performing subjects to the group that were tested on pure medical air.

Eventually, the resurfacing of Fleet Street was complete, and the experiment began. Unfortunately by this time I was due to leave for our year in San Diego, with my continuing contribution based on telephone calls. While I was in the US it seemed a good idea to communicate with the two US laboratories working on this issue that I had identified, one on the west coast and one on the east. I discovered that we had stumbled into a minefield, with the westerners able to obtain effects which the easterners couldn't, even when they crossed over and used each other's laboratories!

I returned, looking forward to the results of our Fleet Street study. We found virtually nothing, other than that smokers appeared to do slightly better on one of the tasks! I assumed this was a chance finding since they were not allowed to smoke immediately before or after the test. So what to make of our initial positive results? A small effect on one or two tests would have been understandable but the sheer size of our effects made that seem unlikely. The weather was cold and there was a heater in the car, but why that should influence one condition rather than the other makes little sense. My main conclusion from this sad story is to reinforce my belief that it is *very* important to replicate experiments before drawing strong conclusions. One of the difficulties of working in the area of traffic pollution is the sheer complexity of the fumes given off, with different types of engine producing different mixtures. Carbon monoxide was assumed to be the major culprit at the time of our testing, but various oxides of nitrogen could well be equally or more unhealthy as can the minute particles generated by diesel fumes that are alarming environmentalists at the moment.

A further concern at the time concerned the presence of lead, leading to the question of whether it was important to reduce lead levels of the petrol used by cars. Some years later, after I had returned to Cambridge, the government asked the Medical Research Council to set up a committee that was tasked with assessing the evidence for the proposal that the lead from traffic fumes has a significant impact on health and cognitive performance. I was asked to join the group. We surveyed the literature and found lots of studies linking the level of lead in the blood of people from areas with differential traffic flow to their performance on a range of cognitive tests. However, people living in heavily lead-polluted areas tended to be poorer and less well educated than those who live in purer environments. It was not possible to decide how much of their poorer performance was due to lead (if any), and how much was attributable to all the other factors, whether genetic or environmental. We decided that there was a need for a "proper" experiment that allowed the effects of lead level to be separated from other factors such as general health and education. This, it was suggested, would be possible by running the study in Edinburgh, where some of the elegant and much sought-after Georgian houses still had lead piping, allowing lead-ingesting children from such homes to be compared with those whose pipes were more recent.

This seemed an excellent solution until the detailed planning began. The standard method of assessing lead levels is through a blood sample. However, the MRC's legal advisors pointed out that it was a crime to take blood from a child except when directly necessary for that child's health, even with the parent's permission. Long discussions ensued as to the relative problems of measuring lead levels in hair, and whether frequency of shampooing was an important factor, or teeth, relying on the tooth fairy to provide samples, but this leaves the problem of which part of the tooth to sample; it apparently matters. At this point, we heard that the government had cut a deal with the oil companies and would be introducing lead-free petrol anyhow!

So, what were the lessons here? Should we have accepted the dubious correlational data used heavily by the environmentalist lobby? I think not. Our job was to evaluate the scientific evidence and if it was inadequate produce something better; good science takes time, and of course replication. Furthermore, it is very rarely the case that a political decision should be taken on the basis of a single or even a replicated scientific result, although it is very important to take into account both the amount and the quality of evidence, particularly in cases where powerful vested interests are involved. An acute political problem can rarely be solved by new research, but what it can do is to focus research on the critical topic, taking the best available evidence and encouraging research that will tackle some of the areas of current interest. Each study, if well designed, will advance knowledge, perhaps also drawing attention to problems that are currently neglected or misunderstood. My next example, the study of memory and anaesthesia, provides an illustration of this.

A particularly interesting request came into the Unit some years after my return as director, from the Professor of Anaesthesiology at Cambridge University. A worrying phenomenon in his field was the occasional patient who claimed to have been conscious during a surgical operation but was unable to indicate this during the operation to the surgeon. This alarming state of affairs is possible because a typical anaesthetic involves three components: the anaesthetic to induce a state of unconsciousness, an analgesic to reduce pain levels and a muscle relaxant to facilitate surgery. It is entirely possible that if some level of consciousness and awareness of pain remained, the muscle relaxant would prevent the patient from responding.

A Cambridge team was investigating an electrophysiological measure to provide an independent indication during the operation of level of consciousness. We were asked if we could help to validate the system by providing a concurrent cognitive measure of level of conscious awareness during different depths of anaesthesia and, on later recovery, to determine whether any memory remained from events occurring during anaesthesia. My postdoctoral research fellow at the time, Jackie Andrade and I were happy to help, presenting material under different levels of anaesthesia, then probing for evidence of memory. A general anaesthetic always has some minimal level of risk, with the degree of risk increasing with the depth of anaesthesia. For that reason, it is important for the anaesthetist to judge a point at which the patient is fully unconscious without requiring unduly large amounts of anaesthetic. The judgement is further complicated by the fact that pain from a surgical incision, for example, might increase awareness if the depth of anaesthesia is too low.

As mentioned earlier, there were, and continue to be, occasional cases of patients who report that they were conscious during the operation but unable to respond because of the muscle relaxant. One way round this problem is to use a cuff on one arm that restricts circulation and prevents the muscle relaxant blocking activity in that arm. This allows the patient to signal awareness by raising a finger. Using this method there is evidence that about 40% of patients show some form of awareness during the process of anaesthesia, a process that does, however, involve a succession of stages. Stage 1 has three phases: the first showing little analgesia or subsequent amnesia for events occurring at this point, leading on to a second phase when the patient can see, hear, taste and answer questions regarding important life events whilst having little subsequent memory of the questions. Phase 3 of Stage 1 involves reduced perception and confusion in reporting life events, particularly those that are more recent. Finally in Stage 2 the patient shows no response to stimulation and is assumed to be unconscious.

Because of concerns about optimising the level of anaesthesia, minimising possible experience of pain while avoiding conscious awareness and subsequent memories, there have been attempts to use electrophysiological measures to support the more traditional behavioural signs of anaesthetic depth. A Cambridge group was investigating one that was based on auditory evoked potentials. A sequence of clicks was played to the anaesthetised participant. The capacity of the brain to reflect individual clicks electrophysiologically as separate events was known to be gradually lost under anaesthesia, hence allowing a potential indicator of depth. The purpose of our study was to validate this measure by linking the electrophysiological response to depth of anaesthesia, level of consciousness and any subsequent ability to remember material presented while anaesthetised.

Our experimental design involved testing each person at each of four levels of the anaesthetic agent isoflurane (0%, 0.2%, 0.4% and 0.8%). We used the isolating cuff technique to allow a finger-raising response to a series of cognitive tasks. We measured awareness by requiring the participant to listen to series of spoken words and respond whenever an item came from a particular semantic category such as animals. This was followed by a memory test which involves presenting a separate sequence of words, some of which would be repeated. Participants were asked to raise their finger if they detected a repeated word, with repetitions coming after delays ranging from 0 to 16 interpolated words. Finally, 10 items from specific semantic categories such as flowers were spoken to be used for a later memory test when consciousness was recovered. We tested only seven people on four separate sessions, one for each level of anaesthesia. All were anaesthetists since the ethics committee argued that only they were knowledgeable enough to give adequately informed consent. At the deepest level, the tester would shout the person's name, and then deliver an electric shock that aimed to simulate the effect of an arousing event such as the surgeon's cut. The junior anaesthetists seem to take a certain delight in imposing this on their professor who was one of the seven participants.

The results for measures of consciousness were clear in showing a gradual decline in responsiveness with anaesthetic strength, with no response at the deepest level from any of the measures. Accuracy of semantic categorisation dropped systematically with depth of anaesthesia, as did performance on the continuous memory task where for all conditions, the greater the number of words interpolated between the presentation of an item and its repetition, the poorer the performance. The electrophysiological evoked response measure also mirrored depth of anaesthesia and showed a significant, though not large, correlation with the behavioural measures.

Episodic memory was tested on recovery using pairs of words, one of which had been presented during the previous test session and one which had not. Performance under air was high with people able to select the previously presented word on 86% of the pairs and under the weakest level of isoflurane, people were still able to detect 63%. However, by the 0.4% level performance was no better than chance while at the deepest level people were simply not able to do any of the tests. When tested on the 10 words from the separate category presented at the end of each anaesthetic session, none could be remembered. Our final test was concerned with testing for implicit memory of the final set by asking them to generate as many items as possible from that category: for example flowers. This also gave a negative result with no tendency for the presented flower names to be produced more frequently. So we ourselves found no evidence of memory from any but the lightest level of anaesthetic.

Our experiment therefore gave broad support to the value of the electrophysiological measure of depth of amnesia while showing evidence of memory for only the lightest level of anaesthesia. That does not of course mean that earlier reports of subsequent memory are necessarily false. They could reflect fluctuations in anaesthetic levels, or perhaps individual differences in susceptibility to the anaesthetic agent.

Viewed from a broader context, the experiment just described represents just one small contribution to a large and growing literature on awareness under anaesthesia to which my own contribution was limited to jointly designing the measures of performance and memory, with the project then being largely taken over by Jackie Andrade. I include it not because of its importance but as characteristic of the way in which the basic tools of a cognitive psychologist can be applied across a wide range of contexts. The psychologist's role is essentially that of a technician providing and adapting tools that were usually developed in the psychological laboratory, and were often designed to answer a theoretical question such as that of whether short- and long-term memory involve separate systems.

Applied psychology is most effective when there is a continuing link between the psychologist and the applied field, preferably extending over a number of years, as in the case of Conrad's contribution to postal and telecommunications field and Ivan Brown's involvement to driver research, both pursued at the Unit over many years. In this connection, I am happy to say that Jackie has continued to keep contact with the field as one of her research interests, one that has, over the years, born fruit both theoretically, in terms of the implications of the work for the psychological study of conscious awareness, and practically through her involvement with the field of anaesthesia. I recently asked her what had happened in this area over the 20 years since our initial work. It appears that the specific EEG method that we used was not developed further but that other similar measures are used, although in the UK principally for research purposes. Jackie suggests that the principal importance of our study was to demonstrate that failure to remember something on recovery did not necessarily mean that it was not experienced. Our participants were able to categorise words correctly at levels of anaesthesia much greater than those resulting in memory. This is important because methods of approaching the issue of awareness during surgery that are currently used clinically still rely principally on the ongoing judgement of the anaesthetist coupled with later questions of awareness which of course depend on memory.

Fortunately, the issue of awareness is now widely accepted as important by anaesthetists within the UK at least. A recently conducted survey across every hospital in the UK and Ireland involved each sending in reports every month for a year. This was then analysed by a committee which included Jackie and one other psychologist. Of 311 reports, 141 were regarded as possible examples and analysed in more detail. The most alarming appeared to be cases who were conscious but unable to respond, terrified that this might be a permanent state of affairs, as in the so-called "locked in syndrome". Situations such as this were most likely to lead to subsequent psychological harm, including post-traumatic stress disorder. Perhaps the most important feature to emerge, however, was that it was not uncommon for patients to fail to understand the difference between sedation, in which the patient remains conscious, and the subsequent state of anaesthesia, leading to the belief that the anaesthetic had not worked. The report stresses the importance of explaining clearly to the patient, exactly what is about to happen and what they can expect to experience. The field continues to develop, and no doubt improved methods of measuring levels of conscious awareness will evolve and become used more generally, driven both by major national efforts such as the survey and by the knowledge accumulated from many different studies such as the one we carried out in Cambridge.

I have described three areas of research, each concerned with a form of environmental stress of practical importance: the effects of fear, of traffic fumes and of anaesthetics. All confront the experimenter with technical challenges and produce complex results, none of which led to immediate practical application. They present a number of general problems for the investigator. The first of these is ethical. The days when fear could be studied by filling a plane with US servicemen and convincing them that they are about to crash are, I hope, long gone! There are also clear ethical limits to degree of stress imposed on volunteers who are often likely to be a self-selected atypical sample of the population. A further major problem in this area is that of controlling extraneous factors, the weather in the case of parachutists and the source and complexity of traffic fumes. Finally, it appears to be the case that people can be remarkably resilient to the cognitive effects of stress, at least over the short term, although very serious effects may well emerge over the long term, as in post-traumatic stress disorder resulting from military combat.

Despite these difficulties, I think it is important to carry out experimental studies that can determine possible *causal* links between stress and behaviour in a way that is not possible using studies based on the correlation between stress and performance. Hence, we still do not *know* that there is a causal effect of lead on cognitive development, over and above the effects of the many other constituents of traffic fumes that were not tackled by the introduction of lead-free petrol. Indeed it now appears to be the case that diesel particles may be an even worse problem. The results obtained in experimental studies carried out under realistic conditions tend to be small, and even when more substantial, need replicating. Even then, they will almost certainly comprise only one of many factors that go into decisions to take action. Such work takes time, skill and patience but is surely worthwhile in linking what we learn in the laboratory to the world beyond.

18
When Long-Term Memory Fails

As described earlier, the work of the Unit combined an interest in developing theory with a willingness to tackle a wide range of individual projects, typically resulting from a request for help. The last two chapters have described my own involvement in a number of such questions in the two broad areas of environmental stress and the law. In such situations the psychologist's task is typically to serve as part of a team, providing scientifically sound evidence on which a response to the question can be made. As will have become clear, obtaining such evidence is far from straightforward, its impact on policy likely to be limited and interpreted in the light of evidence from other sources not only scientific but also practical and political. Any substantial, practical influence is therefore likely to depend on research in the relevant area extending over many years. In my own case, the principal sustained application of theoretical development has been to the neuropsychology of memory through applying the concepts and methods of cognitive psychology to a deeper understanding of clinical deficits. This can then lead not only to the creation of new neuropsychological tests but also to developing ways in which such knowledge can be applied to helping patients cope with their problems.

My involvement in the attempt to link basic cognitive psychology with the practical issues of clinical neuropsychology began in the late 1960s and is still ongoing. The current section, however, will concentrate principally on my time at the Unit, a period when the psychology of memory concerned itself with two highly relevant issues. The first of these was the previously described question of how many kinds of memory it is necessary to assume. While some theorists still claim to explain the whole of memory in terms of a single long-term system, within neuropsychology it was usual to accept the case for multiple memory systems. My own work with Brooks demonstrated that a number of these are preserved in amnesia, while later research has considerably extended the range of such preserved capacities. Subsequent research on normal healthy people has confirmed the distinction between explicit episodic memory and a range of implicit systems as suggested by research on patients although there are still a few theorists who attempt to avoid this distinction.

A second controversy that arose in the field of memory during this period was concerned with the ecological validity of memory research, the extent to which the principles and methods developed within the laboratory would generalise to the world outside. What became known as the "everyday memory movement" first achieved prominence through a meeting in Cardiff on "Practical Aspects of Memory" organised by a group of Welsh psychologists who invited Ulric Neisser to give the opening address. His earlier book *Cognitive Psychology* had introduced the information-processing cognitive approach to mainstream North American psychology, but by this time, he was becoming disenchanted with the narrowness and artificial nature of much of the laboratory-based research that had come to dominate cognitive psychology. In response, he was attempting to do for memory what J. J. Gibson had done for perception, to break away from the laboratory and develop an ecologically oriented approach to memory.

Neisser began his opening address with a frontal attack on what he saw as the mainstream approach to memory claiming that, "If x is an interesting aspect of human memory then x has not been studied by psychologists". A critic might argue that the rest of the conference disproved his claim, since there were literally dozens of papers concerned with potentially important practical real-world aspects of memory, although he was correct in his implication that few would be likely to be accepted by mainstream memory journals with their dominant emphasis on the testing of existing theories.

The conference and proceedings were highly successful, and a second Welsh meeting was held a decade later. This, in turn, led to further US meetings, the founding of a Society for Applied Research in Memory and Cognition and an associated journal. Given the vehemence of Neisser's initial challenge, it unsurprisingly resulted in a repost. In a paper entitled "The bankruptcy of everyday memory", Mahzarin Banaji, a social psychologist, and Robert Crowder, a highly respected but more traditionally oriented memory theorist, pointed to the fragmentary nature of much work in the area and its conspicuous lack of theoretical development. Sadly, having drawn up their battle lines, the two groups went their separate ways and although new journals emerged that tended to specialise in practical aspects of memory, the more traditional experimental journals have tended to remain traditional.

The importance of theoretically driven research and its capacity to operate beyond the laboratory is, however, a crucial and continuing issue within neuropsychology. While it is valuable to use the concepts and techniques of the laboratory to better understand cognitive deficits, it is important to ensure that they are robust enough to be useful to the clinician. Subtle effects may be of great theoretical importance but are likely to be practically useful only if they can be detected reliably in patients who vary in age education and who may well have more than one deficit. My own principal contribution to linking basic and applied research has been to try to use neuropsychological evidence to develop cognitive theory, and then turn theory into practice by developing clinically robust methods of measuring the underlying deficits and wherever possible helping the therapist deal with them.

When I returned to the Unit as director, despite featuring neuropsychology as central to the proposed programme, my own research in the area tailed off. Elizabeth Warrington had moved her research interests away from amnesia and local clinical links were limited to the speech therapy department, where I regularly spent a morning a week seeing stroke patients in the hope of finding a patient with a relatively pure phonological loop deficit. I discovered two patients with interesting reading disorders, subsequently studied by Karalyn Patterson, but saw no relevant memory cases. The opportunity then arose to join a UK-Dutch group of clinical neuropsychologists who shared an interest in Traumatic Brain Injury (TBI), an all-too common condition, typically following a road traffic accident, a sports injury or a fall. These can result in a sudden deceleration causing the brain to swirl around in the skull, potentially sheering the layer of white matter that covers the surface of the brain and serves to transmit information from one part of the brain to another.

The after-effects of TBI range from minimal, with no loss of consciousness to very severe when the trauma can be followed by many weeks of coma, followed by *post-traumatic amnesia*, a state of confused attention and difficulty in retaining new information. This can last for varying periods of time before the patient stabilises at a cognitive level that ranges from virtually normal to severely impaired. Problems of memory and attention are common symptoms of TBI, and are likely to persist through the patient's lifetime. Since TBI is particularly common following road traffic accidents often involving young men, the resulting burden on patient and carer can last for many years. Despite its practical importance, this was a neglected area of research. Unlike the classic amnesic syndrome it tends to be complex both anatomically and in terms of its neuropsychological consequences, making it difficult to draw clear conclusions or indeed to use it to resolve theoretically important issues. As a result it was less extensively researched than the much rarer but theoretically informative amnesic syndrome.

The UK-Dutch group comprised mainly clinical neuropsychologists who were concerned to collaborate in an attempt to reduce this scientific neglect. I was invited along to advise on the memory assessment issues and became interested in a question that was related to the everyday memory controversy. The issue concerned the psychological tests of memory used within clinical neuropsychology. These were typically developed from existing laboratory methods such as learning to associate pairs of words, while visual memory was typically tested by memory for faces and for complex geometric designs. Unsurprisingly, patients tended to object that their difficulties were not in remembering complex designs or learning lists of unrelated words, questioning the relevance of such tests to their problems. Was their scepticism justified?

I decided to tackle this problem and was fortunate enough to be able to persuade the MRC to let me retain two temporary posts from a project that was just finishing. This allowed me to hire a cognitive psychologist John Harris and a clinical neuropsychologist Alan Sunderland. We were also fortunate enough to have the support of the head of neurosurgery at Addenbrooke's Hospital who had an interest in head injury and was sympathetic to our proposed research on whether the standard clinical tests were good measures of the everyday memory of patients. We tested three groups: a group of TBI patients who were about three months post release from hospital, and a second group whose TBI had occurred two to eight years earlier, allowing us to estimate the broad degree of recovery over the intervening years. Finally, we compared both these to another group of road traffic accident patients, matched for age and background but who had suffered fractures and orthopaedic damage but escaped TBI.

We included a range of standard tests of memory and cognition that were known to be sensitive to TBI. The tricky question now, however, was how to measure everyday memory. We opted for two measures: an initial structured interview focussing on lapses of attention, followed by a diary, kept over a period of time, in which such lapses were noted daily. In addition to the patients, we enlisted the help of carers who also reported on the patient's memory lapses using both methods.

Our results were clear in showing the expected deficit across both TBI groups on most of the cognitive measures, with no difference between patients who had been released from hospital about three months earlier and those who were several years post–accident, suggesting that the deficits had become relatively stable within a matter of months. The interview and diary measures of everyday memory problems were closely related, and in the case of assessment by relatives, problems were more severe for both the brain-injured groups than in the orthopaedic controls. Assessments by the patients themselves, however, were less clearly different from those of the control group, suggesting that the TBI patients may well have been forgetting that they had forgotten! A later application of the same design to normal ageing also suggested that questionnaire and diary measures which *depend* on memory are, perhaps unsurprisingly, likely to become less reliable as memory deteriorates.

The crucial question, however, was how well the standard tests predicted the memory lapses observed by the carers. Despite the fact that most of the cognitive measures were sensitive to the effect of brain injury, the only test that was consistently related to memory lapses in both this and a later study on the effect of age on everyday memory was recall of a short story reported in a paragraph like a news report. So, it seems that the patients' complaint that most of the standard memory tests did not capture their problems was correct, apart from the short story measure, which fortunately is widely used clinically.

By this time it was clear that there was considerable interest among clinical neuropsychologists in problems of assessing TBI and a joint symposium was organised and was well attended. One of the presenters was a clinical neuropsychologist from Rivermead Rehabilitation Centre in Oxford, Barbara Wilson. She shared our concern about the relevance of standard memory tests and their capacity to predict everyday problems but unlike us, had already started to do something about it. Barbara had a somewhat unusual background, coming from a disadvantaged family in London, dropping out of teacher training college to marry and raise a family before starting to take courses in psychology in evening classes and then taking a place as a mature student on a university psychology course. She graduated with a first-class degree and went on to study to be a clinical psychologist at the Institute of Psychiatry in London. This is the leading centre for such training in the UK and tends to take a strongly behaviourist viewpoint based on a treatment approach that operates at the level of the individual case. It typically involves careful observation of the patient's problems, followed by treatment based on learning theory of the type developed by B F Skinner in which appropriate behaviour is selectively rewarded. Barbara had begun her clinical career working with learning-disabled people, a context in which such methods were widely employed. She continued this broad approach on moving to Rivermead, focussing on adults with moderate-to-severe cognitive deficits, often following TBI or stroke.

She had already begun to apply the observational aspect of this approach to the detection and analysis of everyday memory problems. After carefully observing the difficulties faced by her patients, she attempted to capture each in a small subtest that would indicate the presence or absence of problems of that type. This resulted in the Rivermead Behavioural Memory Test (RBMT) where measures included remembering the name of a person pictured, remembering a short paragraph, seeing a number of photographs of faces and subsequently recognising them from a mixture of new and old faces, remembering a simple new route, testing the patient's orientation in time and place and finally three simple tests of prospective memory, remembering to do something.

The RBMT seemed to have the promise of solving the everyday memory problem that we had uncovered, so we agreed to collaborate, obtaining funding to finalise the test and to validate it against observations of everyday forgetting and finally to obtain general population norms that would tell us what level of performance we could expect from healthy people of different ages. This would then allow the clinician to compare the everyday problems of an incoming patient with those to be expected of a healthy person of that age and background.

Rivermead was an ideal environment for such a development since it had large numbers of patients passing through, many with memory problems, all of whom would be treated by occupational and physical therapists over a relatively long series of sessions. The therapists were very supportive and agreed to keep a diary noting the memory lapses during treatment of all their patients. In due course we were able to establish that the RBMT was much more strongly related to the observation of memory lapses than the more standardised memory tests that are commonly used. In due course Barbara was able to follow up this initial assessment by contacting patients many years after they had left Rivermead, separating them into two categories: those who could now live relatively independently and those who still needed constant help. The RBMT score while at Rivermead several years earlier was much more successful in predicting which patients would achieve independence than the more standard measures of memory performance.

This does not of course mean that the other tests are of no value. They are very successful in identifying patients with impaired memory, and in specifying and understanding the precise nature of their deficits; both types of measure are important in analysing the patient's problem and planning treatment. However, not all aspects of memory are equally important in coping with life outside the clinic. By selecting and testing areas of everyday life that are likely to challenge people with memory problems, the RBMT is better able to assess the patients' probable capacity to cope. It is now widely used clinically and has been translated into at least 14 different languages.

While the RBMT was designed particularly for the use of clinicians helping and advising their patients, its potential use was much wider, a point that is well illustrated by research on a separate group of patients, people suffering from schizophrenia. I knew little about this disease, other than that it was associated with hallucinations such as voices that appear to come from nowhere, talking to the patient, often very negatively. Patients may also develop delusions, for example that the state is spying on you and attempting to control your thoughts. I did not associate schizophrenia with amnesia, and hence was surprised when approached by a young psychiatrist from Leeds, Peter McKenna, saying that he thought there was a long-term term memory deficit and enquiring as to whether anyone at the Unit might be interested in checking this out. It seemed an interesting possibility and had the added benefit that I could combine it with visiting my elderly mother in Leeds, so I volunteered myself and arranged to make a visit, taking along a few tests.

Peter and I saw the patients in High Royds, a classic rather grand asylum building from an era when it was thought that the best way to treat mental illness was to place patients in elegant buildings within their own grounds. More recently the approach has been to treat as many patients as possible within the community, abandoning the old asylums, which then often seem to be converted into luxury apartments. One of the tests I took was the RBMT. While I had tested many neuropsychological patients, neuropsychiatry was a new field for me and my first patient was something of a surprise. She was a young woman and I got as far as presenting the part of the RBMT that involved showing a female face and learning her name. The young woman pictured looked nothing like the patient, who nevertheless declared "That's a picture of me! Where did you get it from? I don't like this!" whereupon I passed the problem of reassuring her over to the psychiatrist! I did, however, manage to test enough patients to convince me that schizophrenia might indeed have an associated deficit in long-term memory.

We went ahead and set up an experiment using the RBMT to measure everyday memory, together with more standard clinical memory tests and an assessment of overall cognitive performance based on a screening test for early dementia. We found a clear impairment in everyday memory as measured by the RBMT, equivalent to that found in our Rivermead group of brain-damaged patients who had problems that were generally accepted as leading to impaired memory. Performance was also impaired on more standard tests of long-term memory, but on the other hand the general measure of cognitive performance indicated a much less serious overall level of deficit. It is important to note at this point, however, that as is typically found in schizophrenia, there was a relatively wide range of performance across the patients, with some performing well within the normal range.

We went on to extend our investigation and replicate our somewhat surprising result, given that schizophrenia was not commonly associated with amnesia but was widely believed to be linked to an attentional deficit, in which case we might have expected a much greater deficit in our broad cognitive measure. Indeed by this point claims were made that the proposed attentional deficit reflected an impairment in working memory. This view was strengthened by a series of studies based on a technique that came from the animal literature where it was initially based on recording the activity of individual cells in the frontal lobe of awake monkeys. The task involved a visual focus point on which the animal was required to fixate, after which a light came on briefly in one of an array of possible positions. Following a delay a signal instructed the animal to move its eyes to the earlier location of the target. If correct, it then received a food reward. It was found that a successful recall depended on continued activation over the delay in certain individual brain cells within the animal's frontal lobes. This led to the claim that these cells must be the basis of working memory, a claim that did, however, need to be modified in due course when similar cells were found elsewhere within the brain. Within psychiatry, a number of investigators adopted a purely behavioural version of this approach, testing the ability of their schizophrenic patients to remember the location of brief light flashes over a brief delay, finding an impairment, together with a smaller but still statistically significant impairment in the performance of close relatives, suggesting an inherited link.

We ourselves were meanwhile investigating deficits in working memory in our patients using a range of tests based on the Baddeley and Hitch model, and in a later study using more conventional measures of attention. Both studies showed a moderate degree of overall impairment together, as usual in the area, with some patients performing within the normal range. Hence, although it became fashionable to view schizophrenia in terms of a working memory deficit we found the deficit to be relatively small. For a period of time I was regularly invited to give talks on working memory and schizophrenia to meetings of psychiatrists where I suspect, I disappointed (annoyed?) my hosts by proposing that the deficit was much less important than the problems in long-term everyday memory that their patients were likely to encounter. Such long-term memory problems can readily be misinterpreted; forgetting to turn up to an appointment may seem like lack of interest while failure to recognise someone can be interpreted as rudeness, so I do think this is an important area clinically. Why had it not been discovered earlier? Looking back at the very early days when schizophrenia was first identified as a disease, the memory problems of patients were noted but tended to be interpreted in terms of poor attention and lack of motivation, a plausible interpretation but one that needed to be checked before becoming widely accepted.

Much more obvious were the so-called positive symptoms of delusions and hallucinations. These intrigued me, and I wondered if they might reflect a defective link between working memory and long-term memory. Perhaps executive problems might disrupt retrieval, leading to systematic distortions? Patients with damage to the frontal lobes can show a tendency to sometimes bizarre confabulations that are linked to attentional problems. So would those schizophrenic patients who confabulate also be those with impaired central executive capacity? I therefore arranged to see a group of patients with clear delusions, allowing me to get some idea as to the possible links between delusions and other aspects of cognition. I adopted a very unstructured approach questioning their broad view of the world and when their ideas seemed delusional, gently asking why the patient took that view. All seemed ready to talk about their beliefs, which were somewhat diverse.

One patient complained that bad angels were removing his internal organs, resulting in pain. When asked why he thought angels were involved he replied, "It's what they say", explaining that the pain was accompanied by critical voices, who occasionally were contradicted by a good angel who he claimed spoke with a BBC accent. Another claimed to be a world-class Russian chess player although admitting that he could not speak Russian. However when he was in chess-playing mode he could speak Russian fluently he explained. A third claimed to be a reincarnation of Jesus Christ. When questioned about two other patients who made the same claim, he pointed out that they were clearly wrong! Another complained of having his mind and actions controlled by a sinister force linked to the government.

In each case, when questioned in detail, the delusions tended to be broadly coherent and consistent with that patient's abnormal experiences. There is evidence, for example, that hallucinations tend to be predominantly auditory and can be shown to result from internal speech, which is often self-critical. There is also evidence that patients have an impaired capacity to monitor their own actions, leading to a feeling that the actions are being controlled by others. Attempts to explain to the patient that claims of persecution are irrational can readily be explained away on the basis of the cleverness of the persecutors. In other patients, feelings of superiority with no obvious origin can sometimes be attributed to royal birth or divinity, sometimes accompanied by an elaborate internally consistent account about how this may have come about while not being generally acknowledged.

So was the tendency to delusional thinking linked to cognitive deficits? No, the cognitive capacities of the deluded patients tended to be equivalent to and if anything slightly higher than the otherwise matched non-delusional schizophrenic group. I concluded that the patients were simply trying to make sense of some very abnormal experiences such as apparently being criticised by a disembodied voice or having your actions apparently controlled from outside. Unexplained feelings of anxiety could lead to paranoia, while unexpected feelings of euphoria and superiority could lead to claims of greatness. Perhaps the capacity to build these into a consistent and coherent although delusional explanation is possible only with relatively preserved working memory?

What are the implications for treatment? The more positive symptoms of delusions and hallucinations can be controlled through drug treatment, although this requires the patient to comply with the necessary regime and not forget to take the drugs or refuse them because of side effects. There is also some evidence that such symptoms can be helped through cognitive therapy. Unfortunately however, negative symptoms, probably including memory and attentional impairment, tend to be helped less by the drugs or cognitive therapy. Furthermore, poor memory is likely to make consistent compliance with treatment more difficult, suggesting that allowance for probable everyday memory problems should form part of the plans for treatment.

However, most of my neuropsychological work during this period involved patients at Rivermead Rehabilitation Centre on the outskirts of Oxford, which aimed to help adults with brain damage, typically resulting from TBI or stroke. Rehabilitation often involved learning new skills, and hence it was important to detect and understand any learning and memory problems and to bear these in mind, when trying to help the patient.

This should include an assessment of whether the specific treatment is working for that particular patient, basing the assessment on what became known as single-case treatment designs, introduced to Rivermead by Barbara Wilson, based on her earlier experience of applying behavioural methods to helping people with learning disability. Single-case treatment designs all involve first establishing a stable measure of the problem to be treated across several sessions *before* treatment begins. If performance is already clearly improving, treatment may not be necessary. Furthermore if treatment was introduced before establishing a stable baseline, it would be unclear whether any improvement was caused by natural recovery or from the treatment. You would thus not know whether your treatment was working or not and your results would tell you nothing about the usefulness of treatment and whether it should be used with other patients. On the other hand a flat pretreatment baseline, indicating no change in the condition, allows any improvement following introduction of the new treatment to be readily detected, providing clear evidence of its effectiveness, hence also showing its potential for treating other similar cases.

I was impressed by the simplicity of this approach, in contrast to the complexity and expense of the classic randomised control trial, which depends on assigning patients at random to either a treatment group or to an untreated control condition with which the treated patients can be compared. This is the gold standard design within medicine and is ideal for studying the effects of drugs or other treatments of common conditions. However, it requires large groups of broadly equivalent patients. Brain-damaged patients undergoing rehabilitation vary greatly in both the nature and severity of their problems with the result that optimal treatment may vary substantially from one patient to the next. The single-case treatment approach has the advantage that it can be carried out by an individual therapist at the level of the specific patient, allowing a range of possible treatments to be tried and if successful, readily reported and used by others.

I was intrigued by the method and was pleased to work with Barbara on the single-case treatment of a teenager who had been thrown from a horse, resulting in both perceptual and memory problems. As a result of her perceptual problems, she had lost the ability to reliably identify letters visually but could understand them when spoken and put them together to recognise a word: for example, *d-o-g* ... *dog*. She also had a memory deficit which made it hard for her to relearn the visual alphabet. We decided to retrain her using a single-case design devising a treatment in which for each "forgotten" letter, some form of mnemonic was devised. For example the capital letter T could have some "twigs" attached as a reminder of the word tree with T as its initial letter. Groups of letters were trained with performance on the whole alphabet tested at regular intervals. If our training method was successful, only the trained letters should improve, while the other sets should remain the same. She did indeed gradually learn and retained each of the trained letters while showing no improvement on the untrained items, indicating that the training was effective. From time to time she was rewarded with her favourite activity, being taken to see horses in a local field. Her performance was logged each session, and when one group of letters had been acquired we moved on to the next. Looking at the pattern of letters it was clear both to us and her that the method was working. She gradually became what is termed a letter-by-letter reader, spelling out the letters in a given word one by one and then saying the word. At this point she returned to her home in Cornwall, where the task was taken up by an educational psychologist who treated her as he would anyone beginning to learn to read, ultimately with considerable success.

Collaboration with Barbara Wilson had an unexpected bonus, access to a wide range of interesting neuropsychological patients allowing a series of theoretically oriented single-case studies. As explained earlier, the rare patient with a specific and precise cognitive deficit can be extremely valuable in further understanding the defective component of memory. Such patients are rare, and locating them depends on the presence of a neuropsychologist who not only sees many patients but is astute enough to realise the potential theoretical importance of such rare cases and a willingness to collaborate in their detailed investigation. Barbara combined this role with a strong further commitment to rehabilitation and to developing methods of applying scientific knowledge to helping patients cope with their problems.

I will describe several such cases together with their scientific implications before going on to discuss the application of a combination of cognitive and behavioural psychology to their treatment. The first patient, who we will call Keith (not his real name), was someone with a very pure long-term memory deficit. This purity of deficit was remarkable given his medical history, which was very stormy. He was a company director in his late fifties who suffered a life-threatening brain infection from which he had eventually, after many setbacks, recovered remarkably well. His intelligence test scores were in the very superior range; he performed well on tests of perception and on tests of executive capacity and attentional control. He showed good short-term verbal and visual memory performance as measured by span, the number of items that can be held and immediately recalled, and he performed well on the Peterson short-term forgetting task. On the other hand he showed severe impairment on everyday memory as assessed by the RBMT and on delayed recall of a short prose passage, while his free recall of lists of 10 words showed the characteristic amnesic pattern of preserved recency, as shown by good recall of the last one or two items, combined with very poor retention of earlier words. He was also severely impaired on standard clinical memory tests involving remembering unrelated words, or complex abstract figures.

Again, as is classically the case, Keith showed preserved capacity for implicit learning as measured by the pursuit rotor task, learning to keeping a stylus in contact with a moving target, and had a normal capacity to show improvement in speed of assembling a 20-piece jigsaw puzzle over successive trials. He showed a normal improvement with practice in speed of reading words printed in mirror orientation and preserved priming as measured by the capacity to "guess" previously presented words such as STAMP given the initial letters ST---, despite his failure to remember having encountered the words. All of this indicated that Keith was a classic example of a pure amnesic patient.

This allowed us to ask a theoretically important question concerning the relationship between episodic memory, memory for specific experiences that is clearly defective in amnesic patients such as Keith, and semantic memory, accumulated knowledge of the world. In arguing for this distinction, Tulving had pointed to a number of features in which the two types of memory differed, one being the preservation of semantic memory in densely amnesic patients. However, it could be argued that this is not a fair comparison since the evidence of preserved semantic memory was based on knowing the meaning of words and having a normal capacity to recall features of the world such as the colour of bananas, or how many inches there are in a foot. However, it is important to note that these capacities are all based on knowledge of the world acquired *before* the onset of amnesia. In contrast, evidence for episodic memory came from an impaired ability to remember specific new information or events that occurred *after* the onset. A fairer comparison would be based on the capacity to remember specific episodes from before: for example a wedding or winning a race at school. Such events would not necessarily be expected to be remembered as well as semantic knowledge that is in constant use, but their existence at a level comparable to that in healthy people would challenge Tulving's claim.

We first demonstrated Keith's preserved semantic memory as shown by his excellent vocabulary, his capacity to generate examples from a category such as animals and his speed and accuracy of sentence verification, supporting the claim that semantic memory can be preserved when episodic memory is grossly impaired. We went on to test Keith's autobiographical memory using a method, invented in the 19th century by the polymath Francis Galton, whereby a word is presented, for example *river*, and the patient is asked to recollect a specific personal event associated with *river*, perhaps, for example, falling in the river while getting out of a boat. Keith's recollections were spontaneous, fluent and rich in detail despite focussing on specific events of the type that characterise episodic memory. He could, for example, remember his wedding many years before in considerable detail, including, for example, the bridesmaid's dresses.

Our results from Keith and other amnesic patients suggest that episodic memories *can* be preserved in amnesia, provided they were formed *before* the onset of the amnesia, as of course is the case for material used in most tests of semantic memory. After the onset of amnesia, both episodic *and* semantic memory acquisition are impaired, as reflected in the failure of amnesic patients to update their knowledge of facts such as the name of the current US president. Our results invalidate the claim that amnesia provides clear evidence for separate semantic and episodic memory systems, as opposed to a single system operating under different conditions. It does not, however, prove that they *are* the same, a point I will return to later.

It is also important to point out that the capacity to recollect earlier episodes is not always preserved in otherwise classic cases of pure amnesia. A second highly intelligent cognitively well preserved but densely amnesic patient again showed good semantic memory but showed grossly impaired episodic memory for events prior to his illness. For example, he knew he had been at university and had been in the navy but could not remember in what order and had very little recollection of any specific events that had happened during those periods. It became clear that we knew far too little about autobiographical memory and we then began to study it more extensively.

Impaired autobiographical memory can be seen as one form of a condition known as *retrograde* amnesia, the term referring to amnesia for events prior to the onset of the amnesia. It often accompanies *anterograde* amnesia, the impaired capacity to acquire new memories but as with Keith, both do not always co-occur. Retrograde amnesia commonly follows severe concussion and may extend back for different periods of time depending on the severity of the TBI. Earlier memories are typically better preserved than more recent, while events immediately before the concussion are often never recovered. Most research studies up to this point had measured retrograde amnesia using memory for public events on the grounds that such information could readily be verified. Examples include a test based on remembering the names of people who had each become briefly famous during a specific time period, while other tests have used news events, television programmes that appeared for only one season or winners of classic horse races. There are, however, two major problems with this approach, one being that people differ considerably in their knowledge of the particular area tested. The other problem is that if a test is to continue to be usable, it needs to be regularly updated and appropriate new norms collected since items that were very recent five years ago will of course now be more distant and harder to recall.

A good measure of autobiographical memory had the promise of avoiding these issues, and provided we probed appropriately regular recent events, such as last Christmas, the test would not need constant updating. We set about creating such a test with Michael Kopelman, a psychiatrist with prior training in psychology who was working on patients with alcoholic Korsakoff syndrome, a condition that is associated with both anterograde and retrograde amnesia. We wanted our test to be usable across a wide adult age range and chose to divide it into three sections: childhood, early adulthood and recent events such as holidays and the previous Christmas, all periods that are likely to be applicable to most of our patients. For each period we divided the questions into two categories: episodic, for example remembering a *specific* event that happened in your first school, and more sustained and semantic knowledge, such as remembering the names of your first teachers. For most patients, performance on semantic and episodic questions proved to give broadly the same result but occasional cases do occur when a patient can remember notable public events but not personal, or the reverse as in the case of an Italian lady. She was good at recalling family events but failed to remember even the most dramatic public events such as the assassination of the Prime Minister, one exception being the wedding of Prince Charles and Diana, which she seemed to have converted into a personal event of which she disapproved, describing Diana as being just like the wretched girl who had married her own son!

Michael Kopelman validated performance on our test by questioning the patient's relatives, finding little evidence of confabulation, even in Korsakoff patients who have a reputation for confabulation; they were much more likely to say that they just could not remember. There were exceptions, however, in the case of patients with frontal lobe damage who sometimes showed evidence of florid confabulation. These will be discussed further in Chapter 20. We published our test as the Autobiographical Memory Inventory and it has since been widely used. A number of similar autobiographical scales have subsequently been developed, some considerably more detailed than our own, though not reliably more sensitive according to a recent study by Kopelman.

By this point it was still not clear whether semantic and episodic memory involve different underlying systems or simply different ways of interrogating the same system. However, the process of attempting to solve this problem had led to the development of a useful clinical test and had helped in the opening up of autobiographical memory as an interesting and previously neglected area of neuropsychological research, one that continues to be vigorously pursued using a range of new methods within both psychology and neuroscience.

I had myself however, unlike my colleague Barbara, done virtually nothing that might actively help patients to cope with their memory problems. Many aspects of learning and memory had been found to be preserved in amnesic patients, but these were all of an implicit type that were far from easy to use to alleviate the deficits in explicit episodic memory, the memory for specific experiences and events that seems very important for living independently. Reflecting on the results of my study with Neil Brooks and on the various demonstrations of intact implicit memory that followed, it seemed to me that many of the preserved capacities seemed to be measured in terms of enhanced speed of performance or in a greater degree of precision, whereas tasks measured in terms of error rate seemed to be particularly vulnerable to amnesia. Could it be that episodic memory was needed to recall and then correct errors?

We decided to test this by setting up a task in which people were urged to guess if they were uncertain, common clinical practice on the grounds that people usually know more than they think they know. We compared this with a condition where errors were explicitly avoided. To achieve this we used the stem completion task described earlier as an example of preserved learning in amnesic patients. Errorful learning involved presenting the first two letters of a five letter word and asking the learner to guess what the word might be. Words were presented and tested by giving the first two letters and asking for the word to be "guessed", a task that we knew could show learning, even in densely amnesic patients. We deliberately chose words that allowed several possible completions such as STamp, STart, STrip and SToop, all sharing the first two letters. In the errorful condition, people were given the first two letters of each of a list of words and encouraged to guess. We ensured several unsuccessful guesses before providing the answer that was to be remembered. In the errorless condition we simply gave the first two letters and immediately announced, for example, that "The word is *stamp* please write that down". We tested one group of amnesic patients, comparing them with a young and an elderly group. We found that the errorless condition clearly helped the patients, when compared to the condition in which errors were allowed. The young group showed no such advantage, whereas the healthy elderly showed a slight errorless advantage.

As Barbara pointed out, the idea of errorless learning had already been proposed, based originally on operant conditioning studies using pigeons, and had subsequently been used to help people with learning disability. A search of the literature, however, suggested that it had fallen out of favour, one text suggesting that it should be used only if a standard errorful approached failed; unwise since by that time of course, the errors would be well established. We and colleagues went on to carry out a further four single-case studies. In one, an amnesic man who had lost access to the name of 36 objects achieved 33 out of 36 using the errorless method, compared to 19 when errors were possible. Two other single-case studies showed a clear advantage in using the errorless approach to learn the names of therapists, while a fourth example involved learning to put the date and time into a memory-aiding device, something that we had previously shown to be extremely sensitive to amnesia. Using the standard method of repeatedly demonstrating the task led to complete failure after 13 trials, whereas an errorless method that began with the first two steps and then provided sequential written instructions led to perfect performance which was well retained.

Recent literature reviews suggest that errorless learning is being used increasingly widely and successfully, not only in dealing with patients with memory problems but also in the area of language therapy. The effects are not enormous, but they seem to be positive and real. Why does it work? This remains an open question, but my own view is still that it capitalises on implicit memory while avoiding the need to remember and eliminate previous errors. I suspect a secondary factor, however, is that patients understandably hate repeatedly making mistakes despite the previously widespread advice to "guess, you will probably remember more than you think".

In conclusion, in contrast to our useful but limited contribution to answering the sporadic applied questions described in the chapters on the law and on environmental stress, a sustained commitment to the application of the concepts and techniques of cognitive psychology to problems of memory impairment has proved both practically useful and theoretically rewarding. Our attempt to understand amnesia provided evidence directly relevant to a series of important theoretical distinctions including the need to separate long- and short-term memory and the contrast between implicit and explicit memory. Our work also has theoretical implications for both the semantic-episodic distinction and for the concept of autobiographical memory. Happily, our work with patients has also contributed to clinical practice, potentially helping the treatment of future patients through the development of tests focussing on each of these distinctions, together with the collection of norms that allow the severity of any deficit to be assessed in patients when compared to the performance of healthy people. Finally, speculation about how preserved memory can best be used to help patients has led to the increasingly widely used errorless approach to new learning in people with memory problems.

19
Working Memory and Language

A central feature of the working memory model was that it should have the potential to be applied to important cognitive capacities and to skills extending well beyond the laboratory-based tasks on which it was developed. Language was an obvious example. We therefore decided to use the simplest and best understood component of the model, the phonological loop, and to explore its role in the way in which we process language. This had the advantage of tackling an important question on which there was already extensive research, and one which was of obvious practical interest.

At about the time we began developing our three- component model, psycholinguistics was were commanding considerable attention within the cognitive field, influenced strongly by Noam Chomsky's aim of using the analysis of grammar as a basis for understanding the mind. There were initial speculations that sentences needed to be held in STM while they were being "unpacked" grammatically. Indeed, one study appeared to provide evidence that sentences were held as a sequence of words, followed by the syntactic markers necessary for unpacking. However, after an initially promising study, support rapidly vanished following papers from both linguists and memory researchers criticising the experiment and failing to find the predicted effect when the relevant factors were properly controlled.

We ourselves began with what we regarded as a rather simpler question. Is the phonological loop involved in reading? Our volunteers read passages of prose under normal conditions, or while suppressing articulation by repeatedly uttering a single word such as "the". The task was to understand a sentence and decide whether it made sense or not. A typical sentence might be *She doesn't mind going to the dentist to have fillings, but does mind the pain when he gives her the injection at the beginning.* Half of the sentences were made anomalous either by substituting inappropriate words such as *rent* for *pain* or switching the order of two words such as *pain* and *when*. We expected that preventing subvocal rehearsal by requiring repetition of an irrelevant word would disrupt storage within the phonological loop, leading to slower processing and more errors.

Somewhat to our surprise, people seemed to read as rapidly when suppressing subvocal articulation, as under normal circumstances. However, they did significantly less well in picking out the mistakes. We found similar effects when we moved from single sentences to a proofreading task that involved detecting errors in longer prose passages. Rapidly repeating the word "the" increased the error rate, while other potentially distracting tasks such as tapping or ignoring a sequence of spoken words had no effect. These results suggested that subvocal articulation fulfilled a backup function providing a check on accuracy but was not directly involved in comprehension.

In order to get some idea as to what form this backup might take, we moved on to a simpler task known as lexical decision, which required people to judge whether a cluster of letters comprised a word (e.g. *carrot*) or a non-word (*currot*), responding as rapidly as possible. We found no effect of suppressing articulation on speed or accuracy of performing this task. The same result was obtained when people were asked to judge whether two words sounded the same (e.g. *scene-seen*) or differed (e.g. *scone-scene*). We found that people could perform this task with no disruption from suppression, even with non-words (e.g. *chaos-cayoss*). Similar results were reported around the same time by Derek Besner in Canada. However, people did encounter problems in deciding whether two items rhymed or not (e.g. *bean-seen*), suggesting that the need to actively strip away the initial consonant before making a decision was one that did rely on some form of articulatory coding.

We were surprised by the ability to make speedy and accurate lexical decisions under suppression, given that suppression impaired memory span and removed the phonological similarity effect for visually presented items. Both of these suggested that suppression prevented visually presented items being converted from a visual to a phonological code. So why was it still possible to make rapid and accurate judgements about individual words such as *wait* and *weight*? In order to account for this apparent discrepancy, we proposed two types of verbal coding: one based on the *auditory* representation of a word or non-word which we termed the "inner ear" and the other based on *articulatory* coding which we called the "inner voice". Making a simple auditory matching judgement was possible using the "inner ear", while short-term memory or active manipulation, as in stripping away the initial consonant of words before rhyme judgements, appeared to demand articulation of some kind. Importantly, it appears to be possible to create an auditory representation of printed material despite suppression, and also to understand it even when misspelled. Try reading the next sentence while rapidly repeating the word "the".

Meaning kan be kleer wen speling is attroashus and speach is privented.

The balance of evidence therefore suggests that despite its importance for memory, the phonological loop does not play a necessary part in fluent reading. Might it, however, play a part in the process of learning to read? This possibility had occurred to me several years earlier when I was introduced to someone who helped children with reading difficulties at what was then termed the London Word Blindness Centre. This term clearly suggested that their difficulties reflected visually based reading problems, but when I asked whether such children had poor digit spans, I was intrigued to hear that this was indeed the case. Some years later, I was invited to give a talk at Bangor University by Tim Miles, the Head of Department who was an expert on helping children with reading problems, by then, more commonly termed dyslexia. I asked Tim the same question, and he described the pattern of deficits that he typically found in children with reading problems. They included reduced digit span as one part of a cluster of deficits that could well reflect a limitation in the operation of the phonological loop. We decided to collaborate, and I began to work with Tim and a young lecturer, Nick Ellis, in Bangor, together with my postdoctoral colleague Bob Logie in Cambridge.

The possible link between verbal STM and learning to read was already a very lively area. My old boss Conrad had noted in his work on congenitally deaf people, both that their digit span was low and that they had considerable difficulties in learning to read. He suggested that verbal STM might play an important part in learning to read by allowing *sequences* of sounds to be maintained. This is potentially an important capacity for acquiring the skill of reading where, during the early stages at least, it is necessary to convert a sequence of printed letters into their appropriate sounds which must then be maintained in the correct order until the word has been decoded. Work at the Haskins Laboratory in the US had followed up Conrad's work, studying poor readers with normal hearing and testing the hypothesis that their reading delay was also associated with failure to use phonological coding. They found that their sample of poor readers had reduced memory spans and also failed to show the normal phonological similarity effect, whereby similar sounding letters such as *b g d c p* were harder to remember in the right order than a dissimilar sequence such as *k r w l s*. They proposed that poor readers, like Conrad's congenitally deaf group, were failing to use verbal short-term memory (STM).

We decided to explore this further, taking advantage of Tim's contacts within the field of dyslexia and testing at a school for boys with reading problems. We tested a group of boys from the school, comparing them with two other normal reading groups: one group comprised younger children matched for reading age, and the other comparison group comprised normal readers of the same chronological age as the dyslexic boys, and hence at a higher reading level. We recruited these two comparison groups from schools in Cambridge, initially with some difficulty. When we approached the Chief Educational Psychologist we were refused cooperation and warned that dyslexia was simply a label used by middle-class parents as an excuse for the poor performance of their children. I invited him to meet for lunch when we could explain our project further, and over a pint and a sandwich pointed out that we were simply testing the *memory* performance of Cambridge children, whereupon he was happy to agree. I was relieved to hear a few years later that he had left Cambridge and that dyslexia was no longer a forbidden concept.

Following on from the Haskins work we opted to test three features of relevance to the phonological loop, namely digit span, starting with short sequences and increasing length until the sequences were too long for the child to recall correctly. The point of breakdown provided a measure of verbal short-term memory. Next, we looked at the effect of phonological similarity; if the Haskins group was right, we should find the dyslexic group insensitive to this standard effect. Finally we tested the speed with which they could repeat short sequences of words to check for problems in articulation. When compared to the other children, we found our dyslexic group was equivalent in memory span to the younger children of the same *reading age* but had reliably shorter spans than of children of the same chronological age. A similar pattern occurred for speed of articulation, with both the younger and dyslexic groups repeating material more slowly than the age-matched children. However, we found that all three groups showed a clear phonological similarity effect, suggesting that they were indeed all using the phonological loop.

It turned out that the Haskins work was misleading as it resulted from using the *same* sequence length for all groups, a length within the range of good readers but very difficult for the poor readers, with their reduced span. It proves to be the case that when sequence length becomes substantially greater than span, virtually everyone abandons the use of the phonological loop. So, what could we conclude? Our dyslexic boys appeared to be using the phonological loop in the normal way but did have both reduced span and slower articulation. Our earlier hope that their problems might be solved by simply training them to use the phonological loop vanished, but it did seem as if the phonological loop might well play some role in developmental dyslexia.

An alternative source of ideas about the psychology of reading was provided by studies of *acquired dyslexia*, reading problems following brain damage, for example after a stroke. This was a very active area in the UK, profiting from a theoretical model developed at the Unit by John Morton. Consequently, acquired dyslexia in adults was at that time a particular concentration of strength within the Unit. Two main forms of acquired dyslexia had been identified, with the possibility of other less well-studied varieties. The two forms were linked to the proposal that fluent readers could rely on two ways to read. One of these was assumed to be based on the initial stage of learning to read, which teaches the child to turn visually presented letters into spoken sounds, which then benefits from the existing link between spoken language and meaning; the term *surface dyslexia* was applied to disruption of this route.

A second route was assumed to develop subsequently in the fluent reader, whereby a rapid and direct link develops between the printed word form and its meaning, allowing the earlier letter-to-sound route to be bypassed. It was presumably this direct route that allowed our fluent readers to understand prose while suppressing articulation. It also allowed some patients with reading problems to apparently understand words that they could not read aloud, sometimes making errors that were related to the meaning of the correct word while being visually very different. Hence a patient might read *chapel* for *prayer* and *parrot* for *canary*. The term *deep dyslexia* was applied to this condition. Such patients typically found it more difficult to read abstract than concrete words, and, unlike surface dyslexia, patients could not read out pronounceable but meaningless non-words, such as *dosk* and *wug*.

Encouraged by the way in which such cases could be explained in terms of models of normal adult reading such as that proposed by John Morton, some investigators suggested that a similar pattern might emerge for developmental dyslexia. Given our ready access to a population of boys with developmental dyslexia, we decided to explore this possibility, focussing particularly on the types of reading errors made by boys with problems, comparing the resulting pattern with those made by younger boys of the same reading age and with the types of errors reported for patients. The results were clear. Our dyslexic boys showed the same pattern as younger normal readers: words were easier to read than non-words, regular spelled words were easier than irregular, short were easier to read than long and words learned early in life were easier than those encountered later. There was some similarity to the pattern found in surface dyslexia but even more similarity to the pattern found in normal early readers.

Our results seemed clear: dyslexia in children did not resemble that typically found in brain-damaged adults. Furthermore it was perhaps not too surprising that problems in *learning* to read might not be the same as those resulting from brain damage in a fluent reader who had already learned to read and had practiced the skill for many years. We were therefore somewhat surprised when we tried to publish our findings, at the hostility of several of the journal referees, who seemed indignant at our failure to support their particular hypothesis.

I subsequently discovered that this was all too common in the field of dyslexia, populated by a relatively large number of theorists, all with different interpretations that they often seemed to hold with considerable passion. Two or three theories were visually based, while another proposed wider problems in skill acquisition. In the auditory domain, one attributed dyslexia to an impaired capacity to perceive rapid auditory changes and at least two focussed on phonological aspects of reading. I suspect that the reason for this diversity is that reading is a complex skill or combination of skills that can take many years to acquire and can probably break down at more than one point. Each theorist tended to focus on a particular feature of the reading deficit which they argued was crucial, typically testing samples of children with reading problems and finding that their proposed crucial deficits did indeed occur. Unfortunately however, all too few investigators included anyone else's tests in their studies, perhaps understandably, given the wide range of alternative proposals.

A further problem concerned the question of whether deficits regarded as causing reading problems might actually be the result of poor reading, rather than causing it. One deficit that is clearly associated with dyslexia, for example, is *phonological awareness*, the capacity to reflect on the spoken form of words, using this to break them up into their constituent sounds, regarded as an important step in reading development. Measuring phonological awareness, however, is a complex task, typically using a range of tests from simple rhyme judgement to the complex spoonerism task. This was named after Dr Spooner, an Oxford don who is said to have had difficulty in maintaining the order of the initial consonants of words, for example transforming the phrase "the dear old queen" into "the queer old dean". The test involves taking two spoken words and requiring the listener to exchange the initial consonants and then pronounce the new pair: for example transforming *hot* – *rat* to *rot* – *hat* or *bring* – *girl* to *gring* – *birl*. This certainly relies both on working memory to hold and manipulate the words while processing and also on analytic verbal skills that seem to be acquired *during* the process of learning to read. The latter point was demonstrated by studies of illiterate elder daughters within a Portuguese fishing community who were traditionally kept from school to look after the family home and hence never learned to read. They were otherwise intellectually quite normal but could not do complex phonological awareness tests, suggesting that such awareness develops as a result of learning to read.

A few years later I was on the grant committee of an organisation that had funded three or four groups, each claiming to test their various plausible hypotheses as to the cause of reading problems. When the time came to renew the grants, each put in a proposal for further work which was then refereed by, amongst others, the rival groups. Without fail, each rubbished the others with the result that none of them were funded. Despite its practical importance, this degree of conflict within the area was new to me, and certainly not characteristic of the memory field where differences certainly existed but tended not to be pursued with such venom.

There are a number of reasons why passions tend to run rather high in the field of reading and its disorders. First of all, literacy is clearly an enormously important topic within education and indeed within society more generally. Failure to learn to read fluently will result in a persistent handicap, while the acquisition of literacy in previously preliterate group is likely to open doors to education and consequent improvements in living standards more generally. If you feel that your answer to the question of optimising reading is valid, then it is tempting to regard other people with very different approaches as potentially delaying progress by introducing confusion to an already complex area. Furthermore, as mentioned earlier, learning to read is likely to involve the interaction of many different subskills, such as perceptual, cognitive and motivational, together with the influence of an appropriate teaching environment and family support. It is therefore unsurprising that evidence for several types of deficit can be found in children with reading problems.

Finally, the ultimate practical aim of much research on reading and its disorders is presumably to improve the way in which reading is taught and to help children with reading problems. There is a huge literature on the psychology of reading, and this has led to the development of pro-grammes to capitalise on earlier laboratory-based research and to apply it to the teaching of reading. In Britain at least, such work has had a positive influence on government policy with a clear evidence-based emphasis on phonics, associated with clear overall improvements in national reading standards. Doing good educational research is difficult with the result that policies may often be based on persuasion rather than evidence, a situation not helped in some educational systems by decisions taken at a political level, open to lobbying with potential financial implications in a lucrative publishing market.

It is therefore extremely important that psychologists continue to do scientifically credible field research in this very difficult area, a good exam-ple being the work that was done in my current department by Margaret Snowling and her team on developing and evaluating reading systems, and by Dorothy Bishop in Oxford on keeping a close eye on such developments and related claims and maintaining a crucial link to the public through her blog. Given that my own principal interest in the area was that of working memory however, which is only one of several contributors to the under-standing and remediation of reading problems, I decided to retreat from the battlefield and concentrate on other possible impacts of working mem-ory on language and its acquisition.

I decided to look elsewhere for interesting problems but did drift back into the field of reading a few years later while pursuing the separate but related question of which factors influenced a child's capacity to learn new words. It involved a project carried out with Susan Gathercole who had joined the Unit following a postdoctoral post with Donald Broadbent in Oxford. As part of our vocabulary project, we included measures of reading in a longitudinal study which followed up a range of normal Cambridge children over a three-year period. The dominant theory of the cause of dyslexia within the field at that time invoked a deficit in phonological awareness, the capacity to be aware of the sounds that make up a word, and to be able to manipulate them.

Our own study included both a test of phonological awareness based on rhyme judgement and separate tests of verbal short-term memory. By chance, two of the five schools we tested used a different teaching approach from the rest, which seemed to lead to a slower rate of learning, despite starting with children of comparable ability to the other three. As a result, these schools had reached a level of reading at the end of two years that was equivalent to the other three schools at the end of year one. This natural experiment allowed us to separate out the effect of age from that of reading stage, resulting in the discovery that *both* STM and phonological awareness contributed to reading but at different stages of learning. Phonological STM seemed to play an important role at a point where children were learning letter-to-sound correspondences, while phonological awareness became relevant somewhat later.

So, how important is the phonological loop to reading? When learning to read, the phonological loop does seem to be important, and reduced verbal memory span certainly tends to be associated with reading problems. In the case of the fluent reading of relatively straightforward prose, the answer seems to be "not very", other than as a backup in tasks such as proofreading where it does indeed seem to be useful. We still suspected, however, that despite our earlier results, a grossly impaired phonological loop might possibly play a role, at least in dealing with complex sentences.

The opportunity to explore this further cropped up with an invitation to study a patient who appeared to have a severe and very pure phonological loop deficit. The invitation resulted from a collaboration between the Unit and neurologists at the University of Milan, a group that had developed a major reputation under the leadership of the professor of neurology, Ennio Di Renzi. Ennio founded the journal *Cortex* and developed an extremely effective group of neurology-based neuropsychologists, initially using a relatively standard test-based approach. They contacted the Unit with a view to our hosting some promising young neuropsychologists interested in learning more about cognitive psychology. This led to two extensive collaborations, one focussing on Alzheimer's Disease, which I will describe later, and the other focussing on short-term memory with Giuseppe (Beppe) Vallar and Costanza Papagno. Beppe had discovered a patient PV, with a very clear and pure deficit in short-term verbal memory of the type studied by Shallice and Warrington that had played such an important part in the argument for separating long- and short-term memory. We decided to check first of all whether PV's memory deficit could adequately be described by assuming an impaired phonological loop component of working memory. If so, we could then begin to investigate any more general consequences of such a deficit, thus providing insight into what broader capabilities might depend on the loop.

I travelled to Milan on a number of occasions, carefully planning and preparing the experiments with Beppe in Milan before travelling over for the day to Turin, where PV had a small antique and gift shop. When we arrived she would put up the "closed" notice on the shop door, and we would test her across an elegant table surrounded by antiques and upmarket gifts, the most unlikely laboratory in which I have ever worked.

After a hard morning's work we would all three go to a nearby restaurant and reward ourselves with a splendid Italian lunch. It is not a bad life being a scientist sometimes!

We duly found that the longest sequence of spoken digits that she could repeat back was two and that she showed no phonological similarity or word length effect and had a very limited recency effect in the free recall of a list of words. All of these were consistent with a phonological loop deficit. Her performance on standardised tests showed that her long-term memory was normal, as was her visual working memory and her level of general intelligence. So PV seemed to offer a golden opportunity of finding just what function the phonological loop might serve: What tasks could she *not* do, in the absence of an adequate phonological loop?

We began with our earlier question of language comprehension. We tested this by asking her to decide whether each of a series of sentences was true or false, varying the length but keeping constant the broad grammatical form of the sentence. With short sentences, she was fine and hence could correctly accept a sentence such as *Ships are lived on by sailors* but reject *Sailors are lived on by ships*. However, when the sentence was lengthened by adding verbiage, for example, *Sailors, it is commonly believed, and with some justification, are frequently lived on by ships*, she made many errors in contrast to a group of healthy people of equivalent age and intelligence who had no difficulty in dealing with the greater length. This was a start, but it seemed unlikely that the phonological loop has evolved specifically to deal with badly constructed prose. What other function might it serve?

One possibility was suggested by our earlier observation that phonological STM seemed to play a part in children's learning to read. Perhaps the loop was important in phonological learning more generally: for example in acquiring new words. As an adult, PV would already have a good vocabulary and so would not be too handicapped, but a child in a similar situation might well be seriously disadvantaged. We decided to test for this possible deficit by teaching PV new words from a foreign language, Russian. We tested her ability to learn eight new words and their meaning: for example *flower – svieti*. In order to check that this was not a general LTM problem we also required her to learn eight pairs of unrelated words in her native language: for example *table – castle*. We knew that this type of learning relies principally on semantic coding, which should be preserved in PV's case. It was, with both PV and the healthy control group learning all eight Italian pairs in five trials. Learning Russian was very different; the controls took 10 trials to learn all eight words, by which time

PV had not mastered a single one. We had finally found a potentially important function for the phonological loop, namely new phonologically-based learning.

We did of course need to check this, not easy since patients such as PV are rare. So we did the next best thing by using healthy subjects and interfering with the operation of their phonological loop. One set of experiments required people to suppress subvocal rehearsal by repeatedly uttering an irrelevant word during learning. Another series compared the learning of long and short foreign words, while a third series varied the phonological similarity of the words to be acquired. All three of these methods of disrupting the operation of the phonological loop slowed down the rate at which people could learn new foreign words while having no effect on learning to associate unrelated pairs of native language words.

The next step was to ask how widely our new finding could be generalised; did the link between reduced memory span and vocabulary acquisition only apply to extreme cases learning foreign words or could it be applied more widely to children learning their native language? A hint as to how to pursue this came through a talk at the Unit by a linguist, David Crystal, who described a group of children with Specific Language Impairment (SLI), who had substantially delayed language, together with normal non-verbal intelligence. Susan Gathercole and I decided to explore the possibility that these children might have a phonological loop deficit and we were fortunate to discover that one school in Cambridge happened to specialise in helping such children.

Those in the group we studied were eight years old at the time but had the language development of six-year-olds. As expected, they had reduced digit spans and when tested on children's verbal memory battery proved to have particular difficulty in hearing and repeating back unfamiliar non-words. We decided to follow this up by creating a new instrument: the Non-word Repetition Test. This involved the tester reading out a series of non-words ranging in length from two syllables e.g. *ballop* to five e.g. *altupatory*, where in each case, the child had simply to repeat back the non-word as spoken by the tester. We compared our children with normal eight-year-olds, and with a group of six-year-old children whose level of language development was the same as our target group. When tested on non-word repetition, the performance of the language-impaired group decreased rapidly with the length of the non-word and was substantially poorer even than that of six-year-olds. If a child cannot temporarily maintain the form of a new and unfamiliar spoken word, it is perhaps unsurprising if their vocabulary development is slower.

The next question was whether the effect was large enough to influence vocabulary development within a normal population of children, or was its effect limited to a small disadvantaged group. To answer this question we tested a total of 118 Cambridge children starting school at the age of four and five, following them over a four-year period. We used a standard vocabulary test whereby four pictures are shown to the child and the name of one of them spoken; if the child knows the word they must point to that picture. The test starts with words learnt very early in life, gradually becoming harder as words acquired later are introduced. We also tested the children on our newly developed non-word repetition test, and across a series of studies found a gratifyingly high association between non-word repetition and vocabulary for ages four, five and six, becoming less though still statiscally significant by age eight. There was also a link with intelligence, but allowing for this, there was still a robust association between our phonological loop measure and the number of words the children knew.

Of course, showing that non-word repetition is correlated with vocabulary does not prove that the link is causal. One might equally well argue that having a good vocabulary already helps you cope with and repeat unfamiliar new words. There is, however, a way of teasing this apart by testing the same children over several years. If the phonological loop is the driving factor, then performance on repetition should predict *future* growth in vocabulary over the next year, whereas if vocabulary is what drives the relationship, there should be a stronger link between vocabulary on year one and non-word repetition a year later. When tested over several years we found that during the early stages, non-word repetition appeared to drive vocabulary growth, suggesting that the phonological loop is crucial, but as vocabulary develops the association becomes more equal, suggesting that although the phonological loop plays a dominant role during the early years, existing word knowledge does in due course begin to help the child to learn new words.

Further evidence in support of this two-way relationship comes from studying the repetition of longer and more complex non-words by older children. Here, sequences that follow the broad pronunciation rules of English, such as *confrantual*, are easier to repeat than those that have less support from existing language habits, such as *perplisteronk*. Evidence that the phonological loop still makes a contribution comes from the fact that people with high digit or word spans are no better than low span people on word-like items but have a clear advantage on items with an atypical letter and sound pattern. These gain less support from similar known words, and hence depend more for maintenance on a contribution from the phonological loop.

You will note that we have consistently relied on the non-word repetition test rather than digit span, which performs a similar function but is slightly less effective in predicting vocabulary. We think that this is because digit span makes use of the existing familiar sound patterns that are present in the number names. The order of sounds *within* the number names is already familiar; hence the main contribution of the phonological loop is to maintain digit order. This is likely to place less demand on the loop than that of holding a non-word in which the order of sounds within the whole sequence will be new.

So, at last we felt able to refute the suggestion of a rather unsympathetic colleague who regarded the phonological loop as lacking in practical significance, describing it as "a mere pimple on the face of cognition", later suggesting that it was a rather lower part of the anatomy he had in mind. Indeed, the loop seems to provide an important tool for the acquisition of language more generally although, happily not the *only* tool since people with a reduced phonological loop can in due course develop extensive vocabularies. The later stages of language acquisition probably depend more on other factors such as executive resources and exposure to a rich language environment.

Native language learning is by no means the only function of the loop, an obvious extension being to second language learning, as the case of PV demonstrated. I came across a clear example of this whilst spending a sabbatical semester at the University of Texas in Austin. I had been testing a young man Rajan, a mnemonist who had a remarkable facility for remembering sequences of numbers and who had for a while held the world record for the most decimal places recalled of π, the symbol representing the ratio of a circle's circumference to its diameter. I found his memory for other materials to be good but not outstanding when compared to most other graduate students. One student however, SR, initially declined to be tested on the grounds that he had a terrible digit span. That sounded interesting, so we persuaded him to be tested using the same tests we had used for PV. SR's digit span was four, not as low as PV's but dramatically down in comparison to his six fellow students whose spans ranged from 8 to 12. His span for words was less dramatically lower than that of his colleagues and he showed both phonological similarity and word length effects, suggesting that he *was* using the phonological loop. He seemed to be otherwise comparable to his colleagues with normal visual short-term memory and a high IQ of 128.

The next and crucial question concerned the impact of SR's phonological loop limitations on long-term learning. On a test of visual and verbal recall and recognition, his visual scores were normal, but his capacity to recognise names he had just seen or to learn the names of four individuals was clearly impaired. Finally, like PV, we asked him to learn eight foreign words and their English equivalent, or eight pairs of English words all presented auditorily. Like PV, his word-word learning was normal, while across the five trials needed by his colleagues to learn all the foreign words, he showed no evidence of learning. He told me that at high school he had desperately tried to learn both French and Spanish in order to qualify to enter a programme at the Universoty of California Los Angeles but had made absolutely no headway despite his obvious intelligence. Eventually he was allowed in as a special case made by the academic support group that was helping him. He did very well at UCLA and was, when I tested him, an extremely promising graduate student.

The link between working memory and second language acquisition appears to have been noted by the language teaching community, and I was delighted to discover, while writing this section, a recent meta-analysis covering some 79 studies of working memory and second language learning involving 3707 learners, finding a very solid positive link with clear contributions from both the central executive and the phonological loop. It has been a long journey, but the phonological loop managed to justify itself in the end!

20

Boston and the Central Executive

I had been directing the Unit for about 10 years when the opportunity to take a three-month sabbatical arose. I justified it on two grounds. My plan was to spend most of the time at Bolt Beranek and Newman, the US institution that most closely resembled the Unit in combining basic and applied research, but which functioned as an independent company, reliant entirely on earning its living through research contracts. It seemed to offer an interesting potential complement to the way in which we organised things, and to offer the long-term potential of possible collaborations. The second aim was to respond to an invitation from a prestigious Oxford University Press series to write a book summarising a decade of research on working memory and attempting to tie it together into a more coherent theoretical framework. In this connection I was pleased to also be offered a link to Harvard by W.K. (Bill) Estes, a very distinguished experimental psychologist who had first established himself in the latter part of the era of rats and behaviourism. He then went on to elaborate his ideas through research on human learning, developing a mathematical approach that provided the foundations to a good deal of current work on human long-term learning and memory.

It was an important three months for me and worth, I believe, describing in some detail both as a personal experience and through the progress, and lack of progress, on my two missions. It allowed me to lay the foundations of the book *Working Memory*, which consolidated the model, in particular forcing me to be more explicit about the concept of a central executive, although in the interest of coherence, I will go on to describe developments that go far beyond the three-month visit.

Domestically, my time in Boston was divided into two parts: one living in Cambridge with Hilary and two of my sons, and a second part living alone, out on the New England coast at Cape Ann in a colonial-style inn. My visit began in the summer, which meant that our children were out of school, and we were able to arrange a house, car and pet swap between the two Cambridges. We offered our modern terrace house in the centre of town; our rather modest car; and our cat, a large and lazy ginger tom. In return we received a detached house and yard close to Harvard, a Saab car and two dogs. We seemed to be getting the better of the deal until we met the two dogs. We thought that our children would enjoy walking them, but alas this proved impossible since one, a Pyrenean Mountain dog, was huge and liable to set off into the traffic if he saw a cat across the road. He was also rather neurotic and would refuse to eat if his food had been touched by the second dog, a tiny but greedy Yorkshire terrier with hip problems. Looking after them seemed to involve a considerable degree of ritual, particularly when giving them the various pills that they were supposed to take every week. We were, however, very fortunate in the splendid house in a wonderful location.

After a few weeks, Hilary and our boys went back to England, and I had to find somewhere else to live. Rents in Cambridge were quite high, and it occurred to me that this might be an opportunity for a change of scene. I discovered that I could get a much better deal if I commuted northwards up the coast to Cape Ann, where I found a small very attractive town called Manchester-by-the-Sea, very different from Manchester, UK. I stayed in a colonial-style inn, where, given the time of year, I was usually the only guest, travelling in and out on a magnificent streamline train, somewhat dilapidated since its heyday in the 1930s, which took a very scenic coastal route through to Boston. Latterly, I was lent a car by my generous host at BBN, Ray Nickerson, which allowed me to dice with the rather hair-raising Boston traffic and on weekends to travel around New England.

Because Manchester was very small, and I seemed to be the only out-sider, I got to know quite a bit about it. In character it seemed very much like *Tarbox*, the town described in John Updike's novel *Couples*. That, I was told by my landlady, was because the novel was based on the town and the behaviour of a range of local couples, although I later discovered that Updike himself lived at a different small town on Cape Ann. I went with my landlady to a town meeting where issues affecting town governance were discussed and decided by interested townspeople. I asked whether this mode of governance really worked and was assured that on the whole it did, provided decisions did not conflict with the interests of the wealthy Greek family that owned the local supermarket and much of the town's other property. I seem to recall that the main topic of discussion was what to do in case of a nuclear attack, but that could be a confabulation.

Manchester-by-the-Sea was an ideal location for my favourite method of writing, allowing me to dictate a first draft while walking through attractive countryside and along the rugged coast. This was studded with large villas, built when Manchester was favoured by Boston society as its location for summer residence, and later often used by foreign embassies escaping the heat of Washington DC. Inland there were wooded hills threaded through by trails with the occasional wall or abandoned farm building left over from earlier days when the hills were farmed, before being abandoned as people moved west to easier and more fertile land.

Back in Boston I was enjoying my time at BBN, supplementing my MRC salary with funds from working on a joint project with my host, Ray Nickerson, and enjoying meeting the range of distinguished cognitive psychologists who were there at that time. I was particularly intrigued by one project on which Ray was a principal investigator. It was held jointly with Harvard, was sponsored by Luis Alberto Machado whose unusual position was Minister of State for the Development of Human Intelligence and funded by Petroleos de Venezuela. It had the rather ambitious aim of raising the national IQ. Venezuela was oil-rich at the time but education-ally underdeveloped. The minister decided that he would invite proposals from groups who might potentially introduce a system that would raise the overall IQ of the country. Harvard and BBN initially declined the contract as far too ambitious but agreed to a more modest proposal to design and launch a teacher-led, one-year course on thinking skills. I gather that the project was completed, a Venezuelan course developed and in due course a US equivalent.

I also thoroughly enjoyed the weekly meetings that were my main link with the Estes lab, also attended by Ed Smith from BBN and Jay McClelland who was visiting from Carnegie Mellon University in Pittsburgh. Ed was at the front rank of cognitive psychology and subsequently moved to Michigan, where he and his colleague, John Jonides, developed the foundations for using brain-imaging methods to study the neural basis of working memory. Jay, on the other hand, was a central figure in the development of compu-tational models of long-term and semantic memory, playing a particularly important role in developing approaches based on parallel distributed pro-cessing models of language.

Meanwhile I began to explore the way in which applied research was funded in North America. I contacted two or three Boston-based companies that carried out human factors research, explaining my quest. All were happy to see me and discuss the issue of how one might persuade large companies to fund applied research. It turned out that they hoped that I might be able to help <u>them</u>, since they had little direct funding from industry. The standard pattern I was told was that they would have representatives in Washington DC and would watch out for government contracts for which two competitors were typically funded; the aim was to identify and secure one of these, when appropriate. The government was clearly the main source of research funding; gone were the days when companies like Bell Telephone and IBM would fund their own laboratories to carry out both applied and basic blue skies research.

I had higher hopes of BBN, which at the time combined applied research with cutting-edge basic cognitive psychology. I arranged a meeting with their management who I remember as young men in suits. I was disappointed to find that they seemed to have a keener eye to the bottom line than to science, which I suspect they saw as yielding rather unsatisfactory profit margins. I discovered that BBN had recently floated on the stock exchange and appeared to be undergoing a major change in its underlying ethos. I was rapidly convinced, as I suspect were they, that attempting a collaborative link between BBN and the Unit would never work. The flow of innovative cognitive psychology from the lab seemed to tail off over the next few years as they moved more substantially into computer science, where BBN played an important role in creating the Arpanet, which morphed into the Internet some years later. Since that time they have been taken over several times and are now part of Raytheon, a major defence contractor. I suspect that any theoretically orientated links to psychology are long gone.

I returned to find the UK government still very keen to encourage direct contact between research scientists and major companies, something I had wrongly assumed happened all the time in the US. The Unit in fact did have some such links, particularly through ongoing research on human-computer interaction, including one with Xerox, who later located the European branch of their Palo Alto Research Centre in Cambridge, based on the link. The difficulty of building such sustained associations, however, is typified by our subsequent attempt to build a bridge between our own skills and the interests of BP, a company that had interests extending well beyond petroleum. They had a centre focussing on more long-term "blue skies" research, located off Oxford Street in the West End of London that prided itself on being the "University of the West End". Both sides started with enthusiasm and good faith, but it gradually emerged that their needs were some considerable distance from basic research, and that the APU staff involved tended to spend their time on committees. Perhaps the most difficult aspect occurred, however, when my counterpart at BP who was enthusiastic for a collaboration moved; his successor was understandably less committed to the project, which gradually lapsed.

We continued, however, to have very fruitful links to a wide range of practical users of our skills; these tended to be based on individual contacts rather than on formal top-down structural agreements. Furthermore, such long-term links were more likely to flourish in connection with government-controlled institutions such as the Transport and Road Research Laboratory and the Post Office, tending to wither following privatisation. A good example followed the sale by the government of the telecommunications section of the General Post Office. Under the resulting private ownership, even very applied research was liable to come into conflict with the ever-increasing focus on next year's balance sheet and short-term gain, making sustained collaboration increasingly difficult.

At a more institutional level, one way in which governments could continue to be informed by science was through long-standing committees of experts in the relevant area, tasked with taking a long-term view and, on occasion, able to sponsor applied research. Such bodies came under the general term QUANGOs (quasi-autonomous non-governmental organisations). However a subsequent Conservative government decided that such organisations were a waste of public money and proceeded to systematically abolish them, relying instead on their favourite means of control, "market forces", resulting in an ever-increasing number of private companies created to look after "the public interest". It is clearly important to link basic and applied research, a process that can be lengthy and too uncertain of outcome to be readily fitted into a commercial framework in a highly competitive environment. Successive British governments have certainly been aware of this but too often have opted for short-term top-down solutions driven ideologically rather than through any deep understanding of the processes involved in developing and applying science.

In the meantime, independent of the politicians, the world of applied science was changing rapidly, a fact that was vividly represented within Cambridge. A friend who worked as a science writer on the local newspaper won a national prize which allowed him to choose to follow up a story anywhere in the world. He opted to visit the other Cambridge in Massachusetts, which was witnessing an explosion of newly founded science-based companies. Why was Cambridge, England, not showing a similar expansion, he asked? He delayed his trip for a year, by which time exactly the same was happening all around him. Cambridge, England, was witnessing an ever-growing number of young companies, particularly in the areas of computer science, information processing and subsequently biotechnology.

Unlike Oxford, Cambridge had resisted any tendency for commerce to invade the city during the 19th and early 20th centuries, remaining largely as an East Anglian market town with a university. Cambridge today is very different, like its sister city across the Atlantic, hosting an ever-increasing number of technology companies that benefit from the steady flow of bright graduates emerging from the university. Prosperity has clearly increased, at least as reflected by the number of restaurants and expensive ladies frock shops, unfortunately accompanied by major traffic problems and on my last visit, an apparent lack of shops to sell useful things like batteries. That, I suppose, is the price of progress.

To return to Boston, progress on my proposed book proved rather more encouraging than my attempt to build bridges between the Unit and industry, although progress slowed down when I returned to my duties of Unit director, and the book only emerged a year or two later. In writing the book, I found it relatively easy to bring together research on the phonological loop that had characterised our initial 1974 paper, combining it with research on visuospatial memory carried out at Stirling and later back in Cambridge. Things were coming together quite nicely when I realised that I had said nothing about the central executive, probably the most crucial part of the model, a clear case of Hamlet without the prince.

Avoiding the central executive had not been entirely accidental since it depended on some kind of theory of attentional control, and we realised that creating such a theory would be a lengthy and daunting task. I therefore began to look around for existing theories of attention that I might adopt. They were not hard to find, notable examples being those of Anne Treisman with its earlier origins in ideas such as those proposed by Broadbent, while another exciting and influential approach to attention was that of Michael Posner whose elegant research was beginning to combine cognitive experimental psychology with its neurobiological underpinning. However these and several others in the field were all focussed on perception, concerning themselves with factors that determine how information from the world is selected, filtered and made available to awareness. I needed a model that was concerned with action and the capacity to *manipulate* and *control* such information. I knew of only one such theory, that proposed by Donald Norman and Tim Shallice, who were both interested in the question of attentional control but for rather different reasons.

Norman was principally interested in understanding slips of action. Such mental lapses can be relatively trivial, for example driving to the supermarket on a Saturday morning only to find yourself on weekday automatic pilot and arriving at your office instead. Occasionally however such lapses can be devastating, as in a recent case of pilot error at an air display resulting in the plane crashing on a nearby busy road. Norman saw such slips of action as giving clues as to how we control our behaviour and navigate through the complexities of everyday life.

Tim Shallice, on the other hand, was principally interested in the role of the frontal lobes of the brain in controlling behaviour. This was a classic problem since some patients could suffer substantial lesions in these extensive areas with little apparent effect. A classic case from the 19th century was that of Phineas Gage, who had the misfortune to be in an explosion which drove an iron bar through the front of his brain, leaving him apparently intellectually unimpaired, although his personality changed from staid and upright to that of profane ne'er do well. Hebb carried out research on patients who had had surgery to the frontal lobes to "treat" a range of behavioural problems, a strategy that was sadly common during the earlier years of the last century. On standard clinical tests, such patients often seemed to be intellectually normal.

On the other hand, some patients with frontal lobe damage clearly had problems that seemed to reflect difficulties in attentional control. The best way of giving a flavour of these is to describe RJ, a patient who I studied in collaboration with Barbara Wilson at Rivermead. Patient RJ was an engineer who had suffered substantial damage to both left and right frontal lobes following a road traffic accident. He had major problems in attentional control, which sometimes led him to have great difficulty in breaking away from a particular action or activity, for example repeatedly making the same error when attempting to cut lengths of tape during occupational therapy; when the mistakes were pointed out, he crossly responded, "I know I shouldn't be doing this". A similar perseveration occurred in his personal memory on occasion. When asked, for example, how his accident had occurred, something he could almost certainly not actually remember, he correctly reported that he had been driving to a project at the Steel Company of Wales when he overtook a car and was hit by an oncoming lorry. He said, "Then I stopped and he stopped. I said I am sorry mate it was my fault; no the driver said it was my fault, but I insist it was my fault, no said the driver", with multiple repetitions of this conversation before eventually he managed to break out of the loop and continue.

RJ's attentional problems were not limited to perseveration and could often show the opposite pattern of failing to focus and control his actions, sometimes resulting in what is known as utilisation behaviour. This occurs when an object in the environment evokes a response, regardless of whether the response is socially appropriate: for example reaching over and drinking someone else's tea. This can be bizarre as in the case of one patient who, noting a hypodermic syringe on the desk, reached over and proceeded to attempt to inject the doctor interviewing him.

Our principal interest was on the role of the frontal lobes in memory, which in RJ's case was substantial. He had great difficulty in controlling retrieval from memory as required: for example in the task of generating as many animal names as possible in a specified time. RJ's response to this request was "dog" followed by a long pause "there must be thousands of them!" "...... did I say dog?" This was not because he had lost the names of animals since when asked, for example, for an Australian animal that hops, he readily came up with "kangaroo"; his problem was that of initiating and controlling memory search.

Not only can frontal lobe damage interfere with the attentional control of retrieval, it can also impair the capacity to evaluate what has been retrieved, potentially leading to confabulation. On one occasion, while home for the weekend, he turned to his wife and asked, "Why do you keep telling people we are married?" "We are married, we have three children", responded his wife. At this time it was very unusual for people to raise a family and not be married. When RJ again rejected the idea, she showed him photographs of the wedding to which he replied, "That chap does look like me, but it is not me because I am not married". An hour or so later he had completely forgotten this and made no such claim. It might seem as though RJ simply had a rather distorted sense of humour. This is unlikely to be the case because he would act on his confabulations, attempting to retrieve a suitcase from a non-existent roof space or marching out of Rivermead pushing a fellow patient in a wheelchair in order to show him the sewage works that he was involved in building. He had indeed been involved in such a project but long ago and some distance away.

In essence, the Norman and Shallice model for the attentional control of action was very simple. It proposed two separate but interacting systems. One of these was based on well-learned habits, together with rules that would automatically adjudicate when two such habits were in conflict, following a well-established conflict resolution process used in existing computer models. It is this system that is assumed to allow an experienced driver to complete a familiar route and then have no memory of the journey, presumably because most attention was focussed on other matters. Such a system would automatically avoid other drivers, stop at red lights and follow the well-learned route. Suppose, however, that the route was blocked by road repair works; in this case the second system would become involved in active and conscious problem-solving, attempting to plan an alternative route.

It is this component termed the Supervisory Attention System (SAS) that Shallice proposed was dependent on the frontal lobes. Extensive evidence from neuropsychological patients, and latterly from imaging the brains of normal people while performing complex tasks, suggests that the frontal lobes do indeed play a central role in organising behaviour and controlling attention. They are probably also necessary for focussing attention while also allowing us to switch between tasks when appropriate and to timeshare between two or more activities. Shallice's SAS seemed therefore to be an excellent candidate for the central executive; adopting it allowed me to complete my book with at least a semblance of covering our three-component model of working memory.

A common objection to the central executive, however, is that it does not actually *explain* anything, simply functioning as a homunculus, a little man in the head to whom all the complicated aspects of working memory can be assigned. My response to this is that homunculi can indeed be useful, not as an explanation but as a marker and reminder of a series of issues that will ultimately require explanation but that are currently beyond the current focus on more tractable areas. In our case, treating the central executive as a homunculus allowed us to concentrate on the phonological loop. If a model is to continue to grow however, it is important to attempt to specify the tasks performed by the homunculus and one by one to explain them, ultimately allowing the homunculus to retire. Shallice and colleagues have attempted the task of achieving such an explanation of the SAS component of their model, using both neuropsychological data and computational modelling, resulting in a hypothetical system of some complexity. I myself, however, opted to take a rather simpler approach.

I began by proposing a number of tasks that any executive worth its salt would need to accomplish, going on to explore each in turn. The first was that of focussing attention in the performance of complex tasks. A good example of this seemed to be the game of chess which I studied in collaboration with Trevor Robbins, a distinguished neuroscientist in the Cambridge (UK) department and an extremely talented chess player.

We were helped by a number of undergraduate chess players, involved as part of the research component of their degree training. Our study was prompted by reading a paper in which STM for complex chess positions was shown to deteriorate after a brief delay filled by backward counting, the task typically used to prevent rehearsal in the Peterson short-term forgetting task described earlier. The conclusion drawn was that performance depended on verbal memory. It seemed to us much more likely that the executive load of backward counting was responsible, rather than disruption of the phonological loop. We therefore set up a series of experiments in which chess players tried to remember positions after a delay filled by various activities chosen to disrupt different components of the working memory model.

We were able to test players ranging from a modest college chess club level to grandmaster, finding as expected that memory for chess positions increased with expertise and was influenced by secondary tasks designed to disrupt working memory. Preventing verbalisation by articulatory suppression, however, had no effect whatsoever. Disrupting the visuospatial sketch pad did impair performance but not nearly as much as resulted from a range of tasks that were known to make demands on the central executive.

We found a similar pattern of results when the task was changed from memory to selecting the optimal next move. Interestingly, although the more expert players were always better, they showed exactly the same pattern of disruption by the concurrent tasks as more modest college players, consistently suggesting maximum dependence on the central executive, a lesser role for the sketch pad and no verbal involvement. A later unpublished study required players to decide, from a briefly presented middle game, whether black or white was winning. Surprisingly this was not affected by our concurrent tasks. The experts were consistently better, but people seemed to base their assessment on a rapid intuitive judgement, presumably based on long-term memory and reflecting their degree of prior experience. The role of long-term memory was well illustrated by one of the experts who correctly identified one specific game, taken from a much earlier world championship, also pointing out that we had changed one or two pieces! It seemed therefore as though the visuospatial sketch pad was involved for obvious spatial reasons together with the central executive but that when the situation became complex and a rapid decision was required, there was a simple and apparently rapid reliance on long-term memory.

A second proposed capacity of the executive was to divide attention between two simultaneous tasks. An opportunity to pursue this further came with the invitation from neurologist colleagues Hans Spinnler and Sergio Della Sala in Milan to collaborate on a study of Alzheimer's Disease. This is of course an increasingly prevalent disease of old age which combines amnesia with more general cognitive dysfunction, probably including impaired executive function. My Italian friends had a very effective assessment and diagnostic system but were interested in asking more theoretically oriented questions about the disease. We began by using relatively standard measures of memory, finding the expected deficits, together with preservation of recency in free recall, as found in amnesic patients. We then decided to study the capacity of the patients to divide attention between two tasks performed simultaneously, comparing them to healthy people of similar age and background and to a young group.

Measuring dual-task performance is not straightforward. It is generally held to be very sensitive to age, a conclusion, however, that typically results from studies combining two tasks, both of which show an age-based decrement. Not surprisingly, adding two decrements results in a larger overall age decrement. We decided to avoid this problem by careful equating level of performance of our patients with that of healthy comparison groups on each of the two tasks by making the tasks for the healthy harder so that error rates for all groups were the same. A second potential pitfall is to have two tasks that load on the same subsystem, phonological or visuospatial in which case the results will tell us about overloading that subsystem rather than about the central executive. We therefore opted to combine a visual and a verbal task. The verbal task was digit recall using different sequence lengths selected to ensure that error rate was the same for young people, normal elderly and Alzheimer's patients. We combined it with a visuospatial tracking task, keeping a stylus in contact with a moving light where we adjusted the speed of target movement until performance was equated across the groups. Somewhat surprisingly, under these conditions there proved to be no effect of normal ageing on task combination, a result that we have since repeated several times. Our patients, however, while performing at the expected matched level on the individual tasks, found it extremely difficult to combine them. Later studies have shown that this remains the case, even when the two tasks are made very much easier for the patients.

A later study pursued the idea that the central executive was frontally-based by studying other patients, selected as having frontal lobe lesions. The patients were then divided into two groups based on whether they did or did not show the broad pattern of general attentional and behavioural disruption as shown by patient RJ described earlier in this chapter. Those showing such disorganised behaviour performed badly on our dual-task measure, while the other group did not, despite having frontal lobe damage. Both groups were, however, impaired on other tasks known to be dependent on the frontal lobes, such as generating words from a category such as animals and on a non-switching reasoning test. Our results suggest that the frontal lobes control an attentional system with a range of separable executive capacities, just as Shallice had proposed, and that the ability to divide attention is one of these. A quite separate study carried out by Nicholas Alderman on head-injured patients with behavioural problems identified a subgroup who did not respond to a standard reward-based treatment programme. The one task that distinguished this subgroup from the rest was dual-task performance. Perhaps, combining current activity with awareness of its longer-term consequences is a form of dual tasking?

A major strength of our dual-task measure is that, provided levels of difficulty are adjusted, it does not show an age effect, unlike most other symptoms of Alzheimer's Disease such as poor memory, where diagnosis involves detecting the difference between normal age-related impairment and its exaggerated form in dementia. A particularly clear indication of the sensitivity of the dual-task measure comes from a study by Mario Parra of a rare group of Colombian patients suffering from an inherited form of Alzheimer's Disease where it is possible to test genetically which family members have the gene and will proceed to dementia. Mario found that dual-task performance identified such patients in their early 40s, before other measures such as amnesia had begun to appear. Two of our original team, Sergio Della Sala and Robert Logie, now at the University of Edinburgh, have continued to develop clinical aspects of the dual-task measure and are in the process of attempting to provide a version that would be readily accessible to a general practitioner attempting to decide on the presence of dementia. However, making such a test simple and robust enough to be used in general practice and then going through the processes of being officially sanctioned is unfortunately a lengthy and complex process.

A third function that we suggested might be required by the central executive was the capacity to switch between tasks. This was an area that had been little studied since the 1920s when a series of experiments by Arthur Jersild simply required people to alternate between adding a digit and subtracting a digit from successive numbers. He found that people were much slower when required to alternate adding and subtracting than when no switching was required. Interest in task switching had recently been revived by Stephen Monsell in Cambridge, UK, and Alan Allport in

Oxford using relatively complex designs that measured time to respond very precisely. We ourselves were more interested in robust effects that would readily be usable in the clinic and reverted to Jersild's method, using a column of single digits requiring one to be added to each or subtracted from each. Like Jersild we found that completing a column comprising only additions or subtractions was clearly more rapid than alternating adding and subtracting on successive digits. We then asked questions about the role of the various components of working memory in performing each of these tasks.

We focussed specifically on the phonological loop and the central executive by either having people repeatedly utter a three-digit number to disrupt verbal rehearsal or count backwards from that number in threes, thus adding an executive demand. We expected that only counting would have a major effect on performance but to our surprise, we found a substantial effect of articulatory suppression, an effect that was only slightly increased when the executive demand of counting back in threes was added. The decrement was almost entirely on processing speed, with very few errors in any condition. Further studies by ourselves and others subsequently produced similar results.

So, what were our conclusions? At one level they seemed obvious, namely that people were keeping their place by subvocally uttering "add-subtract-add-subtract", but the implications were more far-reaching. The first is that switching in this task does not seem to depend heavily on the central executive since adding a substantial attentional load had little more effect than suppression. That does not of course mean that the executive will never be involved; indeed a classic test for frontal lobe damage is the Wisconsin Card Sorting Task, a concept-forming task reflecting the capacity to switch between sorting categories: for example from sorting on the basis of the colour of objects on cards to sorting by their shape or by number. It suggests, however, that although the requirement to switch between tasks may be conceptually the same across a range of activities, the way in which switching is achieved need not be. If that is the case, then regarding task switching as a specific function of the central executive may not be a particularly promising line to develop.

By this time task switching had become very popular, although typically focussing rather narrowly on a limited range of laboratory tasks based on those initiated by Monsell and Allport, coupled with the attempt to develop very detailed micro-theories. We ourselves wished to ask much broader questions using our simple methods, leading to problems when we attempted to publish our results, with one referee calculating how little time it would take for us to run our particular experiment and declaring "No pain no gain!". As someone who thinks science should be fun, I task-switched to a less masochistic line of research, leaving the micro-modellers to micromodel. There may be a general task-switching factor at the heart of the central executive, but I doubt it.

An important positive effect of our switching results, however, was the realisation that the phonological loop could be used to *control* behaviour, not simply to store verbal information. This was a point that had been emphasised many years earlier by two eminent Russian psychologists, Alexander Luria and Lev Vygotsky who studied the role of "self-talk" in behavioural control. An elegant study by Luria, for example, asked children of different ages to press a bulb when a red light came on but not for a blue light. Before the age of three, children press for both lights, despite being able to repeat the instruction. They can, however, perform the task if the instruction "press" accompanies the red but not the blue light. A few months later they themselves are able to say "press" at the right time but do not perform the action. By the age of five they both speak and act appropriately, eventually reaching a stage at which overt speech is no longer required. Luria also showed a similar pattern of problems in responding to instructions in patients with brain damage, together with improvement following the development of verbal self-cueing. Overt self-instruction is used in some East European approaches to helping patients recover from brain damage, where the patient begins by following the spoken instructions of the therapist, later learning to articulate such instructions themselves and eventually controlling behaviour without overt speech. This important line of research has continued to influence developmental psychology but until recently was largely forgotten within experimental cognitive research on adults.

One final capacity we proposed for the central executive was that of interfacing between working memory and long-term memory. Our original 1974 paper had shown that the requirement to concurrently remember six digits led to marked impairment in the speed of interpreting and verifying sentences such as *A is not followed by B, BA* and we later showed that deciding on the truth of simple sentences such as *Shoes are sold in pairs* or *Shoes hold religious beliefs* is slowed down in a similar way. Could we perhaps extend this to prose comprehension more generally? Indeed, could we use the concurrent executive load method to measure the readability of prose passages? Readability was commonly measured by a method known as the Cloze technique which involved, for example, deleting every fifth word and requiring a group of people to guess what that word was. Prose that was independently judged as more readable typically led to fewer errors in guessing the missing words, presumably because it was relatively predictable and required little extra processing beyond what was already known.

We began by comparing three passages which varied in Cloze readability: a simple fairy story for young children, an explanatory piece on a tropical disease and a paragraph from a philosophy text. We then required people to read them silently while at the same time performing a range of executively demanding tasks and then tested memory for their content. We fully expected that the more demanding the text, the greater the disruption from the concurrent task as measured by reading speed and amount remembered. However, while the less readable the prose, the slower it was read and the less was recalled, the effect of the demanding concurrent task did not differ across passages, nor was the memory task differentially impaired. It appeared to be the case that comprehension and executive processing ran in parallel. We did not even try to publish this, totally unexpected result. Negative results are always hard to publish, particularly when unexpected for the very understandable reason that they may have resulted from some flaw in the experiments. I was about to change jobs and had other fish to fry but as will become apparent, we did return to this puzzling result later.

It was clear by this point that the homunculus was far from ready to retire but while our progress towards our understanding of mechanisms underpinning executive control was clearly limited, our efforts did make one important point. The concept of a central executive was not simply a convenient way of getting rid of awkward questions but could serve as a springboard for investigating the nature of executive control, generating important questions to which the answers were sometimes quite unexpected. In short, our homunculus was serving as a tool for further investigation rather than an excuse for maintaining the status quo.

So, what had we learnt? The fact that it is necessary to focus attention to perform complex tasks is not of course surprising; however the demonstration that the three-component model could be used to tease apart and separate the role of the central executive from those of verbal and visuospatial processing in an area as complex as chess was encouraging. It has led to the use of similar dual-task methodology across a wide range of situations and tasks, both basic and applied. Our proposal that the executive might be required for multitasking was also encouraging; the model provided a basis for separating out this specific function from cognitive overload more generally and led to our fortuitous discovery that task sharing reflects a specific basic deficit in Alzheimer's Disease but not in normal ageing. Our attempt to treat task switching in a similar way was in itself disappointing, suggesting that switching may not be a process that depends on a single underlying cognitive function. A bonus, however, was the realisation that the phonological loop could serve as a means of controlling behaviour, linking our own findings with earlier Russian work on this topic.

Probably the least successful of our four attempts to specify the functions of the executive was that of linking working memory and long-term memory, which led to some quite unexpected results. As is often the case however, the most unexpected results can often be the most productive. It encouraged us to keep chewing away at this particular problem, which, together with a range of related difficulties, eventually led to a major change in the basic model and introduction of a fourth component, the *episodic buffer*, of which more later. It was some time after my return from Boston before the book was finally published.[1]

Note

1 Baddeley, A. (1986). *Working Memory*. Oxford: Oxford University Press.

21
Psychology around the World

In the 60 years since I set sail for Princeton, psychology has changed enormously, not only in its methods and concepts but also in its global reach. In the 1950s, experimental psychology was largely confined to North America and a relatively small number of European countries where it still flourished despite disruption from the Second World War. German psychology, extremely strong in the 19th and early 20th centuries, had suffered greatly following the rise of the Nazi party, which favoured an approach to psychology that was preoccupied with racial superiority, leading to the emigration of the Jewish scientists who formed a substantial part of its psychological elite. Since that time, European psychology has gradually recovered, while an experimental or cognitive approach to psychology is now relatively widespread throughout the world, although still most strongly concentrated in North America. The chapter that follows attempts to use my own travels as a way of reflecting these changes at the same time as conveying a little of the pleasure that I have derived from the opportunities my job has given me to travel, meet and work with a wide range of colleagues.

Apart from family holidays, the bulk of my travel has been academically related and given the strength of experimental psychology in North America, much of it has involved travel to the USA or Canada. The five occasions when I spent a period of months or more in the US are described elsewhere, but travel to workshops and conferences have allowed many more visits. My interest from school days in geography and history persists, and I would typically extend my visit for a day or two, hire a car and look around. Checking the atlas, I note that I have been to every US state except for three, North and South Dakota and Delaware (which I may have visited without noticing!).

Memories that stand out are the pleasure of driving across the high plains with the Rockies in the distance, listening to the country music stations of the small towns we passed and the subsequent majestic scenery in the American and Canadian Rockies. I also remember unexpected pleasures, such as finding small towns in Wisconsin that echoed their European origins, one built by Cornish miners that still makes good Cornish pasties, while another nearby appeared to have been transplanted from the Alps. Both were encountered by accident while tracking down some wonderful buildings by Frank Lloyd Wright. My US memories are not all so idyllic: desperately trying to get to the airport in New Orleans, while roads were progressively cut off by rising floods (not the devastating recent flood I should add) or arriving in New York after dark, attempting unsuccessfully to contact Bell Labs by telephone and then driving off in the pouring rain. I seem to remember I arrived, but I don't know quite how.

The post-war situation in Europe was very different. A few prominent figures from the pre-war generation survived and were still active in the 1950s, including Albert Michotte in Belgium who worked on perceived causality, Paul Fraise in France who worked on time perception and of course Jean Piaget in Switzerland whose influence on developmental psychology grew rapidly in the post-war years, although he would not, I suspect, have regarded himself as an experimental psychologist. However, despite the devastating effect of the Second World War on psychology in many parts of Europe, the war had a positive effect within the UK and North America where the need to tackle practical problems provided a useful stimulus and test bed for existing theories.

In the post-war years however, experimental research with an applied flavour became less prominent in the US where many psychologists returned to purely basic studies. Applied research did continue to develop in Britain and in the Netherlands where two notable centres combined experimental psychology with its practical application. One had industrial links to the electronics company Phillips in Eindhoven, while the other was a government-based laboratory at Soesterberg. It was from here that in 1966, Andres Sanders, a young experimental psychologist, organised a meeting of psychologists from Europe and North America who were actively interested in the newly developing fields of human information processing and "performance theory", publishing the proceedings of the conference under the title *Attention and Performance*. This became the name of the group that went on to organise more than 20 subsequent meetings. During the early years, I myself attended several of the meetings and chose to publish what I regard as some of my best papers in the proceedings. I subsequently lost touch with the group, which tended to focus on classic information-processing methods, typically using reaction time measures, whereas my own approach has been rather more eclectic and less tightly constrained. The early meetings, however, played an important role in providing links between scientists both within and beyond Europe and North America, and in my case, also led to what has become a very long-standing association with psychology in Sweden.

Sweden remained neutral during the war and hence escaped the disruption of the field that occurred in most of Europe. Given its population size, Sweden has a relatively small number of psychology departments and historically has coped with this challenge by focussing on a limited number of topics, generating a sufficient critical mass in each as to have a clear international impact. One such area was perception where there were strengths both in sensory psychophysics and in the development of an ecological approach related both to the ideas of Egon Brunswik mentioned earlier and to pre-war Gestalt psychology. Also related to Brunswik's approach were studies of decision-making. Psychophysiological research was also strong. A group in Stockholm was at the leading edge of research on stress, combining behavioural measures with measures based on neuroendocrinology, while a group in Lund was at the forefront of efforts to observe the operations of the working brain using the newly invented method of positron emission tomography (PET), an early approach to neuroimaging, a field that has developed hugely over subsequent years and now dominates much of cognitive experimental psychology.

Two meetings of Attention and Performance were held in Stockholm, leading to a long-standing friendship with a fellow memory research enthusiast, Lars-Göran Nilsson, then a young lecturer at the University of Uppsala, who in addition to introducing us to the noted nightlife of Stockholm, shortly afterwards organised an international memory meeting. He invited many of the major figures in North American and European memory research including such established figures as Endel Tulving, Bill Estes and George Mandler together with a younger generation of Don Norman, Gus Craik and myself. I have happy memories of various Midsummer Eve festivities, which included our dancing around the maypole watched by our more sedate elders and betters. Lars-Göran went on to become a young professor at the new university of Umeå in the

North of Sweden, in due course developing a very talented group of young memory researchers who themselves then became professors around Sweden, forming another area where Swedish psychology punches above its weight.

A second friend resulting from A&P meetings in Sweden was Slovakian rather than Swedish. Stan Dornic had defected from his department behind the Iron Curtain in Bratislava and acquired a research and teaching position in Stockholm. Stan was a large man with a downbeat sense of humour and a somewhat lugubrious face, which he likened to that of the cartoon character Pink Panther. We became good friends and I enjoyed learning about psychology behind the Iron Curtain where he had been part of an active lab that combined experimental psychology with tackling practical problems although under conditions that Stan found increasingly limiting and claustrophobic.

Having heard from Stan about psychology in what was then Czechoslovakia, I later received an invitation to visit and give lectures in his old institute, which provided a rare opportunity to experience psychology behind the Iron Curtain. I combined my visit with an international meeting on Alzheimer's Disease in Zurich travelling by train, staying over in Vienna, from where I had been advised to travel on to my destination in Bratislava by bus on the grounds that trains across the border were filled with Gypsy smugglers, which led to long waits while the customs officials tried to locate the hidden contraband. I set off in the fog and in due course arrived in Bratislava. My hosts were extremely welcoming and the laboratory quite active in research, although the head of department was still taking a pre-war Gestalt approach to perception, advising me that I could refer to his views as coming from "the Bratislava School", harking back to the 1930s when psychology was dominated by different theoretical "schools".

My principal host turned out to be someone I had heard about from Stan. He was the same generation and was apparently the person in the department who was closest to the communist party. I discovered that he had had a hard earlier life and that the party had enabled him to become educated and successful. A party affiliation was clearly an advantage but not essential, he pointed out, since one person had been appointed professor without being a member! I later met him and discovered the secret; he was a behaviour therapist who specialised in stage fright, a condition apparently not uncommon among members of the party about to address important meetings. I was taken to the opera in a wonderfully restored opera house, returning to my hotel to come across a group of Russians who were visiting a local tractor factory and who suggested that I share their vodka, which I duly did. A bad move since the following morning I was still not entirely sober and had to discuss research projects with each member of the lab, in turn, most of whom had brought goodies for me to eat. I like liver sausage, but I have never found it harder to eat.

I had arranged to fly back to the UK via Prague. My travel expenses were covered but in local currency that could not be exported, so I went on a shopping trip. Prague was a great disappointment; it had obviously previously been a beautiful city, but it was shabby, and the inhabitants were clearly poor, and my attempt to find anything worth buying in the shops was fruitless. I finally spent my travel money on a slap-up dinner in a large hotel, waited on by a flock of waiters who had no one else to serve. When I got to the airport and checked in I was asked for my exit visa. I explained that I had given it up in Bratislava. "But you must have a visa in order to leave", said the attractive young lady at the check in. "And if I don't?" I asked. "Then you must stay!" "_ _ _ Forever?" I asked and laughed, perhaps not a wise thing to do in the circumstances, but she laughed too and waved me through. Subsequent visits to Prague have revealed just how beautiful and prosperous the city is now.

One of the pleasures of my time at the Unit was in the contacts and opportunities it gave for interacting with the growing number of active psychologists throughout continental Europe and the resulting opportunities to visit different laboratories. I was intrigued by the extent to which earlier approaches to psychology were beginning to blend with newer developments but was also struck by the lack of interaction, even in the 1970s, between scientists with similar interests within Europe. One problem was that of language, with a tendency for German investigators to publish in German and French in Francophone journals. However this was becoming much less of a problem, with many investigators having links to one or more US departments. The time seemed ripe to try to develop a society for cognitive psychology that would foster links *within* Europe.

I had had a little experience in setting up regular meetings through involvement in the establishment of an annual informal three-day meeting of UK colleagues interested in working memory. This initially met each year in a pair of cottages in the Lake District used by Manchester University for training mountaincraft to physical education teachers, and which was available via Graham Hitch who had moved to Manchester. It was rather basic, with bunk beds and blankets, and involved self-catering, with Graham and myself cooking full English breakfasts. It had a maximum capacity of around 20 comprising a mix of people at different stages of career. Speaking time was shared equally and the schedule always involved a walk on the second afternoon and dinner in a local pub, allowing plenty of time for informal discussion. It worked well with a wide and varied range of participants.

Unfortunately however, when Graham moved from Manchester to Lancaster, we no longer had access to the two cottages. We tried various venues, which tended to be expensive and rather unsatisfactory. I then spotted a barn that provided accommodation in the Yorkshire Dales and suggested that Graham and I check it out. On the way to the barn, I offered to show Graham one of my favourite places, Troller's Ghyll. A limestone ravine in Wharfedale where my friend and I used to camp; it was said to be haunted by a barguest, a phantom hound with eyes as big as saucers. To see him portended death, but happily we never did! Looking for somewhere to park, we found Parcevall Hall, a Church of England conference centre, a beautiful old building with spectacular gardens. We knocked on the heavy oak door, only to be told that the warden was on silent retreat.

We persevered, rang back later and discovered an ideal setting for our meetings that have continued to return there for well over 20 years. The accommodation is limited to around 30 people, which typically includes two or three overseas visiting students and colleagues from as far away as Brazil, China, Cuba and Japan, who get to see a beautiful part of Yorkshire with great walks, excellent food and a village a mile away with two pubs. Setting up and continuing such informal working memory meetings can be relatively undemanding. Launching a Europe-wide cognitive psychology society seemed a little more tricky; however my various trips to colleagues and departments around Europe suggested that the time might be right.

The opportunity arrived through the existing strong relationship between the Dutch Psychonomics Society and the British Experimental Psychology Society who were due to hold a joint meeting in Amsterdam in spring 1984. I contacted John Michon, a Dutch colleague who I knew from Attention and Performance meetings, to suggest that we discuss the possibility of setting up a society. John had been thinking along the same lines and promptly organised a meeting to which he also invited Paul Bertelson from Brussels, another very active cognitive psychologist with strong international links. We held the meeting over a rather splendid lunch in a hotel overlooking the harbour in Amsterdam, and agreed to go ahead.

We decided that we wanted to grow gradually, focussing initially on already established scientists, attempting to identify one or two people in as many European countries as possible, including Israel and the relatively small range of people with whom we had contact in countries behind the

Iron Curtain. We planned in due course to ask each contact to recommend and recruit two further members, thus establishing a strong core but in due course making membership open to all. In order to select the initial invitees, we took soundings, and in most cases the different sources agreed on who were the appropriate people to invite. An interesting problem occurred in the case of Germany however, which had a number of strong groups working on different topics in different locations leading to different people being suggested by different advisors. Eventually we opted for Wolfgang Prinz who we knew from Attention and Performance, and he proved to be a really excellent choice.

We organised our first conference a year later in Nijmegen in the Netherlands and were delighted to find that virtually all our invitees agreed to attend even though we could not at the time offer them any financial support. We did in fact receive support from an unexpected direction: the US Office of Naval Research (ONR), which funds a good deal of top class basic research in the US. At the time they also provided funds for an established US academic to spend a year in Europe simply travelling around talking to people and finding out who was doing what and where. I discovered from a friend that ONR had helped found the European Society for Social Psychology and decided to approach that year's representative, Richard Snow, a distinguished educational researcher from Stanford who was able to provide help, with no strings attached either before or after.

The meeting, held in 1985, was a great success and led to our setting up an ad hoc committee which became known as "the gang of five" (one more than Madame Mao's dreaded "gang of four"), comprising John Michon; Paul Bertelson; Wolgang Prinz; myself; and Janet Jackson, a Scot who had entered psychology as a mature student in Stirling before moving with her husband to Groningen and working with John. She acted as secretary to the group and was absolutely crucial to its success, combining enthusiasm, efficiency and a maternal concern for the many younger scientists who subsequently joined the society.

John was keen that we should immediately set ourselves up as a formal institution, whereas I tended to favour a much more informal arrangement, minimising bureaucracy. John prevailed, and he was quite right, setting us up as a *"stifting"*, a rather mysterious Dutch legal body that conveniently seemed to allow us to do whatever we wanted whenever we wanted – my kind of bureaucracy! We decided that meetings should alternate between Northern and Southern Europe and accepted the offer to organise the next meeting in Madrid. Over the first few meetings, a number of the organisers had little experience of setting up international conferences, which meant our travelling out beforehand to check arrangements and facilities, a chore that I can fully recommend!

We also decided to set up summer schools with the first being held at Bernried, on a beautiful lake, the Starnberg See near Munich. It was held in a monastery occupied by an order of nuns who specialised in teaching cookery and who had an excellent and well-deserved reputation for their food. We were somewhat concerned that they did not have a similar reputation for wine making, but happily they provided an excellent selection of beers. It was a two-week meeting with a stellar list of lecturers and seminar leaders, generously funded by the Volkswagen Foundation, which allowed us to include three eminent European memory researchers who were then in the US: namely Endel Tulving, Walter Kintsch and Geoffrey Hinton. Both the meetings and the summer schools have continued from that time, with the last three meetings of the society being in Spain, Hungary and Cyprus and the most recent summer schools in Poland, Spain and Italy.

We duly moved the society onto a more conventional democratic basis, which, among other things, ensured that no one served more than two successive four-year terms on the committee. This worked very effectively with the gang of five gradually handing over to new pairs of hands who have ensured that the society continues to flourish, currently numbering some 650 members together with a much wider group who attend meetings. Happily I have not had to rely entirely on my rather shaky memory for this account since much of this, together with developments over the last 30 years, is covered in the society's website under the heading "museum" with John Michon and myself as talking exhibits!

A glance through the issues of any current cognitive psychology journal will demonstrate that cognitive psychology within Europe is currently flourishing and publishing widely. I am not suggesting of course that this is the result of our society; as both George Mandler and George Miller have pointed out, cognitive psychology was active in Europe at a time when much North American psychology was dominated by neo-behaviourism, and while I like to think our society helped, I suspect a major factor has been the broad acceptance of English as the lingua franca of science. Experimental psychology in other parts of the world does not have such deep roots however. I remember talking to Paul Kolers, an eminent Canadian psychologist who in the early 1980s had chosen to take a world tour to find out what was going on elsewhere in the field of experimental psychology. I asked him what he had discovered. "Nothing", he replied, and while I am sure this was an exaggeration, there were relatively few signs either in journal publications or through more informal contacts that the experimental approach had established itself beyond Europe and North America, with the exception of Australia and New Zealand, which had retained contact with the British academic system.

Commonwealth universities were typically established on the basis of the English or Scottish systems and had initially recruited largely from British universities. In the 1950s there were more Commonwealth than British academic jobs advertised in the UK, although this changed dramatically in the 1960s with the creation of a wave of new universities in Britain. During the early years, contact with the Commonwealth was through sea travel, too slow and expensive to allow regular access to conferences and meetings, and a number of Commonwealth universities set up visiting fellowships aimed at maintaining and fostering academic links. The fellowships continued after travel became easier, and I was lucky enough to be invited on three such visits, one to the University of Guelph in Canada; one to the University of Otago in Dunedin, New Zealand; and one to the University of Queensland in Australia. In each case I took the chance to travel around and visit other universities, finding the atmosphere not unlike that in the UK, with a traditional academic culture of small departments with a single professor, though already changing rapidly to the larger and more research-oriented pattern that is typical today.

As was implied by the Kolers' comment, there were far fewer opportunities to make psychology-related visits to Asia, South America or Africa. The few visits I was able to make, however, were particularly interesting and I would like to describe them in a little more detail, bearing in mind that they are simply based on my own limited remembered experience. I had always wanted to travel to India, when, at an international congress in Belgium, I ran into a graduate student friend from my undergraduate days at University College London, S.N. Sinha. By the time we met many years later, he had become Head of Department at the University of Jaipur and President of the national Indian Psychological Society. One of the privileges was to invite a speaker to the psychological section of the Indian Science Congress, an annual meeting that since Nehru's day had always been attended by the Indian President. It was to be held in Kolkata (Calcutta) in January and I readily accepted.

I found the city to be just as crowded as I expected but not at all threatening. Despite obvious poverty, the Bengalese seem to be cheery, with a sense of humour and apparently a reputation for producing poets. As I discovered however, they also have a reputation for producing riots, one of which unsuccessfully attempted to intercept the President's motorcade.

Happily, my taxi was not one of those targeted by the crowd as it was terrifying enough being driven into what seemed like a solid mass of cars. Having arrived, I then had the problem of getting past the armed guard at the gate of the university. In desperation I searched my wallet and produced my Bristol University library card, which surprisingly did the trick and allowed me in.

I duly gave my talk and listened to the other Indian presenters one of whom was an occupational psychologist who made a very interesting point about Indian culture and business. He likened the Indian personality to a coconut, rough and tough on the outside but softer and sweeter within, pointing out that this could lead to an unduly abrasive way of interacting with people outside your circle of friends and colleagues. I was later to experience this side of India when visiting Delhi where there seemed much more of a feeling of every man-for-himself than I had found in Kolkota. I enjoyed India however: Jaipur is a beautiful city; my old friend proved an excellent host; and I was pleased to see the splendid sights, including the Taj Mahal, although not the fabled view by moonlight. I saw it in the rain and, because of the requirement to remove shoes, in wet socks.

My impression of psychology in India, however, was that it was at that time rather an academic backwater, with all the government funding going into physics, engineering and computing. Computer technology at the time did not seem to extend to psychology departments where Delhi had a single desktop machine that was locked away and kept under a dust cover. Perhaps the two departments I visited were atypical but the main external links to India seem at that time to be through Hans Eysenck's psychometric work on personality, formed by psychologists who had worked with his group in London. It should be pointed out, however, that my trip was completed over 20 years ago, and there are some welcome signs of change, hopefully accompanied by a greater degree of government support.

A further Asian visit happened in 2003 when I was invited to take part in a cognitive science meeting in Tehran, just before the invasion of Iraq. The US advised its delegates not to attend although our Foreign Office seemed more relaxed about things. I arrived in Tehran in the evening and was somewhat bemused to be separated from the remaining arrivals and mysteriously led along a red carpet. I was later to discover that I was being welcomed as a guest; the Iranian foreign minister at the time was a cognitive scientist whose psychologist brother was involved in organising the meeting I was attending. My Iranian hosts seemed disenchanted rather than concerned with the political situation at the time. A recent government of secular rather than religious orientation had won the previous election but had been unable to break the stranglehold of the all-important religious council. New elections were shortly to occur, and they seemed to take a somewhat fatalistic view that it did not really matter who you voted for. Unfortunately they were wrong. The forthcoming election led directly to Mahmoud Ahmadinejad beginning his rise to power and many years of militantly Islamic national control.

I duly gave my talk and visited both the Institute of Cognitive Science and the Tehran University psychology department where I found bright students doing interesting things but with little contact to current mainstream psychology and very limited equipment. As visiting speakers, myself and two experts on reading from Sweden and Norway were invited to extend our stay and visit the ancient and beautiful city of Esfahan, a city of wide squares and wonderful mosques. On the first day we enjoyed a splendid lunch reclining on cushions in the traditional Persian style, after which it was suggested that we go along to the psychology department, which we duly did. On entering I noted an advertisement for a conference on cognitive psychology. On enquiring, I discovered that we were it! We turned the corner into a lecture hall full of black-robed students, looking like an enormous flock of starlings. It was so unexpected that I did not even have time to be nervous and fortunately had my slides to hand. After the talk large numbers of young ladies fluttered down all brightly and smartly dressed beneath the robes and seeming very much like students anywhere, with the exception that they all wanted our email addresses. Don't worry we were assured, they won't contact you, and they didn't.

A brief sight of another aspect of Iranian society cropped up the following day when we were being shown around the city by a charming man, very cultured and apparently a famous poet. At the end of the day we arrived at a large and beautiful mosque at sundown which our host wanted to show us. There were, however, armed guards who forbad us to enter. Our host insisted that a guard went and consulted their officer; when he returned he grumpily accepted that we could enter. By this time it was dark, and the mosque was unlit and filled with dark shadows. We looked around nervously and were relieved to make our escape.

I returned to Britain just before the Iraq invasion began with a much more nuanced view of Iran and of the contrast between the Westernised and often highly educated minority, and a much more traditional society that apparently is dominant in more rural areas. I occasionally hear from my friends in Iran and a couple of years ago received a parcel containing a copy of the Qur'an combining Arabic on one page with an English translation facing. It came from someone with whom I had discussions about

Islam and who wanted to help me understand. It provided useful counter-evidence a few years later when I had a visitor from Egypt who insisted that there was nothing in the Qur'an to incite violence. My impression is that psychology is surviving despite the reduction in international contact resulting from the more radical Islamic governments of recent years and I am currently involved in an email discussion with an Iranian computer scientist who is keen to try to develop a computer simulation of the multi-component working memory model. He was able to reassure me that the foreign minister who had arranged for me to be looked after on arrival was back running a successful cognitive science institute.

Since my trip behind the Iron Curtain of course the world has changed dramatically and psychology with it. Meetings are regularly held in countries, such as Poland, Hungary, Romania and Slovenia, which were once largely inaccessible, while excellent research in cognitive psychology can now be found in the Far East where I myself have active collaborations with colleagues in Japan and China. These have resulted from visits to the UK by the scientists and in due course their research students leading to joint research that often continues when they return.

One huge change since the early years is the arrival of worldwide communication through the web. It used to be the case that everyone relied on a limited range of journals delivered slowly by mail, followed by the practice of sending postcards to request reprints of articles of particular interest. Now, papers are readily available before they are published, and the number of subsequent citations recorded. I have also recently discovered that I can see who is looking at my papers, when and where, and I find the results remarkable. The 149 visits to my papers in the last month came from 33 different countries from all around the world. The papers are not of course necessarily read, but I assume that the abstract at least is scanned, indicating a range of interest in cognitive psychology that would have amazed Paul Kolers and I hope gratified him; clearly interest in experimental psychology is no longer limited to North America and Europe.

CAMBRIDGE AND TEXAS TO BRISTOL 1990–2003

22

The Episodic Buffer

Once I had become familiar with how the MRC system worked, directing the Unit was not too onerous, although over the years it became more so with the increase in top-down, government-induced bureaucracy. However, the Unit was well endowed with colleagues who were willing and able to carry some of the increasing load; unlike a typical department, we did very little teaching and had no need to become involved in university governance since we were effectively an independent entity though fortunately with the possibility of taking on and supervising PhD students and doing a modest amount of teaching.

As time went on however, I did become increasingly involved in MRC committees, for many years being a member of either the Royal Navy or the Army Personnel Research Committees by which the MRC maintained a link with the armed forces. This proved interesting, and over the years I grew to respect the military personnel with whom I interacted. They were typically sensible, practical and helpful, provided you made a reasonable case for why their regular routine was being interrupted. I was less impressed by the civil servants at the Ministry of Defence in London, an enormous bureaucracy located in a monstrous office block off Whitehall. They seemed remote from the armed forces they were supposed to serve, spending huge amounts on projects that took many years to deliver. Civil service practice seemed to involve moving everyone every three or four years and I got the impression that the best way to be promoted was to ditch what the last chap had been doing and come up with your own ideas that would, in turn, be ditched by the next chap.

Over the years, the navy had funded extensive work at the Unit on sleep deprivation and the development of optimal schemes for the round-the-clock watch keeping. Our work was overseen by the navy's medical division, usually headed by a senior naval medic who was promoted to the rank of admiral, typically in their last few years before retirement. When chairing the naval committee, I duly asked the admiral what sort of work they would like next, to which he replied more watch keeping. Later in the visit we were taken to see a new type of cruiser and having been shown around, met the captain. The naval psychologist accompanying us, a man with a slightly cynical and subversive sense of humour, whispered in my ear that I should ask about watch keeping, which I duly did. "Oh" said the captain, "We just get together before we set sail and see what the chaps would like". I asked if he knew any of the years of research we had carried out on the topic, to which the answer was a clear "No". Fortunately the work was published in good journals and forms part of the increasing fund of knowledge on sleep and its potential disturbance by different watch keeping schedules that are now available more generally. I suspect that applied research often has its impact indirectly, sometime after the project that generated it, part a pool of advice that is already available when subsequent decisions need to be made. I hope so!

I served on a range of MRC committees, including the Neurosciences Board, a group of about 20 academics who were responsible for higher level policy decisions in areas ranging from micropathology of the brain to social psychology. At the time, the hard work involved in evaluating large numbers of smaller grants was covered by a subcommittee, leaving the board to decide on major grants, typically involving programmes extending over five years or more. We also had the job of evaluating MRC Units, which at that time included a number of small groups based on the work of a specific individual which would expect to close on that person's retirement. Increasingly, the MRC wished to reduce these and embed Units in university departments, leaving us to visit and evaluate larger units where the Council had the expectation of long-term continuing research in that area.

Having served on the Neurosciences Board for a few years, I was invited to become chairman. It was one of three major committees that were responsible for the scientific oversight of the Council's work, each typically being granted a proportion of the available government funding. I took it on cheerfully enough; typically once you have been board chairman you are regarded as having served your time and excused further involvement. However, shortly after I took over, the Secretary (Chief Executive) of the

MRC changed from someone whose policy had been to appoint good people and let them get on with it, to a new Secretary whose prior experience was in pharmaceutical industry management, followed by that of running a large MRC Institute. He made two important management changes which in my view led to a greater centralisation of power. One involved shifting from a system in which each board had a Secretary, always an experienced administrator with a PhD and research experience, who typically remained in post for several years and knew their patch extremely well. These individuals were moved to a series of newly created cross-board positions, reducing their contact with their scientific field, and I suspect their influence. The second change was to centralise funding decisions by combining proposals from all of the Boards into a single list for prioritisation decisions at a one-day meeting of the ruling Council of the MRC that he himself chaired. Council membership included a number of chosen advisors, the chairman of each of the scientific boards, together with the previous chairmen. This was where my problems began.

The previous Neurosciences Board chairman had just retired from running the very distinguished Social Psychiatry Unit at the Institute of Psychiatry in London. Because of the structure of the National Health Service (NHS) it was possible to carry out research on social psychiatry in Britain that would be very difficult to do elsewhere. This unit had done classic work on schizophrenia both on its adequate classification (apparently Russia and the US had previously used different rules from the rest of the world), and had also done important work on the role of the patient's family, of how it could help or hinder treatment. The proposed new director was not as distinguished as his predecessor, but the board felt strongly that it was important for the group to continue. Our new Chief Executive disagreed and proposed that the Unit should not be supported. I saw my role as defending the decision of my board and with resolve somewhat stiffened by the previous director of the Unit sitting next to me, I refused to back down. I discovered at that point that I am not a politician. I probably should have offered some degree of compromise, perhaps suggesting postponement, which was effectively what was decided anyhow.

Would my stubbornness create problems for the Unit? To be fair, I do not think it did affect the way in which the Unit was treated. In the normal course of things, as the retiring chair of Neurosciences Board, I would have continued to serve on the Council for a further year. However, given that I had been invited to spend a semester at the University of Texas, I was spared from the crucial meeting for the following year, when I believe a decision to close the Social Psychiatry Unit was in fact made.

By this time the Applied Psychology Unit was running very smoothly, and I knew I could leave it in the capable hands of Ivan Brown as deputy director. I knew little of Texas, although I was aware that the University of Texas had an excellent department and I welcomed the chance to broaden my horizons. This time, Hilary and the family did not accompany me. Hilary could not take time off from her physiotherapy teaching post, so instead we arranged that each of the family would come over for a spell and stay with me. I was to be supported by a professorship endowed jointly by the Psychological Corporation, the company, who at that time distributed the Wechsler intelligence and memory tests that have dominated the field for many years, while a second contribution to the chair's endowment came from Professor Wechsler's widow.

In due course I discovered that the chair had been created for a leading figure in the field of intelligence and individual differences who had later turned the offer down. Eventually it dawned on me that I was in effect taking part in a semester-long interview for a job I didn't want since I already had, what for me was the best job in the world. Out of pride however, I did want to make a good impression and to be offered it. I enjoyed acting as a Texas professor, happily with minimal teaching and an administrative load that simply involved sitting in on committee decisions about a relatively junior new post.

I liked the department and found it friendly and thoroughly enjoyed living in Austin, a very liberal city that seemed to be regarded by the rest of Texas as a hotbed of reds. I managed to find a very attractive small apartment in a group clustered around a swimming pool within easy walking distance of the campus. I discovered that virtually all apartments were let unfurnished but that you can go to what seems like a very large furniture store and rent by the month a whole houseful of furniture extending from beds and sofas to pictures. This did not extend to kitchen utensils, however, which I had to buy, although there was such a wide range of excellent fast food that they ended up unused.

Even though it was possible to walk to my office, it is virtually essential to have a car in Texas and I decided this was one occasion when it might be fun to opt for something large and Texas-style, the sort of car I had never before considered buying and would be unlikely to do so again. I discovered that the husband of one of the graduate students I was teaching had a father who dealt in Cadillacs and was an expert on big cars. He agreed to help, and we scanned the small ads and arranged to look at an appropriately large Buick, LeSabre; we were told that if we wanted to view it we should meet the seller in the car park of a specified supermarket. This seemed an odd arrangement, but my friend approved the car and the price, and we drove off, although I was somewhat nervous as to whether it might have been stolen. There was in fact evidence of a previous owner, an army major who I decided to telephone. He breezily confirmed that it had been his car and that it was fine, which indeed it was. It had a monster engine, pale blue velour seats, a stereo that would deafen an army and air conditioning that could practically make ice cubes!

I discovered, however, that I needed to pass a Texas driving test. I hate driving tests and was not reassured by the crackle of gunfire that erupted shortly after the test began. Fortunately it came from the police firing range, not a hold up or shoot out! I had many happy hours in my monstrous car, driving myself and my family as each arrived around Texas and neighbouring states, finding the natives friendly, provided you said you liked Texas. On the whole I did; perhaps because I come from Yorkshire, which is the largest English county where we also have some of the less endearing characteristics of Texans. I particularly enjoyed the trip with Hilary to the Big Bend National Park and the Rio Grande near the Mexican border, while my least favourite destination was Houston, an unlovely oil city that regularly seemed to greet me with enormous thunderstorms and torrential rain. No doubt it has its redeeming features but none that I discovered during my brief visits.

On the other hand I really liked Austin and the surrounding Texas hill country. In addition to the thriving music scene, there were lots of interesting people, and I was made very welcome. Academically the department was excellent in a range of areas but was relatively weak in cognitive psychology, an area they hoped to strengthen. I became involved in the attempt to remedy this by appointing a relatively junior non-tenured new staff member. The process could not be more different from that typical in Britain at the time, whereby applications would be assessed and references taken, followed by the interviewing of all candidates on the same day and a decision for what would effectively be a position with lifetime tenure. The process of the University of Texas diverged substantially. The various candidates were evaluated individually with each assessment extended over several days, culminating in a lecture, after which all the senior professors in the department including myself would sit around the table and discuss that candidate's suitability. The discussions were fair and open-minded but almost invariably at least one member of staff would have grave doubts about the appointment. And the process was still continuing when I returned to Cambridge. Neither the UK nor the Texas system seems ideal.

I taught a course on memory for a group of very good and very pleasant graduate students and was in due course familiarised with various potential advantages of the chair in Texas. This included an invitation to a reception for millionaire donors to the university. Don Foss, the very amiable head of department explained that it was relatively easy to obtain funding for specified research projects from the wealthy Texan alumni or, more probably their wives since the husbands tended to support engineering. I was in due course asked if I would like to continue as the Wechsler Professor and if I had been looking for a job, I might well have considered it very seriously, but I explained that I already had what for me was the perfect job. My explanation was accepted in good grace and I was asked to who I would attempt to attract in their position. I suggested a name and in due course the individual was appointed but did not stay very long, perhaps because of the difficulty of building up a viable cognitive group, given their appointment system.

I returned to Cambridge in 1991, some 17 years after I had taken over the Unit's directorship. In three years' time I would reach the Council's statutory retirement age of 65 and have to move out of the Unit to leave a clear field for my successor. I knew that I wanted to continue to do research, so how? I felt confident that I would be offered a room in any of several good departments of which four seemed to be attractive. The simplest would be to remain in Cambridge where it seemed likely that I would be welcome to join the psychology department with an emeritus (retired) status that would involve a little teaching and a possibility of continued research. I would also continue to be a fellow of Churchill College and enjoy chats with my distinguished fellow fellows. A second possibility might be to go to Oxford as had Conrad and Broadbent, while a third was to return to my original department, University College London. In each case however, I knew I would be competing for research space with the up-and-coming young scientists attracted to these leading research departments, who needed to get grants to further their careers. Another option was to choose a department that was improving but would welcome my input and perhaps also provide a salary that might supplement the half-salary pension I could expect.

There was one obvious department, Bristol. Bristol is an attractive city with a good university and a psychology department that had been seriously underperforming. They had, however, just appointed a new head of department, Martin Conway, together with his wife, Susan Gathercole. Both had been on the research staff at the Unit, so I knew them well, before they moved on to the University of Lancaster where they had flourished.

I was pretty sure that Martin would do a good job of building up the department and I had worked extensively with Sue on working memory and language. Finally, the Vice Chancellor (Chief Executive) was a distinguished mathematician and theoretical statistician who I had known as a fellow PhD student. He was reputed to like the idea of attracting people from Oxbridge and my being a Fellow of the Royal Society (the UK equivalent of the US Academy of Sciences) probably also helped. We met and agreed to the following plan. I would apply for a five-year programme grant with Sue Gathercole, which, if successful, would cover my salary up to the age of 65, whereupon Bristol would provide half a salary until I was 70. This guaranteed me a full-time research appointment for several years that was financially advantageous both to the university and myself. Importantly, it had the feature that since I was being appointed from outside the university system, I did not set a potentially awkward precedent that might encourage others within the university to attempt to escape the statutory need to retire at 65. I duly approached the MRC CEO and he seemed as pleased to see me retire as he had been to have me miss my final year on the Council after our unfortunate disagreement, adding that I should consider a move away from the so-called Golden Triangle of Oxford, Cambridge and London. I readily agreed!

In choosing a topic for our grant, I bore in mind the fact that Sue and I had worked on applying the working memory model to language learning and reading in children, an area in which she had become extremely strong. I had recently been involved in jointly editing a Handbook of Memory Disorders and noticed how difficult it was to find anyone with expertise in memory disorders in children, although there was excellent work on specific disorders such as autism and Down Syndrome. We therefore came up with a proposal that had three main aims. One was to develop and evaluate a series of tests based on the components of the working memory model that could be applied to school children, predicting that working memory limitations within the school population would be linked to academic problems. The second was to use the working memory model to look at two groups of children with specific genetic disorders, Down Syndrome where there was already some evidence of potential phonological loop limitations and Williams Syndrome where the deficits appeared to be more visuospatial. The third strand of the project was aimed at further theoretical development of the working memory model. The grant was funded, and Hilary and I duly moved to Bristol.

I tend to be an optimist and regarded the change as the opening of an exciting new chapter, but I must confess that moving from running a group of a 100 people in a laboratory where I had spent 30 years of my working life was not an altogether easy transition. In domestic terms, we moved from a house to a flat, an apartment in a very elegant regency terrace in Clifton, an area that had been developed by the merchants of Bristol in the 18th and 19th centuries, above the harbour and within a 10-minute walk of the university. We had splendid views, although the 40 steps up to our flat could be tedious when loaded with shopping from the supermarket, but once there, it had light airy and extensive rooms. Towards the end of the Second World War the terrace had become quite dilapidated and I understand that our particular house was occupied by a brothel, until a fire caused it to cease business! The Council were apparently preparing to tear down the old terrace, but enough keen young people bought houses and began to renovate them for the terrace to be saved, in our case by the work of two very talented young architects.

My wife, Hilary, had, by this time, left teaching and completed a PhD on learning styles before moving in Cambridge to a post concerned with the teaching of meditation-based mindfulness techniques to stroke patients. On moving to Bristol she was able to obtain a post at a memory clinic concerned principally with Alzheimer's Disease, a job that she enjoyed. We sold our cottage in Norfolk, eventually buying a house some two-hour drive away in Devon on a beautiful tidal creek of the River Dart. It had been built in the 17th century as a classic farmhouse, with one half devoted to housing animals while the other housed the family. It had an asbestos roof which we later replaced with thatch, its original roofing, and as in Norfolk, it was the place where I did most of my writing.

The Bristol department was very friendly and welcoming and did not require me to do either teaching or administration. Initially this seemed ideal, but eventually, I discovered that I was getting bored and upped my research and writing rate, together with taking on some supervision of undergraduate research projects and PhD students. I discovered that I work best and am happiest when I have just a little more to do than I have time to do it. I missed my Cambridge office with its splendid view across the croquet lawn to the orchard, but this was somewhat compensated by the fact that the Bristol department is in a residential area very close to shops, a museum and concert hall, together with several tolerable pubs, one of which hosted a very convivial departmental get together on early Friday evenings.

My research situation was very different from that at the Unit where I typically worked closely with a single postdoctoral colleague, together with a varied series of other collaborations often based on applied projects.

Here, I was responsible for a team, jointly with Sue who looked after the links to test development and education. Sue's component of the project went extremely well, resulting in a battery of tests that separate out the verbal, visual and executive components of working memory, together with norms that indicate the levels of performance to be expected within the normal population of healthy children of different ages. Furthermore, she was able to demonstrate that our earlier observed links between phonological loop deficit and language development were replicated within the general population with a combined deficit of the phonological loop and the central executive being particularly problematic for the development of language and reading. Research by Sue and others suggests that mathematical difficulties are often associated with visuospatial limitations, while executive problems are more generally disruptive of academic development. She has gone on to expand this approach over subsequent years at the Universities of Durham and York, more recently taking over from my successor at the Cambridge MRC Unit, becoming Director of what is now known as the MRC Cognition and Brain Sciences Unit.

I was able to attract a young postdoc from Cambridge, Chris Jarrold, to develop our proposal to apply the working memory model to the study of Down and Williams syndromes, and he rapidly became the lead investigator on this part of the programme. Ursula Bellugi of the Salk Institute in Southern California who had already done classic research contrasting Down and Williams Syndrome was a friend from my days in San Diego and we were able to invite her over to discuss our programme and give a lecture to which we invited carers from the Down and Williams Syndrome communities. This helped us get started, and in due course, Chris with a little help from myself, was able to apply the working memory model, suggesting a particularly marked phonological storage deficit in the Down Syndrome group, while people with Williams Syndrome had a more marked limitation in the visuospatial subsystem. Interestingly, the spatial deficit also applied to language with an impaired capacity to use spatial adverbs such as *above* and *below*. Our programme formed part of a very welcome general increase in research on memory disorders in children and when our Handbook reached its second edition, we were able to include three good chapters on the topic. The department was sufficiently impressed with Chris to offer him a proleptic appointment as a lecturer to take effect once the grant was over. In due course he was promoted to a full professorship and recently responded to the pressure of his colleagues to become department head, having just received a mid-career award for research from the Experimental Psychology Society.

So, the grant as a whole went very well, but what about my own contribution? My attempt to develop the working memory model and put more flesh on the central executive was not going well. It was a period when lots of exciting things were happening in the area of working memory, notably including a series of studies in which differences between individuals in working memory performance were used as a means of throwing light on the underlying processes. This approach had originated back in 1980 with a paper by two scientists from Carnegie Mellon University in Pittsburgh, Meredith Daneman and Patricia Carpenter, both of whom were interested in the possible role of working memory in language, attempting to tackle this problem by developing a measure of working memory capacity. They reasoned that the essence of working memory was the need to combine storage of information with its manipulation, devising a task which they termed working memory span. This involved presenting a series of sentences which people had to read, after which they had to recall the final word of each: for example *The old man was bitten by the fierce dog; Despite the mild spring the summer was terrible that year,* after which the response should *dog year.* This proves to be a surprisingly difficult task with typical spans of around three sentences.

Span was found to correlate highly with performance on the language comprehension component of a graduate student selection test, a result that has now been replicated many times. It might of course be argued that this simply predicts one language test from another. However, later studies showed that replacing sentence reading with simple arithmetic computations, each followed by a word, led to very similar results and that even very simple letter or digit processing also works, provided the task combines memory with processing that is demanding enough to fully occupy attention. Finally, not only has this and similar results been replicated many times, but working memory span has also proved to be closely related to performance on standard intelligence tests, the main difference being that working memory span appears to depend more on processing speed, whereas the reasoning component of tests appears to have a stronger contribution from prior experience.

The new span measure evoked considerable interest from working memory theorists who reasoned that if the process underlying this apparently simple task could be identified and analysed, then we might be approaching an understanding of the cognitive basis of human intelligence. Two laboratories were particularly active and creative, that of Randy Engle then in South Carolina and of Akira Miyake in Colorado. Both adopted a strategy of testing large numbers of people on working memory span and then relating performance to a series of cognitive tasks that each might give a clue to its cognitive basis. Results were then subjected to multivariate analysis, at that time a relatively new statistical technique in the field that provided a measure of the contribution made by each of their tasks to explaining working memory span.

The method seemed very promising and in collaboration with a statistically sophisticated colleague I attempted to follow suit, using a number of tests and focussing on a range of different cognitive capacities, adding one further variable, a comparison between younger and older people. Age tends to impair performance on a range of tasks, and I reasoned that this might potentially prise apart variables contributing to working memory capacity. Our first experiment, carried out in fact before I left Cambridge, produced interesting though slightly unexpected results. The second experiment produced results that were at least broadly similar. Then came the third study in which I changed one of the tasks, only to find that the whole pattern had changed. The interesting though somewhat unexpected pattern produced by the first two experiments had resulted in an ingenious and fairly plausible explanation. The pattern of results that suggested our hypothesis had now completely vanished. Why?

I decided that I needed a rather better understanding of the statistical analysis, and this was provided by my colleague, who reminded me that the patterns suggesting links between the various tests that had been selected to reflect different aspects of working memory were based on correlation, the extent to which variation in one was reflected in the performance on other tests. This was based on at least two aspects of the measures, one being the *validity* of the test, the extent to which it gave a true measure of the assumed underlying memory component. It is important to recognise that no tests are process–pure and that all reflect to a greater or lesser extent contributions from factors other than the target variable. This is particularly likely with measures of the central executive, which is itself almost certainly made up of a number of separate sub-processes. A second test requirement is that a measure is *reliable*, that it will give the same answer when tested again and again. Here, measures of executive skills create difficulties since they may reflect the capacity to find *new* solutions to a range of problems, with such solution times being much more variable than occurs in more routine tests such as those involving measures of storage capacity or speed of routine operations. It seems that adding a new test to our battery had somehow disturbed the balance of correlations found in our two previous studies. Not being statistically inclined, I decided to leave this complex area to my more competent colleagues.

Improved statistical methods were indeed developing. An important innovation was that of ensuring that each capacity was studied using several relevant tests. This allowed the experimenter to check that such tests were indeed measuring a broadly coherent concept and to derive a single measure based on the whole range of tests, thus increasing both the reliability of the overall score and its validity as a test of the proposed underlying capacity. I waited with interest to see what would emerge. Separate studies based on broad test batteries were carried out by groups led by Engle, by Miyake and also by Sue Gathercole and independently by Chris Jarrold. I was relieved to note that all came up with a broadly three-component solution that mapped quite well onto the executive, visuospatial and verbal components of our original model. Indeed a previous analysis of a huge amount of data from the intelligence test field had also come up with this broad pattern. There were, however, differences at a more subtle level, suggesting that the visuospatial system was more closely associated with executive processing than was the phonological loop system. I assumed that this is because the loop is capable of holding information by subvocal rehearsal, a process that is helpful while demanding relatively little executive capacity in contrast to that of maintaining a representation of visual items. Of more central importance, however, was whether this method could be used to analyse the executive component into its constituent parts, and if so whether the different laboratories would agree as to exactly what these comprised.

Using the newly developed statistical approach, Miyake and colleagues derived a number of separate measures concluding that one central feature of working memory was the capacity to resist interference from potentially distracting stimuli, dividing such interference into two categories. One of these, *prepotent inhibition*, is the capacity to resist the influence of *existing* tendencies such as that of automatically moving gaze when a new stimulus appears. The second type, *distractor inhibition*, refers to the capacity to resist potential interference from other sources such as earlier unwanted items in a memory test or other kitchen utensils when searching a drawer for a can opener. At this point Miyake moved away from the analysis of working memory concentrating instead on looking for the genetic basis of executive processing using large populations of twins as a method of analysis. Other groups, however, have subsequently adopted Miyake's measures and his interpretation although I am not aware of any direct replication.

Engle and a lively group of collaborators were using a somewhat different approach, testing the working memory span of large numbers of their undergraduate students and instead of using the whole sample, selecting subgroups that were either particularly high or particularly low in span.

They then compared the performance of these two groups across a number of carefully selected activities, hoping to identify those cognitive capacities that were most closely associated with working memory. To summarise briefly an extensive and ingenious research programme, Engle, like Miyake, proposed that an important component of working memory lies in the capacity to inhibit potentially distracting information, which might come either from earlier competing memories or from concurrent disruption. Both Engle and Miyake also tend to assign major importance to the capacity to retrieve information from long-term memory. This is consistent with the conclusion drawn by others from neuroimaging studies, which tend to show a wide area of brain activation when people perform working memory tasks.

Other theorists such as Pierre Barrouillet and Valerie Camos in Europe have shown that tasks based on processing very simple material such as letters can predict a wide range of cognitive capacities just as well as the more typical sentence span task, provided the processing load is enough to disrupt ongoing rehearsal. They propose instead that performance depends on the capacity to retain material in a limited capacity short-term store by attention-based rehearsal while resisting disruption by the demanding concurrent task. More recently, the old question of whether such forgetting reflects memory trace decay or interference has entered into the controversy, so far with no clear resolution. Perhaps time will tell?

In conclusion, although such large-scale, multi-test studies continue to be useful, they do not yet seem to have come up with general agreement as to how best to think about the processes involved in executive control. Indeed attempts to provide an answer to this question by Tim Shallice using neuropsychological data and by Klaus Oberauer, who has recently proposed an ambitious computational model of working memory, suggest that the answer is likely to be highly complex. In my view at least, the central executive homunculus still has a great deal to do before we know enough to justify its retirement.

It has to be said, however, that my own work around this time did not seem to be making much progress. Much of it was a continuation of work described earlier; despite our demonstration of an unexpectedly large influence of the phonological loop on task switching, attempts to come up with more general principles that might characterise a specific executive capacity for switching proved frustrating, leading us to suspect that switching might depend on different processes in different circumstances. Our attempt to disrupt prose comprehension using a concurrent executive task continued to produce negative results, although a study by Beth Jefferies, a very talented PhD student, now a distinguished professor here in York, did give some clues, finding that although memory for triads of sentences comprising coherent prose was unaffected, remembering three meaningful but unrelated sentences did show some impairment. We interpreted this as suggesting that working memory might be needed in the attempt to form new links between the three sentences to create a meaningful chunk, a process that we do repeatedly in comprehending normal prose.

This suggestion was reinforced by data from two rather unusual amnesic patients studied in collaboration with Barbara Wilson. Typically, patients with amnesia can repeat back single sentences but do very poorly on recalling a prose passage either immediately or after a delay. This was not the case, however, for Keith, the very pure amnesic patient described earlier, or a second patient: a highly intelligent lawyer whose amnesia was coupled with frontal lobe damage. Both were atypical in being able to show normal memory for the whole paragraph if tested immediately but lost everything after a brief delay. How could they manage this? Perhaps, if you have a sufficiently capacious working memory and good language skills it might be possible to create and temporarily maintain the coherent chunks comprising the story? But that raised the question of just where within our three-component system this coherent story was being held. At this point we assumed the executive to be a purely attentional system, while neither the sketch pad nor the phonological loop had anything approaching the required capacity.

A further problem was created by evidence that immediate memory for verbal material could be impaired simultaneously by both phonological and visual similarity. How could our model explain this, given that the phonological and visuospatial subsystems had no method of sharing information, other than through the central executive, which, as mentioned, was assumed to have no storage capacity and no general capacity to combine information based on visual, verbal or indeed semantic coding? Finally it was also clear that the existing model would have even greater difficulty in explaining how people could perform the sentence-based working memory span test that had become so influential. It was clearly time for a rethink.

A feature of the development of cognitive psychology in the 1960s was the tendency for theoretical models to be represented by a series of boxes signifying components such as memory stores, linked by arrows indicating the flow of information from one box to the other. This has some resemblance to electronic circuits, perhaps initially giving a spurious feeling of scientific respectability, regardless of the quality of the underlying model.

This led to the criticism that when the theorist encountered a problem, he or she simply added another box. Graham Hitch and I had resolved to try and keep our model as simple as possible, adding new components only if absolutely necessary. I felt that the time had finally come, however, to add a further box, arguing that one box in 25 years was surely not overindulgent! I called the new component the *episodic buffer*, hoping to capture in the title two of its important features.

First of all it was assumed to hold episodes, integrated chunks of information that importantly, unlike the existing subsystems, were not limited to a single coding dimension. Hence it could contain integrated episodes or concepts that combined visual and verbal information together with their semantic associates. A simple example might be a ringing alarm clock, combining its shape, its sound and its function. It was assumed to serve as a buffer store, providing a limited capacity system that would allow information from various sources to be combined, held temporarily and made available for manipulation by the central executive. Finally, I assumed that the episodic buffer was accessible through conscious awareness, and that information was capable of being maintained by an attentional rehearsal process which others had also assumed and termed *refreshing*. This involves focussing attention on the episode within the buffer, in short keeping it in mind. The store was limited in capacity, probably to three or four episodes or chunks, but the chunks themselves could be quite rich both in physical features and in their links to long-term episodic and semantic memory.

Finally, I proposed that retrieval from the buffer was through conscious awareness. In doing so, I was taking a position on the classic question of the nature of consciousness and linking it to the multicomponent model. I assumed that conscious awareness was a mechanism that had evolved to allow different aspects of experience, including ongoing perception and information from both episodic and semantic memory to be combined and made simultaneously available for possible manipulation by the central executive and hence used to plan and determine future action. My proposal that the buffer was responsible for binding features into new concepts or episodes and making them available to consciousness was not a new one; something similar had already been proposed by Bernard Baars, who proposed that conscious awareness was like a stage on which various actors, the contents of awareness, appear and interact, becoming available to an unseen audience.

I gave a talk based on my proposals at an international meeting and was invited by an editor in the audience to submit a paper to the influential journal *Trends in Cognitive Sciences*, not somewhere I normally publish. I did so and waited for the criticisms. To my surprise and relief, my proposal appeared to be welcomed and has been widely cited in the subsequent years; indeed I have just heard that it has been chosen to be reprinted in the 40th-anniversary edition of the journal, another surprise! In my own mind however, it left a major doubt as to whether I was simply providing another convenient homunculus that could explain any awkward findings without leading to any new knowledge. The only way to answer that particular criticism was to attempt to use it as a theoretical tool and demonstrate that it could indeed be helpful, not only in dealing with existing problems but also in generating new knowledge. At this point our five-year grant was coming to an end, and Sue and I decided that we should bid for a continuation.

The way in which our research had developed was very different. Sue's very practical and systematic research was leading to clear advances in the application of the concepts and methods of working memory to education, and she naturally proposed to continue this programme. My own work was more fragmented with future development depending on being able to demonstrate that the concept of an episodic buffer could be used positively rather than simply offering a way of escaping awkward questions and unexpected results. We decided to put in separate grant proposals as in due course did Chris Jarrold.

Meanwhile, while awaiting the result of our applications, I was able to respond to an invitation to spend a year at the Center for Advanced Studies in the Behavioral Sciences attached to Stanford University in California. The Center was the place where the original term *working memory* had been coined and where Atkinson, who had extended the term to his influential modal model, had spent time as a fellow. It provided a wonderful opportunity for attempting to survey developments in the field of working memory, to consolidate the case for the revised model and to explore its broader implications. I readily accepted.

23

Patients, Parasites and Mobile Phones

A good deal of any scientist's work is likely to comprise papers that *confirm* expectations, gradually edging forward your particular field, responding to criticisms, investigating possible limitations and hopefully extending the scope of the underlying theory or model. Provided a model is well supported by existing evidence a result that departs from expectation, although rarely welcome, can be more informative than one that confirms prior assumptions, provided that it answers a well-posed question, and is based on sound experimentation. The best way of ensuring this is by repeating the study, preferably with some variation on the basic method or material so as to increase the generality of your findings.

Unexpected negative results have continued to play an important part in developing the multicomponent working memory framework ever since our first series of experiments. We expected that blocking short-term memory with the need to rehearse an unfamiliar digit sequence would dramatically disrupt reasoning, comprehending and learning. There were effects but far smaller than existing theories would predict, causing us to rethink and resulting in the three-component model. A more recent need to dramatically change my theory, however, occurred in the area of long-term memory. Some years ago, I was asked to give a talk at a retirement symposium for Elizabeth Warrington, who had first introduced me to neuropsychology. It was suggested that I should talk about amnesia, which put me in a difficult position since neither I nor Elizabeth had worked on the topic for several years. Elizabeth had moved on to open up a whole range of new topics through her identification of patients with theoretically important specific deficits, while I had reached the view that attempts to decide between various explanations of amnesia in recent years had not led to any further great insights. I concluded that the results could be explained relatively simply in what I regarded as a modal model of amnesia, a simple framework that captured most of what people believed to be the case. I *did* want to contribute to the celebration of Elizabeth's career, and decided that I would present my simplified model. My amnesia talk was somewhat constrained by the fact that I had forgotten my slides! However, with a little hand waving I survived without too many awkward questions.

A few days later I was contacted by Faraneh Vargha-Khadem, a developmental neuropsychologist at the Institute of Child Health in London, suggesting that I might like to see a patient of hers. Faraneh is an Iranian whose father was exiled on religious grounds; she completed a PhD under Donald Hebb in Montreal and in due course moved to London where she was instrumental in building up a major group concerned with developmental cognitive deficits in children. I duly travelled up to London and, as she suggested, met Jon, a remarkable young man who was born prematurely, suffered from perinatal anoxia, resulting in memory problems that began to be obvious around his fifth birthday. Neuroimaging showed that his hippocampus was only half the normal size, a fact that was reflected in greatly impaired episodic memory with a pattern of deficits that was directly relevant to my simple model of amnesia.

My modal model basically assessed the balance of evidence on a series of theoretical issues and came up with the following broad account. I assumed first of all that amnesia was a failure of memory traces to consolidate. Second, I proposed that the same memory traces underpinned both semantic and episodic memory, with semantic memory representing the overall sum of accumulated episodic memories. Finally I assumed that recall and recognition represented access to the same unitary system, with recognition simply providing more extensive retrieval cues. A further implicit assumption was that general intelligence comprised a combination of executive working memory skills and semantic knowledge for which, given my prior assumptions, episodic memory would be necessary.

Jon's case refuted three of these assumptions. He was clearly amnesic when tested by recall, could not remember ongoing events from his daily life and performed badly on standard verbal or visual recall tests. When tested by recognition however, his memory appeared to be normal. We were able to confirm this using the Doors and People Test, which had recall and recognition components matched for difficulty. This was a test that

I myself had developed some years before to provide separate but matched measures of recognition and recall of both visual and verbal material. I wanted it to be patient-friendly and based it on material from everyday life such as pictures of door scenes and on people's names. It seems to have worked and to be used quite widely clinically, although its range is limited by the fact that the names are UK-based. It had already been shown that it could detect separate visual and verbal memory problems from patients with damage to their right versus left temporal lobes but the chance to test its capacity to separate recall and recognition using comparable measures was still untried. We duly found that Jon's visual and verbal recall were both very poor, while his recognition memory was at a high average level on both. So much for my claim that memories based on recall and recognition were basically the same!

A second assumption of my simple modal model of amnesia was that semantic memory, knowledge of the world, was based on the gradual accumulation of individual episodic memories. This was supported by the fact that classic amnesic patients appeared to stop accumulating new knowledge at the onset of their amnesia. Hence they would not know who the current US president was, and if asked what common items, such as a pint of milk, would cost, they tended to give a price from long ago. It was clear from talking to Jon, however, that his semantic memory was not grossly impaired; he was well able to discuss current politics. He was clearly very fond of books, notably those by Terry Pratchett and could tell you about the fantasy Discworld underpinning them. We were able to confirm Jon's excellent semantic memory using standard measures such as vocabulary knowledge and speed of verifying statements about the world. Finally, I had assumed that grossly reduced episodic memory would hamper the development of intelligence. This was clearly not the case; Jon's IQ was well above average as reflected by standard tests and conversation; on one occasion, for example, he presented a well-argued case for a single world currency.

In short, Jon's pattern of deficits was quite inconsistent with my assumptions that semantic and episodic memory represented the same system, that recall and recognition were basically the same and that the development of intelligence depended on episodic memory. I was not the only one to be surprised by Jon, who is set to challenge the classic amnesic patient HM in terms of the number of papers that are based on studying his case. Like HM, Jon's challenge to existing theory was based directly on the anatomical question of the role of the hippocampus in long-term memory. The early view based on both lesion studies in animals and on neuroanatomical evidence from patients seemed to suggest that the hippocampus was essential to both recall and recognition. However a number of cases were beginning to appear that seemed to challenge this view, suggesting that a closely linked but separate structure, the perirhinal cortex might be capable of accumulating evidence of familiarity that would be sufficient to allow recognition memory, while accepting that the hippocampus is necessary for the type of recollection that underpins episodic memory. One of the reasons for failure to note this earlier is that the two structures are anatomically very close together with the result that damage to one is typically associated with damage to the other.

Importantly, Jon has a well-preserved perirhinal cortex, with his impairment limited to the hippocampus. It seems plausible that recognition memory could be sufficient to develop knowledge of the world, although not capable of forming a rapid association between an episode and its specific context, a link that is necessary to retrieve that specific memory. Consequently Jon may "know" that a word in a list that has just been presented is familiar, but he does not remember encountering it. For example most people will sometimes remember that a word such as "dog" had been presented because it evoked a memory, perhaps of an aunt's dachshund. Jon can judge familiarity but does not have any recollection of the experience of encountering and processing the items that seem familiar. This process of recollection is typically accompanied by a particular pattern of brain activity, a pattern shown by Jon but only for the very few atypical remote memories, rare events that appear to be associated with recollection of their origin.

Over almost 20 years, I have continued to work with Jon and Faraneh from time to time, although more recently on his working memory rather than long-term memory. This is unusual, more typically, as research progresses, questions are answered, patients move on and people change jobs. When we moved to Bristol, my work on Alzheimer's Disease with colleagues in Milan was becoming less as was my involvement in research on schizophrenia. In both cases, however, an opportunity to set up new collaborations emerged in Bristol. In both cases it was related to the question of whether the central executive could be regarded as comprising a number of separable processes.

Earlier work with colleagues from Milan on Alzheimer's Disease had investigated central executive performance and identified the capacity to divide attention and perform two tasks at once as particularly vulnerable. As you may recall from Chapter 20, we found that this capacity was relatively preserved in normal ageing, provided the total level of attentional demand was equated across ages. While in Bristol however, I was able to investigate this further, resulting from the fact that Hilary had moved to work in a memory clinic in Bristol shortly after we arrived. She formed part of a team led by Gordon Wilcock, professor of geriatric medicine, and Romola Buck, the senior clinical neuropsychologist, a team with considerable expertise in diagnosing Alzheimer's Disease and an interest in research. We obtained a grant to explore further the suggestion from our earlier work that the central executive component of working memory could best be regarded as comprising a number of separable processes rather than a simple pool of attentional capacity. This was the first and indeed the only time that Hilary and I worked together, and we were both a little apprehensive. However, once we agreed not to discuss research first thing in the morning while I was still waking up, it was fine! I looked after the planning and write-up and Hilary looked after data handling and the all-important area of patient recruitment and testing where her clinical skills proved crucial. We replicated our dual-task effect, showing that it could not be interpreted in terms of level of difficulty and was not characteristics of other equally demanding attentional tasks. This resulted in our only joint publication supporting our earlier proposal that the central executive is best seen as an alliance involving a range of separable subprocesses.

Probably the most exotic research I was carrying out over this period, however, arose from a rather unexpected invitation to take part in a multinational study of the potential impact of parasitic infection on the cognitive abilities of Third World children. Although I had done rather little work with children, I had experience in developing and applying neuropsychological tests which might feasibly be adapted for use with children. I duly accepted and attended a meeting in a grand house in the Hudson Valley north of New York, originally owned by one of the millionaire "robber barons" of the early days of capitalism. The meeting was organised by the McDonnell Foundation who have a policy of identifying promising but neglected areas and providing research funding that has the potential to open up that field. In this case they chose to study the impact of parasitic infection on the cognitive development of Third World children. The United Nations did fund anti-parasitic drug treatment, but there was little evidence of either the cognitive impact of any deficit or the effect of treating the infection. The foundation invited a number of potentially interested scientists including developmental psychologists, others skilled in psychometrics and the measurement of intelligence and experts in public health and tropical diseases. One of this latter group, Sally Grantham-McGregor, seemed particularly appropriate to the project having working on the impact of malnutrition on cognitive development in the Third World.

Sally had had an unusual career for a research scientist. As a young medical student in London engaged to a member of the England rugby team, she had elected to spend a year in Canada, travelling out via Jamaica, where she fell for an older man, a Jamaican, who she married and stayed on in Jamaica. She went on to bring up their two boys, gradually developing a scientific career with the MRC Tropical Metabolism Research Unit at the University of the West Indies in Kingston, Jamaica. She showed a talent for research, specialising in the effects of nutritional deficit on the development of Third World children, gaining an international reputation despite her relative isolation and prejudices in some quarters against women scientists. I found her methodology more rigorous that is often found in either psychology or epidemiology, despite the problems of psychological testing under very challenging conditions across the Third World. I was pleased when she agreed that we should collaborate. We put in a proposal to the foundation and it was duly supported.

We chose to carry out our initial study in Jamaica where Sally had an excellent team and good contacts across the community. We decided to investigate the effect of whipworm (*Trichuris trichiura*), which was known to be prevalent in poorer communities in Jamaica and was thought to impair cognitive development, based on a previously reported association between the worm burden and cognitive performance. However, children with the greatest worm burden also tend to be poorer with lower levels of hygiene and nutrition. Attempts to separate out the relative importance of these variables statistically were often made but were rarely entirely satisfactory. In common with the other investigations funded by the foundation, we therefore planned to use a more powerful experimental method whereby an initial assessment of worm burden and cognitive function would be made. This would be followed in one group by drug treatment to remove the worms, while a second group would remain untreated, after which both groups would be retested. The treated group should then be free of worms and if the worms were responsible for cognitive impairment, their test performance should improve relative to the untreated group. For ethical reasons this second group would receive treatment after the end of the experiment.

It was arranged that I would fly out to Jamaica with a suitcase full of possible tests that might form the basis for a battery that would provide a broad assessment of cognitive capacity, suitable for testing Third World children who might be preliterate and from a range of cultural backgrounds. Testing Jamaican children proved very different from my previous testing experience. The school system was very authoritarian, and the children tended to be shy and reticent, particularly when confronted by a strange Englishman asking them to do unfamiliar things. I was given a few tips such as sit *beside* the child, don't make eye contact and use nicknames rather than given names. I had developed a version of our Speed of Semantic Processing Test that was based on verifying sentences carefully designed such that any Third World child would have the knowledge to answer, such as *The sun shines during the day* versus *The sun shines at night*, frequently referred to as "the Silly Sentences Test". However, we found that the responses of some children to all the sentences was an obedient "Yes Sir!" We duly changed the test from statements to questions, measuring the time to complete a list of such sentences.

It was difficult to induce the children to say more than a very few words making the standard memory test of story recall impractical. We opted instead for one test requiring memory for lists of 12 common words together with a second test that involved learning the meanings of a short list of words in French, a language spoken on nearby islands. Testing involved the experimenter speaking the word and recall involved simply pointing to the appropriate one of the range of pictures. We also included a speed of visual search test which involved searching for targets in rows of pictograms representing familiar objects or creatures. After some adjustment, the tests seemed to be working well and I returned to the UK leaving Sally and her very impressive team to continue to collect data. Preliminary results suggested that the tests were relatively reliable and correlated at an acceptable level with reading, spelling and arithmetic, suggesting that they were indeed measuring mental capacities that were educationally important.

We duly tested the lowest streams of five schools from inner Kingston. Measures of socioeconomic status revealed no extreme poverty, three-quarters had TV but only one quarter had running water, with cooking mainly dependent on kerosene stoves. Worm infection determined by faecal samples showed only light to moderate levels with only the Silly Sentences Test showing a statistically reliable association with worm burden and even this was removed when differences in socioeconomic background were taken into consideration. We concluded that the tests seemed to be working well, but that the level of infection was much lower than expected and probably too low to have much cognitive impact, good news for Jamaica but not for the project.

It was decided that we needed to move to a location with much heavier parasitic loads. Selecting a suitable location was complex as it would require approval from the relevant government together with local contacts and infrastructure that would allow us to mount a substantial carefully controlled study. It was eventually decided that the project would move to Tanzania and would be a collaborative effort between ourselves and a team focussing on individual differences and education headed by Robert Sternberg from Yale and a UK parasitology group who had existing links with Tanzania. The focus of the study moved from whipworm to two tropical parasites that were common in the region, schistosomiasis and hookworm. Schistosomiasis, sometimes known as bilharzia, is a waterborne disease spread by parasitic worms that are released from infected fresh water snails. It is particularly common in children who are likely to play in contaminated water, leading to abdominal pain, diarrhoea and ultimately liver damage and kidney failure. It affects 200 million people worldwide and is particularly prevalent in Africa. Hookworm also involves parasitic worms that live in the intestines of the host. They suck blood voraciously, and heavy infection can lead to anaemia and potentially to problems in physical and intellectual development. It is typically contracted through the soil with children in bare feet being particularly vulnerable. It is estimated to affect around 500 million people, again principally in Africa.

The study was based 40 miles north of Dar es Salaam in the town of Bagamoyo, previously the principal outlet for the Arab slave trade, later achieving importance as an administrative centre when Tanzania was a German colony. Today, although it still has some splendid buildings, it feels neglected, a mere shadow of its former importance but ideally placed for testing rural schools, which were likely to have heavy parasitic burdens. The tests were mainly based on those developed in Jamaica, together with a more educationally oriented approach taken by Bob Sternberg's group. A set of socioeconomic measures was developed based on the very different culture, with, for example, the type of roof being a very important indicator of wealth and status. Standard measures of height, weight and health status were included together with measures of the load of the two relevant parasites.

The study began under the local direction of Katie Alcock, a young postdoctoral fellow from Oxford who had built up a team, with local support from the professor of psychology at the university in Dar es Salaam. She began to collect preliminary data, and in general things seemed to be working, although Sally and I were somewhat concerned at the degree of responsibility being placed on Katie's willing shoulders, particularly as a young woman in a strongly male-dominated Muslim society. It was agreed that we would visit the project and hopefully lend a little weight to her requests for more help from Dar es Salaam. It was an exciting opportunity as I had never been to any area of Africa other than Egypt. My wife, Hilary, accompanied me, and we added an extra holiday week for a safari afterwards. It was indeed a fascinating experience; we landed in Dar es Salaam and took a taxi to what we were assured was one of the better hotels. It did not feel that way, and we were warned not to go out after dark! We were then collected and driven over deeply rutted roads to Bagamoyo where the project was based in an old but elegant house built originally by Arab merchants. We ourselves stayed at a rather pleasant hotel in rooms that comprised huts in traditional native style.

The leading Tanzanian member of the local research team was Chacha (pronounced like the dance), a tall and imposing figure who had previously been a school headmaster in his home country near Lake Victoria. He was clearly clever and very competent and had joined the group through being a student at the university in Dar. He was tall and very dark, mentioning that the locals referred to him as "the black man" and appeared to be somewhat afraid of him. We duly helped with the local diplomacy and visited one of the test sites, a fishing village, several miles away along extremely bumpy roads. The village had no electricity and the school room was extremely basic, but the tests seem to run smoothly apart from a break when we saw a procession of people carrying what appeared to be a white bundle. It turned out to be the body of a fisherman who had just drowned.

Our most dramatic memory came as a result of going to the bank to draw out local currency. We asked to be driven there but were assured that it was entirely safe. My wife and I together with Sally were walking back when three young men approached us saying "jambo" (hello), then suddenly grabbed the bags of the two women. I instinctively responded by shouting very loudly and attempting to hit them with a rucksack, a rather flimsy weapon since it only contained a paperback book and our money! Happily, they ran off, and I began to chase them, rapidly concluding that I did *not* want to catch them! I was even more convinced when my wife pointed out that they had a knife. We left the project running relatively smoothly, and Hilary and I flew north to Arusha near the Ngorongoro Crater, a magnificent wildlife park in what remains of huge volcanic crater. We saw incredible wildlife, with the highlight being two bull elephants fighting and later a lioness using our Land Rover as cover in order to stalk and ultimately kill a wildebeest.

Having developed the tests, my involvement subsequently was much less, but the partnership went on to test a total of 906 children aged between

9 and 15 years from 10 different schools. A total of 272 children were identified as having moderate to heavy parasite loads and were compared to 117 uninfected participants. Level of infection proved to be correlated with wealth as measured by house and possessions, a factor that had been left out of many earlier studies. When comparing high-, medium- and low-infection groups, digit span forward and backward turned out to be significantly associated with parasitic burden, and there was some evidence of impairment on the Silly Sentences Test for a subsample who were both infected and undernourished.

There was, however, no evidence for improvement following treatment, and possibly even a suggestion of the opposite. Could it be that the body adapts to the parasite, reaching a modus vivendi which no longer works when the parasite is killed? A possibility but certainly not one that was strongly supported. Another possibility is that the effect of parasitic infection is principally on level of energy and motivation, with a child capable of performing cognitive tasks over the short term but lacking the ability to persevere in a more extended educational context. Overall therefore, the results of the programme could be seen as somewhat disappointing. Unlike the Jamaican study, parasite burdens were significant and were associated with reduced cognitive performance. However, removing the parasites did not lead to an immediate increase in cognitive abilities, a result that would have produced the strongest evidence of a causal link between parasites and behaviour. From my own viewpoint, the results were more encouraging in that we had shown that cognitive tests that correlated with academic performance could be adapted for use with Third World children under very basic conditions.

Probably, the most gratifying example of test development, however, came from a problem encountered in the educational rather than the cognitive component of the project, not initially in fact my own concern. This resulted from the earlier decision to use a translation of an existing US Test, The Wide Range Achievement Test, which measures a number of academic skills, including reading. Preliminary testing, however, indicated that our Tanzanian children scored either perfectly or at chance on the reading subtest, making it too insensitive to detect differences in reading performance between children or indeed any subtle improvement following treatment. It should be pointed out at this stage that existing reading tests in English typically involve either the ability to read out passages of prose, unsuitable for very early readers, or reading out individual words, some of which have an irregular link between their spelling and their pronunciation, such as *have* (in contrast to a regular word like *save*), or *high* (versus *sky*). This approach does not, however, work for regular languages, where such spelling-pronunciation mismatches do not occur. This proved to be the case with the local language Kiswahili, which has a very regular mapping of printed letter to spoken pronunciation. The translated reading test thus simply separated children who had learned the rules, regardless of whether a word successfully read out had been understood or not.

In a rather hurried attempt to find an alternative method of testing reading, I suggested a task known as lexical decision, whereby the child would be presented with a series of items, some real words and some non-words, and would be asked to pick out the words. Originating as a laboratory test, this had proved useful in investigating dyslexia in brain-damaged patients, where it was shown that some patients who could not read out words could nevertheless pick them out from non-words and showed signs that they had been understood. We hurriedly put together a test comprising familiar Kiswahili words and similar-seeming non-words, extending it to letters for younger readers by mixing real letters with letter-like items. A version for older readers was based on sentences where the child had to decide whether a simple written sentence was true or false. Our test resulted in a range of scores showing a bell-shaped distribution, as one would expect of a good test rather than the two extreme peaks found before. It also correlated with teachers' judgements of reading skill and with performance on other measures of academic achievement and was duly adopted by the Tanzanian study.

However, although our new reading test gave plausible results, this does not in itself provide very strong evidence for its validity as a method of testing reading in children. A stronger test of the method would be to construct an English version and use a sample of English children to compare it to existing reading tests based on the more conventional approach. At a later point therefore, Susan Gathercole and I produced an English version, the Reading Decision Test, duly showing that it correlated well with standard tests of early reading, was quick to administer and allowed a whole classroom full of children to be tested at the same time. We went on to collect norms which indicated the levels to be expected from children at different ages and having obtained very positive comments from teachers, we went ahead and published the test. Unfortunately it arrived at a time when teachers were being bombarded with national tests of literacy and numeracy; the last thing they wanted was to administer yet more tests and our splendid new test totally failed to be adopted.

The obvious target for such a test, however, was in countries with highly regular languages for which early reading tests based on irregular spelling could not be used. Some years later an opportunity arose through collaboration with colleagues in Brazil. We developed a reading test in Portuguese, which has regular letter-sound mapping. The project went well, the results are now published and discussions with a Brazilian test publishing company are ongoing. The lexical decision method is applicable to any language in the world, so I hope that our serendipitous finding will be picked up and used ever even more widely.

One consequence of retiring from directing the Unit was that I received fewer invitations to serve on committees and appointment boards. This could be seen as a blessing, although on the whole I quite enjoyed the opportunity it often provided to find out what people were doing in other areas of science and its application. I was therefore intrigued to be invited to become a member of the National Radiological Protection Board, a body responsible for overseeing the protection of the public from the potential negative effects of radiation. I was to replace a social psychologist and felt that I was probably not the right person. However, I suspected that if I declined they might simply decide to manage without a psychologist, so I agreed, assuming that in due course I would suggest someone more appropriate. In fact I discovered that my breadth of experience in applying psychology and interacting with other scientists was more important than a competence in social psychology, and I served on the board for two successive terms. It proved to be a very interesting experience. Our principal role was to oversee a substantial government organisation with a high international profile that was concerned with measurement and monitoring of radiation in all its forms from sunlight to nuclear fallout and beyond. The organisation was largely staffed by physicists and the board itself was strongly oriented towards physics and medicine.

I found that I could play a useful role principally by asking questions, sometimes technically very naïve questions but which could prove to be very pertinent. This was particularly the case in issues of developing their website, where my experience from the Unit in human computer interaction and design of information proved useful. The overall pattern of issues was beginning to change from those in which physical measurement was critical to questions involving interaction with the public in connection, for example, with skin cancer due to sunbathing and radiation from the radon, a gas that is gradually emitted by the underlying granite rock in certain parts of the country, potentially accumulating in house basements and increasing the risk of cancer. This raised complex questions of what and how best to inform the public in regions of potential danger and how to help them take appropriate action.

A similar type of problem concerned the public perception of risk: for example, from the proximity of electric power lines. From time to time there would be reports in the press of clusters of cases of cancer in people living adjacent to electricity pylons or nuclear power stations where deciding whether this provided evidence of a genuine threat depended on expert statistics from very able epidemiologists. One of these was Sir Richard Doll who had been the first to demonstrate the carcinogenic effect of smoking. Then in his 90s, he proved to be extremely astute, providing reassuring evidence that it is possible to make a useful contribution long after the statutory retirement age of 65.

The most intriguing experience from my time on the board resulted from being asked to be its representative on a national committee set up to evaluate the safety of mobile phones, which were at the time becoming more and more common. This was leading to widespread concern regarding the potential effects of radiation on both phone users and on people living in proximity to distribution masts. It was a very hard-working committee that included two excellent neuroscientists, whereas I myself simply had to serve as an observer monitoring fair play from the viewpoint of the Radiological Protection Board. The committee reviewed a huge range of evidence from physics to psychology and neuroscience, inviting presentations from a range of experts followed by a series of open public meetings. It rapidly became clear that there was virtually no robust evidence that radiation at the levels emitted by mobile phones or masts had any effect on the brain. Indeed the only clearly detrimental effects were those of distraction from telephoning while performing other activities such as driving, something which Ivan Brown had demonstrated at the Unit many years before and that had become even more firmly established over subsequent years. Furthermore it was clear that the problem came not from the physical demand of holding a mobile phone while driving but from the attentional distraction of concentrating on the spoken interaction rather than the driving environment.

Our task included a series of public meetings around the country, which proved to be very interesting. In general, people were worried more by phone masts than mobile phones. The phone user has a choice, whereas people rarely have a choice about having a mast outside their house. Most companies tended, when possible, to try to hide them in church steeples or other non-obvious locations, but the situation was somewhat different in Ireland. Here the roll-out of the networks came rather later and was dominated by a company that had itself just arrived on the scene and was much less sensitive to public opinion. As a result, there was considerable opposition both north and south of the border, some of it justified because of the way in which the masts had started to appear in unexpected places and some because of deep-seated if irrational fears. For example, one lady declared that she needed to wrap herself in kitchen foil every night to avoid the radiation, and next morning found it full of small radiation holes!

The report duly emerged, providing a balanced review of the available evidence, concluding that there was at present no clear evidence of potential physical or intellectual harm resulting from using a mobile phone. However, on what was termed "the precautionary principle", it was recommended that the exposure in young children should be kept at a minimal level. They did, however, recommend that mobile phones should not be used while driving, arguing that even hands-off telephoning was potentially highly dangerous. The report was duly presented to the press and public at a meeting in Whitehall. Besides the Chairman of the Committee, I noticed a figure like a displaced orchestral conductor clearly much concerned with how the meeting should go. I concluded that this was probably the government's chief spin doctor although happily he did not need to do much spinning. In due course, driving while telephoning was made illegal but unfortunately only for handheld telephones. When we questioned this decision we were told that the police had objected that a broader ban would be unenforceable because of the difficulty of detecting hands-off telephone use while driving, claiming quite reasonably that a law that cannot be enforced is not likely to be a good law. The frequency of telephoning while driving was reduced but unfortunately by no means entirely removed. However, as applied research goes, this has to count as a win. Meanwhile, Hilary and I were preparing for another year in California.

24

Working Memory in Context

Neuroscience, Emotion and Philosophy

Hilary and I arrived in Stanford, California, in September 2001, having the good fortune to be supported by a fellowship from the Center for Advanced Study in Behavioral Sciences, an independent institution with close links to Stanford University. Stanford is a world-class university, founded by Leland Stanford who made a fortune from railroad development in the 19th century, locating it on land surrounding his stud farm around 20 miles south of San Francisco. It was co-educational, had no religious affiliation and has been extremely successful, producing multiple Nobel Prize winners and more recently forming the hub of Silicon Valley with its graduates and sometimes its dropouts being responsible for many of the multinational information technology firms that have come to dominate the world.

The Center is on a hill just off the campus. It hosts up to 40 fellows who spend a year there, working on their own academic projects. Each fellow is provided with a very pleasant office and has only two duties. The first of these is to continue to meet fellow fellows over an excellent lunch, while the second is to give one talk and attend the talks of others, not an onerous task! My initial aim was to write a book on working memory for the general reader and in this connection I was put in touch with a US literary agent who agreed that this might be a worthwhile enterprise. Not unreasonably, she wanted an outline of the book and I tried several, each emphasising how important working memory was, one linking it to the development of cognitive science, a second attempt linking it to intelligence neither of which enthused her and eventually I tried a more autobiographical approach somewhat similar to the present book, evoking the rather crushing response that "That's all about you, who's going to be interested in that?" We agreed to part company and instead I wrote a more academic book which was eventually published as *Working Memory, Thought and Action*. It caused me to think much more deeply about working memory and proved to be a very good way of spending my time at the Center.

A very attractive city has grown up around the university with excellent shops and restaurants but with very expensive housing. The Center helps fellows find local accommodation tailored to their resources, in my case somewhat more limited than most of my US colleagues. As a result we were located in a relatively modest but very comfortable apartment in the town of Los Altos, about five miles south of the university. This proved to be an intriguing experience. We discovered that our apartment was in a dormitory town for Silicon Valley, largely comprising spacious and elegant homes on extensive plots. Los Altos has model community facilities including an excellent library and museum. The town council meetings were open to all and were broadcast direct to the community, chaired by a Mr Lear whose parents had bestowed on him the first name of "King", while his sister had the equally memorable though less regal name of "Shanda Lear"! Los Altos had an immaculate though expensive supermarket and several coffee bars, one also served beer when we arrived but seemed to have signed the pledge a month or two later and reverted to coffee. The semi-rural town had the feeling of a high tech utopia but was to my mind at least just a little boring; but then who knows what might go on behind the neat gardens and immaculate, Hispanic-tended lawns? Checking its website recently I was intrigued to discover that its earlier inhabitants have included founders of Apple (Steve Jobs), Google (Sergey Brin) and Facebook (Mark Zuckerberg).

We bought a small car, resisting a later radio suggestion to "Buy your wife a jaguar for Christmas"; I assume this referred to the car, though this being California, you can't be sure! Our car allowed me to commute in and provided a way of touring extensively over the very attractive North California countryside. When the time came to leave, a colleague suggested that I sell it through a new system called eBay, just invented by one of his students. It all sounded a little risky, so we ended up passing it on to one of next year's intake at a bargain price. If only I had known!

I was settling in nicely when I switched on the car radio on my drive to the Center on 11th September to hear of a massive terrorist attack in

New York. When I arrived, people were clustered around a television with news coming through of multiple plane hijackings and attacks on the Twin Towers in New York, the Pentagon in Washington, while the plot to hit the White House was apparently prevented by the courage of the doomed passengers. We heard that President Bush had flown westward, which I assumed was a pre-planned response to a nuclear attack and its consequent radiation. He later appeared on TV giving, what to my mind was not a particularly impressive speech. The media rallied around the flag, however, transmitting a feeling that anything remotely critical would be unpatriotic. There were TV programmes in which one person after another stood up and simply declared "I am an American!" Visiting a redwoods forest a few days later, we were intrigued to encounter a group of people all standing together and singing "God bless America". The sheer audacity of the attacks and massive loss of lives shocked the world and must have seemed even more threatening to a country that up to then seemed invulnerable to the bombing attacks committed by terrorist groups in Italy, Spain and Germany and by the IRA in Britain. Among the fellows at the Center we had experts who gave impromptu lectures on terrorism, Afghanistan and other related topics, which probably made us for a while the best-informed group outside Washington. Gradually, life in our ivory tower above the campus resumed and we continued with our various projects.

The Center provided a very congenial and stimulating environment, one that was very appropriate for my own project since the term *working memory* first appeared in a book originating from the Center, while my own office had previously been occupied by Richard Atkinson, whose use of the term stimulated our own concept. I decided that one aim would be to update my 1986 book by reviewing the current state of research after which I would try to place the concept of working memory in a broader context, including the role of emotion and discussing the implications of working memory for the philosophical problems of consciousness and free will. Such topics had previously seemed to me to be beyond the reach of psychology. However, developments in neuroscience were beginning to persuade me that this need not be the case.

This line of thought was encouraged by the fact that a number of my colleagues were addressing broadly similar issues. Jeffrey Gray, a psychologist from London and Oxford, was writing a book on consciousness, while two distinguished social psychologists, John Bargh and Roy Baumeister, had what appeared to be totally opposite views on free will. Meanwhile, I found a common interest in emotion among fellows from a range of other disciplines and we set up an emotion discussion group. Another fellow, Robert Bjork, was a long-standing friend in the memory field and together we arranged a very useful series of seminars with colleagues in the Stanford psychology department. He and I planned a joint memory text that eventually emerged some seven years later, not with Bob but with his ex-student Michael Anderson together with Michael Eysenck as a third co-author.

A major bonus of my year at the Center was the weekly meetings where each fellow would, in turn, give an account of his or her research. Most of the topics were quite new to me and ranged from the social behaviour of ant colonies to the aims and influence of Second World War films. Although the name of the Center suggested an emphasis on *behavioural* sciences the preponderance of fellows came from social sciences and the disciplines of sociology, philosophy, history, politics and economics. My own background in experimental psychology with links through the MRC to neuroscience and biology left me unprepared for some of the methods adopted. The approaches taken seemed to fall into two broad categories: the psychologists and some of the anthropologists and social scientists favoured an experimental approach, attempting to answer questions by comparing groups that preferably differed only along the dimension to be studied. The alternative approach was to study a specific group or event, to come up with an interpretation and then defend that view, rather like a lawyer presenting and defending a case.

I can see why this largely descriptive approach might be taken in historical studies, but even here comparisons would surely be valuable. A case in point concerned a study of conditions in a Dublin prison during the Irish famine. They were clearly not good, but it would have been useful to be able to compare them with conditions at the time in the London or Glasgow prisons. More worrying was the absence of comparison groups in a project involving several fellows investigating methods of assessing and changing opinions on issues of government policy using focus groups over a number of repeated sessions during which the groups were advised by "experts". When asked how they chose the experts and what would happen in the absence of such input, crucial, I suggested, to a balanced interpretation, it was claimed that answering such questions would be too expensive, a rather worrying response as it seemed as if there were plans to extend this approach to practical politics. However, most talks were fascinating, regardless of whether they were entirely convincing to the more hard-headed members of the fellowship.

I decided to begin my attempt to broaden the scope of the working memory model by considering the way in which it might be influenced by emotion. As you may recall, I developed an interest in this topic as a result of my diving research and my somewhat unsatisfactory attempts to study performance in dangerous environments, leading later to our setting up a cognition and emotion group at the Unit to which we were successful in attracting some very talented clinical researchers with an interest in cognitive psychology. They included John Teasdale and Mark Williams who both worked on depression, and Fraser Watts and Andrew Mathews who worked on anxiety. Although my direct collaboration with the group was rather limited, I followed their work with great interest and pride as they published a highly influential book, *Cognitive Psychology and Emotional Disorders*, founded the journal *Cognition and Emotion* and were instrumental in further developing and testing a form of therapy for depression based on *mindfulness*, a treatment originating in the field of transcendental meditation, an approach that is now hugely influential.

I began this part of my project by reviewing research on the influence of anxiety on working memory, a topic that was related to my own earlier work. However, a good deal had happened in the field of emotion since my limited attempts to make theoretical sense of the results of our experiments on performance in dangerous environments. One line of development was through neuroscience as typified by the work of Joseph LeDoux who developed an animal-based approach to understanding the effects of fear and anxiety. His extensive body of research can be very briefly summarised as follows. First of all, he made a distinction between *emotion* reflecting a physiological state and its psychological representation which he referred to as *feelings*. He himself was principally concerned with understanding the physiological basis, proposing that the process of converting the emotion into feelings was attributable to working memory, leaving open the precise mechanism. Fear was assumed to depend on activation of the amygdala, a small area deep in the brain which responds to signals of threat by readying the organism for fight or flight. Information from the senses could reach the amygdala in two ways: either by a very rapid direct route or via a more circuitous route through the cerebral cortex, which was capable of registering the extent and nature of the threat in more detail.

This broad overview was backed up by studies of anxiety in patients who can be divided into two broad categories: those with specific phobias and those with a more generalised anxiety state. Phobias are fears generated by specific objects or situations; some are common and often relatively mild, such as spider phobia, while others, fortunately rarer, can be highly disruptive. One woman, for example, was terrified of birds. She worked in a large shed-like building and was constantly worried that birds would get in, a fear that seriously disrupted her working life. She was also liable to misinterpret cues in the environment: for example, a piece of flapping plastic as a threatening bird. Perhaps even more disruptive is agoraphobia, a fear of venturing out into a potentially crowded and threatening world, something that can prevent the sufferer from ever leaving home. While these are relatively specific, some patients suffer from General Anxiety Disorder, a condition in which the patient is constantly on the alert for any potential threat; hence a couple of barks from the next-door dog might be interpreted as an attempted break-in.

Results from both patients and the general population are broadly consistent in suggesting that General Anxiety Disorder probably represents a malfunctioning of a basic biological system for warning about potential danger. Consistent with LeDoux's views, it does seem to involve a rapid pre-attentive capacity for detecting potential threat, together with a slower component that is based on a more detailed evaluation. Specific phobias, on the other hand, represent learned fears resulting from some form of earlier experience, although it has been suggested that evolution has made avoidance of certain danger-related natural stimuli such as spiders and fungi more readily associated with anxiety.

From a working memory viewpoint, a central question is the extent to which fear and anxiety interfere with cognition, and through what route. The most probable mechanism is through attentional disruption, whereby danger signals interrupt and override ongoing processing within the central executive. Such a mechanism is clearly helpful in the case of genuine threat but needlessly disruptive when the threshold for sending the alarm signal is unduly low. This can either be because learning has made specific signals such as a harmless spider unduly alarming or in the case of General Anxiety Disorder, setting the overall threat detection system at an inappropriately sensitive level, a level that might be appropriate for a healthy person in a threatening environment but is inappropriate for everyday life. An important feature of such a threat detection system is that it operates at a level below conscious awareness, serving as a kind of gatekeeper. That suggests that people may be influenced in making later responses by anxiety-provoking stimuli: for example words such as "death" and "cancer" when presented too briefly to be consciously detected. This is indeed the case.

An alternative to studying patients is to make use of the substantial differences in anxiety as a trait within the general population. Using this approach, Michael Eysenck and colleagues required groups selected as high or low in trait anxiety to read a passage of prose after which they were tested on its content. Initially, there was no difference between groups of anxious and non-anxious people in their understanding of the passage, although eye movement measures showed that anxious individuals did tend to backtrack more frequently when reading the text. When this was prevented by presenting one word at a time, the anxious group appeared to besubvocalising more extensively. Impaired comprehension was only finally seen when subvocalisation was prevented by the requirement to repeatedly utter an irrelevant word. People can be very good at finding ways to compensate for stressors at least in the short term.

Most studies of the effect of anxiety on performance use both physiological measures such as heart rate and skin conductance together with subjective assessments of both a general tendency to be anxious and the level of anxiety at the time of the experiment. Subjective reports and evidence from physiological measures usually agree but there are cases in which the two diverge and people with a physiological indicator of anxiety do not report themselves as anxious. This raises the question of whether disruption in performance is caused by the physiological state, in which case both groups should show impaired performance or by the psychological state in which case only a people reporting anxiety should show a decrement. It proved to be the case that impaired performance was linked to the subjective feeling of anxiety rather than the physiological state of the individual, supporting the distinction made by LeDoux between physiological emotions and psychological feelings.

Within the working memory model, a potential interpretation is to suggest that fear stimuli gain access to either the central executive or the episodic buffer, competing with information currently being processed, and demanding priority. This suggests some form of threat detection system that is able to disrupt ongoing thought processes. The level of threat necessary to trigger interruption in executive processing will differ among individuals as reflected in their chronic trait anxiety level and by the specific situation. For instance a dark street in an unfamiliar city with a higher threat level might lead to an increased likelihood that an unexpected sound would gain access to the central executive, potentially interfering with ongoing thoughts.

However, it is also clear that executive processes can intervene to reduce disruption by selecting an appropriate strategy. One of these is to focus attention on a demanding task, hence limiting the attention to potentially anxiety-provoking features of the surrounding environment. In collaboration with John Teasdale, we found that mind wandering, the tendency to attend to irrelevant features rather than the task in hand, decreases when people have to focus on demanding tasks. However, as people become more skilled, the tasks need less attention, leaving room for other thoughts or features of the surroundings to enter awareness. This makes sense of our diving study in which performance on an intellectually undemanding manual screw plate task was more disrupted by anxiety than by a reasoning test requiring constant attention. In recent years, such mind wandering has become a major area of research.

To summarise, phobic and clinically significant anxiety symptoms can be seen as resulting from the malfunctioning of a basic system for warning of potential danger. Phobias result from an inappropriate learned fear response, while chronic anxiety states may result from an unduly low setting of a general threat detection system. Both lead to a tendency for the functioning of the central executive to be disrupted by irrelevant non-threatening stimuli: in short, by unjustified worry.

Having found it relatively easy to link the multicomponent model of working memory to ongoing clinical research on anxiety, I then attempted to apply the same model to a second hugely important emotional disorder, namely depression, finding this to be a much more challenging task. Clinically assessed depression is not simply extreme sadness or low mood state. It typically will also involve any or all of a range of symptoms including lack of energy, disturbed sleep, complaints of poor memory and disrupted social relationships. In contrast to a potentially life-saving fear and anxiety system, none of these seem to reflect systems that are of evolutionary value. The pattern of cognitive deficits linked to the two clinical states also proved surprisingly different between anxiety and depression, particularly bearing in mind that depressed patients were often also anxious. A prominent feature of anxiety is that it biases attention towards potentially threatening words or stimuli. Depressed patients, on the other hand, show little evidence for such hypersensitivity, showing no evidence of attentional disruption from very briefly presented emotional words, and little effect when the stimuli are clearly seen.

Autobiographical memory also shows differences between anxiety and depression. It is relatively unaffected by anxiety but has an important effect on patients suffering from depression. When in a depressed mood patients tend to be able to recall only negative memories. The effect is related to the context-dependent memory described earlier in divers whereby what is learned underwater is best recalled underwater. Depression favours recall of negative memories, making it hard to recall positive events in any detail. Given that such negative memories are likely to increase the patient's depression, helping break out from this vicious circle forms an important part of a range of cognitive treatments. Unlike anxiety states, therefore, that can readily be linked to a useful system for avoiding danger, it is hard to see how this pattern of deficits could have any evolutionary survival value. I initially hoped that my account of the effects of anxiety disorders might be adapted to cover depression. When this proved difficult. I put the issue aside while considering another challenging question; working memory is essentially a system for controlling action, but what controls working memory? In short, why do we do anything? Attempting to answer this question led me into territory that I would normally have avoided as philosophical quicksand, but which I found myself cautiously tackling.

One source of evidence on the nature of action control came from neuropsychology with the description by Anthony Damasio of a small number of patients who, typically following frontal lobe damage, appeared to have recovered their cognitive capacities virtually completely but nonetheless led chaotic lives. The classic case from the 19th century was that of Phineas Gage, the railroad foreman described earlier, who had the misfortune of having an iron bar driven through his eye socket and frontal lobes following an explosion, resulting in well-preserved cognition but deterioration in character. Damasio's cases were of course much more thoroughly investigated, allowing stronger conclusions to be drawn. One case, for example, involved a businessman who, following the removal of a tumour from his frontal lobes, continued to perform well on a wide range of psychological tests and returned to his job but was quite unable to cope, continuing to fail at a succession of jobs and in his social relationships. The simple task of choosing a date for next appointment proved too complex for him although when a specific date was proposed, he readily accepted it. Damasio explained such patients in terms of what he termed the *somatic marker hypothesis*. This assumed that actions are governed by rewards and punishments associated with different features of the world, allowing people to steer their actions appropriately. Like LeDoux, Damasio separated the idea of physiological emotions from psychological feelings, also proposing that the latter depend on working memory in some unspecified way. He suggested that the area in the frontal lobes damaged in such patients was essential for evaluating the feelings associated with success and failure and that damage to the evaluative system meant that adequate decisions were unlikely to occur.

In discussing this view at the Center, someone pointed me to a very similar proposal by David Hume, the great 18th-century Scottish philosopher. Hume saw our perceived world as comprising objects and features that were not neutral, but which each had a value or valence which could vary in its negative or positive values reflecting its association with pleasure or pain. He, like Damasio, proposed that we steer our way through life using these positively or negatively valenced features to direct our actions, not by reason but by our "passions", which for Hume included not only strong emotions but also much milder feelings, what he termed the "quieter passions of benevolence and love of life which may be known more from their effects than from their immediate feelings or sensation".

It occurred to me that combining the views of Hume and Damasio might offer a plausible interpretation of depression if one assumed that initiating an action involves some form of hedonic judgement based on the balance of pleasant or unpleasant associations, allowing one path to be evaluated as more favourable than another. Assuming that this hedonic detection system operates like any other perceptual system, one might propose that it has a neutral point and that this may be set appropriately or inappropriately. Too high a threshold would result in otherwise mildly positive situations being perceived as negative, while the opposite setting of the midpoint of the hedonic detector would result in an unduly positive view of the world. Note that this assumes a problem with the evaluative *setting* of the hedonic system, not a problem in using this information to make decisions as found in Damasio's patients.

Let us assume that the neutral point in depression is misplaced, with the consequence that otherwise relatively neutral stimuli are interpreted as negative. This could result from a number of circumstances, one being genetic, with some people born with a tendency to see the world in sombre tones, like a friend who, on being awarded career tenure, declared, "Oh dear, I'll never leave now!", while some people seem always to be cheerful. The neutral point could also be disturbed by life events: either being in an uncontrollable negative situation or as a result of a dramatic change in one's circumstances – the death of a spouse, for example. Given that the mechanism is biologically determined, it is plausible to assume that it could be manipulated pharmacologically, hence the short-term effectiveness of certain drugs. As mentioned earlier, depression is accompanied by an inbuilt tendency to retrieve negative thoughts, creating a downward mood spiral. Helping the patient to break free from this vicious cycle as in cognitive behaviour therapy could be seen as enabling the reestablishment of an appropriate neutral point in the hedonic detection system.

From an evolutionary viewpoint, depression could therefore be seen as the malfunction of an absolutely essential system for decision-making. Furthermore it is a system that is likely to involve working memory in bringing together a whole range of features varying in their valence and operating at different levels. These might range from the immediate, "Should I eat this

cake?" to the more long-term "I really need to slim" with further complications at other levels "Would it seem rude to say no?" and "How much do
I care about my general health?" It seems likely, however, that these might
typically operate implicitly, outside the direct control of working memory
so that you find that you have reached out and bitten into the cake without
thinking. Working memory is, however, likely to be involved in complex
and important decisions, such as buying a house, where you might want
to balance out, for example, the attractiveness of the location versus its
convenience and the number of bedrooms versus its overall appearance,
coming up eventually with an overall decision based on combining and
balancing all of these, a process that is likely to be heavily dependent on
working memory.

I have focussed so far on a possible mechanism for decision-making and
its potential malfunction in depression. What are the broader implications
of this approach to a theory of action? The Norman and Shallice hypothesis
assumes that action is determined by two main processes: existing habits,
on the one hand, coupled with the operation of the supervisory attentional
system. This, in our model, depends on the capacity of the central executive to manipulate and evaluate the relevant information. Our actions are
certainly determined in part by habits and cognitive preconceptions such
as prejudices and stereotypes as assumed by the Shallice model. However,
behaviour is also subject to control and manipulation by the central executive in conjunction with the episodic buffer, the subsystem that allows
material to be made available to conscious awareness. This, in turn, leads
to an even more challenging question. What is conscious awareness?

My neighbour at the Center, Jeffrey Gray, was writing a book on
exactly this question, dividing the problem into two halves, which he
termed the easy question and the hard. The easy question is in fact far from
easy as it concerns the way in which the brain creates and utilises conscious
awareness as part of its function. His hard question concerned the nature
of what philosophers term *qualia*, the actual experience of redness of a rose
that goes beyond the physiological processes that underpin colour vision.
Historically, this has underpinned the philosophical question of how the
physical body and non-physical mind interact.

While I agree with Jeffrey on the easy question, I currently take the
view that the hard question is not a useful one to ask. The body-mind
problem is one that has plagued philosophy for centuries. It formed the
core of an influential book published in 1949 by the Oxford philosopher
Gilbert Ryle who argued that the dualist separation of body and mind
proposed by Descartes and termed by Ryle "the dogma of the ghost within

the machine" was the result of the conceptual error of treating mind and body as polar opposites rather than as different facets of the same thing. He uses the example of a visitor to Oxford asking where the university is. It is in fact distributed throughout the city, a unitary organisation but not in any single place, and even if it were contained in a single building, the university is far more than bricks and mortar. For Ryle therefore, conscious awareness and its physiological basis are not two logically equivalent systems that then have to communicate with each other in some way but rather are different aspects of the same system. This is probably the dominant view within neuroscience and psychology, although not the position accepted by Gray.

My own view was that Gray's "hard question" of how to explain the conscious experience of the redness of a rose could be left aside, allowing genuine progress to be made on the question of how consciousness is achieved by the brain. My assumption is that consciousness has evolved as a successful way of dealing with a range of practical problems. As to the question of qualia, why we experience a rose as red, my answer would be "why not?" I see it as analogous to the question of why peacocks have large tails and why crocodiles have strong jaws. These are evolutionary solutions arrived at randomly over many many generations, shaped by the environmental niche into which they have evolved. Consciousness is a very valuable tool for a wide range of activities including creative innovation and social interaction but in its human form has been around for a relatively short period of time and sadly may not be around for anything approaching longevity of the crocodile!

In the working memory model, consciousness is associated with the episodic buffer which serves the purpose of binding together information from long-term memory, perception and the various components of working memory into integrated episodes or chunks. Such a view of consciousness is relatively common in the field, typified, for example, by the previously mentioned proposal of Bernard Baars who likened conscious awareness to a stage on which various cognitive activities are made available. Genuine progress has been made concerning the neurobiological basis of conscious awareness and its link to the initiation of action, a link that is by no means as simple as might be assumed. There is, for example, evidence that the physiological initiation of an action may occur before it is available to conscious awareness, a phenomenon entirely consistent with the Norman and Shallice proposal that action is controlled at two levels, one of which is automatic and not necessarily open to conscious awareness.

Suppose we assume that the episodic buffer is the seat of conscious awareness, does it have a specific localisation within the brain? There is no basic reason why it should be localised and indeed, one might argue that, given its biological importance, a single location might be more vulnerable to possible damage than a distributed system in which consciousness arises from the combined activity of a range of different systems, with damage to one leaving the overall system still able to function. Hence, a loss of access to vision still allows touch and sound to provide some form or orientation in space. A good example of this is provided by the phenomenon known as <u>blind sight</u>. This can result from damage to the occipital lobes of the cortex, an area at the rear of the brain responsible for the early stages of vision where damage can leave the patient apparently blind in a large part of the visual field. However, despite lack of conscious awareness, if asked to guess whether an object is present in the blind area of their visual field, patients are often correct and if required to reach out and grasp the object, will form their hand differentially for a horizontal versus vertical bar, showing that the information is sufficient to guide detailed behaviour in an appropriate way. The effect extends to reading, with the presentation of words such as *doctor* in the blind field facilitating the speed of responding to an associated word such as *nurse* in the conscious field. The capacity for newly acquired information that is not available to consciousness is of course also characteristic of memory in amnesic patients, where having seen a word such as STAMP, the patient cannot recall or recognise it, but when given the initial letters ST, they will guess *STAMP*.

Does it, however, matter whether information is consciously available or not? It certainly does, because conscious availability allows the material to be considered and integrated into a broader plan and utilised to achieve that plan. The fact that amnesic patients have implicit memory does not help them very much in orienting themselves in time and place or in planning their day-to-day life nor are blind sight patients able to make extensive use of information in their blind field. Within the working memory model, such implicit information does not have access to the episodic buffer and cannot be actively and productively manipulated by the central executive in order to plan future action.

I found that I arrived at a concept of consciousness very similar to that proposed by Bernard Baars who proposed that the conscious control of action relies on the availability of what he terms a global workspace, a working memory. Consciousness combines information from a range of different perceptual channels, linking them to information from long-term memory. The resulting conscious awareness is necessary for explicit learning and episodic memory, although it does not of course guarantee such learning; amnesic patients are certainly aware but not capable of adequate long-term storage, probably because the links set up within the episodic buffer fail to be consolidated within long-term memory. Consciousness is also needed for the monitoring and motor control of novel actions although well-practiced movements require less and less conscious attention.

Control of action may operate at a range of different levels, reflecting both immediate and long-term goals which may vary in degree of awareness and extent of control. To take a simple example, breathing is automatic but can be synchronised with fluent speech and may be consciously controlled as in the case of a scuba diver attempting to conserve air by breathing slowly. However, ultimately breath control is automatic, and we cannot commit suicide by holding our breath. Levels of conscious and unconscious control may conflict in brain-damaged patients as in the case of the so-called *anarchic hand sign*, where one hand behaves normally, while the other appears to have a mind of its own. Sergio Della Sala reviews a total of 139 such cases, including one involving a young woman dining with the clinician and her family. Her right hand behaved normally, while her left hand reached out and grabbed a pile of fish bones and thrust them into her mouth. Another patient buttoned her clothes with one hand, while the anarchic hand proceeded to unbutton them.

I concluded that working memory plays a central role in cognition by bringing together information from a range of sources and integrating it into multidimensional representations within the episodic buffer. This normally makes the information accessible to conscious awareness, allowing it to be used for future action. However, such action depends on a range of subsystems, some perceptually based and others reflecting long- and short-term memory, potentially controlled by an executive system that itself operates at a range of different levels of control, some short-term, such as positioning the hand to pick up a piece of chocolate, a second level planning to eat it, and a third being concerned with the need to slim, potentially countermanding the other two.

By the end of my year at the Center, I was surprised at the extent to which my attempt to place the multicomponent working memory in context had led me to consider such a wide range of social and philosophical issues; I had doubts about the plausibility of my views until I began to discuss them with my colleagues at the Center, only to discover that they were less radical than I feared but also less novel. Unsurprisingly we were all to some extent responding to the zeitgeist, the intellectual climate of the time, with our year at the Center allowing time and intellectual space to absorb it and combine it with our own ideas. The resulting book eventually emerged in 2008.[1]

Note

1 Baddeley, A. (2008). *Working Memory Thought and Action*. Oxford: Oxford University Press.

25

Exploring the Episodic Buffer

I returned from Stanford to a department that was undergoing some rather rapid changes. Martin Conway had initially proved to be a very effective department head, and had substantially increased its reputation for research. This particularly applied in the area of memory for which it was probably the strongest department outside North America, with an expertise not only in working memory but also in Martin's area of autobiographical memory, on social aspects of memory, on ageing and latterly on semantic memory and semantic dementia. However, by the time I returned it had lost no fewer than five of its more experienced memory staff to appointments elsewhere, notably including both Martin Conway and Sue Gathercole who moved to chairs at the University of Durham. There was no obvious successor to Martin as department head and attempts to agree on suitable candidates proved unsuccessful.

At one point, while we were still in California, a proposal came through to appoint a husband and wife team who were academically strong as individuals but would fail completely to fit into the existing department. In exasperation I remember saying to Hilary, "If they come I will leave!" "Where would you go?" Hilary asked. "York", I declared without thinking, expecting her to resist the idea of moving north. In fact she seemed quite receptive to the idea, so I thought about it in more detail. York had a number of attractions as a consistently good research department in a very attractive city that I knew well from childhood. Furthermore, my old friend and colleague Graham Hitch had just moved there and seemed to have settled in well. So, having done my unsuccessful best to help solve the appointment problem in Bristol, I sounded out Graham and in due course Hilary and I were invited up for discussions. By this time, I was into the first year of my next grant, so I would be bringing a postdoctoral fellow and a secretary for the next three years. Was York prepared to do a similar deal to the one that I enjoyed at Bristol? Here, a problem arose due to my age, well past the normal retirement point. York had a new Vice Chancellor (VC) who appeared to be unwilling to commit the university directly; however, the department was allowed to employ me through its own funds as a "consultant professor", paid on a monthly basis. Had I been simply responding to the attitude of the new VC, I would have stayed in Bristol, but I really liked the idea of joining what was a friendly and active department and working again with my old friend Graham.

The current head of department was Andy Young, someone I had known for many years and who had for a period held a senior position at the Unit. He was very welcoming and suggested that, like everyone in the department, I should do some teaching to which I happily agreed since it made me feel more a part of the department than I had in Bristol where I had been excused all activities other than research. The teaching load proved to be light and enjoyable, comprising a joint course with Graham on practical aspects of memory and the supervision of undergraduate research projects and in due course PhD students. I found PhD supervision considerably more enjoyable after being convinced by Andy Young that it was not necessary to stick to what I perceived as the traditional Cambridge role where the student functions as the lone scholar, typically seeking guidance only when necessary. I was happy to move to an approach that was closer to an apprenticeship whereby the student and supervisor start by working together and the student becomes gradually more and more independent, an approach I found much more satisfying than the more hands-off Cambridge model.

Despite not formally being a member of the university, I felt more integrated into the department than in Bristol, attending departmental staff and teaching meetings. However I felt that I should not play any part in appointments given that it was uncertain how long I would stay beyond the end of the three-year grant. In fact I have now been there for 14 years and have seen the retirement of most people who were in the department when I arrived! Curiously enough, despite being too old when I joined the department the administration decided that I was no longer too old some 10 years later when it was discovered that my invented post as consultant professor would not allow my research to be included in the increasingly important REF, (Research Excellence Framework) the national research assessment that occurs every five years and has a direct effect both on the funding received from the government and the overall profile of the department and university. It is nice to be no longer too old!

How did all this affect my research? I decided that the simplest way of getting a broad view of my time in York would be to look at my published output over the last, very varied 20 years, during which I first moved from the MRC to Bristol with two postdoctoral fellows, followed by four years with a single fellow and a decade with no grant support. I was therefore surprised to discover that my publication rate has remained remarkably constant at around five papers per year. What had changed, however, is the way in which the various papers were achieved. An important factor has been the resumption of collaboration with Graham Hitch. Working with Graham is a real pleasure; we have broadly similar ideas but different areas of strength. I have a tendency to come up with plenty of ideas, but when one does not immediately seem to pay off I am inclined to rush off and try something else. Graham is more grounded and persistent. He also has mathematical and related skills from his first degree in physics, compensating from my total lack. Since we last worked together he has been involved with Neil Burgess, a neuroscientist, who like Graham, has a background in physics, in developing a computational model of the phonological loop that provides an account of how serial order is stored and retrieved. Graham also has experience of working with children and has continued his interest in working memory and mathematics. He is an excellent teacher, particularly good at encouraging students to think for themselves, whereas I am more inclined to present the answer and then explain than to engage the student directly. The chance of working together was a major bonus and continues to be; Graham has now retired but comes in one day a week and, like me, does most of his writing when away from York.

When I first arrived, Richard Allen, the postdoctoral fellow and I had completed the first year of a four-year grant to attempt to put flesh on the admittedly rather vague concept of the episodic buffer. Richard had just completed a PhD in York based on an approach to working memory using individual differences between people to throw light on underlying mechanisms, an important approach that was particularly influential at the time in the US through the work of Randy Engle and Akira Miyake. He thus brought skills that I lack in addition to being an excellent experimentalist. It was clear from the referees' comments on the grant that awarding it was a close-run thing with scepticism as to whether the concept of an episodic buffer would prove empirically useful, followed by an eventual decision to give me the benefit of the doubt. I was therefore intent on demonstrating that the concept *could* prove a useful tool in further understanding working memory and in doing so I can think of no better colleagues than Graham and as it turned out, Richard. We worked together for the remainder of the grant and have continued to do so since that time with Richard moving to a post at Leeds University, about 25 miles away and continuing to be part of our group while successfully developing his own independent research career.

I myself have not had grant support for most of the last decade and consequently our research programme has depended heavily on working with visitors, typically visiting PhD students funded from abroad to work with our group in York for periods of up to a year. During my time in York I noticed that Graham and I have published jointly with visitors from at least seven different countries, namely Brazil, China, India, Italy, Japan, Norway and Spain, mainly on topics related to working memory, often leading to collaborations that extend beyond the return home of our collaborators. Publications from jointly supervised York-based PhD students cover a rather wider range of topics, including attention, music, serial order and eyewitness testimony. Finally, we have developed a way of gradually building up a research programme based on supervision of the undergraduate research projects that form an important component of a UK psychology degree, using careful replication as a way of ensuring the reliability of the resulting findings.

The initial aim of our grant proposal was to attempt to demonstrate that the concept of an episodic buffer could be used productively to investigate the nature of working memory, using the model to generate questions which, if answered, would have implications that were not limited to our own theory but would be applicable to the field more generally. We decided to focus on the central issue of the binding together of features from different sources within the episodic buffer to create the multidimensional episodes that form the basis of conscious awareness. I had initially seen such binding as an active and attentionally demanding process, heavily dependent on the central executive. There were precedents for this type of assumption in earlier models of the role of visual attention in perception as in the case of Ann Treisman who proposed that attentional capacity was required to bind together visual features such as colour, shape and location to create a perceived object. It seemed likely that even more attention would be required for novel semantic binding: for example combining the concepts of ice hockey and an elephant allowing you to imagine an ice-hockey-playing elephant, potentially allowing you to answer questions about its optimal position – a body-checking defender or perhaps in goal? I assumed that the process of binding would be attentionally demanding, and the link between the episodic buffer and the central executive would be crucial. For that reason my initial model had omitted any direct links from the buffer, to the visuospatial sketch pad or to the phonological loop (see Figure 25.1). My assumption was that we could test this assumption of a single link by using dual-task methods to disrupt each of the proposed components, predicting that if this assumption was correct, then disrupting the central executive would dramatically interfere with the operation of binding within the episodic buffer, while disrupting the visuospatial and phonological subsystems would have little effect. We were thus using the model to ask further questions rather than simply as a post hoc explanation of existing results.

We approached the question by using our well-established method of independently disrupting the visual, verbal and executive subsystems of working memory, using tasks that were carefully chosen to focus on each subsystem separately, articulatory suppression to disrupt the phonological loop, visuospatial tasks to disrupt the sketch pad and more demanding versions of each to load the central executive. Since we wanted our results to be general rather than specific to a particular type of material, we carried out parallel verbal and visual experiments, one series looking at the binding of words into phrases within connected prose, while the other looked at the binding of features such as shape and colour in visual working memory. I will begin with the verbal studies that link directly to the previously described and puzzling lack of evidence for a clear impact of demanding cognitive tasks on prose comprehension before moving on to visual working memory, an area that has become extremely popular in recent years and has come to occupy a good deal of our own research time.

You may recall that we had previously expected that a demanding concurrent task would interfere more with the comprehension of a complex passage from a philosophy textbook than with a more readable description of a disease or an even more accessible fairy story but found no evidence for this. A PhD study by Beth Jefferies of immediate memory for groups of sentences looked slightly more encouraging in finding an effect when the task involved remembering three unrelated sentences. The concurrent load, however, had little effect when the three sentences fitted together semantically as in coherent text.

We decided that we needed to focus at the more manageable sentence level, using a variable that we knew would influence recall, namely the difference between the excellent immediate retention of sentences and the much shorter span for disconnected jumbled words. This difference is usually attributed to the ease of binding together the words comprising the meaningful sentences into a smaller number of multi-word chunks as proposed long ago by George Miller. However, immediate memory span for words is around five, compared to around 15 words for meaningful sentences. This makes it very difficult to interpret any differences found because of floor and ceiling effects, a sequence length that would be suitable for sentences would be too difficult with unrelated words even without concurrent tasks, while a length appropriate for scrambled words would lead to perfect performance on sentences. We found a way around this using what we described as "constrained sentences" whereby both conditions repeatedly used the same limited set of nouns and verbs. This meant that the words themselves would be readily available in both cases, but the *order* in which they occurred would constantly change, making it important to focus on the very last presentation rather than relying on long-term memory, which would likely be misleading because of its including many different orders of the same words. This was successful in reducing memory span from around 15 to about 7 crucial words. In the sentence case the words were linked together in a coherent way in contrast to their randomised order in the comparison condition. This produced sentences that were hardly deathless prose but did make sense such as *The old pilot sold the green bicycle to the tall soldier*, while other sentences might use some of the same words in different order. *The old soldier gave the green book to the tall sailor.* These were about as hard as shorter scrambled sequences such as: *soldier, book, tall, green, gave.*

We carried out a number of studies of which I will describe just one. This used the N-back task, a convenient way of varying concurrent executive load. It involves presenting a stream of items, for example digits, of which the participant must continually repeat either the last item, a very easy task, the one before (harder), or two-back (much harder). This places a substantial executive load on working memory as you constantly have to encode and remember two new items while recalling the earlier one. It can be used as a verbal task as with a sequence of digits, or as a visual task using locations of dots within a matrix. In the simplest zero-back form, it occupies and blocks use of the phonological loop or visuospatial sketch pad respectively, while placing little demand on the central executive, and while the one- and two-back make increasing executive demands.

The results of our various experiments were very clear. All the tasks had some effect on the accuracy of word list and sentence recall and as expected, the verbal tasks were more disruptive of verbal memory than the visual. Furthermore the two-back tasks were clearly more disruptive than the one-back or zero-back for both verbal and visual concurrent tasks, given the greater attentional demand. However, these effects were no greater for the sentences than for the scrambled word lists. This suggests that the tasks were impairing *overall* memory performance but did not interfere with the capacity to *bind* the words together into chunks. We concluded that working memory was certainly necessary for short-term verbal memory and that phonological storage was particularly important but that it was *not* necessary for the crucial task of binding. We proposed that language-based binding went on in long-term memory with the episodic buffer serving as a passive system for storing the *results* of the binding and making them available for immediate recall. We finally felt able to accept our essentially negative prose memory results, having shown clearly through this and a number of further experiments that comprehension did *not* depend on working memory. This is yet another example of the way in which unexpected negative results, given that they are reliable and replicable, have led to a change in the multicomponent model.

A good deal of our research over this period has, however, focussed on visual working memory, an area that I myself had tended to neglect following my earlier research, using relatively complex visual imagery tasks in contrast to much of our verbal research using simple memory span. I was however, intrigued while at Bristol, to receive a paper to review by Stephen Luck and Edward Vogel describing an elegant series of experiments on visual working memory using a much simpler method that involved remembering an array of coloured shapes, followed by a test item with the requirement to judge whether it had formed part of the previous set or not. Using this simple change detection method it was possible to demonstrate that performance dropped systematically with number of items beyond two and to look separately at performance when only colour (e.g. red) needed to be retained, only shape (e.g. triangle) or crucially when the correct binding of both colour and shape was required (red triangle), where a red square or a green triangle should evoke a "no" response. A careful series of experiments resulted in a finding that was particularly relevant to our episodic buffer programme, namely that it was no more demanding to remember a bound object comprising two features (a red triangle) than it was to remember the individual features of red or triangle on their own. This suggested that binding was automatic. Their conclusions did not agree, however, with the result of a similar study from Ann Treisman's laboratory which suggested that the need to remember two bound features such as colour and shape was *more* attentionally demanding than retaining just a single feature.

While Luck and Vogel and their many successors approached the topic of visual working memory via methods often stemming from perception or visual attention, we ourselves have tried to tackle similar questions using approaches initially developed to tackle verbal short-term memory within our broader working memory framework. We began with the question of whether the binding of features, for example colour and shape into coloured objects, depends crucially on the central executive. As in our study of the binding of verbal material in sentence recall, we asked whether a concurrent task loading the central executive will disrupt the binding of shape and colour, as would be suggested by the work of Wheeler and Treisman, or whether, as suggested by Luck and Vogel, such binding is automatic.

We conducted a series of experiments based on the Luck and Vogel approach in which an array of coloured shapes was presented, and memory was probed by presenting a single item with the need to decide whether it had or had not appeared in the remembered set. We used a range of concurrent tasks that aimed to disrupt the phonological loop or sketch pad alone, or which also placed demands on the central executive. Our results were parallel to those we had found in sentence memory. Demanding executive tasks did indeed impair *overall* memory performance, but this effect was no greater for binding, remembering which shape goes with which colour, than it was for remembering only shape or only colour. Thus our results broadly supported those of Luck and Vogel rather than those from Anne Treisman's laboratory.

A clue as to why this might be the case came from a later experiment in which we again used visual stimuli involving coloured shapes, but rather than showing them all at the same time, we presented them one at a time sequentially. We tested by probing one item from each list, again requiring a decision as to whether or not it had been in that list. We obtained a very interesting result; when we probed the very last item, our results were as before: a concurrent attentional load had no greater effect on binding than on retention of single features. However, on earlier items there was a clear difference suggesting that while attention was not required to bind features into objects, it *was* needed to maintain the bindings of earlier items, which appear to be fragile and to depend on attention for adequate maintenance against interference from other items in the sequence. It made sense of the apparent conflict between the results found by Luck and colleagues, who probed with a single item, and those of Wheeler and Treisman, who tested by presenting the whole array, potentially requiring the scanning of several items before detecting the presence or absence of a different item. The items remembered presumably need to be maintained during scanning, a process that is potentially dependent on attention, hence interfering with the capacity to maintain the bindings.

The fact that we failed to find an involvement of the central executive in setting up the initial binding, however, surprised us, leading to a series of experiments in collaboration with a Norwegian visitor Pål Karlsen in which we attempted to make the process of binding more demanding. In one study, we presented a colour and a shape in separate locations: for example requiring people to combine a red blob with an uncoloured triangle after a sequence of such pairs being tested by a coloured shape – a red triangle (yes) or a red square (no). Another study presented the colour first followed by the shape, while a third experiment involved binding a visual shape with a spoken colour. All of these made the task harder and in all cases an attentional load affected overall performance but had no greater effect on binding than it did on remembering the individual features of shape and colour.

Despite our failure to disrupt binding, we were pleased that introducing methods from the verbal short-term memory tradition did seem to yield interesting new results. This approach was further reinforced by the suggestion of Taiji Ueno, a Japanese student who first visited our group as an undergraduate, later continuing his work in parallel with a PhD in Manchester, and now continuing after returning to Japan to take up a post there. Taiji suggested that we should explore the effects of presenting a suffix on performance. The suffix effect is a well-established feature of verbal short-term memory that occurs when a spoken list of items is followed by another spoken item that is to be ignored. In the absence of a suffix, the last item is particularly well retained, an auditory recency effect sometimes attributed to a temporary sensory memory system known as echoic memory. Presenting a further unwanted spoken item, the suffix, largely removes this advantage, while a non-vocal suffix such as a tone or a burst of white noise has little effect. When the digits are presented visually however, auditory suffixes do not disrupt the recency advantage. Taiji suggested that a similar effect might be found if our coloured shapes were followed by a *visual* suffix.

We duly found impaired performance, both when we used the standard method of presenting an array of coloured shapes and when we used our sequential method. In the latter case, the suffix effect principally disrupted memory for the last item presented. We also found that the visual suffix effect proved to depend crucially on the nature of the suffix. If it was made up from a combination of features that *might* have come from the remembered set of features, it had a much more dramatic effect than if it comprised a different shape in a different colour. We found clear disruption from a single potentially appropriate feature even when bound to one that was inappropriate. This suggests some kind of attentional gating mechanism that will accept as proof of appropriateness a single feature, regardless of the presence of an unwanted feature. Perhaps surprisingly, our research could be seen as using memory to study attention rather than using attention to study memory, a conclusion further reinforced by a second series of studies conducted with Vivian Hu, a visiting Chinese PhD student, who like Taiji continues to collaborate after returning to take up a teaching post.

The topic we investigated with Vivian was the role of attention in prioritising the recall of one item over the others. Here again, the sequential presentation method proved particularly useful; we initially showed that telling people that one of a sequence of four items was particularly important was sufficient to enhance performance, on that item. However, the final item continued to be well remembered, regardless of priority suggesting an automatic recency effect. Our next step was to use a concurrent counting task to reduce the contribution of the central executive. This interfered with the capacity to prioritise items but had little effect on recency. In contrast, a suffix influenced recency but not prioritisation.

Our complex pattern of results can be explained by distinguishing between two types of attention. One is a relatively automatic *perceptual* process that is reflected in the capacity to bind the features into objects and is disrupted by a suffix if it comes from the same broad visual category. This can be distinguished from a second central executive-based attentional capacity that is necessary for manipulating stimuli and is necessary for strategic control as reflected in prioritisation. A similar distinction has been made when approached from a purely attentional rather than memory-based viewpoint by Marvin Chun at Yale and Nilli Lavie at University College London.

By this stage it had become clear that our initial hypothesis, that the episodic buffer depended on the central executive and was not accessible by other routes, was inconsistent with the evidence from both the binding of words in sentence recall and the binding of features in visual working memory. In both cases however, our evidence suggested that overall memory performance *was* dependent on the attentional contribution from the central executive, with performance consistently dropping when the central executive was loaded by a concurrent task such as counting backwards. It was the binding of features itself that did not appear to depend on executive processing. We concluded that in the case of language, the binding was dependent on over-learned syntactic and semantic operations within long-term memory, while in the case of the visual tasks, binding appeared to be dependent on processes operating before information reached the executive. We concluded therefore that the buffer was essentially a passive system that received already bound information from a range of sources which include perception and long-term memory, holding this information and making it available to conscious awareness in a form that allows it to be used actively for planning further action.

Our current view of the multicomponent working memory system is shown in Figure 25.1, which separates the active and attentionally limited executive from the passive but equally important episodic buffer. The buffer has limited storage capacity, a capacity that is determined by a number of integrated chunks of information that it can hold. It serves the important function of allowing information in many different forms, namely visual, verbal, perceptual and memory-based, all to be combined and made available to conscious awareness.

We now see the phonological loop and visuospatial sketch pad as systems that bring together separate streams of verbal-acoustic information on the one hand and visuospatial and tactile on the other, allowing the streams of information within each of the two subsystems to be integrated and then combined in more complex multidimensional chunks before being fed into the buffer. You will note that the phonological store accepts information in a number of forms, including not only acoustic but also secondary linguistic information from lip-reading and sign language, an assumption for which there is now considerable evidence. The visuospatial system also combines information from a range of sources that extend beyond the directly visual and spatial to information from joint and muscle receptors

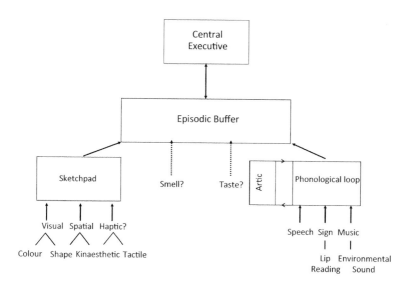

FIGURE 25.1 The current version of our working memory model.

and from touch, which itself combines information from a number of separate tactile receptors, some detecting pressure, others vibration, others temperature while yet others are pain receptors.

My current view of rehearsal is that the capacity of the phonological loop to rehearse by subvocally reproducing the digits or words being remembered may not be typical of rehearsal in general. Because we are using digits or words that are already known, subvocalisation can recreate the fading trace, after "cleaning it up" when any decay occurs, provided deterioration has not gone too far. Hence, if we are remembering digits, recalling a fragment such as *−ee* can be reconstructed and rehearsed as *three*, a process that may well occur automatically. This is not of course possible if the digits are in an unfamiliar language as Fergus Craik showed many years ago by having British people remember Finnish digits leading to a greatly reduced span. Provided the number of items is small, articulatory rehearsal can operate without placing too heavy a load on executive processing. This contrasts with other dimensions such as vision or touch, where it seems most likely that rehearsal depends on a process termed *refreshing* whereby attention is focussed on the material being retained, a process highly dependent on the limited-capacity central executive. You may note two dotted lines in Figure 25.1 connecting taste and smell to the episodic buffer. These represent a speculation that these sensory systems may have their own direct route to the buffer and that it may be possible to maintain such stimuli temporarily by the same process of active refreshing, although I know of no current research that is relevant to this issue. To summarise, our current view therefore is that working memory sits at the interface of perception, long- and short-term memory and attention, making bound chunks of information available for conscious manipulation.

The multicomponent model is often contrasted with the *embedded processes* model proposed by Nelson Cowan who regards working memory as the focussing of an attentional spotlight on the currently activated portion of long-term memory. Importantly, he does not deny the importance of our more peripheral phonological and visuospatial storage systems and has in fact done important work on what we would term the phonological loop. However, whereas my own approach began with verbal short-term memory and was gradually extended to address the more challenging attentional component, Nelson began with the study of attention only later applying it to memory. His particular focus has been on the number of chunks of information that can be held in focus at any given time, arguing that it is limited to three or four rather than the seven suggested by George Miller in the 1950s. He and I agree that his model can be mapped onto the central executive as the controller of the attentional spotlight, central to Nelson's theory and that the episodic buffer is equivalent to the activated temporary storage system resulting from such attentional focus. Our main disagreement concerns our own assumption that information must be downloaded into a *separate* buffer system, whereas Nelson assumes that the operations all occur within long-term memory.

We both agree that there will almost always be a long-term contribution to the operation of working memory. Even a simple digit span task will need to retrieve the digits from long-term memory, relying on extensive prior learning, hence the greatly reduced span in a foreign language. We also agree that the concept of *activated long-term memory* does not provide an explanation of working memory. It does, however, serve Nelson as a theoretical placeholder denoting problems to be solved later while he concentrates on analysing the attentional component, much as our initial concept of a central executive served as a reminder of the necessary complexities of attention, while we focussed on the simpler phonological loop subsystem. Unfortunately our two approaches to working memory are often misinterpreted, with our own model seen as purely concerned with short-term storage, while Cowan's is misrepresented as simply activated long-term memory. Working memory involves both; the crucial questions concern how the temporary and long-term components work together to provide a crucial link between perception, memory and action.

A further useful distinction has been made by Klaus Oberauer in an ambitious attempt to produce a mathematical model of working memory. He distinguishes between procedural and declarative aspects of working memory. Declarative working memory refers to those aspects that are open to conscious awareness, within our model through the episodic buffer. They may be contrasted with the operations performed on the contents of working memory: for example the procedural skills required to articulate and rehearse the contents of the phonological loop or the procedures that allow the performance of a strategy, such as favouring the first item. These are all likely to be dependent on long-term procedural skills which are assumed by our multicomponent model but not currently analysed in any detail.

I have described just a few examples of the way in which we have used the concept of an episodic buffer to investigate in more detail the operation of working memory. Each has been selected to make a single simple point that has typically resulted from a much more extensive series of studies. We ourselves opt to fit the results into the broad multicomponent memory framework. It is important to note, however, that our new findings are consistent with other theoretical frameworks, including some of the increasingly detailed theoretical developments in the study of visual working memory. We are pleased and reassured by the fact that a line research based on the very speculative concept of an episodic buffer together with methods originally developed to study verbal working memory are leading us to conclusions that are similar to those of our colleagues with backgrounds in visual perception, attention and neuroscience.

Such a conclusion would have surprised and perhaps shocked me at the start of my career when I accepted the dominant approach to the philosophy of science, which asserted that scientific theories should be precisely formulated and lead to specific predictions which would decide between one theory and its rival. I suspect that this is still held by many in the field, who assume that Cowan and myself cannot both be right, and that what is needed is a crucial experiment or set of experiments that will decide which approach should be pursued and which abandoned. As mentioned earlier, I rapidly discovered that in my own case, what worked was not an attempt to create theories like Newtonian physics, with the involvement of postulates, equations and mathematics, as was once widely regarded as highly desirable, but rather to see theories as equivalent to maps, ways of making sense of an area and providing a basis for further investigation, only abandoning the map if it proves unproductive in its capacity to account for what we already know and lead to further interesting discoveries. Maps are not realistic representations of terrain but rather reflect different ways of representing important features, towns and roads in one case, geology in another and political control in a third. The three will not of course always agree, politics does not follow geology, but it makes no sense to say that one is correct and other wrong.

So, has our simple three-component model provided a good map? Given the extension to a fourth component, I think it has. First of all, as I hope this chapter has shown it has proved and continues to be fruitful in leading to interesting and tractable questions which when answered add to our knowledge in useful ways. It is a very broad model that has allowed the detail to be filled in gradually by ourselves and others, and a mark of its success is the fact that our conclusions are compatible with those of colleagues who tackle the same question from different viewpoints. One example is our conclusion that it is appropriate to assume two aspects of attention, one perceptual and the other executive, which ties in neatly with conclusions from colleagues such as Chun and Lavie who have tackled the same question from a viewpoint of visual attention. Finally, and I think importantly, our model has been simple enough to be readily understood and applied in a wide range of areas including education, neuroscience, occupational psychology and medicine, offering broad conceptual tools, together with a toolbox of methods that allows their relevance to be directly tested.

26
Summing up

From Behaviourism to Cognitive Neuroscience

I began this book with a brief account of growing up, leading on to an overview of the developing scientific movement that became known as the cognitive revolution. I will begin this final chapter with a brief account of the satisfactions and frustrations of continuing to work as a scientist at the other end of life concluding with the general question of what has happened to the cognitive revolution in the intervening years.

So, what do I do these days? While I try my best to ignore it, a major constraint on my research ambitions is obviously my age. Research is essentially a long-term relatively slow activity taking years rather than weeks. It also costs money, in the case of most neuroscience and much social science, substantial sums of money, typically committed over a minimum of three years, with a year or so before to work up the grant and a year after to write up all the results. While I have survived some 19 years beyond the standard UK retirement age of 65, at no point beyond this could I guarantee that I would continue to be active for long enough to justify grant support for the next four years.

Fortunately however, I work in an area of cognitive psychology that is not expensive, and my style has been to operate through collaborations, typically with one or two other people rather than through large research grants. During my 20 years at the Unit, I worked with a succession of individual postdoctoral fellows of high quality, together with a range of unfunded outside collaborations: for example with neuropsychologists or with interested groups from outside psychology, such as divers or anaesthetists. This style of operation continues to serve me well, although without the postdoctoral fellow I was fortunate enough to have during my Unit years. I have, however, had the good fortune to continue collaborating with two people who were once postdoctoral fellows, Graham Hitch my first and Richard Allen my last, both of whom have gone on to establish highly successful independent careers but who are happy to devote some of their efforts to a continuing collaboration with myself and with the rather fluid group of visiting PhD students, postdoctoral fellows and undergraduates interested in working with us.

I am fortunate enough to continue to have a part-time appointment but to have retired from the increasingly onerous load of teaching and, in particular, administration that is currently inflicted on academics in the UK and, I suspect, worldwide. This allows me to devote most of my time to writing and research, which includes supervising undergraduate research projects. My wife and I divide our time between York, where we have a terrace house near the centre, and a very active and friendly village some 18 miles north in the Howardian Hills, in very good walking country where I do most of my writing. Finally, the absence of long-term grant commitments has at least one advantage; it leaves me free to explore new topics. Hence, while a good deal of my time continues to be spent in continuing to explore working memory as discussed in the previous chapter, I have time to tackle a range of other questions, simply because they seem interesting.

While some such projects may be limited in scope, others can extend over several years, potentially resulting in a genuine theoretical advance. One example of this is a series of studies, prompted by my relatively harmless addiction to photographing doors, an obsession initially resulting from the need to design a clinical memory test of visual and verbal recall and recognition. The resulting *Doors and People Test* appears to be liked by patients and reasonably widely used. I was, however, left with an unbridled enthusiasm for snapping doors wherever I travelled, based on the pretext that they would provide ideal material for later visual memory experiments. This eventually led to a small grant from the UK Experimental Psychology Society to turn the results of my relatively harmless obsession from shoeboxes full of pictures into a computer-searchable database of over 3000 doors. Having justified the grant by pointing out that the psychology of memory is almost entirely based on studies of words, Graham Hitch and I felt obliged to look for possible differences between visual and verbal memory. We used a series of student projects to tackle the question of whether the Craik and Lockhart levels of processing effect that was developed using words would also apply to non-nameable pictures. As you may recall, processing words "deeply", by tasks involving elaboration and focussing on meaning, greatly increases ease of later remembering them. Would "deep" processing also help people remember doors?

To answer this question we needed a deep task that was applicable to both doors and words. We noted that one of the most powerful processing effects among the many verbal studies came from requiring a judgement of pleasantness. Over a long sequence of studies we found a consistently modest positive effect of judgement of their pleasantness of door scenes versus physical judgements such as size or colour for doors and for a range of other visual stimuli such as clocks, mobile phones and natural scenes. Perhaps more surprisingly, we found much less consistency across verbal materials. The typical substantial deeper processing advantage occurred when we used the concrete nouns such as "castle" or "rabbit" that dominated earlier memory research, but we found much smaller effects for less semantically rich materials such as rare animals or people's names.

Our results led to a paper making the first major change for many years to the widely used levels theoretical framework. We based our revision on the distinction between semantic and perceptual encoding of memory stimuli. Semantic coding such as would be necessary for judgements of the pleasantness of concrete familiar words activates a wide range of associated features. A word like "dog", for example, might evoke not only the general image of dogs but also memories of specific encounters with dogs, of dogs owned by your family or perhaps of being bitten, all of which might be involved in judging the word's pleasantness. Perceptual encoding of a visual stimulus such as a door scene is known to be rapid and visually extensive but has little potential for activating rich semantic features that will distinguish it from the many other doors in the list and hence shows only a modest gain from deeper processing.

I am pleased to report that one of the reviewers of our paper was Fergus Craik who supported our extension of his original levels framework, the first for many years. We are currently trying to develop ways of predicting the potential of words to benefit from deeper processing, borrowing methods from studies of semantic memory. We are also trying to understand what makes a picture memorable, an issue being extensively studied in artificial intelligence (AI) by groups interested in automatic object and face recognition. The situation at the time of writing is that neither people nor machines are very good at predicting which pictures will be best remembered. The field is developing rapidly within AI, although the usual questions arise as to whether a successful computer answer to the question can be generalised to the way people process and remember pictures.

Another extended programme emerged from an invitation to develop a test of long-term forgetting. This was prompted by the recent demonstration of a subsample of patients who appear to combine good memory when first tested with very rapid forgetting over the next few days or weeks. Such a patient would have a genuine and potentially disabling memory problem that would remain undetected by most current assessment procedures. One case involved an academic who claimed to have no memory of a conference he had attended two weeks before. I can imagine commenting that I myself regularly had the same experience! In his case, however, delayed testing showed a dramatic loss of information acquired very efficiently a week before. This pattern of accelerated long-term forgetting occurs in some but by no means all patients suffering from temporal lobe epilepsy and may also occur more widely but go undetected. This is because the standard picture for patients with memory disorders is that learning is impaired, but, perhaps surprisingly, forgetting is not. Hence patients suffering from the classic amnesic syndrome or from mild Alzheimer's Disease have great difficulty in acquiring new material but retain what they have learned as well as healthy people. For this reason, most existing memory tests do not extend beyond delays of an hour or so and are not suitable for the repeated testing over the longer delays that are needed to detect such long-term forgetting. As I enjoy developing memory tests, I was pleased to accept the invitation to join an informal group of neurologists, neuropsychiatrists and clinical neuropsychologists focussed on developing suitable tests.

My own suggestion involved a variant of the Wrecks Test, designed in Los Angeles many years before to test the effects of cold on trainee divers. As you may recall, they were asked to remember five shipwrecks, each of which had five features: type, ship name, depth, sea bottom and surroundings. It worked well for divers, but it seemed unlikely that our patients would share their interest in wrecks. We therefore replaced the wrecks with crimes, which the abundance of popular TV programmes suggests are of universal interest. The resulting Crimes Test comprises five crimes, each with five features: the crime, the victim, age and sex, the criminal and the location; for example *An elderly Russian lady who was entering the cathedral had her handbag snatched by a young girl.*

The five crimes proved easy to remember and yielded four 20-item memory tests without needing to repeat any of the questions, hence allowing four separate tests, one immediate and the others after various delays. We found that delayed tests could be carried out by telephone with no loss of accuracy, while the test showed only modest forgetting over periods up to a month. An equivalent visual memory test was designed based on questions about four doors, the type (e.g. factory), colour, surround, what was above the door and what was in front. Again the test seemed to work well, being easy to learn and showing little forgetting over delays of up to a month.

I then had a worrying thought; perhaps each test served as a rehearsal, with a single question evoking memory of the whole crime or door scene? I duly called on a group of student volunteers to help test this possibility by comparing retention after a month, either with intervening tests after 24 hours and a week or with no intervening tests. For both crimes and doors the unfilled month's delay led to substantially more forgetting than found previously. It became clear that the act of testing the memory had helped to maintain it: How?

Psychologists have been studying forgetting since Ebbinghaus's classic forgetting curve published in 1885. So what does the literature have to say on the issue? There appear to be situations when testing makes memory extremely vulnerable, leading to increased forgetting, particularly in animal studies of memory trace consolidation. On the other hand, situations also occur in which testing clearly enhances later retention, leading to a flurry of recent papers demonstrating a positive effect of testing for delayed recall of educational material. Yet other situations lead to enhancement of the items that are tested together with an active suppression of untested items, while our own results suggest maintenance of the existing memory rather than active strengthening. Under what conditions do these various outcomes occur? It is far from clear since these various and apparently contradictory effects tend to have been studied in relative isolation. We clearly need a better theory of forgetting. When is memory maintained, when is it boosted and when and why is it disrupted?

In an attempt to stir up interest in the study of forgetting, my old friends Sergio Della Sala, Bob Logie and I recently organised a symposium and discussion meeting on *Forgetting as a Forgotten Topic*, which led to wide interest, lively discussion and signs that a nucleus of us plan to tackle some of the neglected issues. Furthermore, one of the major practical problems in studying long-term forgetting may have diminished, namely that of ensuring over a matter of days or weeks that people will return to the laboratory for repeated memory tests. The recent extensive development of web-based testing means that they can be contacted and tested with no need for face-to-face contact, provided of course that various forms of "helping" their memory, by surreptitiously taking notes, for example, are avoided. Technological help will not in itself solve the various underlying problems, but by making experimentation easier, it will allow application of the method known as *converging operations* whereby a question that cannot be answered with certainty using any single experiment can be tackled by using a series of experiments, each having different limitations. If they all give the same answer, then the conclusions can be accepted. We plan to use this approach in developing suitably modified versions of the Crimes and Four Doors Tests.

Probably my most exotic current project concerns an attempt to investigate the memory of people who have learned the whole of the Qur'an by heart. A neuropsychologist friend suggested that this might be reflected in the structure of the learner's hippocampus, just as the years of geographical learning by London taxi drivers that goes into their acquisition of "the knowledge" are reflected in the size and structure of their hippocampus. I suspect that we will be unable to recruit enough memorisers to test this particular hypothesis, but I think it is an intriguing question and have indeed already benefited by learning something about the Qur'an, how and why it is learned. As with the Bible its early preservation relied entirely on memorisation, first by the Prophet himself who was illiterate, as were most Arabs at the time. While few could read and write, there was a strong memory tradition, with oral recitation meaning that the community could correct deviations, which it was suggested made preservation more reliable than reliance on the few literate people to transcribe it accurately, an interesting though rather debateable assumption. Furthermore, when the printing press was first invented, it did a very poor job of transcribing Arabic script, again making memory at least potentially more reliable than printing.

I also learned that someone who wishes to become a Hafiz, or Hafiza if female, a person who has committed to memory all 6000 verses of the Qur'an, will start with the last chapters, which are apparently the most basic and simple, with chapters becoming more complex as they approach the beginning. That presumably means that when relying on memory, expertise will be related to the amount learned. This can obviously not be guaranteed for all learners, particularly since some who aspire to becoming a Hafiz may not understand the language of the text they are memorising, which, to be spiritually valuable, has to be the original Arabic. This should, according to what we know of the psychology of memory, make learning in non-Arabic speakers very difficult. But who knows? Even if the proposed brain imaging study proves overambitious, it would be interesting to investigate just what is learned, how it relates to understanding the meaning and whether extensive practice influences the learning of other materials.

In the meantime, I am enjoying working in a truly multicultural team comprising my neuropsychologist friend Narinder Kapur, who comes from a Northern Irish Hindu background but was educated in a Catholic school; Faisal Mushtaq, a lecturer at Leeds University, a Muslim whose parents were born in Pakistan; assisted by a black visiting student from London, Rashaun Black whose strongly Christian parents were born in Jamaica; together with myself, a lapsed Protestant brought up in the Church of England.

So, my own research bumbles along, but meanwhile what happened to the cognitive revolution? George Miller initially hoped that the two seminal conferences in 1956 might herald the birth of a new integrated field in which linguistics, psychology, anthropology and computer science might all combine into a unitary discipline. Perhaps sadly, this proved illusory. Each area had different roots and while they had interests in common, these were not sufficient to create a new integrated field. Instead, however, there has been substantial cross-fertilisation with ideas and methods from one field influencing others, sometimes in unpredictable ways. One way to track this is through the individual contributors to the 1956 meeting that Miller saw as the origin of the cognitive revolution.

Perhaps the most straightforward development was that of signal detection theory, the application of a statistical decision approach to psychophysics as presented by John Swets. This has been widely adopted, not only in perception but also, for example, in memory, where, together with a number of modest refinements, it is simply accepted as a standard way of analysing data. A contrast to the solid and widely appreciated contribution made by signal detection theory is provided by Chomsky's presentation of his theory of transformational grammar. It radically changed the field of linguistics and began to influence neighbouring fields such as cognitive psychology, based on its claim to provide a royal road to understanding the human mind. It gradually became clear, however, that this was not the case; the linguistic intuitions on which it was based did not provide a solid foundation for a broad empirical psychology of language. Chomsky's ideas did, however, spark a very substantial interest in the field of psycholinguistics, which continues to flourish as a more empirically based discipline that has happily extended its scope beyond the intriguing though limited field of syntax.

To return to the launching of the cognitive revolution, the presentation that initially seemed to provide the clearest link between cognitive psychology and computer science was that given by Allen Newell and Herbert Simon who described an approach to psychology based on the assumption that the way forward was to create grand overall models of psychological functioning based on computational modelling, explicitly rejecting the less ambitious attempts to understand specific but more limited aspects of cognition that characterise most research in experimental psychology.

They proposed a computational model entitled the General Problem Solver which aimed to account for the way in which humans solve a whole range of different problems. It was based on a programming language involving *production systems*, each of which was based on a set of If-Then rules specifying that if specific condition A occurred, then this would result in action B. They showed that by bringing together such basic subcomponents, it was possible to simulate the solution of a wide range of problems. They and their followers tended to make the further assumption that unless a theory could be simulated as a computer model, it was not an adequate theory. This implicitly assumes, however, that theorisation should be limited by the current state of computer science, not an approach that was widely popular, or is indeed plausible.

A second problem with this approach was the assumption that the resulting models would necessarily reflect the way in which the relevant cognitive tasks were performed by humans. It rapidly became clear that this was not the case, as illustrated, for example, by the development of chess-playing programmes, which were successful but did not appear to reflect the way in which humans play chess. Furthermore it became clear that solving a given problem could potentially be simulated in a range of different ways, leaving the question of which, if any of the models applied to human cognition. Finally, the approach led to highly complex systems using a programming approach that was by no means universally accepted. This led to a gradual isolation of the advocates of this approach, making it less and less relevant to mainstream cognitive psychology. The broad field of AI has of course become hugely influential as an engineering discipline concerned with solving practical problems, often of considerable complexity. It has been much less successful in its early claims to provide scientifically justified explanations of human cognition.

A rather different potential influence of computer science was represented by the group from MIT who attempted to produce a computer simulation of Hebb's hypothesis regarding the principles underlying learning. This proposed that a synapse linking two neurons is strengthened when both the input and output neurons are activated at the same time, summarised by the phrase "neurons that fire together wire together". Attempts were made to build networks capable of learning based on "units" that were sometimes seen as analogous to neurons. Such "neural nets", however, initially appeared to meet a problem when two different inputs to the same unit were simultaneously active. A way around this was eventually developed in the 1980s, leading to the influential movement that became known as *connectionism*. The approach differed from earlier versions of AI in assuming that processes could operate in parallel rather than sequentially, as assumed, for example, by the production systems approach.

Much of this work developed within cognitive psychology, reflecting ambitious attempts to create models of language comprehension and reading. They were often based on the process of *back propagation*, analogous to the mechanism proposed by Hebb, although this appeared to lead to learning that was too slow to be biologically plausible. All the while however, computing power had been increasing dramatically year by year and it was recently discovered that back propagation, previously rejected as inadequate, was now feasible, given the massive computing power now available. Consequently methods developed within the cognitive psychology-computer science borders by scientists such as Geoffrey Hinton and David Rumelhart are now having a massive impact on the world through the process known as *deep learning*, currently being applied to a wide range of tasks that previously could only be carried out by people. This area of the application of computer science is leading to a flood of automation that is arguably the most significant practical impact of the cognitive revolution. However, as with the earlier serial processing developments in AI, such achievements may not reflect the way in which the brain tackles such problems.

My own interest in the cognitive revolution is clearly as an experimental psychologist concerned with cognitive psychology in general and human memory in particular. In my case, the main influence of the cognitive revolution has been through the information-processing approach prompted by the ideas of Claude Shannon and Norbert Wiener in the US and Alan Turing and Kenneth Craik in the UK. In my own case, the influence has come through their broad ideas rather than detailed modelling. Hence concepts such as encoding, retrieval, parallel processing and inhibition proved theoretically valuable without the need to specify them in precise behavioural terms, or indeed to simulate them either mathematically or by computer. The freedom to develop broad answers to questions while allowing detail to be filled in by further research has underpinned the development of the multicomponent working memory model, allowing the model to flourish over a 40-year period and to be applied to a wide range of other areas from paleoarchaeology to neuroscience and from psychiatry to education.

Progress in developing the cognitive psychology of long-term memory has been extensive but sporadic. During the 1960s the cognitive approach was increasingly influential, with the breakaway from the deadening limitations of an all-embracing interference theory. Major developments included the recognition of the role of organisation in encoding together with Tulving's elegant demonstrations of the importance of retrieval, followed by his later proposed distinction between semantic and episodic memory. Progress continued into the 1970s with the widespread recognition of the distinction between explicit and implicit memory systems, an important and wide-ranging conceptual development that originated in neuropsychology and went on to influence the whole of cognitive psychology as reflected, for example, in Daniel Kahneman's book *Thinking Fast and Slow*.

Since that time however, the cognitive psychology of long-term memory has shown a comparative theoretical lull during which individual research topics became popular without leading to very much theoretical development. These were often generated by important practical issues, such as the unreliability of eyewitness testimony and the dangers of false memory, but have often led to a flurry of laboratory-based studies, making worthwhile but limited contributions to theory though often somewhat remote from the practical application that prompted them. An example of this is the Deese-Roediger-McDermott false memory effect, which involves removing a critical word such as *sleep* from a list of 16 or more associates such as *dream*, *wake* and *night*. When tested, people tend to falsely remember that *sleep* had been presented. This is a robust and interesting effect that I suspect has gained a good deal of popularity as a research topic from its being labelled as "false memory". This might suggest that it impacts directly on the important practical issue of induction of false memories of childhood abuse in the legal and therapeutic fields, a link that to my knowledge has not been well established. The effect is of course valuable as a kind of memory illusion, demonstrating that people can be absolutely sure that they remember something which in fact never happened. Whether the reasons are at all closely related to the occurrence of false memories in the clinical context, however, remains questionable.

In contrast to the relatively limited theoretical development in recent studies of long-term memory, there has been a very substantial shift of attention to the question of its neural basis. I should at this point say something about my own views on the relationship between cognitive psychology, cognitive neuropsychology and cognitive neuroscience since it will clearly influence what follows. I am by trade an experimental psychologist with a particular interest in cognitive psychology and its potential applications. I regard neuropsychology as that area of psychology concerned with the influence of the brain on what I am happy to call the mind, although others might prefer to refer to it as behaviour. In my own case this has involved collaborating with neuropsychologists with access to patients with brain damage. Much of our work was conducted at a time when we ourselves did not have good access to brain scans which were expensive and not always hugely informative. Patient PV, for example, who I studied with Italian colleagues, had a very precise and limited cognitive deficit but a relatively broad cortical lesion. Despite this lack of precise localisation, she and other patients defined in terms of "purity" of cognitive deficit rather than anatomical localisation have had a major influence on theoretical development.

Other neuropsychologists, however, were much more directly concerned with neuroanatomical localisation, a good example being Brenda Milner whose work linking cognitive function to anatomical localisation was important in helping guide the work of neurosurgeons. My own much more limited applied work has been more closely related to the assessment and neuro-rehabilitation of patients who often had a complex pattern of disabilities that were not readily localisable. Whereas neuropsychology is principally focussed on psychology, and in my case with the implications of brain damage for general theories of memory, many current investigators would probably regard themselves principally as neuroscientists, focussing on the brain rather than the cognitive processes themselves.

The link between brain and cognition is clearly of central importance to psychology and the rapid development of neuroimaging technology has proved a magnet to cognitive psychologists in recent years. What is less clear, however, is the extent to which it has yet enhanced our understanding at the level of cognitive psychology in contrast to work on patients with lesions, which has, I believe, already proved of major theoretical significance. The dominant method of neuroimaging applied to cognition in recent decades has been fMRI (functional magnetic resonance imaging), which detects the distribution of oxygen in specific brain areas by its influence on the surrounding magnetic field, as an indicator of the blood flow in that region. It then attempts to link this to the performance of specific cognitive activities: in short, to map cognition onto its underlying brain function. The comments that follow particularly apply to this method.

After an initial period of enthusiasm, I have become increasingly sceptical about much of the work in this area. On what do I base my scepticism? It is certainly not lack of interest since I have been involved in at least five separate fMRI-based collaborations, each of which attempted to ask interesting questions about memory. None of them was successful in this aim, some because of problems of equipment change, a problem which is understandable but irrelevant to my main point, but others because of unreliability of results. Data from one study appeared to suggest activation in certain areas of the brain as the source of the irrelevant speech effect in short-term memory, while a second very similar experiment activated quite other areas, something my colleagues suggested was entirely explicable but was not apparently predictable in advance. Another attempt to replicate an interesting finding of direct theoretical relevance proved fruitless, with other investigators also finding difficulty in replication.

Finally, my attempt to find good examples of the value of neuroimaging in connection with our recent memory text proved frustratingly difficult, with claims of obvious difference between conditions seeming far from obvious to the untutored eye. Reading the papers would often lead to a long list of areas activated under various conditions, followed by often complex post hoc explanations as to how these were to be interpreted theoretically. Given the complexity of the data and the flexibility of the underlying theory, it is virtually always possible to devise an explanation and then move on to another different experiment, potentially requiring a different explanation.

As a cognitive psychologist, I regard it as important that we are ultimately able to link theories based on behaviour to their underlying brain mechanisms. Doing so will, however, depend on combining good psychology with good neuroscience, not an easy task with systems as complex as working memory. My early hopes were that neuroimaging studies in the area of working memory would produce results that are replicable and that map onto coherent well-established results from both patients and healthy people. Sadly this has not been the case. In the case of working memory, after some promising early studies using positive emission tomography, the situation appears to have simply become less and less clear.

I assume that one reason for this is that most of the neuroimaging designs are essentially correlational, deciding what areas are activated during what tasks. Scanning experiments are expensive and the range of behaviours readily studied within the scanner somewhat constrained. This can result in a tendency to identify a particular convenient task with a specific theoretical construct. However, most working memory tasks are not process-pure but involve many different systems, a problem that is tackled in behavioural studies by using the previously described method of converging operations, whereby a wide range of interrelated studies are needed before drawing theoretical conclusions, an approach that is apparently either not recognised or perhaps too expensive to be feasible in fMRI studies. Working memory tasks tend to activate many areas of the brain; visually presenting a sequence of words, for example, is likely to activate areas concerned with visual, phonological and semantic processing, together with frontal areas involving executive control. That does not, however, mean that these areas are all of central importance for a given specified task such as the immediate recall of short sequences, which behavioural studies suggest is critically dependent on the phonological rather than the semantic aspects of the words.

Having stressed my disappointment regarding the contribution of fMRI to the current understanding of working memory, it is important to note the very real progress in applying other methods to the rapidly developing field of visual working memory where the work of Steven Luck, Edward Vogel and their colleagues is particularly exciting. I suggest that their progress is based on two related factors. First that it has typically used scalp-based electrophysiological measures which have been developed over many years and are relatively inexpensive, readily allowing replication. Second, their work combines a thorough understanding of both the electrophysiological measures and psychological theory, allowing well-designed theoretically targeted experimental studies to be carried out.

Neuroimaging has of course been used widely to study long-term memory, one influential example stemming from a suggestion by Tulving in the 1980s that an important use of episodic memory is to allow what he termed *mental time travel*, using the past to plan the future. Much of the evidence offered in connection with this concept is based on neuroimaging studies demonstrating that brain areas involved in thinking about the future are also those involved in recollecting the past. Further evidence comes from the observation that amnesic patients often have difficulty in thinking about the future, while it has also been suggested that mental time travel may be uniquely human.

However, while Tulving made an important point about the wider usefulness of episodic memory, I suspect that much of the excitement has come from the term he invented with its suggestion that we all inhabit a time machine. The simple claim that we use memory to plan the future has rather less appeal. It is also significant that much of the work has been based on anatomical overlap of areas involved in future planning and those involved in long-term memory. Surely however, semantic memory and working memory will also be involved, but these tend not to be seen as central to our time machines. Amnesic patients tend to be poorly oriented in time and place – not a good position for planning the future. Finally as tends to happen with abilities deemed to be uniquely human, subsequent animal studies seem to provide evidence for a capacity that resembles episodic memory, notably as shown by the hiding by scrub jays of food for future use and of its time-based retrieval based on the nature and durability of the food. Of course we cannot be sure that the birds have the recollective experience that Tulving himself claims is essential to episodic memory, but this makes the claim for human memory uniqueness virtually untestable.

However, while I am not convinced that neuroimaging has made a theoretically cogent contribution to our understanding of the complexities of mental time travel, it does offer a valuable supplement to studies of conscious awareness. Consider, for example, Tulving's suggestion of a crucial distinction between *remembering* an item, accompanied by recollective experience and simply *knowing* that the item was recently presented. The demonstration that these two subjective responses behave differently across a range of memory studies was considerably strengthened when they were seen to be accompanied by quite distinctive neural activity that exactly fitted both behavioural and patient evidence. Note that this requires consistency of neural signal rather than specific anatomical localisation. If a given pattern of activity consistently occurs when people claim to be having a specific experience but not when they report a different experience, then it is plausible to use the neural pattern as evidence of that subjective state in further investigation.

A good example of this occurs in a line of neuroimaging research that is broadly related to the study of semantic memory using a method known as *multivoxal pattern analysis* (MVPA). This uses powerful machine learning methods to extract features of the electrical activity of the brain that are associated with a particular type of input: for example pictures of cars, based on presenting many different car pictures to the person in the scanner. Once it has learned the "concept" of a car, the system can "identify" new car pictures that were not part of the original set, purely on the basis of the neural pattern of activation in the brain. While this is impressive, the sceptic could argue that it simply demonstrates that there is indeed a consistent neural pattern of some kind that corresponds to our concept of a car. The next stage is to use such patterns to investigate the underlying neural processes. Hence, while I think neuroimaging will have an important impact on the psychology of memory in the future, its contribution so far appears to be less than is the case for its influence on other research areas such as perception, action and attention. No doubt this will change in due course.

So, given its potential importance, if I were starting my career again, would I choose to work using neuroimaging? I think not. It is important to work in areas that play to your strengths and minimise your weaknesses. One way of doing this is to work with others whose strengths complement your own. I have gained enormously from working with a very wide range of colleagues who not only complement my own skills but also help generate the enjoyment and enthusiasm that I regard as a crucial part of scientific research. In my own case, my weaknesses include limited mathematical skills, a lack of interest in technology and a preference to avoid areas that are already heavily populated, all characteristics of the current neuroimaging scene, together with a tendency to jump from one idea to another when things look a little dull.

So what are my strengths? Looking back over my career, I seem to have quite good intuitions about what people will do in an experimental situation and why. I suspect that I might have flourished during the brief period when introspectionism ruled, though I would rapidly have become frustrated by the difficulty in deciding which apparent insight was valid and which was not. I would also have been frustrated by the large and important areas of mental activities that are not available to conscious awareness. During my own career, the lasting influence of behaviourism meant that my introspections largely remained unspoken, perhaps appropriately since I accept that they should only be influential when supported by replicable experimental evidence. They have, however, continued to provide a useful though fallible guide.

A second strength is that I really enjoy collaboration in general and particularly when exploring a new area where my own skills can be combined with those of my collaborator. A related strength has been a broadly based curiosity coupled with an enjoyment of the challenge of developing reliable measures in complex areas beyond the laboratory, together with an enthusiasm for locating them within a broad and coherent framework. I like the concept of a "naturalist-scientist" proposed by Edward Wilson who began his career studying ant societies around the world, in due course leading through evolutionary theory to sociobiology and a major role in environmental politics. Wilson describes himself as a "naturalist-scientist, in agreement on the need for strict logic and experimental testing but expansive in spirit and far less prone to be critical of hypotheses in the early stages of investigation" (Wilson, 1995, p. 345).[1] He contrasts his approach with the predominant tendency for biology to focus on explanation at the molecular level, very important but by no means the whole story.

Looking back over my own career, I would therefore regard my approach as that of a psychological naturalist, if there is such a thing. I have been fortunate in working in a job that allowed me to investigate a range of interesting fields and attempt to make sense of them within a broad framework, a framework that was constrained enough to suggest further questions while being flexible enough to allow more detailed elaboration without the need for major change. I have always thought of myself as an explorer, producing an approximate map of a new and fascinating country, leaving others with more appropriate skills to come up with a more detailed mapping. If I were starting now, I would probably not choose to work in memory, which I think we already understand reasonably well from a broad psychological viewpoint. I might instead be tempted to explore an area that has been neglected virtually since Freud: namely that of psychological energy. Cognitive psychology is concerned with control, but what is controlled? Why do we do anything?

I would begin by doing some natural history. People differ in the extent to which they appear to be energetic. Why, and how important is this? It is clearly related to emotion but in my mind is separate; being angry is no doubt more likely to be linked to energy than is contentment but you can be angry and exhausted. Energy fluctuates throughout the day; does this simply reflect level of general arousal or does energy imply something more directed? States of health are clearly reflected in energy level; can this be used to develop viable measures, both psychological and physiological? How do these relate to the basic metabolism that turns nutrients into energy? All rather a tall order, so I would probably begin on a small scale by using observation and simple rating scales to investigate both the general population and the selected groups.

A diagnosis of attention deficit hyperactivity disorder, for example, implies a combination of three factors, attentional control and hyperactivity, typically together with a behavioural problem that led to a referral for investigation. There is already evidence that the attentional component fits reasonably well within broad working memory framework, but what about hyperactivity? Are there people who are hyperactive but with good executive control and a high level of general intelligence? I suspect there are but that they will not show behavioural problems and hence not be reported. If so, they might well provide some hints as to possible positive effects of high energy levels. At the age of 84, I am not going to be the one to develop a theoretical concept of mental energy, but I assume someone will and that its initial stages will provide ample scope for some psychological natural history.

Note

1 Wilson, E. O. (1995). *Naturalist*: Island Press.

INDEX

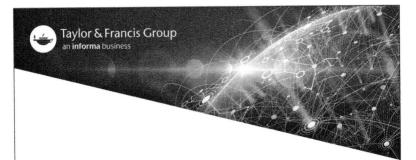